PRIMITIVE SOCIETY

PRIMITIVE SOCIETY

BY

ROBERT H. LOWIE, Ph.D.

PROFESSOR OF ANTHROPOLOGY
University of California

LIVERIGHT

NEW YORK

1947
BLACK AND GOLD EDITION
LIVERIGHT PUBLISHING CORPORATION

* * *

COPYRIGHT, 1920, BY
HORACE LIVERIGHT

COPYRIGHT, 1947, BY
LIVERIGHT PUBLISHING CORPORATION

* * *

All rights reserved—no part of this book may be reproduced in any form without permission in writing from the publisher, except by a reviewer who wishes to quote brief passages in connection with a review written for inclusion in a magazine or newspaper.

LIVERIGHT PAPERBOUND EDITION   1970

*Manufactured
in the United States of America*

PREFACE

THIS book was written originally in order to familiarize social scientists with the contemporary views of anthropologists concerning social organization. Cultural anthropology had by that time crystallized its criticisms of the earlier ambitious schemes of unilinear evolution—very much as experimental biologists had registered their protests against extravagant speculation concerning the development of animal species. It was clear that diffusion had taken place at every level of culture and had thus interfered with whatever sequence of events might be regarded as inherent in the nature of society. Since Lewis H. Morgan's *Ancient Society* (1877) systematically embodied the older unilinear evolutionism that postulated laws of development, my book inevitably grew into a persistent critique of Morgan.

Further, there was an immense and very important body of ethnographic facts which Morgan and other writers had neglected until they were fully expounded in Heinrich Schurtz's *Altersklassen und Männerbünde* (1902). The earlier scholars had concentrated their attention on the family, the clan, marriage, and correlated customs. It remained for Schurtz to point out what a large part is played in primitive society by the equivalents of our masonic lodges and social clubs, by age and sex grouping. In my book I tried to do justice to both ranges of fact, those treated by Morgan and those described by Schurtz.

The reception accorded to *Primitive Society* on its appearance varied considerably. Some readers were repelled by the "negativistic" aspects of the book; others felt swamped by the mass of detail. Dr. W. H. R. Rivers, the leader of British investigators in this field, found that "the number of omissions and errors is very small," and that the book "will be of the greatest value to students as a record of early forms of social institution." On the other hand, he held that I had not gone nearly far enough in my diffusionism (*American Anthropologist,* 22:278-283, 1920). While Rivers complained of my historical pusillanimity, Professor A. L. Kroeber (ib., 377-381) criticised the "negativistic attitude toward broader conclusions," the failure to realize the limited scope of the results attained, the "comparative sterility" of the tendency *Primitive Society* represented. The concluding sentences read: "After all, honesty is the primary virtue, and Lowie's soberness is a long advance on Morgan's brilliant illusions. But one sometimes sighs regretfully that the honesty of the method which is so successfully exemplified here is not stirred into quicker pulse by visions of more ultimate enterprise."

The general American consensus of opinion was favorable. *Primitive Society* was accepted as fairly representing the spirit of American anthropology; aversion to glib generalizations seemed a merit rather than a defect. This type of reaction appeared in various oral and written comments by Professor John M. Cooper as well as in full reviews by Elsie Clews Parsons (*The New Republic,* Nov. 3, 1920) and Edward Sapir (*The Freeman,* June 30, 1920; *The Nation,* July 10, 1920). Sapir hailed my effort as "the first work of major scope in its field, of those intended for a wider than strictly anthropological public, that breaks definitely with the classical evolutionist tradition"; as being within its special sphere "the clearest and most balanced expression we yet possess of the present temper of American anthropology." He accepted it as what it purported to be—a historical-minded presentation that fought shy of both psychological and pretendedly historical formulae. He declared that "the book blends in the most skilful manner, the concrete presenta-

PREFACE

tion of selected features of primitive societies, the discussion of the larger, theoretic aspects of these features, and the still wider bearing of the facts and discussions on his philosophy of social development."

From abroad came some abundantly appreciative comments. Father Wilhelm Schmidt of Vienna, the leader of the German diffusionists, wrote me a flattering letter and contemplated having a translation prepared. This, however, was prevented by the financial status of the Central European countries. An anonymous reviewer in *The New Statesman* compared me with a chambermaid sweeping out the cobwebs from a long-closed room. Bronislaw Malinowski was persistently eulogistic. Occasional remarks by Messrs. Claude Lévi-Strauss, Alfred Métraux, Paul Kirchhoff, Erland Nordenskiöld, and others have indicated that the book was widely read and exerted some influence. On the other hand, it was hotly denounced by many admirers of L. H. Morgan.

Whatever the ultimate verdict may be, it is clear that *Primitive Society* has filled a definite need. It still seems to have no rival in English and continues to be used as a text in various American institutions. As late as 1935 Payot (Paris) published a translation by Mme. E. Métraux under the title of *Traité de sociologie primitive*. I own a Japanese version, apparently issued not many years before World War II, and am credibly informed that a Chinese translation also has appeared.

Retrospectively, a few remarks seem in order in connection with the present edition. An extraordinary wealth of new material has come to light during the last quarter of a century, and to some extent there have been areal syntheses by competent anthropologists. Professor A. R. Radcliffe-Brown's summary of what is known about *The Social Organization of Australian Tribes* (The Oceania Monographs, No. 1, Melbourne, 1931) is typical; so is Paul Kirchhoff's masterly article on relevant facts from the forest regions of tropical America (Die Verwandtschaftsorganisation der Urwaldstämme Südamerikas, *Zeitschrift für Ethnologie,* 63:85-193, 1931). The admirable researches of Martin Gusinde in Tierra del Fuego and of Curt Nimuendajú in the interior of Brazil have revealed unsuspected institutions among the simpler New World natives. A host of able investigators have labored in Oceania and Africa, each of which areas now has a journal specifically devoted to its ethnography. It would be tempting to incorporate these new data into a revised picture of primitive life, but at the time this is not feasible. I must content myself with a series of corrections and addenda.

At the same time I think the reader can be assured that so far as the main propositions of the book are concerned he is not likely to be led astray. The universal importance and chronological priority of the individual family (as against the clan) are accepted by all responsible contemporary scholars—Richard Thurnwald, Wilhelm Schmidt, Radcliffe-Brown, the Malinowski school. Probably no one now believes that promiscuity in the strict sense of the term has existed in recent millennia. Individual property of some sort seems to be a general phenomenon of primitive society. The old argument that matriliny must have preceded patriliny because in early times paternity was uncertain has become worthless as tribe after tribe has become known that is totally indifferent to physiological paternity. Finally, there is still no evidence for anything remotely resembling a true matriarchate.

On the other hand, I should be the last to deny that several approaches other than mine are equally warranted and doubtless better suited to some tastes. In Professor Thurnwald's five-volume work, *Die menschliche Gesellschaft* (Berlin and Leipzig, 1931-1934) the synthetic description of a number of diverse peoples is especially appealing, as is the inclusion of higher civilizations. The symposum edited by Drs. M. Fortes and E. E. Evans-Pritchard on *African Political Systems* (London, 1940) deals ostensibly with only one department of social life, but with an extremely important one that is connected with virtually all others. Corresponding syntheses for comparable areas would be invaluable. In his several publications Father Wilhelm Schmidt (e.g., *Völker und Kulturen,* 1924) has the great merit of envisaging the totality of human cultures from a unified historical point of view. Though some of his reconstructions are assailable, his work represents a major effort to see social history as a whole; and, as Eduard Meyer, the great historian of antiquity, has rightly said, the basis of all historical investigation is always universal history.

So far as my own inclinations go, adhering to the scheme of the book as originally planned, I should under favorable circumstances expand it by utilizing the new empirical data from all over the globe for a historical reconstruction, primarily limited to each major area. I should then compare the results and test how far they severally suggest a parallel development. This possibility I should further check by drawing upon the civilizations—classical, Chinese, Arab, Egyptian—for which the sequence of events can be determined with the aid of written sources. On this basis a reasonable historical sociology might be founded, rivaling Father Schmidt's, but with closer attention to the empirical findings within each continent.

By way of supplementing this historical line of inquiry I should like to resume Tylor's statistical approach. In recent years it has actually been cultivated by Professor G. P. Murdock and his colleagues at Yale, but to date not enough has been published to permit an assessment of the results.

. . .

Finally, a word of explanation concerning the final paragraph of *Primitive Society,* which has been rather generally misinterpreted. The sentence in which civilization is called "that thing of shreds and patches" had no bearing on anthropological theory. It was written in a period of disillusionment after World War I, a sentiment very intelligible at the present moment. I was casting about for something derogatory to say about *our* civilization, and as an admirer of Gilbert and Sullivan naturally bethought myself of the phrase in question. It is true that I did not believe, nor do now, that *all* elements of a culture are necessarily related by some organic bond; on the other hand, ever since 1915 my treatment of kinship terms ought to have absolved me from the charge of viewing culture as *only* a fabric of shreds and patches.

Robert H. Lowie

Berkeley, July, 1947.

CONTENTS

CHAPTER		PAGE
	PREFACE	v
I.	INTRODUCTION	1
II.	MARRIAGE	14
	Marriage Prohibitions. Means of Acquiring a Mate. Preferential Mating.	
III.	POLYGAMY	40
	Polygyny. Polyandry. Sexual Communism. Hypothetical Sexual Communism.	
IV.	THE FAMILY	63
	The Bilateral Kin Group. Looseness of the Family Unit. Matrilocal and Patrilocal Residence. Sexual Division of Labor. Segregation of Unmarried. Sexual Segregation. Adoption. Summary.	
V.	KINSHIP USAGES	80
	Mother's and Father's Kin. Parent-in-law Taboo. Other Taboos. Privileged Familiarity. Taboo and License. Teknonymy.	
VI.	THE SIB	111
	Types of Sib organization. Unity or Diversity of Origin. Sibs of Higher Order. Totemism.	
VII.	HISTORY OF THE SIB	147
	Priority of the Family. Origin of the Sib. The Sib and the Dakota Terminology. Mother-Sibs and Father-Sibs.	
VIII.	THE POSITION OF WOMAN	186
	Theory and Practice. The "Matriarchate." Matrilocal Residence. The Economic Interpretation. Correlations with Stages of Civilization	

CONTENTS

CHAPTER		PAGE
IX.	PROPERTY	205
	Primitive Communism. Tenure of Land. Chattels. Incorporeal Property. Inheritance.	
X.	ASSOCIATIONS	257
	Andaman Islands. Australia. Masai. Banks Islands. Pueblo Indians. Crow. Hidatsa.	
XI.	THEORY OF ASSOCIATIONS	297
	Schurtz's Scheme. Sex Dichotomy. Age-Classes. Varieties of Associations. The Plains Indian Age-Societies. General Conclusions.	
XII.	RANK	338
	Bravery. Shamanism. Wealth. Caste. Conclusion.	
XIII.	GOVERNMENT	358
	Australia. Polynesia and Micronesia. Melanesia and New Guinea. Africa. North America. Democracy and Primitive Organizations. Tribal and Territorial Organization.	
XIV.	JUSTICE	397
	Collective Responsibility. Criminal Motive. Weregild. Evidence. Australia. Ifugao. Eskimo. Plains Indians. Polynesia. Africa. Conclusion.	
XV.	CONCLUSION	427
	CORRECTIONS AND ADDENDA	442
	BIBLIOGRAPHY	443
	INDEX	451

PRIMITIVE SOCIETY

PRIMITIVE SOCIETY

CHAPTER I

INTRODUCTION

PRIMITIVE society is in a sense coextensive with primitive civilization. For civilization or culture, to substitute the ethnological term, is according to Tylor's famous definition "that complex whole which includes knowledge, belief, art, morals, law, custom, and any other capabilities and habits acquired by man as a member of society"; whence it follows that a complete consideration of society involves a study of all the phases of civilization. No such stupendous task is here attempted. I will limit myself to those aspects of culture known as *social organization,* i.e., I will deal with the groups into which society is divided, the functions of these groups, their mutual relations, and the factors determining their growth.

Yet so closely are the several departments of civilization knitted together that concentration on any one of them to the exclusion of all others is an impracticable undertaking. Recent events have familiarized us with the mutual dependence of apparently disparate branches of culture. Military operations cannot be successfully conducted without the activities of the laboratory scientist and of the husbandman. In stages of lesser advancement the same principle holds. If we wish to study social organization it is impossible to ignore industrial factors because often society is organized precisely along industrial lines, into guilds of blacksmiths and architects, shipwrights and tattooers. Our concern, however, will not be with the technical processes employed by these artisans, even though they are characteristic of the society to which they belong; we shall rather deal with the position of each body in the community, its comparative status of superiority or inferiority, its prerogatives and duties as one of a number of parallel or intercrossing aggregates. Similarly, if we have occasion to take notice of religious corporations, interest will not center in beliefs or observances, but in the position which the several groups occupy in the general polity. If we were to view Christianity from this angle, differences as to auricular confession or the theory of transubstantiation would figure mainly as group labels, while the rise to ascendancy in the state of one body of believers, the degradation of another, the disabilities of a third, would primarily engage our attention. Nevertheless it is impossible to anticipate how much knowledge of religion proper would prove necessary to illuminate the main problem, and unawares we might find ourselves plunged head over heels into the subtleties of scholastic disputation. It is not otherwise with savage peoples, and in order to gauge with accuracy the character of a social organization it is sometimes essential to take note of data representing all other phases of aboriginal activity.

Scientifically the study of primitive societies does not require justification. They *exist* and as part of reality Science is bound to take note of them. But the manner and spirit in which they have been regarded in the past have differed widely, and it will not be amiss to consider some of the ideals pursued in their investigation.

For one thing, it is possible to assume a predominantly monographic attitude. Some students fix their gaze upon a single people at a single epoch of its existence, and endeavor to describe this one culture with the utmost fidelity. In the higher reaches of this type of work the ethnographer becomes an artist who sympathetically penetrates into the latent spirit of his culture and creates a picture after the fashion of Gobineau's Renaissance. That is the ideal of humanistic research acclaimed by the philosopher Windelband and his school. To them each manifestation of human history represents a unique phenomenon, an absolutely indefinable set of values that can merely be experienced through the visionary's intuition and then transmitted in fainter tints to his public. Ethnographic effort conducted in this spirit would result in a gallery of cultural portraits, each complete in itself and not related with the rest.

Such an attitude toward the data of civilization is by no means inconsistent with scientific aims, and inasmuch as it reveals the subtler phases of culture it may even contribute indispensable elements to a complete description of reality. But it is equally true that Science cannot rest content with this aesthetic immersion in distinct manifestations of human society. Indeed, a student passing successively from one of these reproductions to another would imperceptibly yield to a mental exercise quite different from the impulse that fired the painter in plumbing the individuality of his subject or from his own initial attempt at re-creation. Spontaneously comparison of later and earlier pictures would blend with merely absorptive processes. Against the martial cast of one culture would stand out the devotional twist of another or the blot of money-madness in a third. Resemblances would be noted as well as differences, and the question would imperatively obtrude itself how both are to be explained. In other words, phenomena would be not merely apperceived by themselves but viewed in their relations.

In part it would be a problem of causal relations. It is natural to suppose that like phenomena must have like causes and accordingly it would become the ethnologist's duty to determine these: a priori they might be supposed to lie in racial affinity, or the similarity of geographical environment, or some other fundamental condition shared by the cultures compared. Practically, however, as will appear later, it is not so easy to isolate such determinants amidst the tremendous complexities of cultural data and to demonstrate that they are the significant factors. Indeed, some ethnologists have abandoned all hope of ever unraveling them. But whether the quest of causal relations be a hopeless one or not, one kind of relation can never be ignored by the scientific student of culture—the chronological one. Assume that our cultural picture gallery contains delineations of all distinguishable cultures. It would then embrace separate pictures of the successive cultures of the same people. Aesthetic contemplation might rest content with apperceiving the picture of Japan in 1000 A.D. and the picture of Japan in 1900 as representing two disparate embodiments of cultural ideals as independent of each other as either is of the Italian Renaissance. But that could not possibly be the attitude of the scientific student. To him the fact that one culture has grown out of another, that the same culture has varied with time, is an all-important fact; without a knowledge of the time relations of cultures that are merely links of one chain he would feel that he had missed the most essential part of reality. To put it tersely, whatever else the investigator of civilization may do, he *must* be an historian.

But what kind of an historian shall the ethnologist be? Some eminent savants whose thinking has been moulded in experimental laboratories have prescribed with much emphasis what kind of history is worth while. Accustomed to seeing physical phenomena described in the stenographic equations of the calculus, they cannot conceive of any branch of knowledge as worth a candle unless it conforms to the pattern of celestial mechanics. Says Professor Pearson in *The Grammar of Science:* "History can never become science, can never be anything but a catalogue of facts rehearsed in more or less pleasing language until these facts are seen to fall into sequences which can be briefly resumed in scientific formulae." Applying his tenet specifically to civilization, this author contends that in broad outline the development of man has followed the same course in Europe, in Africa, in Australasia; that it can be briefly resumed in terms of certain basic principles; and that except in so far as the historian undertakes to ascertain these, his efforts are hardly worthy of serious consideration. Similar opinions have been voiced by Professor Ostwald, the chemist, and Dr. Driesch, the zoologist.

The attitude just defined displays a surprising naïveté. No doubt ethnologists and other historians would be greatly at fault if they failed to discover the laws underlying civilization, thus giving to their data the highest degree of coordination to which they are amenable. But the first question is whether any such laws exist and what measure of coördination is feasible. The existence of uniformity in culture history cannot be assumed simply because it would be convenient. Even in physics the investigator is not always fortunate enough to reduce his phenomena to a Newtonian formula. He must theoretically accept the fact that water has its point of maximum density at four degrees Centigrade, as men at large have had to reckon with it practically, without waiting until water shall assume the properties of other liquids. So the ethnologist cannot permit his task to be pre-determined for him. If there are laws of social evolution, he must assuredly discover them, but *whether* there are any remains to be seen, and his scholarly position remains unaffected by their non-existence. His duty is to ascertain the course civilization actually has followed; and the kind of synthesis he gives must depend on the nature of his facts. To strive for the ideals of another branch of knowledge may be positively pernicious, for it can easily lead to that factitious simplification which means falsification. It would be equivalent to insisting that water *must* condense in freezing. If every people of the globe had a culture history wholly different from that of every other, the historian's task would still be to record these singularities and make the best of them; and in contributing his share to the sum total of knowledge he would suffer no loss in scientific dignity from the unmalleability of his material. Without, therefore, at the outset renouncing the search for laws of social evolution, we will emphatically declare our independence of that pseudo-scientific dogmatism which insists on formulating all phenomena after the fashion that has proved serviceable in a diminutive corner of the field of human knowledge. Uninfluenced by any bias for or against historical regularities, we shall attempt to determine what are the facts and what has been their actual sequence.

Here, however, the ethnologist encounters an obstacle from which the historian of the higher civilizations is exempt. The succession of events in primitive communities is rarely a matter of recorded knowledge except for the most recent period, and when positive information extends back to several centuries ago the student considers himself unusually fortunate. This presents a real difficulty but not an insurmountable one. For in addition to the sparse documentary sources the ethnologist possesses a stock of established ethnographic and linguistic fact, and when this is combined with the data of geographical distribution it is often possible to reconstruct history with practical certainty. With regard to phenomena of social organization instances will be supplied in later chapters; I will therefore elucidate the method by a technological illustration. In smelting iron the natives of Madagascar employ the piston-bellows, a type quite different from the bellows of the Negro blacksmiths of the neighboring African continent. In a splendid example of historical reconstruction Tylor pointed out that the piston-bellows occurs also in Sumatra, in other parts of the Malay Archipelago, and the adjacent portion of the Asiatic mainland; and that anthropologically and linguistically the Malagasy of Madagascar are members of the Malay family. Hence the piston-bellows is undoubtedly a Malay invention, which was carried by the Malays to various regions in the

INTRODUCTION

course of their migrations. By thus combining general anthropological knowledge with knowledge of the distribution of a trait Tylor succeeded in establishing the history of a mechanical contrivance beyond any reasonable doubt.

In the historical reconstruction of culture the phenomena of distribution play, indeed, an extraordinary part. If a trait occurs everywhere, it might veritably be the product of some universally operative social law. If it is found in a restricted number of cases, it may still have evolved through some such instrumentality acting under specific conditions that would then remain to be determined by analysis of the cultures in which the feature is embedded. On the other hand, as in the instance of the Malagasy bellows, there may be no law involved but a question of genetic relationship. Finally, the sharers of a cultural trait may be of distinct lineage but through contact and borrowing have come to hold in common a portion of their cultures.

Thus the data as to distribution demand an interpretation, whether in terms of some causal factor, or of tribal affinity or international intercourse; and the answer elicited with the aid of extraneous ethnological information is necessarily cast in historical form. If we were tracing the history of ironwork, we should assign to the Malay bellows a relatively late date because it is a specialized form evolved in a region of Asia remote from the ancient centers of metallurgy; and we should regard the Malagasy bellows as a relatively recent importation because Madagascar represents the farthest outpost of Malay civilization.

Since, as a matter of fact, cultural resemblances abound between peoples of diverse stock, their interpretation commonly narrows to a choice between two alternatives. Either they are due to like causes, whether these can be determined or not; or they are the result of borrowing. A predilection for one or the other explanation has lain at the bottom of much ethnological discussion in the past; and at present influential schools both in England and in continental Europe clamorously insist that all cultural parallels are due to diffusion from a single center. It is inevitable to envisage this moot-problem at the start, since uncompromising championship of either alternative has far-reaching practical consequences. For if every parallel is due to borrowing, then sociological laws, which can be inferred only from independently developing likenesses, are barred. Then the history of religion or social life or technology consists exclusively in a statement of the place of origin of beliefs, customs and implements, and a recital of their travels to different parts of the globe. On the other hand, if borrowing covers only part of the observed parallels, an explanation from like causes becomes at least the ideal goal in an investigation of the remainder. It is therefore proper to justify in the beginning whatever position one is inclined to take in the conflict between the rival theories of diffusion and independent evolution.

The great strength of the diffusionist theory lies in the abundance of evidence that transmission has played an enormous part in the growth of cultures. This is often not merely a matter of inference but of recorded observation, as in the influence of Egyptian on Greek, or of Arabian on mediaeval European civilization. To this vast body of testimony must be added numerous examples of borrowing established by inference but in a manner that admits of no doubt. Whenever a well-defined trait is distributed over a continuous area, the conclusion can hardly be avoided that it has developed in one spot within that area and has thence traveled to its confines. Often that conclusion is corroborated by a quantitative test: the feature in question is found in a state of high elaboration about the center of origin and dwindles towards the periphery. Thus, Professor Boas has demonstrated with great elegance that the Raven cycle of Canadian mythology originated about the northern part of British Columbia and thence traveled southwards. The farther one proceeds from the point of origin the smaller is the degree of elaboration of the cycle until it finally tapers away. This combination of legendary adventures could not be confined to a narrow coastal strip if it were the product of some law of myth-making; and there would not be noticeable that progressive diminution of complexity if we were not dealing with a case of successive transmission to districts farther and farther removed from the fountainhead.

Diffusion must accordingly be hailed as a *vera causa*. But is it the only one? What shall we say when like traits crop up in widely severed regions of which the populations are neither racially related nor have ever been in contact so far as is known? In that contingency the diffusionist must have recourse to the auxiliary hypothesis that contact at one time existed; and he does so because of his conviction that every element of culture is ultimately due to so extraordinary a confluence of circumstances that the conditions for a second invention can never recur. This is the basic tenet of the diffusionist creed that we must face.

It may at once be admitted that some of the arguments leveled at this position in the past have not been especially fortunate. Thus, the duplication of scientific discoveries has been cited to prove that the same feature may develop independently. Yet in general this argument lacks cogency. A careful historical examination usually shows that the co-discoverers both borrowed largely from the same cultural stock, as did Newton and Leibnitz in the discovery of the calculus. Such a case, then, cannot be likened to the independent creation of cultural elements in completely separated areas. Further, when modern scientists duplicate each other's results they are not merely building on the same foundation but are trained workers who consciously seek to add definite stones to the structure. This deliberate striving on the basis of special training is a motive that must be wholly banished in considering the ruder civilizations, and the likelihood of a repeated invention is proportionately lessened.

The weakness of the diffusionist doctrine in its extreme form lies in its lack of discrimination. Few would deny that a highly complex invention could not readily be made several times, but when this principle is extended to the simplest devices and conceptions it flies in the face of probability. It is true that man suffers from poverty of inventiveness and ever prefers to follow the path of lesser resistance by borrowing, but his failing is not so great as is contended. If it were, that admirable adaptation to environment which we occasionally note in widely separated areas could never have taken place. The Micronesians would not have learned to substitute the shell of the giant clam for the stone no longer available on their islands for axe blades; the Andaman Islanders and South American natives would never have learned to stupefy fish with poisonous plants; nor would any of a legion of ingenious industrial processes of strictly limited range have been achieved. Must we assume that the Plains Indian who was able to perfect a highly complex embroidery technique in porcupine quills was incapable of discovering for himself that buffalo dung could be used in fire-making and had to learn it from some alien source? The Hidatsa Indians of North Dakota still cross the Missouri in boats resembling the Welsh coracle, an umbrella-shaped frame being covered with a hide. Must we countenance the assumption that a connection once existed that has merely been obliterated in course of time? We shall certainly not yield to that view if among neighboring tribes there turns up the prototype of the Hidatsa bull-boat,—an improvised raft of tent skins supported by cross-pieces of wood and proving the autochthonous invention of the boat. Again, there is the case of the Australians and the Tierra del Fuegians, both of whom readily noted on becoming acquainted with glass that this material offered a good substitute for stone in the manufacture of certain implements. Thus a fairly long catalogue might be made of simple ideas that are either positively known to have been conceived more than once or that at least in all probability originated independently in two or more places. Indeed, there is not lacking evidence that even more abstruse notions have in rare instances been re-invented. None is more remarkable than the occurrence of the zero figure in the notation of the Maya of Yucatan, an achievement not equaled by the Greeks or Romans and duplicating that of the Hindu without the least possibility of mutual influence.

However, the illustrations cited apply only to a limited section of the cultural domain, that in which mechanical or theoretical problems are solved by intellectual means. The religious, sociological and aesthetic aspects of culture are founded in response to totally different motives. It is conceivable that in these, where there is greater freedom from rational control, where in other words the analogical faculty functions in unrestrained vigor, the chance for independent evolution is lessened or annulled. Indeed, some observers would sooner admit that the most important inventions of mechanical ingenuity could have a multiple origin than that any human mind could independently have retraced the tortuous path that has led to some grotesque mythological conception. Nevertheless the non-rationalistic departments of culture are not lacking in examples of the independent origin of similar features. A single illustration will suffice. No worse affront can be hurled in the teeth of a Kurnai Australian than to call him an orphan; and the same is true of the Crow Indian in Montana. That so harmless a term should be resented as the most offensive imprecation seems strange, but there is an explanation for it. Among the ruder peoples influence is often directly dependent on the greater or lesser number of faithful relatives. The kinless orphan is consequently damned to social impotence and considering aboriginal vanity it is natural that the vocabulary of vituperation should contain no more degrading epithet. It is therefore not only certain that neither the Kurnai borrowed from the Crow nor vice versa, but the reason for the observed parallel is clear from known facts of primitive life.

It is not necessary to multiply instances of this type because an inexhaustible supply of relevant data is furnished by a single department of culture, to wit, language. Linguistic processes belong to the same category psychologically as the processes by which the non-intellectualistic part of culture has come into being, and what applies to them has accordingly a wider application. English has come to approach Chinese in the simplicity of its grammar not because of the direct influence exerted by China on the speech of the British Isles but from internal causes. If the Shoshonean Indian languages of the Great Basin of North America have a dual number it is not because they have borrowed the notion from the ancient Greeks but because it is a notion that can and does arise independently. In this manner a host of instances can be enumerated showing that the same mode of classifying or describing phenomena has been evolved in languages utterly unrelated in origin and wholly disconnected in point of contact. If that is so, even though the reason for the resemblances be forever hidden from our ken, the fact is established that reasoning and classification by analogy can produce analogous results. Accordingly it is sheer dogmatism to decree that such results could not occur in the case of customs or myths.

In short, there is no reason for excluding the possibility of independent development in the study of social organization. I will accordingly treat each case of resemblance on its merits and shall not strike the balance between the rival theories before the close of my investigation.

In the foregoing remarks lies the reason for the important place assigned to matters of distribution in the subsequent chapters. From the range of a phenomenon we know at once whether it can even tentatively rank as a necessary consequence of human gregariousness, while a comparison of linked traits may reveal the conditions favoring its appearance. The distribution of an institution may demonstrate that it has been diffused, and when coupled with other information it may aid in a fairly complete reconstruction of historical processes. When we know only the range of a usage, we may not yet know very much, but we have at least a point of departure for amplifying our information. When we do not know the distribution of a phenomenon with unrecorded history, we know nothing that is theoretically significant.

The knowledge of primitive society has an educational value that should recommend its study even to those who are not primarily interested in the processes of culture history. All of us are born into a set of traditional institutions and social conventions that are accepted not only as natural but as the only conceivable response to social needs. Departures from our standards in foreigners bear in our biased view the stamp of inferiority. Against this purblind provincialism there is no better antidote than the systematic study of alien civilizations. Acquaintance with adjustments in one society after another that rest on wholly different foundations from those with which we are familiar enlarges our notion of social potentialities as the conception of n-dimensional space enlarges the vision of the non-Euclidean geometrician. We see our received set of opinions and customs as merely one of an indefinite number of possible variants; and we are emboldened to hew them into shape in accordance with novel aspirations.

CHAPTER II

MARRIAGE

IF SOCIAL organization is but one phase of culture and can be understood solely in connection with other phases, a corresponding statement holds even more decidedly for any one of the aspects of social organization. We may begin by considering the primitive family, but very soon we find that in order to comprehend its phenomena we must consider what at first seem quite irrelevant series of facts. In parts of Oceania, where a man regularly eats and sleeps at his club, this type of unit affects family life so profoundly that the two cannot well be divorced in picturing either. If, on the other hand, we begin with clubs, we shall very soon be engaged in a discussion of property concepts because membership in these organizations is sometimes equivalent to the holding of a proprietary title. But any treatment of property involves the notions of kinship that determine inheritance of property. And so forth. In short, these several topics are so closely interrelated that none of them can be treated as the basic one from which all others are logically deducible. However we commence, there must be constant anticipation and constant cross-referencing, for by the sheer necessities of exposition we are driven to examine fragment after fragment of an organic whole.

This being so, any starting-point will do. I will select the family as the first social unit to be considered; and will naturally begin by describing the conditions that confront the individual who desires to found a new family,—the social prohibitions and prescriptions to which he has to submit in the selection of a mate and the traditional means of acquiring one.

Marriage Prohibitions

In every part of the world there are restrictions on the choice of a mate based on propinquity of relationship. Those who transgress the rules are guilty of the dread crime of incest. Within the narrowest family circle sexual relations are universally tabooed. There are no tribes which countenance the mating of parent and child, and where brother-sister unions have been recorded they are not the result of primitiveness but of excessive sophistication. That is, in communities where pride of descent obtains in hypertrophied form, as in ancient Egypt and Peru, the sovereign may find no one of sufficiently high rank to become his mate except his nearest blood kin. Such instances are, however, decidedly rare and do not affect the practices of the common herd.

It is not the function of the ethnologist but of the biologist and psychologist to explain why man has so deep-rooted a horror of incest, though personally I accept Hobhouse's view that the sentiment is instinctive. The student of society merely has to reckon with the fact that the dread of incest limits the biologically possible number of unions. He must further register the different ways in which different communities conceive the incest rule. For while parent and child, brother and sister, are universally barred from mating, many tribes favor and all but prescribe marriages between certain more remote kindred. That is to say, while the aversion to marriage within the group of the closest relatives may be instinctive, the extension of that sentiment beyond that restricted circle is conventional, some tribes drawing the line far more rigorously than others. For example, the Blackfoot of Montana not only discountenance the marriage of cousins but look askance at any union within the local band "because there is always a suspicion that some close blood relationship may have been overlooked." The Shuswap and Thompson River Indians of British Columbia deprecate unions of second cousins, the Nez Percé of Idaho even those of third cousins. According to an educated member of the Paviotso of Nevada the most remote cousins are still reckoned by her people as kindred, and consequently matrimony is barred.

This repugnance to in-breeding must be connected with a common primitive usage. A Paviotso, e.g., addresses all cousins, regardless of degree, as his brother or sister. Now among rude peoples there is a great deal in a name and from calling a girl sister to regarding her as a sister for matrimonial purposes is but a step owing to the superstitious identification of things bearing the same appellation. Hence, provided a tenth cousin be *called* by the same term as the first, the incest horror will be naturally extended to her as well.

There are, indeed, far more startling extensions of this sentiment. Frequently there is not merely a rule against the marriage of actual blood-kin but even of individuals between whom no relationship can be traced and who are regarded as kin simply through the legal fiction that fellow-members of a certain social group are ultimately descendants of the same ancestor. The magical potency of the group name doubtless plays a large part here. Thus in Australia a man of, say, the Emu group in one tribe would not mate with an Emu woman of an alien tribe a hundred miles away, though blood-kinship is absolutely precluded by the conditions of the case.

The rule which prescribes that an individual must find a mate outside of his own group, whether that group be the family, the village, or some other social unit, is known as *exogamy*. The contrary rule which makes it compulsory for a man to mate within his group is labeled *endogamy*. Endogamy flourishes where social distinctions have come to be matters of paramount importance. The Hindu caste system is the stock illustration, European aristocracy supplies another. At a lower level of civilization the Tsimshian of British Columbia frown upon the marriage of a chief's relatives with those of a chief's attendant or of an attendant's with commoners. It is only the notion of obligatory marriage within the social unit not the *de facto* occurrence of unions within the group that constitutes endogamy. For example, the young men of Kalamazoo naturally find their wives for the most part among their townswomen, but there is nothing to prevent them from seeking a bride in Ottumwa or Przemysl. It is only where there is lurking the notion of a prohibition that we can speak of an endogamous tendency,—say, in connection with the feeling that a Catholic ought not to marry a Protestant.

Exogamy and endogamy are not mutually exclusive except with regard to the same unit. The Toda of the Nilgiri Hills in Southern India are divided into two groups, the Tartharol and the Teivaliol, between which legal matrimony is prohibited. But each is subdivided into groups which are exogamous. A person of the Pan section of the Tartharol may not choose for his spouse a girl of Teivaliol affiliation, but must seek a Tartharol of some section other than his own.[1]

Means of Acquiring a Mate

Generalizations about primitive tribes are dangerous, but few exceptions will be found to the statement that matrimony with them is not so much a sacramental as a civil institution. It differs, however, notably from modern arrangements in Caucasian civilization in that the contract often binds not individuals but families. This appears clearly in two forms of matrimony known as marriage by exchange and marriage by purchase. In both a girl is treated as an asset which her family will not surrender without receiving adequate compensation.

Among the Kariera of Western Australia the acquisition of a bride is complicated by certain rules of preferential mating. That is, a man is not only forbidden to marry his sister and certain other kinswomen, but is practically obliged to mate with a particular type of cousin or some more remote relative designated by the same term (see below, Preferential Mating). With this limitation exchange is commonly practised. A man, A, having one or more sisters finds a man, B, standing to him in the proper cousin relationship who also possesses a sister. These men each take a sister of the other as wife. This method seems to have a very definite distribution. It is common in Australia and the Torres Straits Islands but rare or absent even in the neighboring region of Melanesia.

Apart from such exchange of sisters, the Kariera elders arrange marriages of the orthodox type between juvenile cousins. The death of one of them may effect a change but the new arrangement will still conform to the matrimonial norm: the prospective spouses will be cousins of the prescribed type, though perhaps more remotely related. In the case of infant betrothals a boy grows up with the understanding that a certain man is his probable father-in-law and as such is entitled to occasional presents and services. But since his fiancée may die, there is a whole group of potential fathers-in-law who are entitled to similar consideration, though in lesser degree; these attentions may be conceived as a form of compensation equivalent to the purchase form of other areas. When a girl attains the proper age, she is simply handed over to the bridegroom. That we are verily dealing with a family compact appears clearly from certain additional elements of Kariera matrimonial life. "Where there are several sisters in a family they are all regarded as the wives of the man who marries the eldest of them." This is a widespread custom known as the *sororate*. On the other hand, a man's wives are automatically inherited by his younger brother or a kinsman ranking

MARRIAGE

as such, a usage technically referred to as the *levirate*. Finally, a man may waive his preëmptive claim on his wife's younger sister in favor of his younger brother.

Compared with exchange, purchase has an exceedingly wide distribution. It is, however, important to distinguish several varieties of purchase which are neither psychologically nor legally equivalent. In some regions woman is to all intents and purposes a transferable and inheritable species of chattel; in others, there will be found only the appearance of purchase, since the price offered is balanced or even outweighed by an equivalent gift or dowry.

To begin with purchase in the strictest sense of the term. Among the Kirgiz, a Turkish tribe of southwestern Siberia, a man will betroth a ten-year old son to a girl and commence forthwith to amass the bride-price, which is as high as 81 head of cattle. This is paid in instalments; only when a large portion has been conveyed to the fiancée's family may the young man visit the girl, and the marriage takes place with the completed payment. Owing to the high amount exacted by the bride's family, few men have more than one wife and very rarely is a woman divorced, though under the Mohammedan law the husband's authority would be unrestricted. Here the woman is quite definitely conceived as her spouse's property and loses contact with her own family.

With the Ho, an Ewe tribe in the interior of Togo, West Africa, there is a series of payments and services which establish a proprietary title to the wife, but there is no complete severance from her family and altogether her social status is distinctly better than among the Kirgiz. Here the initial arrangements are often made even before the girl's birth: a man who likes a woman is wont to bespeak the next daughter she may bear. If the proposal is accepted, the fiancé must give a preliminary present to the prospective parents-in-law, which is followed by monthly gifts of cowrie-shells to the infant girl and horticultural assistance to her parents, together with a variety of other services. At puberty the young woman is turned over to the bridegroom, but if the compensation offered by him appears inadequate the parents will previously annul the contract by sending him a stipulated amount of cowrie money. There can be no doubt that in a certain sense the Ho woman is a form of property; she may serve as a pawn in a creditor's custody and is inherited by her husband's brothers while herself barred from inheriting any of his possessions. Nevertheless in practice the theoretical rigor of these conceptions is considerably weakened. Women may exercise a great deal of influence on their husbands, have been known to leave them in joint rebellion, and are entitled to compensation for supplying their spouses with cotton.

The erroneous notions that might be suggested by the catchword 'purchase' are clearly exposed by a consideration of the Kai, a Papuan people in New Guinea. Here the bride-price, consisting of a boar's tusk, a hog and other valuables, is paid to the girl's maternal uncles and brothers, while the father is merely entitled to a certain amount of work. In a sense the husband again becomes the owner of his wife through the transaction: she is inherited by his brothers or kinsmen, is punishable by her husband for adultery, and in cases of elopement her loss is compensated by a return of the bride-price. But while juridically the wife is nil, her person has not been surrendered absolutely by her kin. If the man breaks his wife's pottery, he must indemnify her family; he is as little entitled to inherit her property as she is to appropriate his legacy; and the children belong definitely to her and her kin. In short, what the man acquires by purchase is an exclusively sexual prerogative; even in return for his wife's economic services he is obliged to do an equivalent amount of work on behalf of the common household.

In contrast to Kai custom stands the *lobola* usage of the Thonga of South Africa. To be sure, here too the suitor and his family acquire a woman through offering a stipulated bride-price (*lobola*),—cattle or hoes; and the widow is as a matter of course inherited by a member of her husband's family,—one of his younger brothers, or sister's sons, or sons by another wife. Indeed, the property concept is consistently applied to a still greater extent. When a man has surrendered the customary bride-price, his wife's family forthwith use it to purchase a wife for an adult son. If, now, the first man's wife elopes, her husband may claim the *lobola;* since it has already been expended in buying a wife for his brother-in-law, the eloper's insolvent kinsfolk may be driven to the point of surrendering this newly bought woman to her fugitive sister-in-law's husband. So far it is simply a case of rigorously applying the purchase principle. But in one respect there is a fundamental divergence from Kai practice: the *lobola* is most emphatically understood to pay not only for the woman but for all her issue, so that a husband may claim restoration of the bride-price if his wife dies childless, while, on the other hand, the offspring of a woman belong to her family provided the *lobola* remains unpaid.

Again a different conception prevailed among the Hidatsa of North Dakota. Purchase was here the most honorable form of marriage for the woman, and only girls never previously married were bought. But though some proprietary right was acknowledged, as evidenced by the levirate rule, its development was relatively weak. The husband had no absolute power over either his wife or the children. He was indeed entitled to wed his wife's younger sisters but on the other hand he frequently figured in the beginning of his matrimonial life as a sort of servant in the father-in-law's household. It is also important to note that the purchase was often no more than an exchange of gifts, the bridegroom's being sometimes exceeded in value by the return presents received from the bride's kin.

This equivalence of dowry and bride-price is by no means

rare in North America. It was characteristic of the matrimonial unions of the Tlingit of southern Alaska. Obviously in such cases we can hardly continue to speak of purchase. The legal conceptions bound up with such usages are interesting. With the Tlingit the children always belonged to the mother's family in case of divorce. If the husband separated from his wife on account of sheer incompatibility, he was obliged to restore the dowry to her parents, who retained his gifts. If, however, the cause was adultery on the woman's part, he was entitled to have his presents returned to him and kept the dowry.

Enough has been said to show the great variability of the purchase concept and the range of juristic notions associated with it in different regions. Before leaving the category of cases in which compensation of some sort is offered for the wife it is well to point out that the notion of service for a bride, which is frequently merely a substitute for purchase or supplementary to it, may display a quite different significance. Thus, with the Koryak of northeastern Siberia service is the established method of winning a bride. Even when the son-in-law settles with the wife's parents, so that they not merely avoid losing the daughter's assistance but gain her husband's permanent support, the rule is not relaxed. The suitor not only must accomplish useful work, but must endure privation and humiliating treatment; his service period is a test of character and skill rather than the equivalent of a bride-price.

Suitors' trials, indeed, play a very prominent part in aboriginal folk-tales, which delight in depicting the hero as overcoming the most extraordinary obstacles. Reality is less romantic, but definite tests are not wanting. Thus, among the Arawak of British Guiana the prospective husband was obliged to prove his marksmanship by shooting an arrow into a woodpecker's nest from a moving boat and to give further demonstration of his mettle by clearing a field and filling a large number of crab baskets within a specified span of time. The idea at the bottom of such tasks is of course to make sure that the young man is capable of providing for a family. This motive occurs as a constant refrain in the utterances of North American Indians, where the skilful hunter figures as the ideal son-in-law.

Common as is the notion that some sort of compensation must be yielded in return for the bride, it is by no means universal. Even in some of the cases cited above a closer examination has shown that the *form* of rendering a consideration may harbor substantially different conceptions. There can be no real purchase where the dowry equals the bridegroom's gifts; nor where the present offered dwindles, as among the Indians of the northwest Amazons country, to a pot of tobacco and another of coca. A number of forms of marriage must be mentioned, however, which lack even the semblance of compensation.

In the first place, there is marriage by capture. Though it plays an exaggerated rôle in the earlier speculative literature of the subject, it is really of distinctly minor importance. For example, the warlike Plains Indians frequently enough captured women of hostile tribes and took them to wife; but the vastly preponderating number of alliances for obvious reasons took place within the tribe. There, however, the appropriation of a woman by force was not so simple a matter because it might at once precipitate a family feud. It is true that among the Northern Athabaskans of the Mackenzie River region there were wrestling-matches between rival claimants, the stronger being entitled to carry off a woman even though she had already been married; and similar practices are reported from the Eskimo on the west coast of Hudson Bay. But, on the whole, social sanction of the rights of brute force within the community is granted by very few peoples. To be sure, there occurs in a fair number of cases a dramatization of bride capture. Thus among the Koryak the bride, often assisted by her friends, resists the groom's advances and he may receive a sound thrashing before reducing her to submission. Such usages were interpreted by an older school of anthropologists as survivals of a condition in which marriages were normally contracted by capture. But it is far simpler and less hypothetical to connect it with other incidents of Koryak pre-matrimonial experiences and to recognize in the symbolic capture merely the final test of the suitor's adroitness and prowess. Elsewhere we may plausibly assume with Dr. Hobhouse that the dramatic performance of capture symbolizes appropriation and "is not necessarily a survival of something more real, but may be rather a legal expression of the character of the act performed."

Secondly, there are those cases in which the young couple, defying it may be the wishes of elders or the dictates of convention, marry by mutual consent, possibly overcoming obstacles through elopement. Instances of this type are reported from everywhere but the implications of such love matches vary enormously. In modern America marriages based on mutual love represent theoretically the highest type, but this notoriously does not hold for the upper strata of European society. There, as among the Kai, legal wedlock and the gratification of the sexual instinct are two distinct things. The latter is abundantly satisfied apart from marriage; marriage is largely dissociated from love in its higher and lower forms and is based on considerations of an economic, social, or political character. The type of union that seems highest to us may thus be regarded by others perhaps as unequivocally inferior in social value. Among the Crow Indians of Montana there was abundant opportunity for philandering at picnicking excursions or similar occasions, and some of the attachments thus formed ripened into more than temporary unions. Yet in tribal estimation such marriages were not to be compared with marriages by purchase, which ranked as more honorable and are said to have had far greater likelihood of per-

MARRIAGE

manence. This doubtless was due to the fact that a man would only buy a woman or girl with an established reputation for chastity. The matrimonial history of a typical Crow might thus consist of several love matches and a single orthodox marriage by purchase, which through the sororate often became polygamous. A woman did not become an outcast by associating herself with a man from inclination: she merely fell short of ideal perfection. Indeed, she would not even rouse unfavorable comment unless she frequently changed mates. A handsome or brave man was expected to have an indefinite number of love affairs, quite apart from anything resembling marital alliances. The matter might be formulated thus, that the more permanent love matches acquired a status superior to mere philandering or concubinage but never attained the prestige of marriage by purchase.

The Crow data suggest a principle of wider application. Generally there is more than one way of acquiring a permanent mate, though the several methods may be graded differently in the scale of public approbation. A Crow may get a wife by buying one or by inheriting his brother's widow, he may enter an alliance of love without payment or legitimately acquire additional spouses through the sororate after purchasing the eldest daughter in the family, or capture an alien woman in an attack on a Dakota camp, or under special conditions legitimately take away a tribesman's wife if she has previously been his mistress. In other regions the particular means may differ but multiplicity is fairly common. This fact renders a numerical estimate of the several methods of arranging marriage in the world peculiarly difficult, and the task is rendered even more onerous by the different connotations of such terms as purchase or service. Shall we reckon the Crow as a bride-buying people because purchase is the ideal mode, even though possibly sixty per cent of all the stable unions may be nonconformist? Or is it permissible to treat Kirgiz, Kai, and

Hidatsa as wife-purchasers without discrimination? Professor Hobhouse has attempted a census of the bride-buying peoples, giving the percentage of pastoral, agricultural and hunting peoples who render compensation for their wives. But though every effort to enhance the precision of sociological statements must be hailed with pleasure, in the present instance it seems foredoomed to failure because of the variability of matrimonial arrangements in the same tribe and because of the varying significance of purchase.[2]

Preferential Mating

While primitive society frequently interdicts unions which to us seem unobjectionable, it often favors and even prescribes the marriage of individuals in a manner foreign to modern Caucasian usage. Several instances have already been encountered,—a type of cousin marriage, the levirate, and the sororate.

When primitive peoples favor cousin marriage, this is nearly always limited to those relatives technically known as *cross-cousins,* while *parallel* or *identical* cousins are barred from intermarrying by the incest rule. The children of a man and those of his brother are one another's parallel or identical cousins; so are the children of a woman and those of her sister. On the other hand, the children of a man are cross-cousins of his sister's children, the relationship being reciprocal. Everyday speech lacks a generic word to include brother *and* sister, but the ethnologist may conveniently borrow the biologist's term *siblings,* which designates descendants of the same parent regardless of their sex. With the aid of this term we may put the matter thus: the children of siblings of the same sex are parallel cousins and are usually themselves called siblings in primitive languages; the children of siblings of unlike sex are cross-cousins and are generally designated by a term expressing greater remoteness of kinship. Cross-cousin marriage may theoretically be of two types: a man may marry either the daughter of a mother's brother or of a father's sister. Practically these two forms may coincide through the fact that the mother's brother by tribal custom usually espouses the father's sister. So far as this is not the case, marriage of a man with the maternal uncle's daughter is decidedly the more common variety.

Cross-cousin marriage has a very interesting distribution. Far from being universal, it is nevertheless reported from every grand division of the globe. In West Australia and about Lake Eyre tribes prescribing marriage with a maternal uncle's daughter jostle others which prohibit any such union. The custom flourishes in several of the Melanesian Islands, notably in Fiji, but is discountenanced in nearby Polynesian groups, such as Samoa. Southern Asia may turn out to be the center where the institution attains its highest development; at all events, it has been fully described for the Toda and Vedda, occurs among various peoples of India and Farther India, such as the Tibeto-Burman Mikir of Assam, and also in Sumatra. Nor is it lacking in Siberia; the Gilyak enjoin the union of a man with his mother's brother's daughter, and it is at least likely that the cousin marriages permitted by the Kamchadal and Tungus conform to the same pattern. While relatively rare in America, this usage is reported from the northern coast of British Columbia, from central California, and Nicaragua; and the fact that in South America Chibcha women have a single word for husband and father's sister's son suggests that they too frequently mated with cross-cousins. Whether this type of preferential mating is countenanced by the Sudanese Negroes, is doubtful; but it is orthodox in parts of South and East Africa,—among the Hottentot, Herero, Basuto and Makonde.

It may be asked what happened in these tribes if a man had no cross-cousin,—if his mother had no brother or her brother no daughter. From our best accounts it is clear that in such cases a substitution of some more remote relative occurred who was reckoned of the same status. This took place, we are told, among the Kariera of West Australia: preëminently it was the daughter of a man's mother's own brother that was his prospective spouse; but failing such an uncle, he would apply to a mother's parallel male cousin or if necessary even to a more remote maternal kinsman provided he too was called maternal uncle.

In this connection an important question arises. If primitive folk commonly extend the term for cross-cousin so as to embrace many more remote relatives, are we not here confronted with a serious source of error? Is it not possible that our authorities have mistaken the native meaning and given the impression that near kin are expected to marry when in reality the form of marriage favored may be that between far more remote relatives or even between fictitious relatives? Fortunately modern investigators have made their records sufficiently specific to render an answer possible. The Toda, the Vedda, and the Fijians definitely prescribe the marriage of actual cross-cousins in the strict sense of the term whenever possible. Thus, nearly 30 per cent of the Fijian marriages tabulated by Mr. Thomson are of this type. With the Toda the figure does not quite come to 12 per cent, but this is explained by the transfer of wives in later life, which follows no definite rule and thus obscures the orthodox arrangement of infant betrothals. Even so there are families rigidly adhering to the norm, with six out of eight unions conforming to theory. Disparity of age is no obstacle, so that a woman of twenty may be wedded to a boy of two. On the other hand, Mr. Gifford informs us that among the Miwok of California local differences have arisen as to the favored degree of the cross-cousin unions. Some divisions countenance actual cross-cousin marriages, others restrict them to cousins of the same status but more distantly related.

Altogether our data suffice to prove that in one's own

generation the incest sentiment cannot be instinctive so far as first cousins are concerned but must be conventional. If it were instinctive, why are unions of parallel cousins generally tabooed and those of cross-cousins frequently enjoined? Why does one tribe permit cross-cousin marriage, while the institution is anathema to its next-door neighbors? Why do some communities license marriage with the daughter of a maternal uncle but under no conditions allow the other variety of cross-cousin marriage (Miwok, e.g.)?

Another question that arises in connection with this institution is to what extent it is not only permitted or even prescribed but obligatory. While the data are generally too meager to permit a general answer, it seems that tribes differ widely in this regard. The Kariera, if I interpret the evidence correctly, make cross-cousin marriage practically compulsory; the Fijians made allowances to individual antipathy; while with the Toda and Miwok other co-existing forms of orthodox marriage share the field with cross-cousin unions.

Can any interpretation be offered as to the essential meaning and origin of this institution? Tylor, following Fison, gives a plausible explanation why marriages of cross-cousins are permissible while those of parallel cousins are tabooed. He assumes that the custom arose in communities subdivided into exogamous halves with fixed rules of descent. In such cases parallel cousins will always belong to the same half, hence will be prevented from marrying by the exogamous law, while cross-cousins will belong to complementary halves and hence remain unaffected by the exogamous restriction. For example, if affiliation be inherited from the father, then the following condition develops. A man and his brothers and sisters all belong to their father's half of the tribe, A. The children of this man and those of his brothers will also be A, hence are precluded from intermarriage. But his sisters are obliged to marry men of B, and their children are all B, hence of the group which the brother's children *must* marry into.

This would be an exemplary solution if cross-cousin marriage were merely the marriage between members of certain groups regardless of degrees of kinship. But, as Rivers has pointed out, and as the data from Fiji, the Toda and elsewhere prove, this assumption is contrary to fact. It is often the *first* cross-cousin that is regarded as the preferential mate, more remote members of his kinship category being only substitutes in case of necessity. This is what Tylor fails to explain. All he shows is that in a dual organization cross-cousins in the strict sense of the term would be among potential mates. He does not explain why the next of kin among these potential spouses are considered preëminently the proper ones and the remainder merely makeshifts. A further difficulty lies in the fact that by no means all of the tribes practising cross-cousin marriage are organized into exogamous halves. The Toda are halved but into endogamous groups; while the Gilyak, Tsimshian and the South African tribes mentioned above lack the dual organization altogether. Further, Dr. Rivers has shown that in Melanesia it is precisely the tribes lacking such an organization which practise cross-cousin marriage, while this institution is absent where the dual organization is in full swing. Hence it cannot be the simple consequence of an exogamous dual system.

For Melanesia Dr. Rivers offers an alternative hypothesis avowedly constructed to cover only the Oceanian data. He assumes that at first the old men in power arrogated to themselves the available women, but later surrendered their marital privileges to their sisters' sons, ultimately substituting daughters for wives. An analogous interpretation, but of a rather less hypothetical cast, is presented by Mr. Gifford. He finds evidence that the cross-cousin marriage of the Miwok is a relatively recent institution and was preceded by marital rights over the daughter of one's wife's brother. These rights, Mr. Gifford plausibly argues, were passed on by inheritance to the man's son, whence marriage with the daughter of the maternal uncle. It is important to note that in consonance with their respective data Dr. Rivers and Mr. Gifford assume different rules of descent, a matter to be dealt with below. In Melanesia it is or was the sister's son, in central California the son that held the position of heir-apparent, hence if cross-cousin marriage is at all the consequence of inheritance rules, as both authors assume, either explanation is satisfactory but applicable only to tribes with corresponding laws of succession.

It is of course conceivable that cross-cousins came to marry each other by a less round-about method. Where the possession of property plays a dominant rôle in the tribal consciousness, as in British Columbia, the motive of keeping desirable belongings within the family circle may well lead to marriage with the father's own sister's daughter or the mother's own brother's daughter, as Swanton suggests. Another, though often related, cause lies in the sentiment of caste, which discountenances union with a person of lesser rank. To be sure, such ends would be equally served by the marriage of parallel cousins. But these, as has been noted, are commonly called siblings and with the primitive tendency to identify what is similarly *named* are reckoned as siblings, i.e., the incest feeling is extended to them. The cross-cousins would thus remain as the next of kin whose marriage, being permissible by customary law, could at the same time preserve the property and the social prestige within the family.

It should be noted that all the explanations offered of late are based on specific conditions. Cross-cousin marriage is in all probability not a phenomenon that has evolved from a single cause but one that has independently arisen in several centers from diverse motives.

Before leaving this interesting institution, a few words must be devoted to its influence on the classification of kindred. Where a man regularly weds the daughter of his mother's brother or of his father's sister, a maternal uncle will normally be his father-in-law, or a paternal aunt his mother-in-law. Hence it is not at all remarkable that in many tribes practising this form of marriage the men designate mother's brother and father-in-law by a single term and also have another single word for father's sister and mother-in-law. This is the case in Fiji and among the Vedda. But the effect of this form of marriage may go farther. Since a man's mate is normally his cross-cousin, we sometimes find that there is no distinct word for 'husband' or 'wife' but one term for both the husband and male cross-cousin of a woman, and another for both the wife and female cross-cousin of a man. Further, a brother-in-law may be called by the same terms as a man's male cross-cousin, while a woman will call her sister-in-law by the same designation as her female cross-cousin. However, by no means all tribes proceed with uniform consistency in this regard, and where other forms of preferential mating coëxist with cross-cousin marriage (as among the Miwok), the influence of the latter may be dwarfed or even reduced to nothingness.

Widespread as is the distribution of cross-cousin marriage, it pales into insignificance before that of two other forms of preferential mating, the levirate and the sororate. Though frequently in association, these customs also occur separately and accordingly are best treated in juxtaposition rather than as a single phenomenon.

Tylor found the levirate in fully one-third of the tribes for which data were extant in his day. Nowadays the proportion found would undoubtedly be far greater. Indeed, it is easier to count cases where the custom is positively known to be lacking than to enumerate instances of its occurrence. In North America it seems to be definitely discountenanced only among the Pueblo groups of the southwest, while even among the neighboring Navaho Indians usage requires a widow to wed her husband's brother or some other one of his close kinsmen. However, the levirate does not everywhere appear in the same form. First of all, a fair number of tribes restrict the widow's remarriage to younger brothers of the deceased husband, as do the Koryak and the Andaman Islanders. Though perhaps most commonly recorded in Asia, the junior levirate is by no means confined to that continent, for it is reported from Santa Cruz (Melanesia) and West Australia. Owing to the inadequate information usually vouchsafed on this subject by observers, we cannot even be sure that the levirate is not commonly of this type. Nevertheless, for some regions our data are sufficiently specific to prove that the levirate does exist in the unrestricted form as well. This holds, e.g., for the Banks Islands and the Torres Straits.

Secondly, the juridical and psychological implications of the levirate may be quite different. With the Thompson River Indians the brother of the deceased had an incontestable right to the widow; in many other places, as among the Thonga, the woman is permitted to choose from among a considerable number of her husband's kinsmen; in still other regions the arrangement appears to be in no sense obligatory. Indeed, the aboriginal attitude is sometimes almost antithetical to what might be conjectured off-hand: the woman is not so much claimed by way of prerogative as she is inherited as an obligation. That is, the brother-in-law is required to furnish protection and support to the widow and her children. This is often the nature of the relationship among the Chukchi and apparently also among the Gournditch-Mara of southwestern Victoria (Australia).

Where there is so much difference in conception and so little exact information, it would be vain to concoct a theory for all the known cases. The one general remark that may safely be offered is Tylor's view that the levirate results from the notion of marriage as a compact between groups rather than individuals. From this principle it follows that when a union terminates by the death of one of the mates, a substitute is automatically supplied by the group of the deceased. Beyond this point we shall have to inquire into the specific conditions of the social environment, the status of woman in the community examined, the accepted methods of acquiring a spouse.

For a large number of cases we can account by the rules prevalent as to the acquisition of a wife. Where the woman is definitely purchased in the strict sense of the term, she naturally forms an inheritable chattel. Thus among the Kirgiz a younger brother inherits the widow even if he is a minor. Similarly, a Kai widow becomes the property of an unmarried brother of her deceased husband; a man from another family wishing to marry her is obliged to offer payment. The underlying conceptions appear with great clarity in Shasta law. Since a man's brothers and kinsmen practically always contribute to the bride-price in this Californian tribe, they establish a secondary claim to the woman, and on the husband's death she naturally passes into the custody of a brother or, failing one, of a more remote male relative.

That property concepts often lie at the root of the levirate appears from other forms of preferential mating which coëxist with the levirate or supersede it. In a polygamous Thonga household of five wives the principal widow is likely to fall to the lot of that one of the husband's younger brothers who becomes master of the estate, the second and third wives go to two other brothers, the fourth to a nephew (sister's son) of the deceased, the fifth to one of his sons, who of course must not be her own. That is to say, those kinsmen who inherit part of a man's wealth also are entitled to inherit a widow. Similarly we find in the Melanesian Banks Islands and on the Northwest Coast of North America in addition to the levirate the rule that a wife may pass into the possession of the deceased husband's sister's son. It can hardly be an accident that in both these regions the sister's son is reckoned the heir-apparent to his uncle's property.

Though this principle explains much, it obviously does not explain everything. Why do we often encounter the levirate in the restricted form? As Jochelson points out, both elder and younger brothers inherit a deceased man's possessions, yet only his juniors are permitted to wed the widow. A common sense explanation suggests itself, but it should not be taken as more than a guess. Other things being equal, the elder brother is likely to marry before the younger, who may sometimes be hard put to it to acquire a mate, either because of an exorbitant bride-price or because available women are scarce. Under such conditions the junior levirate may have arisen on the view that to him who has not shall be given, and this tendency may have been standardized into customary law.

Another limitation to the property conception of the levirate lies in the fact that there are peoples practising it who do not purchase wives and do not regard women as property in the strict sense of the term. In not a few of these cases, however, we may reasonably fall back on Tylor's general principle of primitive marriage as a *family* contract: since from the aboriginal point of view the union of individuals is often largely symbolic of an alliance of groups, a deceased mate is naturally superseded in the matrimonial relationship by a member of the same group.

This assumption gains in weight when we find it also accounting admirably for the complementary custom of the sororate. The Shasta levirate has been described above. It is coupled with the sororate in an illuminating manner. Just as the man's brothers unite to pay for his bride, so the bride's family are jointly responsible for the services normally to be expected from a wife. If she fails to bear children, they gratuitously furnish a sister or cousin as a supplementary spouse; and the same rule obtains after the first wife's demise. There is here involved not merely a right but an obligation on the husband's part: he may marry outside his wife's family only by their specially granted leave.

On the basis of Tylor's theory we should expect the levirate and the sororate to coëxist, and in very large measure they undoubtedly do, while contrariwise the Pueblo Indians who were found to lack the levirate likewise do not practise the sororate. This intimate correlation is rightly insisted upon by Frazer, who has collected instances of the sororate from all regions of the globe. The connection would undoubtedly appear to be even closer were not much of our information on the marriage rules of primitive tribes of rather haphazard character. That is, it may safely be assumed that in not a few instances it is sheer negligence or defective observation that has made writers report one of the two customs without the other. There are nevertheless some noteworthy cases of negative correlation that must be accepted at their face value. While the Koryak practise both customs, the neighboring Chukchi have only the levirate; and the same applies to the Masai of East Africa, who expressly prohibit marriage with two women between whom there is any blood-relationship. Such exceptions, however, are not frequent enough to interfere with the conception of the levirate and the sororate as two closely connected institutions.

The sororate, like the levirate, exists in two main forms, though the principle of differentiation is not the same. A man may be entitled to marry his first wife's sisters during her lifetime; or he may be restricted to marriage with a deceased wife's sister. A precise statement as to the distribution of these two types is hardly possible at present, but in North America the restricted sororate seems to flourish west of the Rockies, while simultaneous wedlock with sisters is common to the east of them. A parallel to the junior levirate is afforded by the probably universal rule of the sororate that a man is merely entitled to wed his wife's younger sisters. This limitation is easily understood when we remember that in primitive society girls are almost invariably married off at or soon after puberty, so that a marriageable girl's elder sister would already be the wife of another man.

Like cross-cousin marriage, levirate and sororate tend to produce a definite terminology of kinship. As Sapir has pointed out, their influence may be exerted in two distinct ways. On the one hand, since these forms of marriage lead to the identification of the stepfather and the paternal uncle, the stepmother and the maternal aunt, it is natural to designate each pair of these relatives by a single term. Conversely, a brother's child becomes the stepchild of a man; a sister's child, the stepchild of a woman. These features were actually found by Sapir among the Wishram of southern Washington. More interesting still is the second method of formulating in language the social usages under discussion. Since the paternal uncle may come to marry one's mother and thus occupy a father's status, he is called father without qualification; and for a corresponding reason the mother's sisters are called by the same term as the mother. Further, it will be natural for a man to class his brothers' children with his own, and for a woman to treat in similar fashion the children of her sisters. Moreover, since a man often marries his wife's sisters, it is not surprising that a single word suffices for these sisters-in-law and the wife; while a woman will have but one appellation for her husband and her potential husband, his brother. These designations actually occur among the Yahi of northern California. Now this Yahi method of designating relatives has an enormous distribution throughout the world, and inasmuch as the levirate and sororate are also very widespread institutions they offer a satisfactory explanation of what from our point of view seems a puzzling phenomenon,—to wit, that a man should have perhaps a dozen 'fathers' and a dozen 'mothers.' Of this matter we shall have occasion to speak more fully later on.

Cross-cousin marriage, levirate, and sororate are by no means the only forms of preferential mating. In fact, incidentally we have already met several others,—the inheritance of a widow by a sister's son or stepson (Thonga), the marriage of a man and his wife's brother's daughter (Miwok). The last-mentioned variety is interesting because it has appreciably affected Miwok kinship terminology. As Mr. Gifford shows, not less than twelve terms reflect this institution. For example, the word *wokli* is applied not only to a wife's brother or sister, but also to the son or daughter of her brother; for since a man marries his wife's brother's daughter, the siblings of this second wife become his siblings-in-law. It is because so many terms of kinship reflect this type of marriage while none suggest the cross-cousin marriage that Mr. Gifford convincingly argues for the greater antiquity of the former among the Miwok.

Though no attempt is made here to exhaust the extant varieties of orthodox marriage, one more additional type may be cited. It is characterized by the marriage of a man not with his mother's brother's daughter, but with the daughter of his mother's mother's brother's daughter. This form of marriage suggests the cross-cousin marriage but differs in diminishing the closeness of relationship by one degree. Restricted to Australia, it occurs both in the central and western sections, its area of distribution adjoining that of the cross-cousin marriage.[3]

References

Note. All titles are fully quoted in the Bibliography, where authors are listed alphabetically and their several publications chronologically; titles of the same year are distinguished by letters. The chapter references cite the author's name if he is represented by a single title; his name and the date if two or more papers or books are listed; and if there are two in the same year, the letter is added. The pages are set off by colons. Examples: Brown: 156. Jochelson, 1908: 739. Rivers, 1914 (b) : I, 123.

[1] Hobhouse: 145. Wissler, 1911: 19. Teit, 1900: 325; id., 1909: 591. Spinden, 1908: 250. Hopkins: 45. Boas, 1916 (a): 498. Rivers, 1906: 34 seq.

[2] Tylor, 1889: 253. Brown: 156. Rivers, 1914 (b): 1, 123. Radloff: 476-485. Spieth: 120, 182-198, 61-66. Keysser: 85-92. Junod: 1, 102-125, 194, 232, 258-266, 480. Lowie, 1917 (a): 46, 74 seq.; id., 1912: 220 seq. Krause: 220 seq. Jochelson, 1908: 739 seq. Roth, 1915: 315. Whiffen: 163. Hearne: 104 seq. Boas, 1907: 466. Hobhouse: 153, 158.

[3] Brown: 190-194. Rivers, 1914 (b): 1, 48, 184, 257, 270, 294; II, 24, 121 seq.; id., 1906: 512 seq. Thomson: 182-201. Seligmann: 64, 75. Stack and Lyall: 17. Frazer, J. G., 1910: II, 188; IV, 141-149. Czaplicka: 89, 98 seq., 107. Boas, 1916 (a): 440. Swanton, 1905 (a): 50 seq., 63, 68. Gifford, 1916; 187 seq. Morgan, 1871: 265. Rivers, 1915. Schinz: 177. Junod: 1, 200, 207, 243. Weule, 1908: 96. Tylor, 1889: 262 seq., 253. Franciscan Fathers: 432. Jochelson, 1908: 748 seq. Man: 71. Brown: 158, 190-194. Reports, V: 245. Teit, 1900: 325. Bogoras: 608. Howitt: 250. Radloff: 485. Keysser: 88. Dixon, 1907: 463. Merker: 47. Sapir, 1916: 327-337. Gifford, 1916: 190.

CHAPTER III

POLYGAMY

THOUGH popularly polygamy is understood to mean marriage with two or more wives, it properly designates marriage of either a man or a woman with more than one mate. What is commonly reckoned as polygamy is accurately called *polygyny,* the complementary institution being *polyandry.* In addition must be considered the union of a group of men with a group of women, a custom known as *group marriage.*

Polygyny

Polygamy is one of those dangerous catchwords that require careful scrutiny lest there result a total misunderstanding of the conditions it is meant to characterize. In every human society the number of male and of female individuals born is approximately equal. Hence in order to have either polygyny or polyandry as a fairly common practice it is obviously necessary that some non-biological factor should disturb the natural ratio. The first thing to do on hearing of a polygamous people is to demand a census of the marriageable members of both sexes. Among the Eskimo such are the rigors of an Arctic sea-hunter's life that the adult male population is seriously reduced, so that polygyny becomes arithmetically possible. Holm reports a settlement in southeastern Greenland with a population of 21, of whom only 5 were males. But the general ratio encountered by this traveler was only that of 114 women to every 100 men. Of the Central Eskimo the Kinipetu (in 1898) numbered 35 men, 46 women, 38 boys, and 27 girls; the Aivilik 26 men, 34 women, 27 boys, 15 girls. West of Hudson Bay Captain Comer in 1902 found 119 men, 123 women, 138 boys, and 66 girls among the Netchillik; and 46 men, 58 women, 41 boys, 33 girls among the Samniktumiut. That is to say, in none of these instances save Holm's first-mentioned settlement is even bigamy possible as a universal institution. Indeed, in Cranz's day hardly one Greenlander in twenty had two wives, Captain Holm never found a man with three, and even an unusually influential Aivilik contented himself with two. In short, even among the Eskimo, who constitute an a fortiori case, monogamy is the rule in practice, though polygyny is permitted; and marriage with more than two women is undoubtedly exceptional.

It is true that from Africa there are reported instances of an extraordinary multiplicity of wives. Even disregarding such anomalies as the Dahomi court, where all the Amazons are by a fiction considered wives of the king, we find well-authenticated cases of men with five, ten, twenty and even sixty wives, and these at least so far as the first-mentioned figure is concerned are described as fairly common. Unfortunately none of the authorities I have seen on the subject deigns to furnish us with data as to the relative numbers of the sexes. From remarks incidentally dropped by them it seems certain that only the wealthy and the eminent men have polygynous households. Thus, among the Kikuyu of East Africa Mr. and Mrs. Routledge found monogamy "quite usual"; two or three wives were common; and the rich had six or seven. It is clear that even so moderate an indulgence in polygyny on the part of the socially distinguished would make it very difficult for many young men to acquire a mate at all. But the consequent hardship is mitigated by two conditions. In the first place, there is the chance of inheriting a wife through the levirate or one of the other orthodox methods.

Secondly, there is a widespread tendency to connive at what we should consider irregularities among young people prior to wedlock. A Thonga is thus in a position to gratify his sexual appetite long before his kin have amassed the amount paid for a legitimate wife.

The African data show that in addition to the biological limitation of polygamy there enter the restrictions imposed by economic conditions. Where the bride-price is of considerable value, even bigamy is practically out of the question for the average man, though it may be sanctioned by theory. The Kirgiz, though converts to Islam, cannot as a rule afford to buy a second wife, and a man hardly ever avails himself of his legal privilege unless his first mate is barren. Similarly, for the vast majority of the Kai the practice of even bigamy is impracticable, though permitted, and it remains largely confined to the chiefs.

Another purely social factor limiting polygyny requires attention. Some peoples practise what is known as *matrilocal residence,* i.e., the bridegroom settles with his wife's parents. Unless the sororate is in vogue, the espousal of a second wife thus becomes dependent on the permission of the parents-in-law. Thus, the Zuñi and Hopi, who practise matrilocal residence but not the sororate, are strictly monogamous. It cannot be said that this custom absolutely bars polygyny, but it certainly strongly tends to limit it. The Yukaghir of northern Siberia tell of instances where a man lived part of the year as son-in-law with one household and the remainder of the year in the same capacity with another; but monogamy was decidedly the prevalent form of marriage.

In seeking to understand the psychology of primitive polygyny we must first of all eliminate the conventional preconceptions on the subject. Polygyny is not by any means a sign of feminine inferiority or felt as a degradation by the women concerned. The husband may be prompted to take a second wife not by an excessive libido but by his first wife's eagerness to shift part of her household duties on other shoulders. "Why have I to do all the work; why do you not buy another wife?" querulously asks the Kikuyu wife. In the same spirit, a Kai chief's consort will have so many social obligations to fulfill that she gladly welcomes the arrival of a helper; and similarly a Chukchi woman may even insist that her husband acquire an additional worker. With the Kai, indeed, the possibilities are so ample for gratifying one's sexual desires in adultery that in legal marriage with a second wife the sexual motive is eliminated. In general it may be said that the economic and related factors are far more potent. Among the Thonga it is only the well-to-do that can afford to buy several wives, but the investment yields ample return through the services rendered by them, which not merely suffice to supply the husband's wants but enable him to become a lavish entertainer of outsiders and thus raise his social prestige. In this way polygyny becomes a badge of distinction. In a very different environment, the Mackenzie River basin of northern Canada, the Athabaskans had their women transport goods, and the chief Matonabbee had as many as seven or eight of these servant-wives. Another motive for taking additional wives lies in the universal longing for progeny. When the first wife is barren, it is thus a widespread practice for the husband to espouse a second woman in the hope of gaining issue through her. The sexual factor pure and simple is of course not to be wholly ignored in the discussion, but everything goes to show that its influence on the development of polygyny is slight.

The analysis of polygynous marriages found in a particular tribe will prove illuminating. Among the Reindeer Koryak Mr. Jochelson found that only six per cent of the men had two or more wives each, a single one having three. In the last-mentioned case the first wife had borne children but had been disfigured by illness, and the second wife proved barren. In some of the remaining cases bigamy was resorted to because of the first wife's sterility; in others she had been inherited through the levirate and was considered too old.

It remains to discuss the relation to one another of the several wives in a polygynous family. In Africa, where their number is frequently considerable, each commonly occupies a separate hut with her children and manages an independent household; the Thonga arranges these huts in the arc of a circle and his ideal is to acquire enough wives to complete the ring of habitations within his enclosure. As to the mutual sentiments of fellow-wives, accounts vary. M. Junod, possibly from a missionary's bias, draws a dark picture of domestic bickerings among the women, but no such scenes were observed by Mr. and Mrs. Routledge in East Africa and, as they rightly remark, the separation of wives in independent establishments makes for peace and "places the whole on the footing of a village under one head man." Sporadic instances of jealousy must, of course, be expected to occur everywhere, but when an additional wife is taken at the request of the first the danger is minimized. The same result may be effected by the sororate; at least among the Hidatsa the natives have developed the theory that sisters are less likely to quarrel in this relationship than unrelated women. Among the Koryak and Chukchi our authorities generally found harmony in polygynous families but record occasional instances of ill-temper, and this probably represents the most typical condition wherever polygyny is practised.

Doubtless an important factor in producing harmony lies in the definite superiority all but universally accorded to the first wife. Thus in the Siberian tribes just cited the second wife is to all intents and purposes her predecessor's maid. Precisely the same relationship obtains among the distant Kai in New Guinea, where the first wife sends the other women for firewood or water and orders them to prepare meals for the guests. Similar conditions are reported from the Masai. Here, too, the first wife superintends the others, receives a larger portion of her husband's cattle for use, and is distinguished by the number and value of his gifts.

Altogether a study of the facts leads to a rather different view of polygyny from that which might be assumed on the basis of modern prejudice against the institution. But the one fact it is most important to remember is that while probably a majority of primitive tribes permit polygamy, biological and in some measure social conditions prevent the majority within any one group from availing themselves of their theoretical prerogative.[1]

Polyandry

Polyandry has a far more restricted distribution than polygyny. Indeed, well-authenticated cases may be counted on the fingers of one hand. It occurs in some (by no means all) Eskimo communities and as an occasional device among the Wahuma (Bahima) of East Africa, while its highest development is seen in Tibet and southern India. For those who incline to a purely economic interpretation of social life it may be interesting to have pointed out the differences in economic status among the peoples in question. The Eskimo are maritime hunters, the Wahuma and Toda are pastoral, while only the agricultural, not the nomadic, Tibetans have been found to practise polyandry. In another sense, however, the economic factor enters among the Wahuma and the Eskimo.

Wahuma polyandry is an altogether unique phenomenon. While legitimate, it is not a dominant institution but occurs only under special circumstances and for a restricted period. When a man is too poor to buy a wife alone, he is assisted by his brothers, and these share his marital rights until the woman's pregnancy, when they become his exclusive prerogative.

In this form polyandry does not require a disturbance of the natural ratio between the sexes, but where it is the general custom it presupposes an artificially produced preponderance of the marriageable males. This may be effected in different ways. In certain Eskimo communities the conditions of life are so arduous that female children are considered a burden and are frequently killed shortly after birth; and thus the polygynous tendency due to the perils of masculine life is more than checked. Female infanticide, though apparently not founded in economic necessity, is likewise at the bottom of Toda polyandry. But the agricultural Tibetans do not practise infanticide except when directly influenced by Chinese example; yet they are polyandrous and the Chinese are not. Unfortunately the Tibetan data on this point are far from clear.

Among the Tibetans polyandry is of the fraternal variety, i.e., several brothers share a wife. In cases of barrenness it is interesting to note that a second wife is chosen, who may be a sister of the first. Though our information is not so precise as we might wish, it seems that some economic considerations are potent in the moulding of Tibetan marriage customs. Why, e.g., is polyandry restricted to the agricultural natives and to the fraternal type? Rockhill assumes that the cause lies in the desire to transmit an estate undivided.

Our data on the Toda are far and away the most satisfactory and permit us to gain an insight into what polyandrous life is like. First of all, we find that as far back as trustworthy records extend there has been a marked excess of men over women, coupled with the practice of female infanticide. But this custom has been abandoned in ever increasing measure as a result of Caucasian influence, and accordingly there is a progressive diminution of male preponderance. "In 1871 there were 140.6 men for every 100 women; in 1881, 130.4 for every 100; in 1891, 135.9, and in the census of 1901, 127.4 men for every 100 women."

These official census reports are confirmed by Dr. Rivers' independent genealogical records. For three successive generations these show that the numbers of males for every 100 females were 159.7, 131.4, and 129.2 in one of the Toda divisions, and 259, 202, and 171 respectively in the other and more conservative group. The motive for female infanticide among the Toda remains obscure, for there is nothing in their present or past history to suggest that they were driven by economic necessity. Its obsolescence has affected marriage customs in a most interesting manner, which will be described below.

Most commonly, but not always, Toda polyandry is of the fraternal variety. That is, when a man marries a woman it is understood that she becomes the wife of his brothers, who normally live together. Even a brother subsequently born will be regarded as sharing his elder brothers' rights. In cases of fraternal polyandry no disputes ever arise among the husbands, and the very notion of such a possibility is flouted by the Toda mind. When the wife becomes pregnant, the eldest of her husbands performs a ceremony with a bow and arrow by which legal fatherhood is conventionally established in this tribe, but all the brothers are reckoned the child's fathers.

The situation becomes more complicated when a woman weds several men who are not brothers and who, as may happen, live in different villages. Then the wife usually lives for a month with each in turn, though there is no absolute rule. In such cases the determination of fatherhood in a legal sense is extremely interesting. For all social purposes that husband who performs the bow and arrow ceremony during the wife's pregnancy establishes his status as father not only of the first child but of any children born subsequently until one of the other husbands performs the requisite rite. Usually it is agreed that the first two or three children shall belong to the first husband, that at a later pregnancy another shall establish paternal rights, and so forth. Biological paternity is completely disregarded, for a man long dead is considered the father of a child provided no other man has performed the essential rite.

The statistics cited above show recent approximation to the normal ratio of the sexes owing to the diminishing of female infanticide. It might be supposed that this development would lead directly to monogamy, but that would be failing to reckon with the force of conservatism in the adjustment of social relations. What the Toda have done is to cling to polyandry and temper it with polygyny. Where formerly three brothers shared a single wife, they now tend to share two, in this way adapting themselves to the excess of women as compared with their former scarcity.

Altogether the facts relating to polyandry are instructive in illuminating the weakness of the unilinear theory of evolution, the theory that an inherent law causes all societies to evolve the same customs in a uniform sequence. Toda and Eskimo polyandry are both causally related with female infanticide; so far, then, there is parallelism, the same cause leading to the same effect. But what lies back of female infanticide? In the Eskimo case, the rigors of economic existence in the Arctic; among the Toda the cause of female infanticide is obscure, but we know positively that it bears no relation to the economic life. Again we may compare the ancient Toda and the Tibetan conditions. In both tribes a paucity of marriageable women renders polyandry possible, but that paucity is produced in different ways since infanticide is not practised by the polyandrous Tibetans. In developing their polyandrous usages the Eskimo, Toda, and Tibetans have not been impelled to follow the same series of stages, though *one* stage—scarcity of women—naturally leads to polyandry as its sequel. The fact that the Toda have come into contact with a foreign culture which suppresses infanticide has exercised a greater influence on the history of their marriage customs than any inherent law of social evolution. These foreign influences may ultimately force Eskimo, Toda, and Tibetan alike to adopt compulsory monogamy, but if that result be achieved it will be because all three tribes have borrowed the same custom from the same cultural center not because of some mystical tendency of polyandry to pass through like stages into obligatory monogamy.

Before leaving this type of marriage, it is necessary to discriminate true polyandry from the customs by which men may temporarily waive their marital rights in favor of others. This usage proceeds from the proprietary claim of a man to his wife's favors, which he may therefore yield at his pleasure, either to conciliate a superior or as a token of friendship. Thus, among the Crow a young man would temporarily surrender his wife to a comrade or to an older man whose supernatural powers he desired to share; indeed, such surrender was a normal part of the transaction by which various Plains Indian tribes acquired certain ceremonial privileges. As a matter of simple hospitality this custom is reported from the four quarters of the globe. A Masai visiting a strange settlement at once calls on a member of his own age-class, who forthwith abandons his wife and hut to the visitor; and to mention but one other instance, in various Australian tribes the men consider it a duty to furnish their distinguished guests with bed-mates.[2]

Sexual Communism

If we conceive the recent tendency of the Toda toward combined polyandry and polygyny developing into the dominant form of marriage, we shall have many groups of brothers each united to a corresponding group of two or more wives. The units involved in what has been called *group marriage* may, however, vary considerably according to the size of the groups, their constitution, and the restrictions on marital intercourse which are enforced. If there were a complete lack of incest rules in a community, so that not merely brother and sister but even parent and child would mate without incurring reprobation, we should have a condition of perfect promiscuity. At the other end of the scale would be the definitely regulated marriages of the modern Toda. Since the term 'marriage' is hardly applicable to some of the conditions labeled *group marriage,* I will follow Dr. Rivers' suggestion and substitute as a generic equivalent *sexual communism.* Deferring a theoretical discussion of this condition, let us first consider some of the concrete data.

In the first place we must recognize that far-reaching sexual communism may exist side by side with individual marriage. That is to say, one portion of the community may live according to the former principle, the remainder according to the other. Our own civilization with its connivance at prostitution presents as clear an example as possible. Primitive societies differ mainly in that sexual communism is openly sanctioned within the corresponding limits. The Bororó of the Mato Grosso are divided into the older men regularly married and living in separate huts, and the bachelors inhabiting a special dwelling, where they jointly possess such girls as they capture from the village and for whom they pay to their mistresses' brothers or maternal uncles either arrows or articles of personal adornment. While these Brazilian data are unfortunately inadequate for a full comprehension of the social regulations involved, the Masai situation is perfectly clear. Here, too, there is a segregation of the unmarried warriors, all men below approximately thirty, who cohabit freely with the immature young girls. Each brave has his favorite mistress, who tends his cattle and manufactures objects for his personal decoration. This mistress is never identical with the girl betrothed to a man in childhood, for his fiancée is obliged to dwell in another warrior's camp. So long as the warrior remains in his kraal, his sweetheart remains faithful; but if he absents himself for a single day, his **exclusive**

POLYGAMY

claims upon her lapse and she may choose another lover. In all these relations, however, the tribal incest rules are strictly obeyed. When a bachelor has had his fill of the warrior's life, he leaves the companionship of the kraal and settles down in a separate establishment with his fiancée, provided she has succeeded in avoiding pregnancy, which is considered disgraceful.

Bororó and Masai usages, like the practice of prostitution among ourselves, obviously in no way conflict with the institution of individual marriage, which on the contrary is the normal condition after the period of youthful profligacy. There are, however, tribes from which sexual communism is reported without any such limitations.

The most authentic case is that of the Chukchi. It is important to note first of all that among these people sexual communism is a *general* practice embracing practically all families. Second or third cousins, or even unrelated men desirous of cementing a firm bond of friendship, will form a group exercising marital rights over all the wives of the men concerned. Brothers do not enter such agreements. Bachelors are rarely admitted into the union since this is based primarily on reciprocity. At times sexual communism extends to as many as ten couples. When we scrutinize the concrete data cited by Bogoras, it becomes obvious why the term 'group-marriage' which he used in common with other writers is really inapplicable. The Chukchi 'companions in wives' do not dwell together with their spouses in a communal household. They are members of distinct camps and the obvious object of the institution is to provide travelers with temporary bed-mates. A Chukchi thus has but rarely the opportunity to exercise the potential right acquired by the mutual agreement. "The inmates of one and the same camp are seldom willing to enter into a group-marriage, the reason obviously being that the reciprocal use of wives, which in group-marriage is practised very seldom, is liable to degenerate into complete promiscuity if the members of the group live too close together." In other words, the institution has nothing to do with unrestricted sexual license but is founded on aboriginal notions of reciprocal hospitality. It is true that sometimes a 'companion' takes another's wife, lives with her for several months, and then returns her; or that an exchange of wives may become permanent. But these very facts, while clearly demonstrating that Chukchi notions of conjugal fidelity differ from ours, establish beyond a doubt the individual nature of Chukchi *marriage*. Bogoras records isolated instances of polyandry, but never did he find several companions simultaneously sharing their several wives' services. The exchange of wives does not imply group marriage but merely the succession of one individual marriage after another. Chukchi marriage is individual marriage tempered with the occasional and temporary extension of the husband's purely sexual rights to his fellow-contractors.

Sexual communism as a normal condition, thus excluding individual marriage, has been confidently ascribed to the Urabunna and Dieri, two Australian tribes inhabiting the vicinity of Lake Eyre. Owing to the fragmentary nature of the Urabunna evidence, it will be ignored in favor of that from the Dieri.

Among the Dieri the orthodox form of marriage for a man is union with his mother's mother's brother's daughter's daughter or with his mother's father's sister's daughter's daughter. When a boy and a girl stand to each other in this relationship, they are potential spouses and a childhood betrothal may be arranged by their mothers and maternal uncles; normally there will be an exchange of girls by the two contracting parties, so that a boy in each family is provided with a mate. *No woman is ever the affianced wife of more than one man.* However, after the marriage is consummated, it is possible for the wife to become the concubine of several other men, married or single. Precise statistics showing to what extent and between whom such marital relations obtain are unfortunately lacking, but a number of specific statements by Howitt enable us to form some picture of the resulting condition of affairs. It should be noted that in every case the man and woman indulging in sexual intercourse must stand to each other in the orthodox relationship as defined above. In perfect consistency with this rule we find that brothers who have married sisters may share their wives and that a widower in return for presents takes his brother's wife for his concubine. Moreover, a visitor of the proper relationship may be offered his host's wife as a temporary concubine. Normally, however, concubines seem to be assigned through formal allotment by the council of elders, which confers rights of concubinage on individuals who are potential spouses. In practice, it seems that only men of distinction are likely to have a number of concubines; others will be advised by the dominant elders to confine themselves to a single one. A further check to excessive concubinage lies in the mutual jealousy of the subsidiary mates, each of whom discountenances new relations of concubinage, being permitted to pour hot coals over the mate suspected of contemplating a new liaison. A bachelor's concubine is especially prone to exercise surveillance over his sexual life.

In all this the two most significant facts are: (a) that a wife invariably takes precedence over the concubine when both occupy the same camp; and (b) that the husband—the duly affianced spouse—enjoys an undisputed preëmptive right over his wife. No concubitant can lawfully abduct his concubine from her husband except at periods of general license; he may merely exercise his subordinate rights in the husband's absence or with his consent. Again, a wife may indeed take the initiative and ask her husband to select a properly related man for her concubitant; but if her husband refuses, she has no redress, and contrariwise she has no power of veto when allotted as a concubine.

Inadequate as are our data, which suggest various queries

that remain unanswered, it is clear that what Howitt describes as 'group marriage' does not represent a uniform psychological or sociological phenomenon. It is surely one thing for a man to yield marital privileges to a widowed brother, and something quite different for him to conciliate an honored guest by surrendering his bed; and neither practice bears even a remote resemblance to the formal allotment to one another of potential spouses by a council of elders. 'Group marriage' might rightly be predicated of a community in which groups of men shared marital rights *on equal terms* over corresponding groups of women. No such condition obtains among the Dieri: the husband is the well-nigh absolute overlord over his wife's sexual life, the concubitant a mere substitute. Even 'sexual communism' seems to be a very misleading term for what actually occurs, since communism hardly suggests the complete overshadowing by one partner of the other 'communists.' Moreover, everything we can gather on the subject suggests that while marriage among the Dieri is permanent the actual state of concubinage is ordinarily of quite temporary duration. Finally, the population of the Australian local group is so small that the number of properly related individuals who might become concubitants is extremely restricted to begin with. When we consider the additional restrictions of concubinage by sexual jealousy and the admonitions of elders, both of which factors are stressed by our authority, it is obvious that in the everyday life of the average Dieri man concubinage cannot possibly play the part suggested by the pretentious terms 'group marriage' or 'sexual communism.' There is assuredly a certain amount of fraternal polyandry mixed with polygyny; some surrender of marital prerogatives on the score of hospitality; and still more in deference to men of social prestige. But that the majority of Dieri men live in individual wedlock for the greater part of their lives is obvious. Communism on the Toda plan there may be when two brothers dwell with two sisters; but when a concubitant assumes an absentee husband's place there is at best merely one individual relationship superseding another. Altogether we have seen before that primitive marriage cannot be regarded solely or even predominantly from the sexual point of view; and to leap from the fact that more than one man may have access to a woman to the conclusion that there is an institution of group marriage is little short of absurd, as Dr. Malinowski correctly remarks.

Besides the Dieri and the Chukchi, a few other tribes, such as the Gilyak of the Amur region, have been reported as practising sexual communism to the exclusion of individual marriage. The data, however, are of so inadequate a character that they may be ignored until additional information is available. Considering the extreme paucity of all the reported cases of 'group marriage' and the results of our analysis of the sexual communism found among the Chukchi and Dieri, we are justified in concluding that hitherto no evidence has been adduced to show that any people in the world have in recent times practised sexual communism in a manner destructive of the individual family.[3]

Hypothetical Sexual Communism

However, it is possible to harmonize this verdict with the theory that though primitive tribes no longer practise group marriage they have risen to the practice of individual marriage after passing through antecedent stages of sexual communism. This has in fact been the dominant view among modern sociologists and its historical significance requires a brief examination of the reasons for its vogue.

When evolutionary principles, having gained general acceptance in biology, had begun to affect all philosophical thinking, it was natural to extend them to the sphere of social phenomena. Among the first to embark on this venture was Lewis H. Morgan, whose ethnographical treatise on the Iroquois had established his reputation as an accurate and sympathetic observer of primitive custom. Under the influence of evolutionary doctrines Morgan outlined a complete scheme for the development of human marriage. It was eminently characteristic of the intellectual atmosphere of the period that Morgan's first stage should be a condition of perfect promiscuity, in which sexual lust was unrestricted by any incest rule. Complete lack of regulation of sex life is manifestly the diametrical opposite of obligatory monogamy, and the evolutionary theorist of the day was bent on connecting the most diverse phenomena by a graded series of intermediaries. For the mid-Victorian thinker it was a foregone conclusion requiring only statement not proof that monogamy is the highest form of marriage in the best of conceivable universes; and it was equally axiomatic that early man must have lived under conditions infinitely removed from that ideal goal. So Morgan made no pretense at producing empirical proof of pristine promiscuity, which in fact he assigned to the period when man was still hovering near the border line between humanity and a lower organic stage. He advanced promiscuity as a *logical postulate* precisely as some evolutionary philosophers advance the axiom of spontaneous generation; and thereby placed it beyond the range of scientific discussion.

It was otherwise with Morgan's second stage, that of the 'consanguine family,' based on the intermarriage of brothers and sisters but barring that of parents and children. For this stage, while nowhere observable, as a general tribal usage, was inferred by Morgan as the only possible cause of certain empirical phenomena. In other words, he was here no longer indulging in logical axioms but proceeding in the spirit of the scientists who invented the atom to account for the behavior of chemical substances. The fact which Morgan adduced as conclusive proof of the former intermarriage of brothers and sisters was the Hawaiian method of designating kin. That method is of a simpler character than the one usually found in savage tribes. While many primitive peoples carefully distinguish between maternal and paternal relatives, the Hawaiians not only draw no such distinction but apply their kinship terms so as to include all relatives of the same generation regardless of propinquity. For example, *makua* designates both the parents and all their brothers and sisters, sex being indicated by qualifying words meaning 'man' and 'woman.' Morgan argues that the maternal uncles were called by the same term as the fathers because all *were* fathers in the sense of having free access to their sisters; that similarly all of a man's nephews and nieces were called sons and daughters because all his sisters were his wives, as they were the wives of his brothers; and so forth. It is Morgan's contention that while the customs reflected in kinship nomenclature have a tendency to pass out of existence the terminology itself is more conservative and thus furnishes a sort of palaeontological record of social institutions.

In the first place, while Morgan's inference as to the prior existence of the consanguine family has an empirical foundation, this does not hold for the place he assigned to the inferred stage in his scale. Even admitting that his data prove the former intermarriage of brothers and sisters, we are not compelled by the evidence to assign to that practice *any* particular age. If Morgan does claim a hoary antiquity for this condition, placing it immediately after the reign of utter lawlessness, it is because of the tacit assumption pervading his entire scheme that a unilinear series may be postulated bridging by degrees the gap between promiscuity and monogamy. Only on that hypothesis does it follow that the inferred stage of the consanguine family must come directly after one of antecedent promiscuity and before other types of the family. Yet had Morgan not been smitten with purblindness by his theoretical prepossessions, he might well have paused before ascribing to the Polynesians the part they play in his scheme. For the aboriginal civilization of Polynesia, instead of suggesting by its crudeness an extreme antiquity for any and all of its constituents, must rank among the very noblest of cultures devoid of the metallurgical art. When Morgan assigned to this settled, politically organized and marvelously aesthetic race the lowest status among surviving divisions of mankind he attained the high-water level of absurdity, which accounts of Oceanian exploration accessible even in his day would have sufficed to expose. It is true that missionary reports had described marriages of brother and sister in the uppermost social stratum of Hawaii, but this merely indicates that in Hawaii, as in ancient Egypt and Peru, such unions resulted from pride of blood evolved in an inordinately sophisticated civilization.

Morgan, however, not merely assumes the relative chronology of the consanguine family and his other stages without the slightest empirical warrant, but lays himself open to the still more serious charge of drawing wrong inferences from the existence of the Hawaiian system. Some of the objections against his logic have been forcibly urged by Herr Cunow, whose strictures are all the more noteworthy because of his appreciation and partial acceptance of Morgan's work. To begin with a specific point, Morgan overlooks the fact that the Hawaiian system not merely embraces blood-kindred but also distinguishes from them relatives by affinity: there are thus distinct terms for brother-in-law and sister-in-law and even a specific word to denote the relationship of the husband's parents to the wife's. If the Hawaiian nomenclature represents the consanguine family stage, Cunow acutely argues, then such terms of affinity have no place in it. For with intermarriage of brothers and sisters my wife's brother is *my* brother, while her parents are my own parents or at least my parents' siblings.

The really fundamental error, however, lies in Morgan's assumption that a native term translated 'father' is synonymous in the native mind with 'procreator.' He cannot conceive that a Hawaiian could ever have called the maternal uncle 'father' unless at one time the uncle cohabited with his sister and was thus a possible procreator of her children. But this is to misunderstand the evidence, which does not teach us that the mother's brother is called father but that both mother's brother and father are designated by a *common term* not strictly corresponding to *any* in our language. That such linguistic identification must have for its basis conjugal intercourse with the same mate is an arbitrary assumption, which in fact leads to nonsensical consequences. For as McLennan observed before Cunow, the theory that all 'fathers' are potential begetters involves the parallel view that the 'mothers' whom a Hawaiian reckons up by dozens are believed to have all conceived and borne him. To be sure, Morgan lamely sidesteps the fatal difficulty by asserting that here the native intends to denote a marriage connection rather than a blood-relationship; he calls his mother's sister 'mother' because she is the wife of his reputed father, hence after a fashion his stepmother. This, however, is sheer subterfuge. The extensions of the terms translated 'father' and 'mother' respectively are strictly parallel; they form part of a single system and demand a single interpretation. If the notion of actual parenthood underlies the system at one point, it must do so uniformly; and since this supposition leads to a monstrous conclusion, it must be discarded. The simple explanation of the Hawaiian system lies in Cunow's suggestion that it represents the stratification of blood kindred by generations. Our own nomenclature is not so far removed from this type as might at first blush appear. We group all our parents' siblings under the terms 'uncle' and 'aunt'; the essential difference lies in our segregation of the immediate family circle by using distinct terms for father and mother. It is not difficult to understand how in some societies stressing the age factor, as many primitive communities do, **terms of consanguinity might come to indicate *merely* generation** to the extent of merging the next of kin in the group of their contemporaries.

In short, Morgan fails to prove that the Hawaiian nomenclature must have had its origin in the intermarriage of brothers and sisters; and even if it had arisen in this fashion, there would be no proof that either the terminology or its hypothetical cause is of great antiquity.

On the latter point we can go somewhat further. While the number of primitive tribes following the Hawaiian system of nomenclature is limited, a far greater number follow the Dakota and Iroquois plan of bifurcating blood-kindred according to whether they are maternal or paternal. The Dakota, like the Hawaiians, have a single word for father and father's brother, and another for mother and mother's sister; but the mother's brother, instead of being classed with the father, and the father's sister, instead of being classed with the mother, are both designated by specific terms. Now in scrutinizing nomenclatures in general conformity with the Dakota plan, we discover details of distinctively Hawaiian complexion. A priori these might be accepted as survivals of an older purely Hawaiian system, but specific circumstances prove conclusively that the opposite interpretation is the only possible one. For example, a Crow addresses his father's sister as mother, just as does the Hawaiian. Now the Crow tongue is a specialized representative of the Hidatsa branch of the Siouan family. All the other Siouan languages, including the Hidatsa, discriminate between mother and father's sister; nay, Crow speech itself does so whenever the paternal aunt is not directly addressed. Hence it is quite clear that Crow vocative usage is not a survival but an innovation. Similar recent changes are reported from the Iroquois, the Torres Straits Islanders, the Gilyak of Siberia, and the Timne of West Africa. It is therefore justifiable to consider Hawaiian features as frequently the result of secondary development; and when these specific data are combined with the high cultural status of the Polynesians, they constitute a crushing argument against the priority of either the Hawaiian terminology or of any social customs supposedly linked therewith.

After the discussion of the consanguine family, we may deal briefly with Morgan's evidence for his next stage, which represents what in common ethnographic parlance is called group marriage, viz., a condition in which "the group of men were conjointly married to the group of women." Morgan considers particularly the institution of several sisters sharing a group of husbands not necessarily kinsmen of one another; and of several brothers sharing a group of wives not necessarily related to one another. Group marriage might of course be conceived somewhat differently, though always involving a combination of polyandry with polygyny. Thus, Professor Kohler seeks the origin of the Dakota kinship nomenclature in the custom by which the brothers AAA marry the sisters bbb, and the brothers BBB the sisters aaa. It is, indeed, again the kinship terminology that furnishes the main argument for the speculative ethnologist. As in the previous case of the Hawaiian system, he ignores obvious alternatives and associates our concepts of parenthood with primitive terms bearing a wholly diverse significance. Social phenomena already described amply account for the Dakota nomenclature. In the levirate and the sororate we find usages explaining fully why father and father's brother, mother and mother's sister should be classed together. These phenomena show that kinship terminology is not necessarily expressive of *actual* sexual relations. A man may never come to inherit his brother's widow, either because his brother survives her or because she is married by another brother. Quite regardless of this fact, he is called father by his brother's children, and corresponding considerations hold for the sororate. The fact that conjugal relations with one's mother are theoretically possible for a number of individuals is sufficient to label them all with a common designation. There is no reason for assuming that the natives ever meant to imply more than a like social status when applying like kinship terms.

It is true that Morgan interpreted the sororate as a relic of group marriage, and Frazer has extended the interpretation to the levirate as well. But these are empty guesses, which may be disregarded. Levirate and sororate are real institutions intelligible in their context; they are not rendered one whit more intelligible by conceiving them as survivals of a condition that has never been observed.

To sum up. Sexual communism as a condition taking the place of the individual family exists nowhere at the present time; and the arguments for its former existence must be rejected as unsatisfactory. This conclusion will find confirmation in the phenomena of primitive family life.[4]

References

[1] Thalbitzer: 15, 67. Boas, 1907: 7, 115, 378. Cranz: I, 209. Routledge: 134. Hollis, 1905: 303. Junod: 1, 97, 125-128, 274. Radloff: 484. Keysser: 90, 44. Jochelson, 1910: 110 seq.; id., 1908: 752-755. Bogoras: 598-602. Hearne: 124 et passim. Merker: 27 seq.

[2] Annual Archaeological Report: 112. Roscoe, 1907: 105. Rockhill: 211 seq. Tafel: II, 124 seq. Rivers, 1906: 477-480, 515 seq. Lowie, 1917 (a): 63, id., 1913: 228 seq. Hollis, 1905; 288. Frazer, J.: 34.

[3] Von den Steinen: 388. Hollis, 1905: xvi. Merker: 44, 84. Bogoras: 602-607. Howitt: 163-167, 177-187. Malinowski: 100-123.

[4] Morgan, 1877: Pt. III, especially Chapters II, III, VI. Rivers, 1914 (b): 1, 275 seq. Cunow, 1894: 54, 127 seq.; id., 1912: 50 seq. Lowie, 1917 (a): 118, 162. Kohler: 266. Frazer, J. G., 1910; IV, 139 seq.

CHAPTER IV

THE FAMILY

BIOLOGICALLY every community must rest on the family,—the group comprising a married couple and their children. But biological and sociological necessity need not coincide. It does not follow that the biological family must exist as a unit differentiated from the rest of the social aggregate of which it forms part. Indeed, in such a stage of sexual communism as is pictured by Morgan's school the family would be wholly submerged in a wider group. The matter is thus one not for a priori argument but of empirical fact.

Before undertaking the inquiry suggested by this consideration, we had better briefly scrutinize the family concept as it appears in our own civilization. The first point to be specially noted is its bilateral character, which indeed is involved in our definition. That is to say, the family as a social unit includes *both* parents and in a secondary sense the kindred on both sides. This appears in the duties of parents to their children and also in our laws of inheritance, which recognize the bond with both maternal and paternal relatives. The desirability of emphasizing this feature will become manifest later. In one significant respect, however, the bilateral principle is abandoned in favor of another: our family is patronymic, the wife and all the children taking the father's name. In this way the husband, his sons and their male descendants through males together with wives and unmarried daughters, are segregated as Smiths or Browns from the remainder of their kin. To be sure, this is a point rather of comparative than of practical importance. It would be otherwise if all the Smiths, however remotely related, formed a definite social unit set over against the rest of the community, e.g., if in the inheritance of property the most remote kinsman of the same family name took precedence of such close relatives as married daughters or the sons of sisters. Since one-sided emphasis on the paternal branch of the family is not in vogue with us apart from the transmission of the name, we are justified in describing our family as an essentially bilateral one.

The question, then, that concerns us above all others is whether primitive tribes similarly recognize the bilateral principle in their conception of family life. Whenever they do, we shall be justified in holding that they recognize the family as a social unit regardless of whatever other units may coëxist with it. Let us then first consider the evidence for the presence of the bilateral principle and next pass in review some of the more important factors that tend to mould primitive family life, often causing it to deviate appreciably from the West European norm.

The Bilateral Kin Group

Objective testimony of quite incontrovertible character is furnished on behalf of the universality of the family unit by the recorded systems of kinship terminology. As even Morgan pointed out in a discussion with McLennan, every tribe has terms of relationship for both the paternal and the maternal lines and in so far acknowledges bilateral kinship. But to limit this attitude to the matter of nomenclature would be to understate the case beyond all reason. In by far the majority of primitive tribes both sides of the family are reckoned with not only in vocabulary but in customary law, definite functions being commonly associated with definite types of relationship. Thus, the Hopi unlike ourselves are matronymic since what corresponds to our family name is transmitted from mother to child; but the personal name is invariably bestowed by a woman of the father's kin and symbolically suggests that group. Among the likewise matronymic Hidatsa a variety of social usages bear witness to the importance of the paternal kindred. Thus, sacred objects descend from father to son; the father's relatives are entitled to gifts on all occasions; nicknames are frequently given not for a man's own peculiarities but for those of a father's kinsman; and it is the father's kin that conduct the funeral proceedings. On the other hand, we find the patronymic Thonga assigning a very remarkable position to the maternal uncle. Here the mother's brother lays claim to a portion of the bride price and plays an important part in his nephew's ceremonial life, while the sister's son may appropriate his uncle's food and claim part of his legacy, at times even inheriting one of the widows. To cite but one other instance, the patronymic Torres Straits Islanders permit a boy or man to take his maternal uncle's most valued possessions, while the nephew immediately obeys his mother's brother's injunction against fighting.

The subject of kinship usages is a large one and cannot be exhausted in a paragraph. In the present connection it is simply important to note that both paternal and maternal kindred are regularly recognized and that such a thing as taking the family name of one parent in no wise precludes important social relations with the kin of the other side.

Such social usages as have been cited above involve an implicit recognition of the parent. Both parents are of course also directly recognized by virtue of the sentimental bond connecting them with their children, and further because husband and wife, together with at least their younger children, form an economic and industrial unit. Marriage, as we cannot too often or too vehemently insist, is only to a limited extent based on sexual considerations. The primary motive, so far as the individual mates are concerned, is precisely the founding of a self-sufficient economic aggregate. A Kai does not marry because of desires he can readily gratify outside of wedlock without assuming any responsibilities; he marries because he needs a woman to make pots and to cook his meals, to manufacture nets and weed his plantations, in return for which he provides the household with game and fish and builds the dwelling. In Queensland the father supplies the family with larger game and fish, the mother with yams, grass-seed, fruits, molluscs, and smaller fish. In central Australia there is a similar division of labor and from Dr. Malinowski's compilation of facts it is clear that throughout the continent the individual family on this basis normally constitutes a definitely segregated unit. As Mr. Brown remarks regarding the West Australian Kariera, "the unit of social life in the Kariera tribe was the family, consisting of a man and his wife or wives and their children. Such a unit might move about by itself without reference to the movements of the other families of the local group. In the camp each family had its own hut or shelter with its own fire. The family had its own food supply which was cooked and consumed by the family. The man provided the flesh food and his wife provided the vegetable food and such things as small mammals or lizards." The economic and industrial relations of the Ewe mates are regulated with equal definiteness. It is the husband's duty to furnish meat and fish, and the wife's to supply salt; both share the horticultural work; the woman spins, while the man weaves and mends the clothing.

Such facts might be multiplied indefinitely. On the strength of this universal trait we are justified in concluding that regardless of all other social arrangements the individual family is an omnipresent social unit. It does not matter whether marital relations are permanent or temporary; whether there is polygyny or polyandry or sexual license; whether conditions are complicated by the addition of members not included in *our* family circle: the one fact stands out beyond all others that everywhere the husband, wife and immature children constitute a unit apart from the remainder of the community. In primitive society it is indeed usually the case that an individual owes certain duties to a whole class of individuals from all of whom he in turn expects a definite mode of treatment. But as Mr. Brown admirably points out in the article quoted, there is no confusion as to the intensity of the obligation, which varies with proximity of kinship. Though two dozen paternal uncles and fathers' cousins may be addressed by the same term as the father, it is the real or putative father that preëminently supplies his wives and children with such necessaries as ought to be furnished by the man in accordance with primitive custom. So we have seen that though a man's nth cousin may be called his brother, it is his own brother that inherits the widow through the levirate, and only in the absence of brothers does a more remote kinsman function as a substitute.

The only possible escape for adherents of the theory that the bilateral family is unknown to primitive man is to flee from the patent phenomena of the cruder contemporaneous societies to the obscurities of a remote past. The hypothesis that the family is everywhere a relatively late product of social evolution has already been touched upon from one point of view and will be reëxamined later in another connection. For the present it suffices to establish the present universality of the bilateral family concept.

But this does not necessarily involve the thesis that family life must therefore everywhere assume the same form it does among ourselves. Indeed the fundamental changes brought about within a century in our own family life through economic developments and an altered conception of woman's status would reduce any such supposition to an absurdity. Usages like polygyny and polyandry are bound to affect the character of the family, as has already been indicated. Recalling some data presented in previous chapters and anticipating facts to be more fully treated below while postponing still others for later consideration, I will briefly indicate some of the factors that vitally affect primitive family life.[1]

Looseness of the Family Unit

Even in the higher cultures the individual family is a conspicuously unstable unit. When daughters marry and take up their abode with their husbands or when sons establish independent households, the intimacy of the bond that united them with the parental family is almost inevitably weakened if not wholly destroyed. Among primitive peoples who rarely if ever interpose religious scruples against divorce all sorts of disruptive forces must be reckoned with. Sheer bravado often tempted Crow men publicly to discard their wives on festive occasions by way of exhibiting their strength of soul, and apparently it mattered little whether they had children or not, infants naturally accompanying their mother. Again, two rival military organizations of this tribe indulged in licensed wife-stealing at the beginning of every spring, the sole qualification being that a man might abduct only women with whom he had once been on terms of intimacy. In such a case the husband was without redress and any attempt to resort to force would permanently injure his social prestige.

Notwithstanding such usages, it is important not to confound the actual frequency of divorce with its theoretical possibility. Even among the Crow a chaste woman would be exempt under the accepted restriction of kidnapping, while others would be liable to capture only if married to the member of one of two societies and if a former mistress of a member of the other. The public 'throwing away' of wives was indeed unlimited by such rules, yet in practice a man would hesitate a long while before divorcing a virtuous and industrious wife. Here, as elsewhere, practical considerations interfere very largely with the exercise of an abstract prerogative. A Kirgiz who has paid an enormous price for his wife very rarely expels her, regardless of Mohammedan sanction. Similarly, a Kai husband is unwilling to surrender his wife even in cases of elopement. He has bought her economic services and demands a restitution of her person or the equivalent of her price; and unless her lover furnishes the requisite property, the woman's kin restore her to her purchaser-husband. Even where both sexes are equally free to separate from the conjugal roof it does not follow that divorce will be proportionately common. In the Amazons country a Witoto woman is never blamed for leaving her husband because such unnatural procedure can be due only to gross maltreatment since under the existing conditions a woman without male protection is sure to die. On the other hand, the reprobation meted out to a husband who rids himself of his wife without adequate cause acts as a deterrent on the other side.

The presence or absence of children, though sometimes disregarded, usually exerts a profound influence on the stability of marriage. Barrenness is very widely accepted as an adequate reason for the repudiation of the wife. Conversely, as with us, children tend to unite parents. This is very clearly exemplified by Eskimo conditions. Before the birth of children divorce is countenanced by Greenland society upon the slightest provocation; Captain Holm encountered a woman barely turned twenty who had just separated from her sixth husband. But after children are born the conjugal relationship becomes more stable, and in long-continued unions there is loyal attachment and even deep affection. The latter remark holds true for the Chukchi and according to my own observations for the Crow, though both of these tribes display a strong tendency to sever the bonds of marriage for meager cause.

Difficult as it is to generalize, we shall not go far wrong

in stating that while the primitive family is not nearly so loose a unit as the theoretical power to divorce might suggest it is nevertheless on the whole considerably looser than our own, though its instability diminishes markedly after the first few years of matrimony.[2]

Matrilocal and Patrilocal Residence

Rules of residence exert an incalculable influence on the life of the family, for physical propinquity affects not merely sexual love but all human sentiments. A newly married couple may settle, permanently or temporarily, with the wife's or the husband's family, or they may set up a household of their own. In order to gain a provisional picture of the conditions resulting from these factors, we may begin by comparing the family life of two tribes, the patrilocal Hupa and the matrilocal Pueblo Indians.

Among the Hupa a man looked for a mate in some other settlement and regularly took his wife to his own village. Hence a man and his sons, with his and their wives, as well as the unmarried daughters, were united in one locality, while the daughters on marriage followed their husbands to another village. Thus, a man was born, lived and died in the same place, while a woman spent the greater part of her life away from her native village. This rule of residence inevitably established a unilateral grouping of kin: there was a local segregation of individuals related through their fathers. Nevertheless this paternal line, while objectively distinguished from other kinsfolk through a common residence, was not specifically recognized as a distinct unit by the Hupa. Thus it might come to pass that a man unable to pay the bride-price was obliged to serve in his father-in-law's village and the children of the marriage belonged to the wife's people. In such cases, then, the lapse of the usual patrilocal rule carried with it a quite different association of kindred from that normally produced.

This would of course have been impossible had the Hupa recognized the local segregation of patrilineal relatives as not merely customary but as reflecting the abstract principle that in reckoning kinship there should be a uniform stressing of the paternal side.

A distinctive alignment of kin is effected by the matrilocal rule of the Pueblo Indians, combined as it is with female ownership of the house. The nucleus of the household consists of the maternal grandmother, the mother and maternal aunts, the unmarried brothers of the mother, and all the children of the adult women. The husband of a woman lives in his wife's home but without safe tenure of residence rights: in case of divorce he must leave and will return to the house of his childhood, the one owned by his mother or one of his sisters. This being so, a man continues even after marriage to regard his mother's rather than his wife's house as his home. In this way the children of any family are brought into constant association with their maternal uncles, whose status is admirably described by Miss Freire-Marreco: "They take their places at meals here as a matter of course, invite visitors to eat, behave as hosts and masters of the house; though they do not (if they are married) contribute anything to the material support of our household since they have to supply corn, meat and wood to their wives' homes." They keep their tools and finery under the maternal roof and give advice and reproof to their sisters' children, from whom they have a right to exact obedience.

Thus we find that the rule of residence may produce a stressing of one side of the family and in so far forth interfere with the bilateral symmetry of family relations. Among the Hupa the maternal uncle, living as he does normally in another village, cannot possibly influence the education of the children, which will inevitably be moulded by patrilineal influences. In the Pueblo household, though the father continues to form an economic unit with his wife and her offspring, his authority over the children is at least shared by the men belonging to the house in which he himself lives as a visitor. The status of the spouse himself is thus profoundly affected. Obviously a man occupies a different position under his own roof as regards not only parental but conjugal status. In a matrilocal community he cannot be master of his wife's person in an absolute sense; in any dispute the husband has to reckon with her kin and is liable to be expelled. Further, matrilocal residence naturally limits polygyny except in the form of the sororate.

However, we must not forget that matrilocal and patrilocal residence represent merely the extremes of a series of fluctuating conditions. The Pueblo Indians are in the fullest sense matrilocal; not so perhaps a majority of the people usually so classed. Very commonly we find that a husband begins married life with his parents-in-law, fulfilling to all intents and purposes the functions of a servant, but sets up an independent household at a later stage, say, after the birth of children. This applies to the Hidatsa, the Ovambo of South Africa, the Khasi of Assam. In such cases the influence of the maternal kinsfolk is of course less pronounced than in permanently matrilocal arrangements. Again, there may be no definite rule, the young couple living at will either by themselves or with the wife's parents.

In order to understand the phenomena involved we must resolutely decline to rest content with such classificatory catchwords as 'matrilocal' and 'patrilocal' and study the data both statistically and with reference to correlated usages. For example, in northern Siberia both the Koryak and the Yukaghir suitor serve for the bride, but the former takes her to his own family, while the latter resides with his parents-in-law. There thus seems to be in this respect a clear-cut, unbridgeable distinction between these tribes. Yet the demarcation is not nearly so definite as a bald statement of gross results would suggest. In 11 out of 181 recorded Koryak marriages the son-in-law settles in his father-in-law's house, viz., when there are no sons in the bride's family and her father invites him to take the place of one. On the other hand, among the Yukaghir it occasionally happens that two households exchange daughters and retain their sons. Further, a bride's father who has sons may waive his claims on the husband's residence if he is an only son. Finally, it is customary with the Yukaghir that the youngest son should stay with his parents. The Eskimo data are equally illuminating. Here we encounter local differentiation: the Greenlanders are patrilocal, the tribes of Labrador and Baffin Land at least begin with matrilocal marriage. Indeed, even among the Central Eskimo differences have been observed, some communities following the patrilocal, others the matrilocal rule. Since the former practice on the whole predominates, we may regard it as the more fundamental Eskimo custom. The question then arises what caused the deviations. Here we may fall back upon the general reason that when a suitor is unable to furnish adequate compensation for his bride he naturally becomes her parents' servant. More specifically, we learn from Holm that when there are many sons in a family sometimes only the older ones bring their brides under the paternal roof, while their younger brothers go to reside with their parents-in-law.

By substituting the whole range of observed data for the misleading catchwords, we gain a better insight into the nature of matrilocal and patrilocal residence, nay, we are able to picture the processes that might transform the relevant marriage customs of a tribe. General impoverishment could at any time have made the patrilocal Hupa matrilocal by standardizing their now anomalous makeshift. Contrariwise Professor Kroeber has shown that even in the generally matrilocal communities of the Pueblo area significant deviations develop. Incompatibility between a man and his wife's housemates sometimes leads Zuñi spouses to snap their fingers at the traditional rule and a wife will follow her husband to his mother's home. This migration may produce strange consequences, for since the husband may not have any sisters or only childless ones and the dwelling is always owned by women a house will thus come to pass from the possession of one family into that of another.

To sum up. The mode of residence must in any individual case produce a profound influence on family life because the alignment of kin, the status of the spouses and the relations of the children to maternal and paternal relatives will vary with the matrilocal and patrilocal rule. But we must remember that it makes all the difference in the world whether the rule is followed throughout married life or only for a limited period at its commencement; whether the rule is nearly absolute or admits of modification; and what are the motives that operate in anomalous cases and may under proper conditions rise to ascendancy.[3]

Sexual Division of Labor

It is a commonplace of modern sociology that increasing economic independence has transformed the status of woman and thereby the character of the family. Accordingly, it is not surprising that the sexual division of labor should color the family life of simpler cultures. This division is very largely conventional, i.e., in no way connected with the physiological characteristics of the sexes, as may often be proved by contrasting the regulations of different and even neighboring tribes. Thus, the Southern Bantu rigorously exclude women from their herds, while the Hottentot women regularly milk the cows.

Contrary to the widespread popular notion that primitive woman is invariably a drudge, we find on the whole a rather equitable assignment of tasks. Among hunting tribes the wife adds to the game brought by her husband wild roots, berries, and shell-fish. At a higher level man remains a hunter, while woman takes the important step of not merely gathering but planting and harvesting seeds. In technical ethnologic parlance it is customary to distinguish between agriculture or plough-husbandry and horticulture or tillage with more primitive implements. In Africa and in most horticultural American and Oceanian tribes, gardening with the hoe is woman's distinctive economic employment, as Eduard Hahn was probably the first to point out. On the other hand, the domestication of such animals as the ox was undoubtedly achieved by men. Generally speaking, the care of the herds has remained in the hands of men, who have sometimes jealously guarded their prerogatives. The Bantu taboo against women's entering a corral has been mentioned, and the Toda go so far as not to permit their wives to cook food of which milk is an ingredient. In connection with the domestication of the ox men also developed the use of the plough in agriculture, thus diminishing the relative importance of woman's contribution to the larder.

In addition to economic activities we must consider industrial occupations. Here there is, as already suggested, a great deal of variation even within the same general region. For example, with most of the North American aborigines the dressing of skins is reckoned a distinctively feminine task, but in the Southwest this work is done by the men. In northern Arizona the Hopi men do all the spinning and weaving, while these tasks are invariably performed by women among the neighboring Navaho. With respect to primitive ceramics we are indebted to Dr. Laufer for a generalization comparable to Hahn's: wherever earthenware is manufactured by hand, it is produced by the women, while the wheel-turned pottery is made by the men.

The position of woman in society forms so important a problem that a special chapter will be devoted to it. In the present connection it suffices to note that each people has its traditional conceptions of masculine and feminine employment and that differences in this regard cannot fail to affect the course of the family life. A polygynous Thonga becomes a parasite supported by his gardener-wives; a Kirgiz wife performs the household tasks, while the husband not merely tends the herds but also supplies firewood, tills the soil, and manufactures all household vessels; the Toda woman has hardly any duties besides pounding and sifting grain, cleaning the hut and decorating clothing. It is not a question of woman's theoretical status, for that is doubtless lowest among the Mohammedanized Kirgiz, and probably lower among the Toda than with the Thonga; it is simply a question of what labors are conventionally allotted to each sex. Dr. Laufer has forcibly pointed out how at a higher level of civilization "the forms of Chinese family life and the psychical relations of the members" are radically different from our own because woman never superintends nor even approaches the kitchen, which is always far removed from the center of the house and thus never serves as a family rallying-point.[4]

Segregation of Unmarried

Among the customs often giving to primitive family life a very peculiar cast as compared with ours is the segregation of unmarried young men and women from the remainder of the community, frequently at adolescence, sometimes even at an earlier period. Thus, among the Dravidians of southern India the youths no longer sleep with their parents but in a separate club house, and the girls in a dormitory of their own, superintended by a matron. Every Kariera camp is divided into the married people's and the bachelors' camp, the latter including widowers, the former single women and widows. The Masai usage has already been described by which the bachelor braves reside in a special kraal with the immature young girls, while all married men have settlements of their own.

These customs introduce us to the principle of dividing a community on the basis of age, with or without a farther recognition of a sexual segregation. The relevant problems of distribution and interpretation will receive detailed discussion. Suffice it for the present to call attention to the inevitable rending asunder or at least serious weakening of the family ties where the adolescent children are separated from their parents by these fixed institutions.[5]

Sexual Segregation

Still more drastic in its effects on the family as a social unit is the separation of husband and wife either by the segregation of men in a club house of their own or by exclusion of the women from those forms of public activity which especially engross the attention of the men. This, too, is a subject for ampler treatment further on, but one or two characteristic illustrations must be cited here by way of anticipation.

Among the Hupa the women lived in the family house, where their husbands came to eat meals before and after their daily tasks. In the evening the men retired to the sweathouse, which served not only as a Turkish bath and club but as a dormitory as well. This, however, does not compare with the isolation of the women in parts of Melanesia, such as the Banks Islands, where the men and indeed the adolescent boys not merely sleep but eat apart from the women, membership into the men's club being early purchased to shorten the ignominy of having to feed with the women. Finally may be mentioned the well-nigh universal Australian custom of barring women from attendance at those sacred rites about which most of masculine thought revolves in its more serious moments.[6]

Adoption

The very constitution of the family may be altered by the legal fiction through which parents rear as their own the children of another couple. In many cases the children are related to their foster parents, but this is by no means prerequisite. A common motive for adoption is lack of issue. Thus, a Chukchi couple without offspring will adopt the child, preferably the son, of a relative, and the boy then becomes the principal heir. The sentimental relationship comes to approach very closely that based on the natural tie. With the Crow Indians it is common for men and women to adopt a sibling's child, and if anything there was exaggerated demonstration of affection as if to compensate for the subconscious feeling that after all the tie was factitious. But probably nowhere is adoption so prevalent as in Murray Island of the Eastern Torres Straits group, where children for no manifest reason are adopted even before birth and brought up entirely as members of the adoptive parent, often remaining in ignorance of their real parentage till adult life or even till death.[7]

Summary

Although the character of the primitive family is appreciably altered by the usages sketched above, these modifications do not invade the bilateral principle. A man may spend the major part of his working and sleeping hours away from his wife, but for all that he is linked to her by the common interest in the children of the household, really or putatively his own, and by their economic and industrial partnership; and similar considerations apply to the other conditions mentioned, which often strangely affect the dynamics of family life from a Caucasian point of view. In short, the bilateral family is none the less an absolutely universal unit of human society.

References

[1] Lowie, 1917 (a): 40 seq., 51. Junod: 1, 44, 212, 226, 253, 262. Reports, v: 144 seq. Keysser: 45, 85. Roth, 1906: 6. Spencer and Gillen, 1899: 18. Malinowski: 158-167. Brown: 147. Spieth: 191.

THE FAMILY

[2] Lowie, 1912: 223; id., 1913: 169. Keysser: 86. Whiffen: 165. Thalbitzer: 65, 72. Bogoras: 596.

[3] Goddard, 1903: 56-58. Freire-Marreco: 269-287. Lowie, 1917 (a): 46. Schinz: 304, 311. Gurdon: 78. Jochelson, 1908: 744; id., 1910: 92. Cranz: 1, 215 seq. Boas, 1888: 579. Thalbitzer: 59. Murdoch: 410. Kroeber, 1917 (a): 105.

[4] Hahn. Rivers, 1906: 567. Laufer, 1917: 148; id., *in* Amer. Anth., 1918: 89. Radloff: 462.

[5] Baden-Powell: 172. Brown: 147.

[6] Goddard, 1903: 57. Rivers, 1914 (b): 1, 63.

[7] Bogoras: 556. Lowie, 1912: 219. Reports, VI: 64, 177.

CHAPTER V

KINSHIP USAGES

IN PROVING the bilateral character of the family, I have called attention to the social relations that obtain between an individual and the relatives on both his father's and his mother's side. As a matter of fact, primitive law usually goes much further and establishes definite functions for every relationship not only by blood but by marriage as well. In our society no fixed conduct is prescribed towards a maternal uncle or a sister's son or the husband of a father's sister. In primitive communities, on the other hand, a specific mode of behavior may be rigidly determined for each and every possible form of relationship. From the point of view of any individual this means that his tribesmen are classified into certain categories, each one of which implies an altogether special set of social rules to be observed by him. He is bound to render services to an individual of one class; with a member of another he may jest and take liberties; with persons of a third category he must have nothing to do except through intermediaries; and so forth. Proximity of relationship may or may not count; usually, as Mr. Brown has explained for the Kariera, a savage owes the same type of conduct to a more remote as to a closer kinsman addressed by the same relationship term, but the intensity of the obligation is greater for the nearer relationship. As this author further remarks, a native may be at a complete loss how to treat a stranger who falls outside of the established rubrics. What most frequently happens is that by a legal fiction, or it may be by marriage with a member of the community, the new arrival comes to occupy a definite status. Thus, in a Plains Indian myth a young boy finds a strange girl whom he adopts as his sister; automatically she becomes the sister of his brothers, who accordingly are prohibited from marrying her. In real life these implications are consistently carried out, so that the stranger would be a daughter to her adopters' parents, a sister-in-law to their wives, and so forth. In short, she would be classified for the entire family circle and her social relations would be regulated thereby.

It is largely the character of these kinship usages that differentiates family life among different tribes and divides its operations in primitive society from those of our own; and they are so numerous and diversified that a special chapter must be devoted to the matter. They involve both duties to relatives and claims on their help and property; both strict prohibitions as to intercourse and sanctions of extravagant forms of intercourse. The systematic study of the subject, which owes much to the energy of Dr. Rivers, is still in its infancy; yet something of value may already be extracted from the vast array of detail.

Mother's and Father's Kin

Certain peculiar relations with the maternal and paternal kin must profoundly affect social intercourse. For example, where a mother's younger sister is likely to become the father's second wife through the sororate, the initial attitude of the children towards her is bound to be influenced by the circumstance, and vice versa. Correspondingly, the levirate creates a bond between a father's brother and his brother's son to which there can be nothing analogous in civilized society. There are functions connected with other maternal and paternal relatives equally far-reaching in their effects.

Ethnologists describe under the heading of *avunculate*

the customs regulating in an altogether special way the relations of a nephew to his maternal uncle. These relations often have humorous features to which attention will be paid later. In their more serious aspect they involve an unusual authority on the uncle's part and the inheritance of property not by the son but by the sister's son. Some examples have already been furnished; the Kai suitor must obtain the consent of the girl's maternal uncle, and in the inheritance of Thonga widows it has been seen that a nephew may acquire the wife of his mother's brother. Phenomena of this sort are common. Among the Winnebago of Wisconsin, Dr. Radin informs us, the nephew acts as a servant to his mother's brother and formerly accompanied him to battle as a sort of squire. On the other hand, he was permitted to take liberties expressly forbidden with his paternal uncle, e.g., he might appropriate his uncle's belongings. Among the Omaha the maternal uncle had full control of orphaned children and even during the parents' lifetime showed a parent's zeal in defending them or avenging an injury to which they were subjected. In the Hopi household the mother's brother instructs the children in their ceremonial duties and in the traditional lore. On the coast of British Columbia the nephew goes to live with his maternal uncle, works for him, marries his daughter and becomes his legal heir. From Oceania similar customs are reported. The Torres Straits Islander obeyed his mother's brother more readily than his father, and it was his mother's eldest brother that guarded him at his initiation into the status of manhood. Here, as among the Winnebago, a man might take anything belonging to his maternal uncle. This latter feature is carried to excessive lengths by the Fijians. In Africa the avunculate is also fairly common. Among the Makonde of East Africa the maternal uncle must consent to his niece's marriage and receives part of the bride-price, while it is the sister's son that is entitled to a man's legacy. In Upper Guinea the Anglo-Ewe grant to a maternal uncle greater authority over the children than to their father. The nephew, being a man's heir-apparent, must work for him and accompany his uncle on his travels. Among the probably Hamitic Nandi of East Africa the mother's brother must consent before a boy is circumcised; he is entitled to a cow when his nephew has made a successful raid; and nothing seems more terrible than to incur his wrath.

That some of these resemblances can hardly be due to mere chance, is obvious; but the avunculate is so closely bound up with certain other phenomena of primitive life not yet described that a discussion of its meaning must be postponed. What we are here interested in is the unexpected shifting of what we consider paternal authority on avuncular shoulders and the equally remarkable tendency to make a nephew his maternal uncle's companion and heir. That family life must in large measure assume a different aspect under such conditions, requires no proof.

There are usages equally definite connected with the paternal kin. To Dr. Rivers we are indebted for data on the extraordinary importance assumed in Oceanian communities by the father's sister. In the Banks Islands a man not only treats his maternal aunt with great respect, greater than that accorded his mother, but it is she who arranges his marriage and may definitively veto a projected match. A father's sister may take her nephew's property so far as he has derived it from her brother, and he may appropriate any of her possessions. Her power to forbid or effect marriage is common in Melanesia and even extends to Polynesian Tonga, where this relative is viewed with greater veneration than father and paternal uncle. Concerning this kinswoman among the Thonga of South Africa we hear little, but she is treated with great respect, while among the Toda she bestows a name on a newborn girl. In Hopiland this function is regularly assumed for all children by the paternal grandmother. The Crow have a variety of usages associated with the father's siblings and his more remote kindred or even strangers figuring as his brothers and sisters. All these are viewed with respect; a person would not walk in front of them, regardless of their age or sex. They were preëminently the individuals to receive gifts when the nephew had captured booty from the enemy, and in turn the father's brother would chant his nephew's praises throughout the camp. Names of honor were derived from a paternal kinsman, and nicknames too were based on his rather than one's own deeds. In addition to the foregoing the related Hidatsa had the rule that a person's funeral must be conducted by the paternal kindred.

Vitally as these rules respecting one's attitude toward blood kin affect social relations, they are eclipsed by equally significant and more spectacular regulations of behavior towards the relatives by marriage, notably those connected with a person's parents-in-law.[1]

Parent-in-Law Taboos

Among a great many primitive peoples the husband, and more rarely the wife, assumes an altogether peculiar social relationship with regard to the parents-in-law. There is either complete rupture of all direct intercourse with one or both of them, or intercourse is hedged about with restrictions that may or may not be relaxed either with prolonged matrimony or through the performance of a special act. A series of concrete statements will make the matter clear.

A Yukaghir daughter-in-law must not look into the face of her father-in-law or husband's elder brother, nor must a son-in-law look into his father-in-law's or mother-in-law's face. In giving orders to the son-in-law, who it must be recollected lives with his wife's family, the father-in-law speaks impersonally or by hints. A daughter-in-law must not uncover her body before her husband's father and vice versa, and a similar rule holds for the wife and her husband's elder brother. Other Si-

KINSHIP USAGES 85

berian tribes possess almost identical customs. No married Ostyak woman may appear before her father-in-law, nor the bridegroom before his mother-in-law until he has children; at a chance meeting the face is muffled, and a woman must continue to cover it throughout her lifetime. Before the full payment of the bride-price the bridegroom visiting his sweetheart must turn his back or cover his face if he accidentally meets her father. The Buryat wife never addresses either parent-in-law by name, her face must never be uncovered in the presence of her husband's father or elder kinsman, she must not remove her dress in their presence, nor sleep in the same tent or cross their path or ride in the same wagon. They, on the other hand, must not dress or undress in her presence or utter obscene language before her and must signal their approach so as to permit a decorous adjustment of her dress. The Kalmuk observe similar restrictions, as do the Altaian Turks and the Kirgiz. The Kirgiz woman does not look into the face of her husband's father or elder kinsman and must never utter their names even if these contain designations of common objects. There is an anecdote of a Kirgiz woman who was prohibited from employing the usual words for lamb, wolf, water and rushes because they formed part of the names of her relatives by marriage. Accordingly, in telling her husband of a wolf carrying off a lamb through the rushes on the other side of the water, she was obliged to paraphrase: "Look yonder, the howling one is carrying the bleating one's young through the rustling ones on the other side of the glistening one!"

That a group of tribes occupying adjacent territories in Siberia and with intimate cultural relations should share this set of taboos, is at once intelligible through diffusion. But what shall we say when similar usages turn up in distant Ceylon? There no Vedda may so much as approach, let alone, touch his wife's mother. If he meets her in the jungle, he moves aside off the track. He will not enter a rock-shelter occupied by her alone nor take food from her except through a third party nor speak to her save in the presence of others. Quite similar taboos obtain between a man and his son's wife. Furthermore, all these restricted relatives avoid each other's names, using kinship terms instead.

But this particular type of avoidance extends its sway over the four corners of the globe. In the Banks Islands, Melanesia, the son-in-law must not utter the name of either parent-in-law nor the daughter-in-law that of her husband's father; indeed, any word entering their names is discarded from the vocabulary to be supplemented by makeshift expressions. Further, a man will not jest with his wife's father, or address him familiarly, or take anything from above his head. As for the mother-in-law, he will not even enter a house if she is near the door, and if he meets her in the bush he will turn off the path and make a détour to avoid her. She, on the other hand, must not pass a tree he has climbed, nor drink water from any bamboo he has carried, and if she requires his assistance she must ask for it through her daughter. Transgression of these rules is expiated by money payments. Similar regulations apply to the relationship between a woman and her father-in-law.

Passing to other parts of Oceania, we find that the Bukaua of Huon Gulf, New Guinea, do not permit parents-in-law and sons-in-law to touch each other or utter each other's names. The father-in-law must cover his face if he eats before his son-in-law; should the latter see his mouth open, the father-in-law feels ashamed and runs into the wood. If the older desires to give the younger man a present of betel lime, he may not place it in his hand but deposits it on a leaf. In the Western Torres Straits a person of either sex never mentions the name of the parents-in-law; a man holds no conversation with them except through his wife or in cases of absolute necessity, when he will speak very little and in a low voice; a woman does not give food directly to her father-in-law but only through her mother-in-law.

Probably throughout Australia parallel restrictions occur. Mother-in-law and son-in-law must avoid each other and in some localities she is not even supposed to hear his name spoken. Accidental contact between the two may lead to divorce of the young couple; infraction of the taboo might lead to the man's banishment and in some tribes even the death penalty was inflicted. Among the Kariera a hut or brush is interposed between them as a precaution against a man's looking at the wife's mother, but the taboo breaks down with the lapse of years. Here and probably in Australia generally a woman need not shun her father-in-law.

No less striking are the parallels from Africa. A Zulu covers his face with his shield if he accidentally comes upon his mother-in-law, throws away the mouthful he is eating if she chances to pass by, and must never pronounce her name. With the passing of time, however, the severity of these rules is considerably mitigated. Similar customs are cited by Frazer for various Bantu tribes and also for the Masai. Among the West Africans they do not seem to flourish, though a Matse-Ewe regulation prohibits parents-in-law from eating in the son-in-law's house and vice versa, an infringement being reckoned disgraceful and regarded as preventing the birth of children.

American examples abound. A Crow must not speak to his wife's parents and vice versa. The father-in-law taboo is less exacting, but the mother-in-law rule is still rigidly observed. A man may speak to his wife's mother only through his wife and he must not pronounce her name nor any word forming part of it. The latter taboo involves the use of circumlocution, as among the Assiniboin, where a knife may have to be referred to as "something sharp" and a horse as "the animal we ride." The father-in-law's name may be pronounced but to do so is not considered polite. It was possible in former years to remove the taboo by the formal presentation of a substantial gift to the parents-in-law; among the Hidatsa and Mandan by bringing them an enemy's scalp. Further, a Crow mother-in-law may remove all restrictions after her daughter's death by addressing her son-in-law as her son. There is no corresponding taboo between a woman and her father-in-law among the Crow and Hidatsa, but it occurs among the Dakota, Assiniboin, Kiowa, Arapaho, and Omaha in conjunction with the taboo between son- and mother-in-law.

Contrary to what might be supposed, wherever we obtain data as to the subjective aspect of avoidance, there is no suggestion of hostility between the tabooed relatives, the stress being entirely on the mutual respect shown. An Hidatsa interpreter had married a woman from the Arikara tribe, which does not observe these customs. Accordingly, his Hidatsa friends once saw his mother-in-law speaking to him and exclaimed in horror, "What's the matter with your mother-in-law, Joe? She does not seem to have any respect for you at all!"

From the extremely wide range of parent-in-law avoidance, the absolute universality of these rules might be conjectured on the ground that where unrecorded the customs have merely eluded notice. It is true that a mere absence of statement even in otherwise excellent accounts cannot be taken as decisive on this subject. However, in North America the distribution of the taboo has been systematically investigated of late years, and it appears conclusively that a considerable number of tribes completely lack the custom. Among these are the Nootka, the Arikara, Zuñi, Hopi, various Plateau Shoshoneans, and a number of Californian peoples. On the other hand, avoidance flourishes among the Plains Indians and occurs in the Southeast, among the Southwestern nomads, a number of Californian tribes, and in northern British Columbia.

The first problem that presents itself for solution is one of distribution. How do customs so similar happen to be so widely spread? That we are to some extent dealing with diffusion cannot be questioned for a moment. The Siberian data, e.g., display so far-reaching a resemblance in detail that a single source of origin is the only possible assumption. Again, when we find that of all the Shoshonean peoples of the Plateau area only those in contact with the Northern Plains tribes practise the taboo, the inference is sound that they have borrowed it from their neighbors. But how shall we interpret the similarity of the name taboo of the Kirgiz of Central Asia and the Assiniboin of Montana, with consequent use of paraphrase for words of everyday speech? To my mind, this case is instructive in proving that resemblances may develop independently. For while the taboo itself is marvelously similar, it obtains between different individuals. With the Kirgiz it is the daughter-in-law that must paraphrase words in her father-in-law's name; among the Assiniboin it is the son-in-law who must not utter the father-in-law's name. But so far as the possibility of borrowing goes, this makes all the difference in the world. For by what mechanism can usages of this type be supposed to be disseminated? They surely are not imposed by a conquering chief on a vanquished tribe in the way in which the Chinese were made to wear pigtails. Further, they are of far too intimate and recondite a character to be understood by a random visitor; such a one might note that certain of his hosts shun one another without the faintest notion of their relationship; hence without the possibility of transmitting such a custom to his own people. Certainly, if he observed a woman cutting a male relative by marriage, he would not be stimulated thereby to concoct an innovation for his own people by which a man should avoid his mother-in-law or father-in-law, or transfer the name taboo to a quite new relationship. The custom cannot be so much as comprehended without intimate contact; and if it is not set down as merely a barbarian idiosyncrasy, it will be adopted as it is found. Most commonly, I have no doubt, its propagation must have been the result of intertribal marriage: brought up with the notion that the wife's mother or, for a woman, the daughter's son, must be tabooed and that contrary conduct is ridiculous if not outrageous, a foreigner may by his personal influence come to affect tribal custom. Imitation of his example will thus establish the taboo where it had not been found before but it could not establish what to the concrete mind of primitive man is an utterly distinct practice. Hence I unhesitatingly reject, quite apart from geographical considerations and others based on the probable meaning of the Siberian usage (p. 103), the hypothesis that the Kirgiz and the Plains Indian taboos are historically connected.

The case is somewhat different when we compare, say, the African and Australian, or Melanesian and American data, for here the rules relate to the same individuals and are really remarkably similar. As to certain striking details, however, we must remember that *if* there is stringent avoidance it is bound to take certain forms: e.g., a man then *must* make a détour if he chances upon his mother-in-law. Similarly, if the Banks Islander and the Crow must not use words entering the parent-in-law's name, paraphrase is an inevitable consequence. The specific coincidences are thus not nearly so cogent as they might at first appear to be. In other words, the question is whether the bare fact of avoidance between individuals in the same relationship is necessarily an indication of a single source of origin. The reply will partly depend on the interpretation of the custom, for if it is derived from conditions that may plausibly be regarded as existing in many localities the assumption of independent origin will be greatly strengthened. Waiving this point for the present, I hold that both the probable mechanism of the borrowing process for this trait and its ascertained absence in certain regions negative the probability of diffusion over disconnected continents. Transmission of the usage has been seen to involve an unusual intimacy of contact such as cannot be readily assumed, even if *some* contact be admitted, between Oceania and Africa or between Melanesia and America. It is surely not very probable that a custom which failed to traverse California or to pass from the Hidatsa to the neighboring Arikara and from the Omaha to the neighboring Pawnee should have leaped across oceans. My conclusion, then, is that diffusion has played its part in the history of the parent-in-law taboo but that independent development must be assumed for distinct geographical areas.

Turning next to the problem of interpretation, we find a theory advanced by Frazer which with all its deficiencies cannot be readily ruled out of court entirely. Frazer rightly points out that rules of avoidance are not restricted to parents-in-law but also may apply to such blood kindred as brothers and sisters. All relevant regulations, he argues, must be put under a single head and must be explained as "precautions designed to remove the temptation to sexual intercourse between persons whose marriage union is for any reason repugnant to the moral sense of the community." The explanation, he recognizes, suffers from a serious, though in his opinion not fatal, difficulty, to wit, the taboos restricting the social relations of individuals of the same sex. These, according to his contention, are due to a secondary extension of rules that once applied only to relatives of opposite sex. It is impossible to do justice to Frazer's argument without anticipating what must be said about various other kinship usages. One remark, however, may be offered at this point. Granting that taboos restrain individuals whose union would be incestuous, it does not follow that their purpose is to prevent sexual intercourse between these individuals. It is possible to admit the empirical correlation but to reject the causal interpretation given. To this topic we must revert later.

An explanation of parent-in-law taboos similar in trend but with psycho-analytic motivation has been given by Dr.

Sigmund Freud, whose views merit consideration not only on their own account but as typical of any psychological interpretation of social facts. Freud applies to the data of mother-in-law avoidance the concept of 'ambivalence,' that is, he conceives them as based on a blending of affection and animosity. Some of the hostile motives in the case, he argues, are manifest: the woman's reluctance to surrender her daughter, the suspicions directed against the stranger, her desire to maintain the dominant position created in her own household; the man's resolute aversion from subjection to an alien will, his jealousy of all who preceded him in his wife's affections, his resistance against having his sexual illusions disturbed by the personality of a woman who recalls his wife by many common traits yet lacks the charm of youth and beauty. To these elements Freud adds latent factors of specifically psycho-analytic nature. The aging mother-in-law is prematurely cut short in her own psycho-sexual life and is able to satisfy her emotional needs only by identification with her children's psyche. But identification with her daughter may readily lead to love for the man her daughter loves, and in the resulting conflict of sentiments the hostile, sadistic component of passion is directed toward the son-in-law so as to suppress with greater certainty the tabooed incestuous emotion. On the other hand, the son-in-law is stirred by similar impulses. He has conquered, so psycho-analytic theory will have it, the infantile passion for his mother and substituted an unrelated woman conceived in her image. With the appearance of his mother-in-law there is a tendency to relapse into the juvenile state, which shocks his incest feelings since these demand that the incestuous source of his bride-choice remain barred from consciousness. Inasmuch as the mother-in-law's personality, unlike the mother's, has not been known from the earliest stages, so that her image has not been for years slumbering unaltered in the subconsciousness, it is relatively easy to conquer temptation, which nevertheless remains a reality.

The motive for the avoidance rule is accordingly the prevention of incestuous intercourse.

The first stricture that must be directed against Freud's explanation relates to a simple matter of fact. He paints the subjective state of mother-in-law and son-in-law with the lurid colors that tinge our modern family life but are wholly lacking in the savage relationship. To repeat what has already been said: whenever we gain a glimpse of what the connections by marriage really feel, there is never a trace of hostility: respect is invariably the dominant note in the mutual sentiments, which are thus of a totally different character from the ones that so persistently figure in our comic weeklies.

The data concerning other taboos have of course the same bearing on Freud's as on Frazer's views. But Freud's psychological motivation suffers from a fatal defect shared with all psychological interpretations of cultural data. The facts of psychology to which Freud appeals possess avowedly universal validity, they must accordingly act with equal force in the most diverse, in all communities, except so far as there may be racial differences. But the parent-in-law taboo is found to have a most capricious distribution. In North America the Navaho avoid the mother-in-law, while the neighboring Hopi view the custom merely as a Navaho peculiarity. The Lemhi Shoshoni regard a man as insane if he speaks to his wife's mother; among the Comanche, who are not merely of the same stock but even speak practically the same language, I had great difficulty in making my informants so much as grasp the notion of the taboo. Shall we assume that the infantile sentiments of the Hopi male diverge so widely from those of the Navaho? That the emotional reactions of Hopi and Navaho mothers-in-law will regularly be quite distinct in character? Indeed, in order to adapt the theory to the facts we must assume one type of psychology for the Banks Islanders, Australians, Zulu, Navaho and Lemhi Shoshoni and a different psychology for the Hopi, Comanche, and Arikara. But to conceive this assumption is to reduce it to an absurdity. The psychoanalytic theory falls to the ground because it is a psychological theory, and because we are not dealing with simple psychological facts but with psychological facts socially determined. The reason why a Navaho mother-in-law avoids her son-in-law is not because she individually feels this way or that way about her son-in-law but because she is a member of a society which taboos intercourse between certain relatives by marriage. Any conflict that might conceivably arise in her situation would be a conflict not between one set of feelings and another set of feelings for her daughter's husband but between some personal reaction and the sentiment of blind obedience to an accepted social norm. The question is why social norms differ, and that can be answered solely by correlating the social differences with other differences of a social order.

In this respect Tylor's interpretation accords much better with modern scientific requirements, for he derives parent-in-law avoidance from the rule of residence, i.e., one sociological feature from another. In matrilocal marriage, he explains, the husband is regarded as an intruder and is simply not recognized, corresponding treatment being meted out to the wife in patrilocal communities, while both kinds of taboo occur in the intermediate condition of temporary matrilocal residence. On statistical principles he shows that the matrilocal residence and mother-in-law avoidance actually are combined more frequently than they would be if mutually independent, thus establishing a causal connection between the two phenomena.

Tylor's attempt to introduce rigorous methods into anthropological inquiries must ever rank as an heroic pioneer achievement of the very first order but his statistical results cannot be accepted unscrutinized. Unfortunately the data on which his conclusions are based have never been published, and it is therefore impossible to check them satisfactorily. It is clear, however, from his statements that Tylor takes for statistical units the several tribes for which relevant facts are reported. But this is hardly a defensible method. For example, there may be a dozen cases of the daughter-in-law taboo among Siberian tribes. If in each one of them there has been an independent association of patrilocal residence and avoidance, then the case for a causal nexus is tremendously strengthened. But we cannot take such independence for granted. It is entirely possible that the avoidance rule was a feature already characteristic of certain ancestral Siberian tribes, that in other words it originated but a single time so far as each stock is concerned and has merely persisted in the several branches into which the ancestral tribe has broken up. In addition, it is more than probable that this applies strictly to only one stock from which the tribes of other stocks have merely borrowed the usage in its entire setting. But this alters the logic of the case completely. Let us assume, for the sake of simplicity, that we have a single contradictory case elsewhere to pit against the dozen Siberian cases; let us take some American tribe, like the patrilocal Blackfoot, who lack the Siberian rule and practise the taboo proper to a matrilocal people on Tylor's scheme. If the Siberian cases represented twelve instances of the taboo arising independently from antecedent patrilocal residence, we should admit at once that they completely outweighed the negative testimony of the Blackfoot data. But if there has been historical connection, the twelve Siberian units are reduced to a single one for our purposes and we have *one* case of connection harmonizing with Tylor's theory and *one* case contravening it; in other words, the theory then remains unproved.

This is merely to show that Tylor's results, while based on mathematical principles, may nevertheless be lacking in validity because of erroneous premises, viz., a faulty choice of units. Indeed, if we take larger units, the correlation is hardly favorable to the hypothesis in an unqualified form.

Siberia, to be sure, has both patrilocal residence and the taboo between daughter-in-law and father-in-law; but neither the Australian nor the South African data harmonize with the theory. In both areas the wife goes to her husband's people yet not only is the Siberian prohibition lacking, but the reverse rule holds, viz., the son-in-law taboo, which ex hypothesi should develop only in a matrilocal community. Further, it is rather remarkable that such distinctly matrilocal tribes as the Zuñi and Hopi lack the supposedly correlated avoidance rule, while peoples only temporarily matrilocal like the Hidatsa rigorously observed it as did the patrilocal Blackfoot, who are definitely known to lack the daughter-in-law taboo, which on Tylor's theory should flourish among them.

There is still another oversight in Tylor's interpretation. He explains why both of the parents-in-law and the son-in-law would avoid each other among matrilocal, and why both of the parents-in-law and daughter-in-law should avoid each other in patrilocal tribes. But in many of the recorded instances the taboo is restricted to individuals of opposite sex. In some Australian tribes there is no obstacle raised between the intercourse of father-in-law and son-in-law nor in Siberia between mother-in-law and daughter-in-law; and on the whole these cases are too frequent to be ignored.

Nevertheless, when all deductions are made, I still believe that Tylor's theory contains a valuable element. Residence is not, clearly enough, the sole efficient cause of the parent-in-law taboos but it may well be one of the determinants or act as a cause in the absence of deterrent factors. A finer analysis than any yet attempted may to that extent qualify the negative conclusion reached above. Here a mere suggestion must suffice. The patrilocal Siberian tribes enumerated were shown to enjoin avoidance of the husband's father or male kinsman older than the husband's. But the Yukaghir who are matrilocal not only share the taboo of the patrilocal Siberians, a fact quite intelligible as the effect of diffusion, but also differ practically from all the rest in adding the son-in-law taboo. It is difficult to evade the inference that there is a connection between the unique mode of residence and the unique taboo.

In view of Frazer's reasonable suggestion that parent-in-law avoidance represents but one species of a wider genus, its interpretation is best deferred until we shall have surveyed prohibitions affecting other relationships.[2]

Other Taboos

Since it is impossible to deal with all the recorded kinship taboos, we had better limit our attention to a few thoroughly studied tribes and the restrictions on social intercourse imposed in each case. The consequences of these rules for the everyday family life will be readily imagined.

Probably no people has gone further in this respect than the Yukaghir. In addition to the son-in-law and daughter-in-law prohibitions as met elsewhere we find rules barring speech between the elder brother or male cousin and the younger brother's or cousin's wife; between the elder brother (cousin) and the wife of the younger brother's (cousin's) son; between the elder brother and the wife of his younger sister's son; between the elder brother and the younger sister's husband. But blood-kindred are likewise subject to restrictions: brothers should not converse unrestrainedly with one another, nor brothers with sisters, nor sisters with one another, and this rule extends to cousins. Persons in any one of these relationships must not uncover their bodies in one another's presence, not even if of the same sex, and they must refrain from discussing anything relating to cohabitation. They must not address one another directly nor look at one another, must neither call one another by name nor by a kinship term.

In the Andaman Islands I do not find the parent-in-law taboo recorded but its place is taken by a similar rule.

Until middle age a man evinces great shyness in the presence of his younger brother's wife, never communicating with her except through an intermediary. There is no such prohibition of social intercourse with the elder brother's wife.

The Melanesians prescribe circumspectness of behavior for a number of varying relationships. There is a fairly widespread prohibition of intercourse between brother and sister. In Lepers' Island they never see each other after the girl's puberty tattooing, for she leaves the house to take up her abode with a maternal uncle. If they meet subsequently, the girl gets out of the way and both avoid looking at each other. They never speak of each other or utter each other's names. If the man wishes to see his nephews, his married sister will leave the house before he enters. Anciently the Fijians observed analogous regulations: brother and sister might not speak to each other or play and eat together, and communication was through an intermediary; neither pronounced the other's personal name. In New Ireland, where cross-cousins of opposite sex are classed with siblings, the same restrictions apply to them. In the Banks Islands the sibling taboo is weakened into a rule against mutual jesting, but a host of other regulations are reported. Father and son must not eat together. A man must not take something hanging above his maternal uncle's head but must wait till his uncle is gone. The father's sister is not only treated with distinguished respect as previously explained, but her name is not uttered nor will she pronounce that of her nephew. A husband may call his wife by name but it is considered highly disrespectful on her part to address him correspondingly (see p. 109). Brothers-in-law refrain from uttering each other's names, and so do sisters-in-law; jesting between two individuals in this relationship is considered objectionable.

To take a final example from America. The Crow include in the son-in-law taboo, as commonly happens among primitive tribes, not only the mother-in-law's and father-in-law's sisters and brothers respectively, but also the wife's grandmothers; and the husband's own brothers are subject to the husband's taboos. That is to say, there is a tendency to extend the restriction to individuals addressed by the wife as if they were her parents, and to inviduals occupying the husband's status. Further, a man is obliged to shun his wife's brother's wife, and vice versa. The relations of brothers-in-law are peculiar. They are on terms of the greatest friendship and may indulge in good-humored raillery, but anything savoring of obscenity with a personal application is out of the question between them, and if a man transgresses the rule his brother-in-law may strike him. A man may not speak obscenely in his brother-in-law's presence even if he is conversing with other individuals. Brother and sister are not indeed prohibited completely from conversation, but after puberty they no longer speak freely to each other nor are they supposed to be together alone. A man entering a tent and finding only his sister indoors will depart forthwith. A Crow interpreter once twitted me with the indecency of the Caucasians who dare reproach the Indians with looseness of morals while themselves so shameless as to speak freely with their own sisters. Finally, husband and wife generally avoid calling each other by name except after years of marriage.[3]

Privileged Familiarity

Representing the opposite pole of social intercourse are the series of customs that permit and all but prescribe various forms of often but not always reciprocal familiarity, such as chaffing or billingsgate between individuals standing in a specific relationship. These usages, like others connected with kinship, did not attract systematic inquiry until recent years, and there is little doubt that a far greater amount of information remains to be garnered. At present most of our data come from Melanesia and North America.

The avunculate, despite its more serious aspect, demands

consideration from this angle also. In Fiji the sister's son not merely treats his uncle's property as if it were his father's, but recklessly and wantonly kills his pigs and destroys his plantations for the fun of it. On the other hand, when he seizes stuff at an exchange between his uncle's tribe and another group, he gets a drubbing from his uncle's sons; they are at liberty to beat him but may not recover the property. Among the Winnebago Indians, too, it will be recalled, the nephew may appropriate the belongings of his maternal uncle. With the Thonga the sister's son takes his uncle's food and among the Hottentot the uncle may seize his nephew's property if damaged, while the nephew freely indemnifies himself with his uncle's uninjured possessions.

One of the best-authenticated instances of privileged familiarity is that between brother-in-law and sister-in-law among the Blackfoot and Crow Indians. There is no limit to the obscenity of language that may be bandied back and forth by these connections. As to behavior, I have myself seen a middle-aged Crow romping with his wife's sister in a manner that would strike us as transcending all limits of decency, yet both were quite unconcerned at the presence of the man's wife and adult son.

Of a distinct character is the joking-relationship of the Crow and Hidatsa. The people involved are not necessarily kindred at all but merely children of fathers belonging to the same tribal subdivision (see p. 116). Within this group license runs riot: any member may play tricks on any other and enjoy complete immunity. But the relationship has a more serious function. A man's jokers are also his moral censors. If he has in any way transgressed the tribal code of ethics or etiquette, a joker will suddenly confront him on a public occasion and twit him with it aloud so that he feels like sinking into the ground with shame. Yet he has no redress but to await a chance for requital.

KINSHIP USAGES

Privileged license is reported from Melanesia for a different relationship. In Fiji one cross-cousin may impudently appropriate another's possessions just as a nephew does a maternal uncle's; the despoiled cousin may chide his robber but must not attempt to retrieve his property, for that would be a sign of low breeding. Even if of opposite sex cross-cousins may take liberties with each other, and formerly sexual intercourse between them was condoned. Abusive language among cross-cousins is sanctioned as proper and is accordingly not resented. In the Banks Islands there are localities where brother-in-law and sister-in-law indulged in horseplay, though not to the extent noted for the Plains Indians, definite sexual references being avoided. A Banks Islander, however, may heap almost any indignity on his father's sister's husband, threatening him and mocking him continually.[4]

Taboo and License

The examples of taboos and of license cited from various parts of the world abundantly justify Frazer's contention that it is unwarrantable to discuss parent-in-law restrictions apart from all others. Evidently these prohibitions represent but one special type of a broader class of usages regulating the social behavior of relatives by blood and marriage. That all of the taboos or all of the cases of privilege should have a common psychological basis, is a highly improbable assumption on the face of it. It is clear without argument that the Crow custom permitting familiarity with the sister-in-law differs fundamentally from the phenomenon of the joking-relationship with its blending of serious and comic elements. Hence it is desirable to renounce once and for all a theory that shall embrace all the data cited. The regulations in a particular locality should rather be viewed in conjunction with the whole culture, and whatever interpretations appear from such an inquiry may then be compared with corresponding results from other regions. Since our data are still so inadequate, definitive explanations can hardly be expected at present; nevertheless some inferences may be stated with considerable assurance.

In seeking a guiding principle for the maze of detail we had best begin with a simple case, one where we are not obliged to contend with a multiplicity of regulations possibly based on a variety of motives but where the taboos are few and can readily be correlated with some coëxisting usage. Such an instance is furnished by the Andaman Islands. From there a single taboo is reported, that against social relations between a man and his younger brother's wife; and we are expressly informed that there is no restriction on intercourse between a man and his elder brother's wife. This rule, then, is directly connected with the coexisting form of marriage known as the junior levirate. For this people, at least, we may enunciate the principle that *social and sexual restrictions go hand in hand,* a conclusion adopted in more general form by Dr. Goldenweiser on the basis of Sternberg's unpublished Gilyak data and by Dr. Rivers as a result of his Oceanian researches. I would supplement this statement with another, viz., that *licensed familiarity generally obtains between potential mates.*

Let us now test these propositions by the evidence from several distinct regions. The Crow restrict intimacy between siblings, whose union is of course out of the question; and they permit excessive liberties between a man and his brother's wife, whom he may inherit by the levirate, and also between a man and his wife's sister, whom he could until recently take for an additional wife through the sororate. In Melanesia a similar correlation, positive and negative, has been noted: siblings of opposite sex shun each other, brother-in-law and sister-in-law are on terms of familiarity. From South Africa there comes corroboratory testimony not yet cited. A Thonga woman is free in her relations with her husband's younger brother, whom she may some day wed, but distant reserve characterizes her intercourse with the husband's elder brother, who can never marry her. This is simply the Andaman Island case repeated. But a wife may also be inherited by the sister's son, and we verily find that this nephew may take all sorts of liberties with his maternal uncle's wife even during her husband's lifetime. Finally, a Thonga man shuns his wife's elder sisters, who are not among his possible mates, and treats with the utmost freedom her younger sisters, who may become subsidiary wives.

To these examples I will now add the Siberian parent-in-law taboos. The peculiarity of this set of restrictions lies in the inclusion of the husband's elder brother together with the husband's father: a woman must shun or reverence both in the same fashion. Further, there is (except among the Yukaghir) complete absence of the taboo between mother-in-law and son-in-law and virtual absence of any restriction on relations between daughter-in-law and mother-in-law. These facts are at once intelligible if we conceive the 'parent-in-law' taboo as essentially a brother-in-law taboo based on the junior levirate, which many Siberian tribes share with the Andaman Islanders. The extension of the prohibition to the father-in-law is readily explained from another Siberian trait, the emphasis on sheer seniority in the classification of kin, to the point of disregarding a difference in generation. Thus, the Votyak have a single word for any male kinsman older than the speaker, and the Yukaghir denote by one term the husband's father and the husband's elder brother. On my hypothesis it is clear why the Siberians, with the single exception noted, lack the taboos so frequently found elsewhere. For the mother-in-law is not concerned in the daughter-in-law's inheritance by her husband's kinsmen; nor does the levirate affect the relative status of son-in-law and father-in-law.

The Siberian example is interesting from another angle.

It illustrates the possibility of convergent evolution. The causal sequence in Siberia is: junior levirate, hence taboo between sister-in-law and husband's elder brother; identification of husband's father with husband's elder brother, hence extension of avoidance to the former. From the Assiniboin the daughter-in-law and father-in-law avoidance has also been reported, but since this people neither practise the junior levirate nor identify husband's elder brother and husband's father, the history of their taboo *must* be different from that of, say, the Kirgiz taboo. Thus, the same result may be arrived at through varying stages of development.

To return to the main proposition. The cases quoted yield ample evidence for the reality of the correlation stated above, viz., between social and sexual taboos, and between social license and the possibility of sex relations. But the existence of taboos between members of the same sex indicates that this principle by no means explains all the phenomena with which we are dealing. It is permissible to argue that a rule has been extended from one relative to another when, as in the Siberian case, there is specific evidence to support the assumption. We cannot, however, content ourselves with Frazer's labor-saving assumption that every taboo between members of the same sex has grown out of a taboo affecting persons of opposite sex, an hypothesis rightly repudiated by Dr. Parsons. Such wholesale interpretations will be eschewed by the sane historian in favor of an intensive study of all the taboos of a particular tribe in their normal cultural setting.

At this stage a point temporarily dismissed before again raises its head. If there *is* an empirical correlation between social and sexual taboos, why not follow Frazer's psychological interpretation of the correlation so far as it holds? Why not assume that social relations are tabooed in order to prevent sexual intercourse between the restricted individuals? My answer is that incestuous relations are amply prevented by other factors of a far more basic nature than the taboos in question. If the horror of incest between brother and sister is instinctive, as I assume with Hobhouse, then no social restriction is required to enforce an innate aversion. But even if that hypothesis be repudiated, there are fundamental social laws that preclude incest. In Australia we find matrimonial laws of which the transgression was punished with death even where nothing we regard as incestuous was involved: a man might mate only with a member of a specified class, say, his mother's brother's daughter. Again, in many parts of Melanesia, the tribe is divided into exogamous units, all siblings belonging to the same unit. Under such conditions a man and his sister cannot possibly be mates.

I must confess that in the cases mainly discussed hitherto, viz., those affected by the junior levirate and sororate, the psychological interpretation seems simple. Convention has dichotomized biologically desirable mates into those who are and those who are not sociologically possible. Hence there naturally follows a difference of attitude, which in the one case may degenerate into license, in the other assume the grotesque prudery of avoidance. That is, with certain relations once definitely established as incestuous, I believe that taboos are no longer required to enforce continence but that they are the spontaneous outgrowths of the artificially extended incest horror. Anything that even remotely suggests sexual relations produces a feeling of revulsion and this frame of mind leads to complete severance of intercourse.

But I am not at all convinced that the parent-in-law taboos are always or even frequently to be considered in the same category with the taboos affecting members of the opposite sex and the same generation. For example, the Crow restrict intercourse not only between mother-in-law and son-in-law but also between father-in-law and son-in-law and between two brothers-in-law. It is certainly remarkable that a people far from averse to grossness in their mythology and everyday conversation should exhibit such delicacy in the conduct imposed on a man in the company of his wife's brother. This trait has also been observed among the Blackfoot and Arapaho and may turn out to be of far more common occurrence than might be imagined from our meager records. So far as this region of North America is concerned, then, we may ultimately find that the basic sentiment is one of respectful reserve to be maintained towards members of the wife's family regardless of age; but that a difference in both generation and sex has naturally intensified the feeling in the case of mother-in-law avoidance.

The necessity of viewing all the taboos of a region jointly is especially manifest with regard to name taboos. Considering the superstitions clinging to names in savage communities, where they are usually supplanted by kinship terms in daily intercourse, the existence of such prohibitions in connection with kinship presents no great puzzle, but it is essential to note whose name is tabooed. Among the Toda a man never utters either parent-in-law's name but neither does he pronounce that of either grandparent, and only reluctantly does he mention his wife's. Hence this taboo cannot be regarded as a specifically parent-in-law taboo, and it certainly cannot be connected with sexual restrictions. This interpretation applies equally to the Crow, among whom spouses normally avoid uttering each other's names. Among a Melanesian people the husband is permitted to call his wife by name, but not vice versa; Dr. Rivers' informant plausibly explained this as a sign of female inferiority. The avoidance of the name of a particular relative is thus liable to complete misinterpretation if we connect it merely with a corresponding taboo on the other side of the globe instead of correlating it with corresponding restrictions on the use of names of other relatives in the same society. It is only from this thoroughgoing investigation of particular regions and subsequent comparison of different areas, not from random running of parallels, that we can expect light on the meaning of avoidance rules.

This intensive type of inquiry, if anything, will also illuminate the absence of taboos that might reasonably be expected. Why, e.g., do the Kariera lack a taboo between son-in-law and father-in-law? I do not profess to know but the direction in which an explanation may be sought is worth indicating. It is possibly to be found in the fact that a man's father-in-law is normally his maternal uncle and that the Kariera conception of the avuncular bond precludes avoidance. This explanation would of course be limited to the Kariera and such tribes as share their notions of kinship. At all events, it is clear that if we desire to get at the bottom of taboos we must get to the bottom of the culture of the tribes observing them; and since they may have borrowed their taboos the culture of the entire area must be subjected to careful examination. There is no royal road to the comprehension of cultural phenomena.[5]

Teknonymy

When an Ewe child is born, the parents are henceforth no longer addressed by their own names but are designated as the infant's father and mother, e.g., "Father (Mother) of Komla." This practice of naming the parent (or other relative) from a child was first conceptualized and interpreted by Tylor, who coined a Greek derivative, *teknonymy,* to label this curious phenomenon. Applying the statistical method noticed above, he inferred that teknonymy was causally connected with the institution of matrilocal residence and also with the son-in-law taboo. The son-in-law, he reasoned, is at first cut as a stranger by his wife's family but subsequently gains status in the household as the father of the child born there, whereupon he is addressed, as it were, in terms of the child.

Tylor knew of some thirty peoples who named the parent from the child, though he cites only three,—the Bechuana of South Africa, the Khasi of Assam, and the Cree of western Canada. It has since become clear that teknonymy is far more widely disseminated over the earth. Thus Frazer's compilation proves its occurrence in Australia and New Guinea, in Malaysia, China and northern Siberia, among various Bantu tribes of Africa, in northern British Columbia, in Guatemala, and Patagonia. Even so his list is remarkable for omissions that can be supplied from available literature. For example, in the Andamans, among the peasant Sinhalese and the Henebedda Vedda, the custom has attracted notice, and among the Gold of the Amur a woman always calls her husband "Father of So-and-so." Teknonymy has been found in Fiji and other sections of Melanesia and in various parts of America. Among the Zuñi and Hopi its vogue is unparalleled. A Hopi woman addresses her mother-in-law as "Grandmother of So-and-so" and her father-in-law correspondingly; a man will use corresponding appellations for his parents-in-law. My interpreter never spoke of his wife except as "So-and-so's mother," mentioning the name of any one of her children; she, in turn, referred to him teknonymously. Sometimes a man having no children is called "Uncle of So-and-so."

In the light of our present knowledge Tylor's interpretation appears untenable. For one thing it fails to take into account that the mother, as well as the father, is often referred to in terms of her children. As for the supposed correlation with matrilocal residence, the Australians, the Melanesians, and the Gold, to cite only a few instances, are patrilocal. On the other hand, among the matrilocal Zuñi and Hopi it is impossible to conceive teknonymy as supplanting the son-in-law taboo, because no such taboo exists and also because various relatives beside the father are named from the child. Thus neither of the two assumed correlations holds.

Can a more reasonable hypothesis be advanced? We shall again do well to renounce a generic theory and to attach ourselves to the correlates of teknonymy in its particular manifestations. It is first of all essential to know who refers to whom teknonymously. Among the Gold it is the wife who must so address her husband, while he may call her by name; prior to the birth of her first child, the woman has no way of designating her husband at all. Correlated with this phenomenon we find that a brother may call his sister by name, while she lacks the corresponding privilege, and that among the Gold the female sex is held in very low esteem. It follows that in this tribe teknonymy is a result of the wife's inferior status; it is a natural solution of the difficulty that a woman may refer to her husband neither by name nor by a term of relationship. Obviously an entirely different explanation must be sought in the case of the Hopi. There the abundant use of teknonymy is especially evident in the case of relatives by affinity; and it is hardly an accident that the Hopi vocabulary reveals a surprising paucity of words for precisely these relatives. Here, then, teknonymy may have developed from the necessity of referring to individuals for whom other designations were lacking and may have been secondarily transferred to some additional cases. In short, teknonymy again furnishes a case of convergent evolution, and its multiple sources must be looked for in specific conditions. Still another interpretation will be offered in connection with a phenomenon to be described below.[6]

References

[1] Lowie, 1919 (a): 35-40; id., 1912: 201; id., 1917 (a): 40. Rivers, 1914 (b): 1, 38, 367; 11, 160; id., 1906: 332. Junod: 1, 223.

[2] Jochelson, 1910: 75 seq. Czaplicka: 120, 122, 127, 128. Radloff: 314, 480. Seligmann: 68. Rivers, 1914 (b): 1, 41. Lehner: 426. Reports, v: 142. Howitt: 199, 208, 256, 266.

Brown: 157. Junod: 1, 230. Frazer, 1912: 77-81, 84, 95.
Spieth: 744. Lowie, 1912: 213; id., 1917 (a): 48, 91. Freud,
1912: 30 seq. Tylor, 1889: 246.

[3] Jochelson, 1910: 75. Man: 68. Rivers, 1914 (b): 1, 35-43, 213, 291; 11, 508. Lowie, 1912: 213 seq.; id., 1917 (a): 69, 71, 74.

[4] Hocart, 1915; 641; id., 1913: 101. Lowie, 1912: 204, 215; id., 1917 (a): 42, 79. Rivers, 1914 (b): 1, 40, 45 seq.

[5] Goldenweiser, 1910: 251. Rivers, 1914 (b): 1, 223 et passim; id., 1906: 494. Junod: 1, 228-236. Parsons: 282.

[6] Tylor, 1889: 248. Spieth: 217. Frazer, J. G., 1911: 331-334. Man: 61. Seligmann: 65. Laufer, 1900: 320. Rivers, 1914 (b): 1. 230, 279. Lowie, 1917 (a): 92. Kroeber, 1917: 72.

CHAPTER VI

THE SIB

BESIDES the omnipresent family group we frequently find in primitive societies a type of unit that resembles the family in being based on kinship but otherwise differs fundamentally from it. Following Professor Philbrick, I will call this unit by the good old Anglo-Saxon term *sib,* for the hopeless confusion of nomenclature in this department of our subject imperatively calls for a new word and the one chosen is recommended alike by its alluring brevity and phonetic suggestiveness.

The sib ('clan' of British anthropologists) is most briefly defined as a *unilateral* kinship group. The family is bilateral: to say that an individual belongs to a certain family implies that he recognizes relationship with a certain man as his father *and* a certain woman as his mother. The sib traces kinship through *either* parent to the total neglect of the other. If a tribe is organized into mother-sibs ('clans' of most American anthropologists), every child regardless of sex is considered a member of its mother's sib and takes the maternal sib name if there is one. If the tribe is organized into father-sibs ('gentes' of most American anthropologists) every child follows the father's sib and takes the father's sib name. The other parent, *for sib purposes* counts for nought, just as in European countries outside of Spain the mother is neglected as regards the transmission of the family name. If all men and women inheriting the name Smith were united by their common patronymic into a definite social group set apart from all Browns and Joneses, we should be justified in saying that they formed a sib. If we deny to them that designation it is because in our society there is no bond whatsoever connecting even all those Smiths who are related by blood; in inheritance a closely related Brown takes precedence of a more remote Smith. But for purposes of illustration we may assume a Smith sib founded on actual blood relationship. Such a sib would include the ancestral Smith with all his sons and unmarried daughters, his sons' sons and unmarried daughters and so on *ad infinitum*. In order to convert this unit into a typical primitive sib only one change is required, viz., making affiliation (except for cases of adoption) wholly dependent on birth and unaffected by marriage. The father-sib thus embraces a male ancestor, his children male and female, and the children of his male descendants through males. Correspondingly, the mother-sib includes a female ancestor with her children and the children of her female descendants through females.

From the foregoing there develops at once a significant distinction between family and sib: the former is a loose, the latter a fixed unit. Divorce and migration rend the family asunder; but the sib bond is permanent. This trait is well exemplified by the Hupa phenomena described in a previous chapter. It was shown that through patrilocal residence the children grow up in the paternal village, which the daughters leave only on marriage. Until that time, then, a number of brothers with their children would form the core of a patrilineal sib, held together by a common residence. But owing to local exogamy the very rule that cements the union of the group leads to its partial dissolution when the girls marry. The married woman, whatever her sentiments, is no longer a member of the same social unit when she has settled in her husband's locality. On the other hand, in the anomalous case of a man's serving for his bride the children are counted as belonging to her village, contrary to the normal course of events. But if the Hupa were organized into father-sibs, neither the married woman nor the children of men serving for their brides would lose affiliation with their father's sib, the facts of residence being then irrelevant. Any individual would automatically take the patronymic on birth, preserve it till death, and if a male transmit it to his children.

As a corollary it follows that the sib, while eliminating half of the blood-kin, is far more inclusive than the family with respect to the relatives who *are* recognized. With us a third or fourth cousin hardly ever functions as a member of the family at all; but by the fixity of the sib bond even the most remote kinsman is still known as a member of the same unit, which is most commonly designated by a name borne by all members, thus leaving no doubt as to sib affiliation. The feeling of community thus established is reflected in the terminology of kinship: sib-mates of the same generation usually call one another siblings, and from this, given the primitive attitude towards names, it is but a step to the feeling that marriage between sib-mates would be incestuous. Hence we find as one of the most common traits of the sib the law of exogamy. The intensity of the sentiment that marriage should be outside the sib varies considerably. In Australia it was so pronounced that a man or woman guilty of transgressing the rule would have been promptly put to death; and a stranger would not marry into the similarly named sib of a tribe hundreds of miles away even though actual blood connection was out of the question. In North America, on the whole, the native reactions were of a much milder cast. The Crow would mock offenders, comparing them to dogs, but they took no steps in the direction of punishment. Similarly, the Iroquois evince no horror of sib incest, punishing transgressions with nothing more painful than ridicule, while the Miwok content themselves with pointing out the impropriety of marrying within the sib. But disregarding the character of the reprobation that non-exogamous unions evoke, we may say that exogamy is one of the most common characteristics of the sib.

As already stated, the sense of kinship among sib-mates is associated with a special type of kinship nomenclature, the most remote relatives of one generation frequently regarding one another as siblings. The kinship terminology of tribes organized into sibs conforms indeed with extraordinary frequency to what I have called the Dakota type (p. 60). The correlation was pointed out by Tylor and more particularly by Rivers, who has shown how well such a system of kinship accords with a sib scheme. Given exogamy, a man must marry a woman of some other sib, and his brothers and certain of his cousins are equally eligible mates for her, her sisters, and certain of her female cousins. But brothers and sisters, as well as far more remote kinsfolk of the same sib, are barred from marriage by sib exogamy. Hence it is quite natural that the father and father's sib-mate be grouped together and differentiated from the mother's sib-mates. The alignment of kindred in sibs goes hand in hand with their alignment in terminology. It is therefore plausible to convert the functional connection into a causal one and to say that a sib organization *produces* a Dakota terminology.

Before, however, accepting this view, we must inquire whether there are not other possible causes that could fashion such a classification of kin. And here we may recall that the Dakota alignment is also singularly in harmony with the levirate and sororate (p. 37). There is thus an alternative hypothesis; or possibly sib exogamy and these two modes of preferential mating may be themselves causally connected. To this point we must revert later. But whatever qualification may be made as to interpretation, the empirical fact remains that tribes organized into exogamous sibs have a Dakota type of nomenclature,—one in which collateral and lineal kin on the paternal or maternal side, respectively, are merged regardless of propinquity.

Stimulated by Rivers, I have tested his views in the light of North American data and found that practically all tribes with exogamous sibs have a system of the Dakota type; that some sibless tribes, whether through borrowing or other influences, share such a nomenclature; but that many sibless tribes distinguish collateral and lineal kin. It also appeared from personal investigation that the Hopi, the only Shoshonean people organized into sibs, are likewise the only one with a Dakota terminology. The generalization that the Dakota nomenclature is connected with the sib organization thus stands firmly established, though its meaning cannot be determined without further inquiry into the influence of the levirate and sororate.

To revert to other aspects of the sib unit. The rule of 'once a sib member, always a sib member,' suffers hardly any exceptions as a result of marriage. I know of no case whatsoever in which a man enters his wife's sib; and of the contrary possibility the only good illustration seems to be that of the Toda, where the wife adopts her husband's sib. It is true that the ancient Athenians enrolled a woman in her husband's phratria, but the Greeks were hardly primitive and their regulation seems to anticipate our modern law. On the other hand, adoption plays a more important part. When a man adopts a child, then in a patrilineal community it becomes automatically a member of his sib, and in a matrilineal community of his wife's sib, just as would a real child.

However, it is not these individual adoptions that have most deeply influenced the constitution of the sib. When we investigate by genealogical methods the average sib, we generally find it impossible to derive all the members from a single ancestor. What we discover is a series of independent lines of descent merely theoretically united by a common ancestry. It is of course possible that the native informants have simply forgotten the bond connecting ancestors of the more remote generations, but this explanation cannot apply to all cases. Thus, in taking a census of the Hopi I found that several very small mother-sibs were not composed wholly of individuals related to one another by blood but could be separated into two or three distinct matrilineal groups which regarded themselves as related only by a legal fiction. What we know of primitive logic makes such wholesale adoption quite intelligible. If two men coöperating in a ritualistic performance adopt each other as brothers, their respective sisters would likewise be brought into the mutual relationship of sisters, and *ipso facto* the descendants of the 'sisters' would be viewed as though they were connected through real sisters and theoretically classed as descendants from a single ancestress.

Before closing this preliminary consideration, it is well to solve what may otherwise appear as a puzzle. If the bilateral family is ubiquitous, how can the sib ever coëxist with it? Does it not contravene the law of identity to picture societies which simultaneously recognize both parents and yet ignore one of them? Of course, recognition and neglect refer to distinct phases of social life. As we recognize the mother but ignore her with respect to the family name, so primitive tribes may recognize both parents in a variety of ways yet disregard either for specific purposes.

Hitherto the sib has been considered mainly from a morphological angle; we must now turn to the functions of the sib. These are best illustrated by describing a selected series of sib organizations.[1]

Types of Sib Organization

To begin with a simple case. The Crow Indians are divided into thirteen exogamous mother-sibs. These units are designated by nicknames; one is called 'They-bring-game-without-shooting,' another 'Bad-War-honors,' a third 'Bad-Leggings,' and so forth. Sib-mates not only address one another as though they were blood-kindred even when not related but actually act towards one another as such, gladly giving help when an opportunity offers. Their relations are, however, restricted to the social sphere and do not in any way touch the field of religious activity. The Crow were locally divided into a northern and a southern branch, but in each were found members of all the sibs.

When we turn from the Crow to the Hopi of northern Arizona, we at once meet a very different series of traits. The Hopi, like the Crow, have exogamous mother-sibs and there is a close social bond uniting the members of a sib. There, however, analogy virtually ends. The very names of the sibs are of a wholly different character; they are in no case nicknames but are derived for the most part from natural phenomena, the Snake, Sand, Lizard, Cottonwood sibs furnishing typical examples. Property, which among these sedentary people plays a greater part than with the roving Crow of buffalo-hunting days, is to some extent held by the sib and inherited in the sib. Thus, each sib has its distinctive territory for hunting eagles; and the most important prerogative of assuming certain ceremonial offices descends in the sib, being held by actual blood-kinsmen through the mother. This involves what to us seems an outrage on equitable inheritance rules. For since the Hopi sibs are matronymic and exogamous, father and son are never in the same sib; hence a father cannot pass on his ceremonial privileges to his own child, but must transmit them to his nearest sib relatives, his brothers and his sister's sons. It is in this manner, for instance, that leadership in the Snake fraternity continues to be inherited. The tremendous rôle of ritualism among the Hopi thus colors their sib concept and sharply differentiates it from that of the Crow, where sibs and ceremonies are quite dissociated.

The multifarious functions with which the sib may be invested and the complexities of which this type of organization is capable are well illustrated by the Winnebago of

Wisconsin. Here we encounter, in the first place, what is known as a *dual organization;* that is to say, the entire tribe is divided into two sibs, which in this case are patronymic. These two father-sibs are exogamous like the more numerous sibs of the Crow and Hopi. They are symbolically connected with the sky and the earth, one group being called 'Those above,' the other 'Those on earth.' Besides regulating marriage through the rule of exogamy, these sibs play a part on the warpath, in ball-games, and in one of the tribal feasts, for on all these occasions individuals are grouped according to membership in the two sibs.

An important complication, however, results from the fact that among the Winnebago the two father-sibs are subdivided,—the one into four, the other into eight lesser groups. These are no less father-sibs than the dual divisions. Since nomenclature is of subordinate significance, we might without detriment call the subdivisions sub-sibs, or sections of sibs, or invent a special term for them. I will now, for convenience' sake, call the lesser units 'father-sibs' and give to the larger Winnebago groups the self-explanatory designation of *moieties,*—an old Shakespearean word derived from the French *moitié,* 'one-half.'

The sibs into which the patronymic Winnebago moieties are divided present a number of interesting features. They are exogamous, but in a different sense from the Winnebago moieties or the Hopi and Crow mother-sibs. These latter units are exogamous in their own right, so to speak; the Winnebago sibs are *derivatively* exogamous, i.e., they are exogamous because the larger units embracing them are exogamous. The exogamous feature is really not distinctive of them but of the greater moiety. On the other hand, a number of novel conceptions appear. Each sib not only bears the name of an animal, such as Snake, Eagle, Thunderbird, Bear, but further postulates descent from the animal species in question; and its members carve, weave, or engrave representations of the sib animal, though there is no evidence of any cult in its honor. Further associated with each sib is a set of distinctive personal names. In this respect the contrast with the other tribes discussed is striking. Among the Crow there is no connection whatsoever with the personal name of a child and any sib: the name-giver, a distinguished tribesman, calls the child by a name reminiscent of his deeds or experiences. If he has at one time struck three enemies in battle, the child (whether boy or girl) may be named Strikes-three-enemies. With the Hopi the name likewise depends on the name-giver, yet also on her sib, which is never the child's in this matronymic tribe; for she regularly belongs to the father's sib and bestows a name referring, often in mystic fashion, to her own sib. Winnebago practice differs in that each individual gets a name from a series of appellations belonging to his own sib, such names frequently suggesting the story of its mythic origin. Like the Hopi, the Winnebago attach to their sibs ceremonial functions. Each unit owns a sacred bundle and performs the ritual associated therewith. Finally must be mentioned as a new trait the association of units with political activities, differentiating the sibs from one another. Thus, the Bear people exercise police functions, the tribal chief is invariably chosen from among the Thunderbirds, while the public crier is always of the Buffalo sib.

One more American illustration must suffice. The Miwok of central California are divided into exogamic patrilineal moieties associated with Water or the Bullfrog and Land or the Bluejay. Unlike the Winnebago moieties, those of the Miwok do not comprise lesser sibs. All natural phenomena are divided between Land and Water in rather arbitrary fashion, and this theoretical dichotomy of the universe has its practical counterpart in the assignment of personal names. These are remarkable in referring not directly but symbolically to the bearer's moiety. Ritualistically the Miwok divisions are not nearly so significant as the Hopi or Winnebago sibs. Nevertheless in funerals and puberty performances the alignment follows that of the dual division.

Turning to western Siberia, we find the Ostyak divided into a considerable number of exogamous father-sibs, each constituted of a number of men and their descendants. Although the sibs frequently comprise not only hundreds but thousands of individuals and though many of the members are unable to trace any blood-relationship among themselves, there is a distinct belief in an ultimately common origin. The male sib-mates keep together in their migrations and there is a spirit of brotherliness that makes the rich share their produce with the poor as a matter of course. The sib is not merely a social but also a political unit; each has a headman of its own, whose office descends to his son or next of kin and whose main function is to arbitrate disputes. Several sibs are combined into a sort of league presided over by a prince. Over and above the sociopolitical aspects of the Ostyak sib there remain its religious functions. Each has its distinctive idols kept by a seer or shaman, and the members join in rendering sacrifices and performing other ceremonies.

Passing to still another region of the globe, we encounter a highly developed sib system in Melanesia. In Buin, Solomon Islands, Dr. Thurnwald discovered eight exogamous matrilineal sibs, each definitely associated with some bird, such as the owl or parrot, which members of the sib neither kill nor eat. Indeed, the Owl sib would resent the slaying of an owl by men of other sibs to the extent of precipitating a blood-feud, hence none of the sacred animals is hunted by any member of the tribe. The natives do not trace their descent from the birds but conceive the mystic kinship in a different way: the Parrot sib, e.g., tell of a human ancestress who wedded a parrot and gave birth to a bird of that species. In the Admiralty Islands, the obligations between the sacred animal and its sib are expressly recog-

THE SIB

nized as mutual, so that men of the Alligator sib are believed to be safe from attacks by alligators. In contrast to the Winnebago system that of Buin is quite dissociated from the political organization of the people. To mention but one fact, the succession to the chieftaincy is from father to son in direct contravention of the matrilineal scheme followed by the sib.

To content ourselves with just one more illustration for this provisional survey, the Kariera tribe of Western Australia is subdivided into moieties and some twenty patrilineal sibs lacking distinctive names, but each holding a definite territory by an inalienable right. Further, each sib is associated with a varying number of animals, plants and natural phenomena. Thus, one sib is connected with the rainbow, the white cockatoo, the March fly, two species of fish, and a conch shell. Each of these species or objects has a ceremonial ground of its own within the domain of the correlated sib, and it is there that special ceremonies are performed by both male and female members for the purpose of multiplying the animals and plants in question. Most of these are edible, and it is noteworthy that there is not the slightest restriction as to the killing of the animals or the eating of either animals or plants by sib-mates. As usual, the sibs are exogamous; residence being patrilocal, a boy grows up in his father's sib territory and since he is expected to marry his maternal uncle's daughter his bride will come from another sib and another locality.

These examples should suffice to elucidate the diversity of function that may be associated with a sib system. The sib thus appears as an extraordinarily changeable social unit. It is commonly exogamous but is sometimes only derivatively so (Winnebago). It may be linked with animals and plants towards which a definite attitude is prescribed (Buin) and it may be wholly divorced from any such connection (Crow). It may be a local (Kariera) or a non-local (Crow) unit, a political (Ostyak) or non-political (Buin) division of society. This variability suggests an important problem.[2]

UNITY OR DIVERSITY OF ORIGIN

To Morgan the sib organization appeared to rest on so abstruse a concept that he felt obliged to assume a single origin of all recorded sibs. That is, he supposed that the institution had sprung into existence in one place and thence spread over immense areas. This is especially remarkable because Morgan's theory of a *law* of social evolution according to which all mankind must progress from one stage to another favored the assumption of many independent inventions of like institutions and customs. It may be conceded that if primitive man had evolved an arbitrary and elaborate scheme for separating certain of his kindred to the exclusion of others, it would be improbable for such a grouping to be repeatedly re-invented. Below, however, we shall see that the classification of relatives characteristic of the sib is a very natural one under certain conditions, so that the improbability of parallel and independent sib formation does not hold. Waiving this point for the present, we may inquire whether the resemblances of sibs in different parts of the world are sufficiently far-reaching to call for the hypothesis of a single origin. The variability noted above is hardly favorable to that assumption. The argument would be clinched if we could show that even in a restricted area, such as North America, there are several independent centers of sib diffusion, for then a fortiori one origin for the whole world would be out of the question.

In North America there are four, or possibly five, disconnected areas in which a sib organization flourishes,— the Woodlands east of the Mississippi, the Northwestern Plains, the Southwest, and the Northwest Coast, to which Central and Southern California should possibly be added as a distinct region, though some are inclined to consider the sib scheme there merely a ramification of the Southwestern system. We are, then, confronted with the problem whether these several organizations have evolved independently—whether possibly even within each continuous area there have been several distinct foci for the development of sibs—or whether all the sibs of the continent have sprung from one source.

East of the Mississippi and even including the southern Plains to the west there is an immense continuous area peopled by tribes of varying stock, some of them matronymic, others patronymic, but practically all sharing the institution of sibs. Passing from the Iroquois to the Menomini and Omaha or Choctaw, we cannot fail to note that the sib scheme is largely fashioned after the same pattern. The sibs are commonly named after animals, the same species often recurring in different tribes; each sib has a set of distinctive personal names for its members; and almost every sib system is bound up with a moiety grouping of which the most constant function is the alignment of men in athletic games. Even remote tribes within the region defined share highly specific traits. Thus, the Osage in Missouri have moieties associated with peace and war, respectively, and so have the Creek of Alabama. Exogamy is universal, sometimes as a function of the lesser, then again in association with the major (moiety) sib. The resemblances are too numerous and specific to be explained by chance, but must be explained by diffusion. On the other hand, the rule of descent divides the sib systems of the area into two categories, which also correspond closely to the geographical grouping of tribes if we accept the approved theory that the Iroquois were originally a southern people. Thus the Iroquois may be conceived to occupy one connected territory with the matrilineal Creek, Choctaw, Chickasaw and Yuchi, while the Central Algonkians and Southern Siouans represent another definite geographical area. Given the resemblances mentioned, we certainly can not assume more than one center for the notion of unilateral descent in either region. It is simply a question whether the difference in descent requires two separate inventions of the sib or only one for the entire area. In either case we should have to allow for diffusion. This is obvious if only one center is assumed. But even if, say, the matrilineal Iroquois sib and the patrilineal Omaha sib represent two ultimately independent inventions, there must have been subsequent borrowing, directly or indirectly, because of the character of the shared features. To take but one, sets of individual names distinctive of sibs do not occur for hundreds of miles to the west of the area under consideration, hence their distribution among both the paternally and maternally organized peoples east of the Mississippi and on the southern Plains is a sure sign of borrowing. For my present argument it is not essential to decide whether the Eastern sib area corresponds to a single or a double evolution of the sib, so I will leave the question open.

This question may be waived because the theoretical point involved is settled with ample decisiveness by a comparison of the Eastern sibs with those of the Northwestern Plains. In this region five tribes require consideration,— the Hidatsa and Mandan of North Dakota, the Crow of Montana, the Gros Ventre and Blackfoot of Montana and Alberta. Of these the Blackfoot have an incipient rather than a fully developed sib organization: they have nicknamed localized bands with predominantly patrilineal descent, but without a fixed rule, so that a man may change his band affiliation and that of his children as well. Exogamy also is not absolute and rests on the suspicion that band mates are probably related by blood. In the winter the tribe broke up into the several bands, which scattered from economic motives, while in the summer they united for the chase or ceremonial purposes. This organization is almost duplicated among the Gros Ventre but with one significant modification; corresponding to the band there is a full-fledged sib with definitely patrilineal descent and rigid exogamy. The three other tribes, all members of the Siouan family, regularly trace descent through the mother.

Now, if we assume that all the Eastern sib systems had a single origin and make a corresponding hypothesis for the Northern Plains systems, the two composite photographs of the sib concepts in the two areas reveal hardly the faintest resemblance to each other. The Eastern sibs are almost invariably named after animals and are sometimes connected with their eponyms by descent or definite religious obligations. In the Northern Plains animal names hardly ever occur and never in connection with the notion that there is a mystical bond between the eponym and the sib members. By far the most common appellations of these sibs are of the nickname variety; members are dubbed the Ugly-ones or Those-who-do-not-give-away-without-return or Bring-game-without-killing. Equally important is a difference already alluded to: while all the Eastern sibs have distinctive sets of personal names, such sets are never found in association with the sibs of the Northern Plains. Finally, the moiety frequently found in the East as a ceremonial or exogamous unit and in connection with athletic games occurs only among the Mandan and Hidatsa, and there only as a relatively unimportant aggregate of sibs with hardly any serious function. It is thus clear that the sib systems of the East and of the Northern Plains represent two wholly distinct patterns and there is not the slightest reason for deriving them from a common source.

But by applying established ethnographic knowledge it is possible to go a step further; more particularly can we trace with some assurance the history of the Gros Ventre system. The Gros Ventre are a recent and relatively small offshoot of the more southern Arapaho, a people lacking anything in the nature of sibs. In their new home the

Gros Ventre have been most closely affiliated with the Blackfoot, and the twofold effects of their Arapaho origin and Blackfoot contact are manifest in their culture. As already explained, the Gros Ventre sibs, except for their firmer integration, resemble the Blackfoot bands to a remarkable extent, and if this is taken in conjunction with the known relations of the two tribes there can be no doubt of an historical connection between the Blackfoot band and the Gros Ventre sib. Now the Gros Ventre had no sibs when they broke away from the parent tribe and since they are numerically inferior to the Blackfoot it is highly probable that they were the borrowers and by perfecting notions found among their new neighbors evolved a genuine sib system. At all events, the germ of the system was developed either by one of the two tribes or by both in conjunction. If it evolved independently of the other systems in this region, then the diverse origin of sibs in North America is demonstrated a fortiori.

The Blackfoot-Gros-Ventre sib scheme does represent an independent development. For geographical reasons, if it were connected with any other Northern Plains system, it would be connected with that of the Crow; and as a matter of fact, the great development of nicknames for social units, a feature far more prominent in this trio of tribes than among the Hidatsa and Mandan, suggests that this particular trait has actually been diffused. But there resemblance ends. The Crow are matrilineal, the Gros Ventre and Blackfoot patrilineal; and what is still more important, the Crow units are not localized but are all found in each of the local subdivisions of the tribe. The Blackfoot and Gros Ventre could not derive the basis of their organization from the Crow, because that basis did not exist there; and vice versa. Hence in this restricted area there are at least two sib patterns that evolved separately, making at least three altogether east of the Rockies. A fortiori the general query as to the diversity of the sib schemes of the world is answered, but it may be well to envisage the remaining North American areas.

Conditions in the Southwest have been clarified to an extraordinary degree by Kroeber's acute analysis, one of the masterpieces of ethnographic research, which I will follow in summing up the essential facts. The Zuñi sibs are exogamous and derive their names from animals, plants, and natural phenomena, but there are no taboos after the fashion of Buin nor is any veneration extended to the eponym. Descent is matrilineal. The sibs are associated with ceremonies, not in the sense that they perform rites as units but rather inasmuch as specific ritualistic offices must be filled by persons of a particular sib. These essential characteristics are shared by all the Pueblo Indians, who differ mainly in the presence or absence of moieties over and above the lesser sibs: while on the Rio Grande there is a dual organization not associated with exogamy but with important ritualistic and political functions, in the western section of the area no such division occurs. This difference, however, pales into insignificance in view of the extremely complicated scheme of sibs shared by all the Pueblo tribes and first brought to light by Kroeber's efforts. All the four linguistic groups of the region link together sibs in larger aggregates after the identical and purely conventional plan. Thus, the Hopi class together the Badger and Bear sibs, and so do the Zuñi, the Keresan and the Tanoan villages. Similarly the Fire and Coyote sibs are everywhere coupled. The identity is as far-reaching as could possibly be expected; where a modification occurs, it is usually of an obvious character involving the substitution of a Horn for a Deer sib, or of one bird sib for another. As Professor Kroeber puts it, "a single precise scheme pervades the . . . organization of all the Pueblos." Nothing comparable is found outside this region, hence the system of this area stands out as a distinct historical entity from the sib organizations hitherto considered.

It is, however, possible though by no means certain that the sib organization of southern California is an attenuated outpost of the Pueblo system, as Mr. Gifford has suggested. The geographical concentration of sibs in that part of the state more or less adjacent to Arizona favors that view, and it is supported by another fact. This is the very region of California that is culturally linked with the Pueblo area in other respects, notably through the occurrence of pottery. Nevertheless, there is one serious difficulty in the way of Mr. Gifford's hypothesis: the Californian sibs are uniformly patrilineal, those of the Pueblo tribes are matrilineal. Were there clear evidence that the Californians possess the unique Pueblo scheme of arranging sibs, we should of course be obliged to assume historical connection and a change in the rule of descent. As things stand, the evidence is suggestive rather than conclusive and the question must for the present remain open.

Far to the north, extending from the southern tip of Alaska to the northern coast of British Columbia and contiguous districts, lies the last sib center, represented most characteristically by the Tlingit, Haida, and Tsimshian. The Tlingit are divided into exogamous Raven and Wolf (or Eagle) moieties; the Tsimshian into exogamous quarters, two of which are named Eagle and Wolf, while the remaining two bear names not referring to animals, though they are connected with the bear and raven respectively. Descent is throughout matrilineal. Associated with each of these tribal divisions are series of highly-prized ceremonial privileges conveniently comprised under the heraldic term 'crest' and involving among other things the exclusive right to use designs representing certain animals or objects. The importance attached to the crests gives to Northwest Coast organization its distinctive character. Often a supernatural relationship is alleged with the animals in question, but taboos and religious veneration are noticeably lacking. Nor is it always the eponym from which the principal crest of a moiety or quarter is derived. Thus, the Haida Ravens have the killer-whale for their main crest, and among the Eagles of the same tribe the beaver rivals the eagle crest in importance. Accordingly, in tracing the historical relations of the exogamic divisions of the three tribes the crests prove more significant than the designations; the Tsimshian Ravens turn out to be the equivalent of the Haida Eagles. Furthermore, not all the members of a division need share the same crest. There are matrilineal subdivisions each of which owns its peculiar crests. As a matter of fact, it is these lesser groups rather than the moieties or quarters that are in the strictest sense to be regarded as sibs, for it is they that are preëminently bodies of real or putative blood kin, while the larger exogamic groups are not derived from a common ancestor except among the Haida. Each subdivision or sib is a localized group, presumably at first a matrilineal village community but now dispersed over several villages.

The organization of the Northwest Coast resembles the systems of none of the other areas. It is furthest removed from the system of the Northern Plains, which if diffusion had occurred ought to resemble it most closely since it is geographically nearest. We have already seen that the Plains system in turn is radically distinct from that of the nearest Eastern tribes and from that of the Pueblo region. How borrowing could have taken place under such conditions passes comprehension. Nor is it possible to suppose that the sib idea in a generic form was once generally distributed over North America and has since become differentiated in the several areas, for I shall prove later that the sib never existed outside the regions mentioned. There is then no escape for the conclusion that the sib evolved at least four times in North America and accordingly has had a multiple origin in the world. Below I shall point out that there are several widespread conditions favoring the independent evolution of unilateral kinship.[3]

Sibs of Higher Order

The survey of sib systems given above demonstrated sibs of different order in the same tribe. The Winnebago were found to be divided into two father-sibs, each of these moieties being further subdivided into lesser father-sibs. In British Columbia the Tlingit and Tsimshian exogamous groups comprise each a number of matrilineal sibs and by an allowable extension of the term may themselves be called sibs since there is an undoubted sense of kinship though without a distinct belief in common ancestry. Frequently the higher unit is of a rather colorless character. The thirteen Crow sibs are linked together into five couples and a trio, but the functions of the larger groups, all nameless, are quite insignificant. They are not exogamous, the constituent sibs being regarded as not related but merely as friendly. Similarly, the Zuñi aggregations have no influence on marriage and little effect on social life apart from ritualistic activity.

Where such lesser and greater units coëxist, the question inevitably arises as to their relationship. It is conceivable that the greater evolved from an original sib by subdivision, the fragments still preserving a sense of their former unity and cohering as the sibs of a sib-aggregation, which may or may not be a moiety. It is equally conceivable that social groups once distinct should have come to unite for certain purposes yet preserve a sense of their pristine separateness. Again, it is possible for two radically distinct plans of organization to be coördinated in such fashion that the unit of one system shall embrace several units of the other.

Morgan pronounced exclusively in favor of the first-mentioned course of development; and it must be confessed that there is a good deal to be said on behalf of his theory. It has considerable a priori plausibility; nothing seems simpler than that an increasing sib should split up into segments retaining a certain cohesion. Further, as Morgan pointed out, there are instances of the larger aggregate bearing the name of one of its subdivisions and also of several lesser sibs representing different species of one genus designating the greater division. For example, in the tripartite organization of the Mohegan one third is called Turkey and comprises lesser sibs called Turkey, Crane, and Chicken, respectively; another third is called Turtle and embraces the Little Turtle, Mud Turtle, Great Turtle, and Yellow Eel sibs.

Still more convincing in view of the great importance which the Eastern Indians attach to the series of personal names peculiar to sibs, the Onondaga-Iroquois have a Big Snipe and a Little Snipe sib, which not only suggest fission by the similarity of designation but by the common possession of a set of individual names.

Nevertheless, while fully prepared to accept the occurrence of segmentation, we should not rashly bar alternative explanations. There is no reason whatsoever why both division of a unit and accretion of distinct units should not have occurred in different places and at different periods. The evidence for accretion is in more than one case convincing, in other instances at least suggestive. No one can doubt that the Crow sibs are the fundamental units of their social organization, in view of the almost complete functionlessness of the larger aggregates. Yet it is readily conceivable that in course of time the bond between linked sibs would have grown firmer until one function of the sib after another would have been assumed by the sib couples and trio. In the corresponding Hopi case I was repeatedly told that certain sibs were connected because they had once united for ceremonial purposes. Here, too, the step from mechanical aggregate to an organic synthesis of sibs into sibs of higher order could be readily taken. An extension to a new group of the kinship terms often used ceremonially might contribute to the work of consolidation.

In short, a generic solution of the problem must be rejected, and each case of coëxisting sibs of greater and lesser order must be discussed on its merits.

The third possibility, while of great interest, is largely so in an academic way. It is easy to apply the principles used in comparing sibs of different tribes to sibs of differerent order in the same tribe and prove that they are units of quite distinct character. Take exogamy, for example, as one of the most important and widespread functions. If the greater unit is exogamous, any of its parts must be so by logical necessity; hence it is possible to argue that the lesser unit is not really exogamous, accordingly differs in essence, hence in origin, from the larger group. Contrariwise, the large unit might be found wanting in point of exogamy and be ruled out as a phenomenon distinct from the exogamous sib. Such arguments cannot in the nature of the case be frequently refuted but neither do they establish the historical diversity of the lesser and the greater sib. For, if, say, the process of segmentation *were* to take place in accordance with Morgan's view, the result would inevitably be lesser sibs only derivatively exogamous.

There is another factor that should be considered in this context as tending to obscure the historical relations of the lesser and the greater sib: functions may be transferred from one to the other. Thus, Dr. Goldenweiser holds that the Iroquois moieties were once exogamous, while to-day this function is restricted to the much smaller sib. Contrariwise, a function of the smaller may be extended to the greater unit, and if in full force it would be impossible to reconstruct the actual history of the case.

By far the most interesting type of major sib is the moiety, though it also occurs as a simple undivided sib, as among the Miwok and Yokuts of central California. Again it is necessary to remember that the moieties need not be exogamous. Those of the Hidatsa have nothing to do with marriage, and the Toda moieties are even positively endogamous. Nevertheless it is the exogamous dual organization that occurs most frequently and accordingly demands special attention.

Where there are only two exogamous divisions, there follow by logical necessity certain consequences that sharply differentiate a moiety organization from one with more than two exogamous sibs. Where the number of exogamous sibs is greater (unless special rules are superimposed) a man may marry a woman from any sib not his own. Thus, a Crow may marry a woman from any one of twelve sibs; twelve-thirteenths of the marriageable women of his tribe are his possible spouses. But with only two exogamous divisions a Winnebago is restricted to half the women of his people, a very considerable difference. There is still another implication of social significance. Among the Crow a man has special relations with members of two sibs, of his own (i.e., his mother's) and his father's; but the number of individuals in both relatively to the total population is small. Given a moiety system, a man may have specific relations with all tribesmen, for one half of them belong to his own moiety, the remainder to the moiety of that parent through whom descent is not traced.

A striking feature of moieties is the development of reciprocal services. At an Iroquois burial the functionaries are always selected not from the deceased person's but from the opposite moiety, and the same holds for the remote Cahuilla of southern California. On the coast of northern British Columbia certain festivals are never arranged except in honor of the complementary moiety. It is a puzzling question how this reciprocity is to be interpreted. Is it fundamentally a matter of the moiety or merely incidentally so because either moiety includes one of the parents? The Hidatsa case is illuminating because there we find that in burial it is not the non-exogamous moieties that function but the sib of the deceased person's father. It is thus possible that the Iroquois and Northwest Coast phenomena belong in the same category, and that in these matrilineal tribes reciprocity merely signifies social recognition of the father. Other functions of moieties have already been cited. Those of the Iroquois are characteristic of the Eastern Indians. At such games as lacrosse members of opposite moieties are pitted against each other. At feasts and ceremonies there is a corresponding spatial grouping; one moiety faces the other, each being represented by a speaker.

It was shown above that there is a peculiar fitness in the association of the Dakota type of kinship nomenclature with a sib organization. But that fitness is especially marked when the sibs appear in the form of moieties. Certain features of the Dakota terminology would harmonize in equal degree with *any* sib system regardless of the number of units. For example, that father's brothers and even the most remote of his male cousins, if of the same sib, should be called by the same term as the father might happen as readily in a tribe with fifty sibs as where there are only two. But other features cannot be so well explained from a multiple sib organization. Take, for example, the common classification under one head of the mother's brother and the father's sister's husband. With exogamic moieties and, say, maternal descent I belong to my mother's moiety A, and so does her brother; my father, on the other hand, and his sister are of moiety B, and the latter is obliged to marry a man of moiety A. Thus, the father's sister's husband and the maternal uncle are bound to belong to the same moiety, and if the nomenclature reflects primarily the social organization it is proper that both should be called by a common term.

Still more common is the classification of cousins into parallel and cross-cousins. As Tylor pointed out, this, too, is admirably consonant with a dual organization. Assuming the same conditions as before, we find that if a man belongs to moiety A, his brother will also belong to that group; both must marry women of moiety B, and their children will all be B. Correspondingly, two sisters of moiety A must marry men of moiety B, and their children will all be A. That is to say, parallel cousins, the offspring of several brothers or of several sisters, will always be of the same social group. Not so with cross-cousins. For though a brother and a sister of moiety A must both marry individuals of the opposite moiety, the brother's children by maternal descent become members of B while the sister's retain their mother's affiliation. Thus, cross-cousins are bound to belong to different moieties.

But if we add only one sib, the situation changes. A man of sib A may then marry either a woman of sib B or of C; hence the wives and consequently also the children of several brothers will belong partly to sib B and partly to sib C, and there will be no reason in the sib alignment for classing them together. Thus, the presence of more than two sibs does not explain the most common form of the Dakota terminology nearly so well as does the dual organization. For this reason, among others, some scholars hold that moieties represent the earliest type of sib.

This theory is extremely captivating. Besides explaining the Dakota nomenclature, a dual organization is certainly the simplest that can be conceived. Nevertheless there are important objections to this assumption. In the first place, the distribution of moieties is by no means so extensive as the type of kinship terminology consistent with them. The absence of a dual organization with exogamy in most, possibly in all, parts of Africa, and among many American and Asiatic tribes bids us hesitate before committing ourselves to the hypothesis of a dual division as the earliest form of all sib organizations. It may hold for Australia and Melanesia, but that proves nothing for the rest of the globe. Of course it is possible to assume that moieties once existed where there are now more numerous sibs, but that is arbitrarily to complicate the theory with a baseless auxiliary hypothesis in order to save the simplest interpretation from the onslaught of cruel facts. Then, too, we may reasonably doubt whether a dual organization is really the simplest for primitive man. Logically it undoubtedly is; and historically it would be if a primitive tribe always developed sibs by fission. But if, as we may with great likelihood assume for many cases, exogamous organizations evolved by the fusion of originally distinct bodies, then it is far more probable that matrimonial relations should not be restricted to a single external group but should be established with a number of them, the coalescence of all of which would yield the characteristic community organized into an indefinite number of exogamous and intermarrying sibs, which might subsequently be arranged in opposite halves.

This is not an altogether hypothetical condition of affairs. Among the Toda the moieties are endogamous but subdivided into exogamous father-sibs, so that each Toda moiety corresponds to the whole of an exogamous tribe. Now within the Teivaliol moiety, which embraces six sibs, the one named Kuudr is numerically preponderant to such an extent that in order to observe exogamy its members have married nearly all the available members of other sibs, leaving very few of these to intermarry with one another. Dr. Rivers recorded 161 marriages between Kuudr people and the rest of the Teivaliol as against 16 between members of the other five exogamous groups. "Owing to the enormous development of one clan (sib), the Teivali division has almost come to be in the position of a community with a dual marrying organization in which every member of one group must marry a member of the other group, but there is no reason whatever to think that this is due to any other reason than the excessive development of one clan (sib) in numbers."

The condition approximated by the Toda, viz., a *secondary* arrangement in two complementary units, was according to Dr. Boas attained by the Haida of the Northwest Coast of America. Dr. Boas suggests that several tribes of this

THE SIB

area were formerly characterized by a tripartite organization. Thus, the Tlingit in some localities are not strictly organized into moieties but have a third exogamic unit freely intermarrying with the other two. It is therefore possible that the moieties of the Tlingit and Haida are the result of a reduction in the number of original units, leaving two equivalent tribal divisions.

Finally may be cited the data for the Masai. In British East Africa Mr. Hollis discovered four sibs, the Aiser, Meñgana, Molelyan, and Mokesen; with the exception of the last-mentioned these were also found by Captain Merker on German territory. There, however, the Aiser and Molelyan are after a fashion united in opposition to the Meñgana, whom they nickname 'Gluttons' because of their legendary transgression of a dietary taboo. Apparently the grouping is not basic and has not affected marriage law. Nevertheless it does illustrate how a dual division may arise not as a pristine form of organization but as a later development.

Such concrete data, coupled with the more general considerations given above, lead us to reject the theory that moieties were necessarily or even frequently the most ancient representatives of a sib organization. That the dual organization accords better with the Dakota terminology than other forms of sib organization, is no reason for assuming its uniform priority in contravention of the facts of distribution and definite evidence of the secondary origin of moieties.[4]

Totemism

Brief as has been our survey of sib organizations, it suffices to illustrate the frequency with which sibs bear the names of animals and plants, other natural phenomena being sometimes, though far more rarely, substituted. This mode of designation is fairly often coupled with beliefs and practices revolving about the eponym. Sometimes, as in Buin, the animal is held sacred and there is a strong sense of kinship with it on the part of the sib. Elsewhere, as among the Kariera, groups are not named after plants or animals but are nevertheless definitely associated with them, say, through the performance of rites for the magical multiplication of the correlated fauna or flora. Frequently there is a belief in the descent of the sib from the eponym. All these and similar usages are brought together under the head of *totemism* and the animal, plant or object in question is called a *totem*. Among the Arunta the group associated with an animal or plant is not a sib since membership depends not on that of either parent but on the mother's belief that such and such a child is the reincarnation of a particular totemic spirit. Thus siblings are often members of different groups. Nevertheless, the group activities so closely resemble those of neighboring tribes where the totem group is a sib that it would be unwarrantable to exclude the Arunta manifestations from the category of totemism.

Totemism has a very wide distribution, being found in America, Australia, Melanesia, Africa, and parts of Asia. This extensive diffusion deeply impressed the scholars who first investigated the relevant data, and following the theoretical bias of their time they assumed without further inquiry that all the phenomena labeled totemism represented identical psychological processes and had originated independently in different areas through the psychic unity of mankind. Latterly it has become fashionable in some quarters to deny the possibility of independent cultural inventions, and accordingly we find Professor Elliot Smith broaching the hypothesis that totemism developed in or about northeastern Africa and thence spread to the four corners of the globe.

Opposed as these interpretations appear at first blush, they are united by a common basis, viz., the conviction that totemism everywhere is essentially the same. It was this naïve assumption that led to a series of hypotheses purporting to explain how totemism in general originated, the modifications found here and there being treated as negligible. For example, there was a theory that totemism developed from the practice of animal nicknames. Such appellations were supposed to lead to explanatory legends making the men who had adopted the sobriquet the descendants of the eponym, whence there followed the taboo against killing or eating a member of the species. On the one hand, it was these prohibitions that aroused interest and led to the view that totemism was a form of religion, or even a necessary stage in religious evolution; on the other hand, it was the exogamous character of the totemic sib that was stressed as the 'social aspect' of the phenomenon, which, however, was directly deducible from the belief of the sib-mates in a common totemic ancestry.

It was in 1910 that Dr. Goldenweiser approached totemism from a quite distinct point of view. Professor Boas had repeatedly shown that apparently simple ethnological phenomena were as a matter of fact the result not of primary unity but of secondary association. Thus, when primitive tribes call geometrical designs by animal names it does not follow that their artists attempted to represent animals, and that their sketches were subsequently conventionalized into lozenges or triangles. These patterns can sometimes be proved to have had an independent origin and to have received a convenient designation at a later period. Further, Boas had proved that the resemblances noted between remote tribes were often illusory: they represented no basic likeness comparable to the homologies of the anatomist but rather correspond to his superficial analogies. That is to say, ethnologists had erred in the same sense in which the untutored mind errs when it classifies the whale as a fish and the bat as a bird.

Applying these principles to what had been regarded as a uniform complex of features, Goldenweiser discovered that totemism, instead of being everywhere alike, differed to an extraordinary degree. For example, Central Australian totemism with its emphasis on ritualistic performances for the magical increase of the totem differs *toto coelo* from that of British Columbia, where artistic representation of the totem and the guardian spirit idea are in the foreground of aboriginal consciousness. Passing in review one after another of the alleged criteria of totemism, this author found every one of them wanting in even approximate universality. Exogamy may or may not be coupled with the other features, totemic taboos may be dissociated from a totemic name for the group practising them; descent from the totem may or may not be postulated; and so forth.

Thus no feature or set of features was found to be necessary or characteristic of totemism, hence none was regarded as essentially primary in either a psychological or an historical sense. If, then, there be any bond linking the totemic manifestations of various peoples, it cannot lie in the common possession of certain traits but only in the mutual relations of these traits. Here Goldenweiser reverted to the earlier distinction of a social and a religious phase of the phenomenon. But his inquiry had demonstrated that the religious factor was often of a most attenuated kind; hence in his final formulation a less pretentious term was substituted and totemism was defined as "the tendency of definite social units to become associated with objects and symbols of emotional value"; or as "the process of specific socialization of objects and symbols of emotional value." The socialization of emotional values within groups tracing descent in definite fashion saved totemism from becoming a catchword not corresponding to any reality whatsoever. While the psychological unity of the phenomenon was thus vindicated, its historical diversity was insisted upon. Owing to the heterogeneous character of the totemic complex and the complexities of historical evolution, Dr. Goldenweiser concluded that such resemblances as occurred are the result of convergent evolution. That is to say, in one region one feature had been the starting-point, in another a different one; and only through later combinations of these elements had the complexes come to present the observed similarities. A ready explanation for the frequent combination of certain particular elements was found in the wide distribution of such traits as taboos, animal names, etc., which made their coalescence a matter of mathematical probability.

Before commenting on these views, we had better refer briefly to a far bulkier contemporaneous publication by Dr. J. G. Frazer, in which a painstaking compilation of relevant data is followed by a quite different theory of totemism. With respect to some specific conclusions, to be sure, both authors are in accord. Frazer no less than Goldenweiser dissociates exogamy as a non-essential part of the totemic complex. It is when Frazer derives the totemic complex minus exogamy from a single psychological source, the Central Australian belief that every child is the reincarnation of the totemic spirit supposed to haunt the spot where its mother first becomes aware of conception, that he displays a fundamental departure from the method of his fellow-student. For while the belief mentioned seems to Frazer a sufficient explanation for the taboos, belief in descent, and so on, Goldenweiser regards these residual phenomena as not less independent of one another than is exogamy from any and all of them. Frazer, in other words, does assume an inner nexus among the several symptoms of totemism (apart from exogamy) and regards one of them, the identification of totemite and totem as the basic one. Goldenweiser considers none of the symptoms as fundamental and their combination is to him a conjunction in Hume's sense of the term, an empirical union of traits, rather than an organic synthesis. His stressing of the mere *relation* of the elements to each other is diametrically opposed to Frazer's adherence to a particular symptom.

Further, Frazer's selection of a Central Australian notion as the core of all totemism would impress Goldenweiser as the height of absurdity. He might concede that Frazer's conceptional theory had some application in Central Australia but certainly not that it could hold for other areas whence comparable beliefs have never been reported.

Our random selection of totemic data in the survey of sib organization suffices to corroborate the destructive results of Dr. Goldenweiser's acute analysis. What connects the totemism of the Kariera with that of the Buin? The Kariera totem groups are nameless local sibs with multiple totems, which are neither worshipped nor tabooed but only magically increased. The Buin totemites hold their animals, one for each sib, sacred to the point of avenging an injury inflicted on them by other sibs and have no rites for the propagation of the species. In the one case there is no kinship between totem and sib, in the other a legendary basis exists for the sense of relationship, though there is no belief in descent. The Winnebago, on the other hand, have totemic descent, totemic names for groups as well as persons, artistic representations of the totems, but no taboos or cult. There is not the slightest reason for assuming that phenomena so heterogeneous have had a common origin either historically or psychologically; and if all of them are to be labeled as totemic it will not be for any community of specific traits but for some such highly abstract formal resemblance as that defined by Goldenweiser.

But is Dr. Goldenweiser's definition of the totemic content, attenuated as it is, sufficiently so to cover all cases? I am not persuaded that it is. The Buin totems certainly represent emotional values; those of the Winnebago possibly; those of the Kariera only by a stretching of terms that would convert black into white. Why not content ourselves with noting that the several social groups of one tribe are commonly differentiated by distinct names often borrowed from the organic kingdoms, or by heraldic devices of similar origin, or by distinctive taboos, or what not? Why not abandon the vain effort to thrust into one Procrustean bed a system of naming, a system of heraldry, and a system of religious or magical observances? Each of these might with profit be studied separately and where connections occur their rationale must of course be likewise investigated. But the fact that they represent diverse phenomena should not be obscured by the deceptive caption of 'emotional values.'

In a later paper Dr. Goldenweiser has greatly clarified the problem by a searching analysis of Iroquois totemism so-called. The Iroquois sibs are named after birds and beasts and are the exogamous units of today, though formerly this function was probably characteristic of the greater sib or moiety. But there is no taboo against killing the sib animal, indeed the very notion of such a prohibition impresses the Indians as absurd. Nor is there a trace of any belief in descent from the eponymous species or of any sense of kinship with them. One of the most prominent features of the Iroquois system is the existence of sets of individual names, each sib having its distinctive series; but these names are in no way connected with the animals. It is true that carvings of the eponyms were placed over the doors of houses in which the correlated sibs predominated; yet there is no proof that the right to such carvings was confined to members. Are, then, the Iroquois sibs to be regarded as totemic? Do the Iroquois possess a totemic complex? Goldenweiser's answer is in the negative. Animal names are too common a feature in primitive society, he argues, to permit the inference of a special relation between a species and the group merely deriving from it its name. Only when the name involved a "psychological association with the animal in the minds of the givers or the receivers of the name, or of both," or when the exogamy is traceable to this association, is it desirable to speak of totemism. Otherwise sibs with animal designations have no more claim to be considered totemic than sibs with nicknames, local names, or appellations derived from a human ancestor.

As Dr. Goldenweiser rightly insists, the question is not a purely terminological one. It is at bottom this, whether *merely* naming groups after animals is tantamount to definite beliefs and practices associated with the eponyms. The importance of names for the aboriginal mind is undoubted; but whether it necessarily results in a totemic complex is a matter for empirical inquiry. Dr. Goldenweiser's negative seems eminently reasonable and indeed might properly be supplemented with a refusal to class together the various beliefs and performances. To go through rites for the increase of an edible species is not the same as to regard an animal or plant with superstitious awe, and that in turn differs from a mere taboo.

In a still more recent contribution to the subject Dr. Goldenweiser assumes the position that totemism is after all a specific phenomenon, being characterized by "the association of the totemic content with a clan (sib) system." This is said to be a conclusion based on the introduction of an historico-geographical point of view: Dr. Goldenweiser now argues that the sib and the totemic complex are almost indissolubly linked, complexes without sibs and sibs without complexes being 'very rare.'

I consider this argument to be singularly infelicitous and to contravene some of the most valuable results of Dr. Goldenweiser's earlier studies. It is utterly inconceivable to me how in the light of data, many of which were cited by himself in his critical study, Dr. Goldenweiser can claim an historico-geographical sanction for his astounding generalization. The Crow, Hidatsa, Gros Ventre, Apache all have sibs without even totemic names; and since Dr. Goldenweiser does not repudiate his conclusion that the name by itself does not establish totemism, we may add the Iroquois and at least some of the Pueblo Indians. What Siberian tribe is known to be organized into *totemic* sibs?

And in what sense are the Arunta totem groups sibs? The conclusion that totemism is an "all but universal adjunct" of the sib organization is reached simply by ignoring awkward contradictory facts. It is regrettable that so keen and erudite a thinker should have deviated so far in his latest discussion from the straight and narrow path of historico-ethnographical investigation.

To sum up my own position on the subject of totemism. I am not convinced that all the acumen and erudition lavished upon the subject has established the reality of the totemic phenomenon. Assuredly Professor Boas is right when he points out the tendency of kinship groups to become associated with "certain types of ethnic activities." But this is merely saying what seems self-evident, to wit, that definite social groups do not exist *in vacuo,* so to speak, but must be characterized by some function or other. The question is whether the nature of the associated activities does not matter so long as *something* is associated, and this view I cannot accept as justifiable. For me the problem of totemism resolves itself into a series of specific problems not related to one another. The association of animal names with sibs is one problem and where it appears in a continuous area as in the Eastern United States its historical implications are obvious: there has been borrowing of a mode of sib designation. This has nothing whatsoever to do with the Kariera and Arunta custom of multiplying the supply of edible plants and animals, but that such a usage is shared by Central and West Australian tribes is an important fact with similarly clear historical implications. That sibs fairly often taboo the eponymous animals is a phenomenon of great psychological interest well meriting study. But only confusion can result from envisaging what is disparate under a single head.[5]

REFERENCES

[1] Philbrick: 114. Rivers, 1914 (a). Lowie, 1915: **223** seq.; id., 1917 (b), Chap. v.

[2] Lowie, 1912: 182-246. Radin, 1915. Gifford, 1916: 140-148. Castrén, 1853: 286 seq. Thurnwald, 1912: 316, 327. Brown: 145, 160.
[3] Morgan, 1877: Pt. II, Chap. XV. Skinner: 8-21. Fletcher and La Flesche: 38, 134-198. Dorsey, J. O.: 252. Swanton, 1912: 593 seq. Lowie. 1912: 186-207; id., 1917 (a): 7-22. Wissler, 1911: 18. Kroeber, 1908: 147 seq.. id., 1917 (a): 91-150. Gifford, 1918: 155-218. Boas, 1916 (a): 478-530.
[4] Goldenweiser, 1912: 464 seq. Gifford, 1918: 187. Rivers, 1906: 507. Boas, 1916 (a): 478-530. Hollis, 1905: 260. Merker: 16-18.
[5] Smith: 33. Goldenweiser, 1910; id., 1913: 370; id., 1918: 280. Boas, 1911: Chap. VIII; id., 1916 (b): 319. Frazer, J. G.. 1910: IV, 3-71.

CHAPTER VII

HISTORY OF THE SIB

THE bilateral family is an absolutely universal institution; on the other hand, the unilateral sib has only a restricted though wide distribution. It is true that many of the more highly civilized nations of the world, like the Greeks, are known to have passed through a period in which they were organized into sibs. But this may simply indicate that at a certain level the sib system tends to decay, leaving the always coëxisting family in possession of the field: it does not by any means prove that the sib is older than the family. A survey of the data clearly shows that the family is omnipresent at every stage of culture; that at a higher level it is frequently coupled with a sib organization; and that at a still higher level the sib disappears.

Priority of the Family

This simple statement of fact, however, runs counter to one of the most generally accepted and least warrantable of Morgan's speculations. For Morgan held that the family was a late product which had been almost uniformly preceded by the sib. In his scheme the exogamous sib represents a remarkable reformatory movement that retrenched the intermarriage of blood relatives, gained a foothold through the biologically beneficial results produced thereby, and spread in consequence over an enormous area. In this theory two elements require examination,—the alleged effects of the sib system, and its pretended distribution.

On the former point we can afford to be brief. Apart from the fact that modern biological opinion is by no means agreed as to the necessarily evil results of inbreeding, there are certain obvious difficulties in the way of Morgan's interpretation. It would not be fair to object that sib exogamy does not prevent the union of father and daughter in a matrilineal, and of mother and son in a patrilineal, society. For Morgan believes that incestuous relations between parent and child had been eliminated at an earlier stage, and that the sib merely added to matrimonial restrictions by barring the union of siblings. But what Morgan may fairly be criticized for is his failure to realize that exogamy does much more than proscribe the marriage of brothers and sisters: it precludes sexual relations between certain cousins of the most remote degree of propinquity, nay, even between wholly unrelated sib members while in no way interfering with the relations of even first cousins who are not of the same sib. Cross-cousin marriage is perfectly consistent with sib exogamy; but so are also marriages between certain parallel cousins. For example, in a tripartite matrilineal tribe two brothers of sib A may marry women of sibs B and C, respectively, and their children will not be prevented from marrying by the rules of the sib. What the sib, then, really does is to bar incidentally the union of certain close kinsfolk along with that of remote and putative kindred, while permitting the marriage of certain other close relatives.

The assumption as to the practically universal occurrence of the sib in primitive society requires more extended scrutiny. I shall endeavor to establish the counter-proposition that the sib is lacking precisely among the more primitive tribes and as a rule appears only when horticultural or pastoral activities have partly or wholly superseded the chase as the basis of economic existence. From this, I argue, there directly follows the chronological priority of the family. But in order to give cogency to this argumentation it is necessary to ward off one hostile criticism.

It is an undoubted fact that the peoples of the world do not advance uniformly in the several departments of culture. The Eskimo rouse our admiration by their mechanical ingenuity yet their political and social life is of the crudest order. Architecturally the Maya of Yucatan tower above the Negroes of Africa, but their lack of metallurgical knowledge puts them on a lower plane from another point of view. Accordingly it is conceivable that a very lowly people might distance its compeers with respect to social organization and rapidly climb the giddy heights represented by the family in Morgan's scheme. Hence, it has been asserted, material advancement is no criterion of social progress, and we are not warranted in inferring that the rudest tribes in their general culture also represent the earliest form of social organization.

But this is pushing a legitimate point to a manifest absurdity. Undoubtedly one phase of culture does not absolutely determine another, and we may expect backwardness in one line of activity to be sometimes compensated with progressiveness in another. Yet a moment's reflection suffices to show that the correlation, while not absolute, is nevertheless a strong one. There is no record of a hunting people who have achieved architectural marvels comparable to those of Peru or Yucatan; for scientific and artistic progress a certain stage of technological knowledge, which in turn implies a social division of labor, is a *sine qua non;* and so forth. It may therefore be readily granted that occasionally a very crude culture may go hand in hand with an abnormally intricate social fabric. But that all the tribes which rank as the lowest in the scale of general civilization should in the one phase of culture represented by family life have risen to the high-water mark of attainment, while tribes of a far more advanced status should uniformly have lagged behind in this one particular,—that is a proposition so monstrous that to conceive it clearly is to repudiate it as sheer nonsense. Hence if we really find the family present and the sib lacking in the lowliest cultures almost without exception, we shall obey the dictates of reason in concluding that the family is an earlier and the sib a later development. This inference is of such fundamental importance that its empirical basis must be fully set forth.

The first who threw down the gauntlet to the current dogma by a trenchant application of the principle of cultural appraisal was Dr. John R. Swanton. He confined his discussion to North American data, and I am not aware of a single student in this field who has failed to accept his position. Swanton showed conclusively that virtually all the ruder Indian cultures lacked the sib scheme; while the sib appeared among tribes with a far richer, economic, industrial, ceremonial and political equipment. Thus, the immense sibless region of northern California, Oregon, Washington, Idaho, Nevada, Utah, with all of northwestern Canada save a narrow coastal strip and its immediate hinterland, represents uniformly the lowest grade of human existence on the continent. The Paviotso roaming over the Nevada desert in search of edible roots cannot be compared for a moment with the settled Iroquois, Hopi, or Tlingit in point of general cultural condition.

It may be asked why the complete lack of sibs throughout so vast an area remained unnoticed for so long a time and is still unknown to Morgan's disciples. The reason is an astonishingly simple one. Morgan was a New Yorker and accordingly commenced his researches among the Iroquois, thence proceeding westward through the zone in which the sib organization is dominant. In his time the Indians of the Far West were almost completely unknown for ethnographic purposes, hence his generalization that all North American tribes had sibs was pardonable. Had he begun work in Oregon or Idaho, his entire scheme would presumably have been different. But what was excusable in

1877 is no longer so forty years later; and while a premature conclusion as a result of partial ignorance is but a venial blot on the master's escutcheon, its tenacious championship today must blight the scientific reputation of the epigonoi.

But the North American data do not necessarily agree with the phenomena observed elsewhere; we must consequently look for corroboratory testimony in other continents. Turning first to the southern half of the New World, we find that the lowest culture, that of the Fuegians, is again characterized by the lack of a sib organization. In Asia the evidence is especially suggestive. Sibs are typical of the Turkic peoples, who possess a highly developed system of stock-raising and are renowned for their skill as metallurgists; but they are wanting among the Chukchi and Koryak, whose marginal culture has only recently and partly embodied the feature of reindeer-breeding and was formerly on the level of the seal-hunting Eskimo. The Khasi of Assam, horticultural and tinctured with the political notions of a higher civilization, have sibs; not so the crude Sakai and Semang hunters of the Malay Peninsula. Most convincing of all, the Andaman Islanders of Negrito stock, isolated in the Bay of Bengal, untouched by the waves of enlightenment that carried iron and horticulture even to the remote Philippines, are devoid of the sib institution.

Our knowledge of African sociology is still sadly deficient, but there is no evidence, so far as I am aware, that contravenes my general proposition. Sibs occur in Bantu and Sudanese tribes, often in conjunction with complex political organizations; and they are reported from pastoral peoples like the Masai, who probably mingle Hamitic with other strains and occupy in many ways a relatively high plane. The cruder Hottentot, non-horticultural and representing the last dwindling ramification of Old World nomadism, apparently lack sibs. At least, the reported transmission of the father's name to the daughter and the mother's to the son is completely at variance with the unilateral tracing of descent, by which all the children take the name of one of the parents. Finally, I have found no mention of sibs in accounts of the still more primitive hunters, the Bushmen and Pygmies.

There remains Australia. In the island continent the sib is a widely diffused institution and presumably an old one. But this does not involve the admission that it is older than the family; for here, as elsewhere, we do not find the sib without the family but both institutions side by side. Hence the utmost that can be conceded is that in Australia the problem of priority remains indeterminate. Even were it otherwise, the Australian data would prove nothing for the sequence of stages in other regions, for the Australian culture is by no means more primitive than that of the Paviotso or Andaman Islanders.

In short, with the one notable exception of the Australians the simplest cultures lack the sib and possess the family, and even in Australia there is no evidence that the sib is more ancient than its invariable concomitant.

But here we are once more confronted by a hostile objection. What if the tribes enumerated as sibless are really organized into sibs that have merely escaped observation? To the field-worker the suggestion savors of the closet. There is nothing especially recondite about a sib organization; where it exists it penetrates the social life to such an extent that an inquirer is bound to stumble across it at every corner. An intelligent visitor cannot spend many weeks with people like the Crow or Hopi and fail to note the presence of hereditary and unilateral divisions. When, therefore, prolonged inquiry fails to elicit a trace of such institutions, the only permissible inference is that they are not there. This conclusion attains practically absolute certainty when corroborated by a number of independent investigators. Thus, the Northern Athabaskans have been

HISTORY OF THE SIB

visited by Samuel Hearne—an incomparable observer—and among modern students by Drs. P. E. Goddard, Frank Russell, J. A. Mason, and the present writer; yet not one of them has recorded anything resembling a sib.

But it may be urged that failure to note a sib system is no imputation on the recorder's intelligence, that the system may escape detection simply because it is no longer there, having been destroyed by the impact of civilization. This argument, too, smells of the study-lamp. It assumes gratuitously that sibs have a tendency to pass out of existence readily upon contact with Caucasian ideas. But this does not hold true. The Hopi came into contact with the Spaniards in 1540 but they are still organized into mother-sibs; so the old social system of the Iroquois has weathered French, English and American influence in the heart of New York State; so the handful of surviving Mandan of North Dakota preserve a knowledge of their sibs and the old matrilineal tradition. Californian data are likewise illuminating. The same observers have found sibs in one region and failed to find them in others, so that here at least personal bias is barred. Moreover, it is not at all true that the tribes recorded as sibless have lost all cognizance of ancient custom. The Hupa still maintained the curious division of the sexes by which husbands never slept in their wives' houses in the winter; and the Maidu of twenty years ago still had a great deal to say about ceremonies and their secret society. On the assumption that all Californian peoples formerly shared a sib system, the present limitation of that system to certain regions of central and southern California is not at all clear. Why such nice adherence to geographical continuity when modern conditions are supposed to usher in a period of chaos? On the contrary alternative, however, we can readily conceive the more southern Californians as the extreme outposts of the highly elaborate social structure distinguishing the native tribes of New Mexico and Arizona; or we can assume a local development of sibs in California that has spread only to a moderate extent.

The position that cases of lacking sibs are not due to recent disintegration of native custom can be rendered impregnable with the aid of the heavy artillery of kinship nomenclatures. As an empirical result there has been determined a correlation between the sib organization and the Dakota type of kinship terminology,—that which distinguishes maternal and paternal relatives in the parents' generation but merges kindred regardless of degree of relationship. It has been pointed out that in different regions there is a tendency for the Dakota classification to become even more inclusive so that relatives are grouped regardless of anything but generation. This fact is favorable to the theory I am now attacking. Thus, Dr. Rivers thinks that in Oceania the Polynesians once possessed the sib organization and the Dakota system still found in many parts of Melanesia, and that these features gave way to a sibless organization with a Hawaiian nomenclature. Accordingly the Hawaiian terminology, though not consistent with a sib institution, might be interpreted on the hypothesis that a sib organization once existed in the tribe under consideration; and naturally this view will suggest itself also when a sibless tribe is found with a Dakota nomenclature. It is not by any means a stringent demonstration of the former existence of sibs since there are alternative explanations,— the terminology may have been borrowed, or it may be due to other social causes (p. 37). Nevertheless the argument has the semblance of plausibility.

But what recourse is left to the disciple of Morgan where the terminology, instead of merging collateral and lineal kin, carefully discriminates the parent from the parent's sibling? Such a result is exactly what we should expect from a family organization, in which the father and mother would take an exceptional position sharply differentiated from that of more remote kin. Here there can be no question of recent breakdown of ancient custom or of innovation due to white influence. For it is one of the cardinal doctrines of Morgan's philosophy that kinship terms are more stable than the social fabric in which they originated and may persist for ages after it is rent asunder. Hence if the kinship terminology linked with a sibless organization yields no evidence of former sibs, then there is not the slightest reason for assuming that the tribe was ever organized into sibs since ex hypothesi the terminology would vanish later than the correlated social structure.

I am not urging this point in order to gain a dialectic victory. For in this matter I am of opinion that Morgan was on the right track. Kinship terms represent a linguistic phenomenon, and language is notoriously conservative. We speak of the setting of the sun, though we no longer believe that he moves round the earth. The impact of new conditions may vitally transform and even shatter aboriginal society without ruffling the traditional mode of addressing relatives. A colonial administrator or Indian agent will abrogate human sacrifices and impose improved methods of tillage, but he is not interested whether his wards have one word or a dozen for the father and the paternal uncle. Accordingly, the distinction of lineal and collateral kin would fortify the evidence of observers as to the absence of a sib institution.

Turning now to the concrete data, we find repeated realization of the condition suggested above as merely hypothetical. In California, among various Salish and Shoshonean peoples, and in Eskimo territory, we encounter relationship systems differentiating the lineal and collateral kin. Outside of America there are the Andaman Islanders, the Chukchi and Koryak. In all these instances, then, which could doubtless be multiplied were relevant data on sibless tribes more abundant, the recorded absence of the sib receives the stamp of finality. The dogma of the universality of the sib in primitive communities thus lies shattered.

There is still another line of argumentation that may be advanced on behalf of the view that is here set forth. In consonance with the important rôle which names assume in savage thought the inclusiveness of primitive kinship terms is usually far more than a mere matter of terminology: like designations involve like social relations. It is a misconstruction of this fact that has often favored the mistaken notion that the individual family and individual relationship were non-existent where there were a dozen 'fathers' and 'mothers,' scores of siblings, and so forth. The error lay in assuming that in this connection likeness meant identity. But we have already found that in various contingencies it is the closest relative of the appropriate class that takes precedence. By the provisions of the levirate an own brother inherits the deceased man's widow, other kinsmen being merely substitutes. Cross-cousin marriage in the best-recorded cases means marriage primarily with the real mother's own brother's daughter or with the father's own sister's daughter. Among the Crow Indians all men called brother-in-law are entitled to a peculiar form of respect; but in this regard the real brother-in-law enjoys an unchallenged preëminence. Considering the wide dissemination of the sib concept in Australia, it is especially gratifying to find these results so emphatically corroborated by the most competent of Australian investigators. Mr. Brown, too, finds that while social functions are the same in kind, as he happily puts it, they are not the same in degree; and the difference in degree varies with the degree of propinquity. In short, it is the relations of the narrow family circle that are primary, and there has simply been a secondary extension in attenuated form to wider and wider circles of real and putative kin. The Australian phenomena, whose import has hitherto been left indeterminate, thus fall in line with the data from other regions. In Australia, as elsewhere, the family is basic and primary, the sib relatively unessential and a secondary development. The reversal of the

ORIGIN OF THE SIB

How, then, did the sib originate on the basis of the earlier family concept? In setting out to answer this query we must recollect what the sib really is. The sib is a group of *selected* kin, and the problem is whence comes the principle of selection. Why are certain relatives put together to form a social unit to the exclusion of other kin? In attempting a solution we must scrutinize the social conditions found among sibless tribes in the hope of detecting factors favorable to the development of the unilateral principle; and we must also examine the correlates of sib organizations in search of agencies that may have produced them and tend to maintain them in operation. In my opinion the transmission of property rights and the mode of residence after marriage have been the most effective means of establishing the principle of unilateral descent, and I will endeavor to show how they might originate both a patrilineal and a matrilineal community.

Let us recall once more the data from the Hupa (p. 70). With them residence is patrilocal but not quite definitely so. That is to say, in the majority of cases the paternal grandfather, father, son and son's son of a man are natives and occupants of the same village, taking their wives from without. In other words, the Hupa system actually unites by residence those male relatives who are united in a father-sib. We have here the germ out of which a father-sib might readily develop. Only two modifications are requisite. The patrilocal rule must be made stringent, so that every family shall follow the same principle of segregation; and secondly, there must be a means of fixing the affiliation of the female no less than of the male members of a family. The latter end is most readily effected by the use of a name for the segregated males; that name would naturally come to be given at birth to *all* children born in the village, whether they are male or female; and thus girls as well as boys would bear and retain a patronymic designation. Then it no longer matters whether a woman departs from her native locality; the name alone suffices to fix her affiliation. Similarly, when the principle of patrilineal reckoning is once established in this fashion, the residence rules may decay without affecting the system since a man's membership is fixed once and forever by the group appellation.

A corresponding influence of a common residence is clearly brought out in the case of a South American people. In the Northwest Amazons the social unit is the house community of possibly two hundred individuals. Since marriage is always patrilocal, the normal Hupa grouping of male kinsfolk takes place without exception, and the evolution of a typical sib would merely require the permanent identification of the female children with the house group into which they are born. One additional detail is especially illuminating. Physical propinquity, here as elsewhere, has engendered a sense of particularly close relationship. The children of brothers, being inevitably reared in one house, are regarded as too closely related for marriage, while no such restriction applies to the children of sisters. The house community functions as an exogamous unit permitting and preventing precisely those parallel cousin unions that would be permitted and prevented by an exogamous patrilineal sib.

Professor Speck's intensive researches among the northeastern Algonkian peoples demonstrate the joint action of contiguous residence and common proprietary rights. Hunting-territories are here definitely transmitted from father to son; the wife is taken to her husband's abode; and brothers in some measure share economic privileges. It is obvious that such conditions again effect an alignment of kindred which approximates that of the characteristic father-sib.

The explanation offered for the segregation of patrilineal kin may in corresponding fashion be applied to the assemblage of matrilineal kin. In this connection Tylor has already urged the importance of matrilocal residence. Obviously, whenever the bridegroom comes to reside permanently in the house of his parents-in-law, the children will as a matter of course be associated with his wife's rather than with his people. It has been shown that this is the natural correlate of anomalous matrilocal unions even among a predominantly patrilocal tribe like the Hupa. But the influence of matrilocal residence appears most clearly in such cases as those of the Hopi and Zuñi, where there is not merely matrilocal residence but hereditary transmission of the house from mother to daughter. Grandmother, mother, and daughters are thus united into the core of a social unit, and all children born in the house are naturally linked with this permanent group.

But although matrilocal residence in this form adequately accounts for the evolution of a matrilineal kinship group, there are two serious obstacles to this interpretation as a general theory. For one thing, not a few matrilineal peoples are patrilocal. This is true of the Australians and Melanesians, and also of some African and American tribes. Of course, it is possible to prop up the hypothesis with the auxiliary assumption that all matrilineal peoples were formerly matrilocal but that would be idle conjecture. Secondly, matrilocal residence is often not a permanent condition. If at the expiration of a year or so the young couple set up house for themselves, what motive is there for affiliating the issue, or at least the issue after the first child, with the mother's kin rather than with the father's?

It is therefore desirable to supplement the factor of matrilocal residence and female house ownership with some additional factor that might effect a similar alignment of relatives. Here it seems useful to consider what we know concerning the sexual division of labor. Hahn has familiarized us with the notion that tillage at primitive levels is frequently a feminine occupation. This fact seems to me to have rather significant implications. The girls growing up to maturity will learn from their mother how to cultivate the soil as they learn any other technique characteristic of their sex. But in some cases their exclusive occupation with horticulture may establish a proprietary title to descend from mothers to daughters, and in this way a matrilineal set of female kin is defined. That is the condition which formerly prevailed with the Hidatsa, where gardens were jointly tilled by a woman, her daughters and granddaughters, and where the title descended correspondingly. The female descendants of sisters were thus actually united by common property rights and association in economic activities. Had there been a corresponding segregation of patrilineal kin, say through descent of hunting-territories, as among Dr. Speck's Algonkian tribes, it is possible that the patrilineal principle would have survived or that the clash of systems would have prevented any definite rule of descent from originating. But among the Hidatsa there were no individual hunting prerogatives to be inherited by sons and the residence rules were neither strictly patrilocal nor matrilocal. Hence there was no patrilineal principle to counterbalance the active matrilineal one. Since, then, the garden-owners formed the most definite group, it was natural for any child to have its affiliations indicated from birth by reference to the garden group. In short, there thus developed matrilineal descent and the mother-sib.

It may be asked how successive generations of women could be united in a patrilocal group. The answer lies in the fact that patrilocal and matrilocal residence frequently do not imply a change of either spouse's community but only of his or her dwelling within that community. The Pawnee villages were definitely endogamous, the Kai al-

HISTORY OF THE SIB

lowed a girl to go to her husband's house but hardly ever to another settlement, and in many other instances the majority of marriages were between members of the same local group. Hence, though the domiciliary arrangements in such cases must react on the family life, as pointed out in a previous chapter, they would not affect the segregation of matrilineal or patrilineal kindred in the manner suggested. A Kai woman, though living in a different house from her daughters and granddaughters, has no difficulty in associating with them in her daily employments since they are all residents of one village.

The succession of events outlined for the Hidatsa must not of course be taken to represent a verified historical fact but only an interpretation, which, however, seems to me to enjoy a high degree of probability and to merit examination wherever there are matrilineal tribes in which women perform the work of husbandry. Even in other cases similar considerations apply. The Australians are patrilocal and at least often in the sense that a wife removes to her husband's band. While her husband roams over the band territory to hunt, she gathers vegetable food within the same district. Now in a part of Queensland she is recognized as individual proprietor of certain patches of plants and transmits her prerogative to her daughters. If, as sometimes happens in Australia, the men had only communal rights over the territory while the women established individual ownership over definite sections, we should have a condition favoring matrilineal descent among a patrilocal people.

From the point of view here assumed it is intelligible why a considerable number of tribes should lack a sib system since unilateral reckoning of kinship is found to depend on certain special usages, such as a definite rule of residence, which are common but not universal; and further because there may be a conflict of mutually exclusive unilateral principles, yielding the palm to neither. On the other hand, the frequency of the sib institution seems roughly to correspond to the wide distribution of the causes here reckoned with. Finally, the multiple origin of the sib, which was previously suggested on other grounds, is rendered still more likely if underlying the sib are phenomena such as the residence rule or inheritance law. For in these rules lay the possibility for an indefinite number of independent developments of patrilineal and matrilineal descent.[2]

The Sib and the Dakota Terminology

As noted previously, the empirical correlation between an exogamous sib system and the Dakota terminology is sometimes interpreted in causal terms: the sib is represented as producing the characteristic grouping of kin. There can be little doubt that when a sib organization is once firmly established it will react upon the method of designating relatives: all persons of one's generation and sib will be reckoned siblings, all males in the father's sib are addressed as father, and so forth. But what is true of the sib scheme in full swing cannot possibly be true of the nascent sib. For that *is* simply a peculiar alignment of kindred; and if it coincides with the Dakota system of alignment, the relation between the two is one of identity, not of cause and effect. Consequently, if we desire to understand that alignment we must not rest content with uttering the word 'sib' as though it were some peculiarly illuminating abracadabra, but must penetrate beyond the concept it represents. In the preceding section I have shown how under some conditions a father and his brothers with all their sons and sons' sons may be segregated into a definite social group; and how under other conditions there may arise a corresponding assemblage of a mother and her sisters with all their daughters and daughters' daughters. But for all I have said a father and his brothers, while members of the same social group, might be discriminated in designation,—a very rare occurrence among tribes divided into sibs. Hence it is desirable to show how this and corresponding classifications of kin came into being.

First of all, it may be worth while to point out that a separation of paternal and maternal kin is just as natural for a family as for a sib system. The mother's brother, e.g., is as decidedly the representative of a different social group from the paternal uncle's in one case as in the other. We find accordingly that this distinction is clearly drawn by a number of sibless tribes. Where their nomenclature often differs from the Dakota pattern is in maintaining the distinction between father and paternal uncle, mother and maternal aunt. If we can show how this distinction may vanish, we show how the sib-mates not merely become united into a group but how they come to assume the mutual relations so characteristic of a sib organization.

I am of the opinion that the levirate and the sororate are older institutions than the sib and that by their joint action they can produce and often have produced that very classification of relatives characteristic of the sib and following the Dakota pattern. That they veritably can effect this result, has already been explained; but the chronological sequence I am postulating demands proof. For it would be possible to suppose that levirate and sororate are the consequence rather than the cause of the sib; that fundamentally any fellow-member took the place of a deceased spouse, the brother and sister functioning not by virtue of their family relationship but only as sib-mates. But in the first place this assumption is refuted by the known facts concerning the levirate and sororate. These rules, as indicated above, apply primarily to the real brother or sister. Their precedence is unchallenged among sib-members, who are only substitutes for own siblings. Secondly, the distribution of the levirate and sororate is far wider than the distribution of the sib, and what is more they occur among not a few of the sibless tribes of ruder culture. This fact not only suggests their relative priority but also explains why some sibless tribes share the Dakota terminology of the tribes with sibs. If that nomenclature, though consonant with the sib institution, is not its product but the result of older marriage customs, then where these customs exist the terminology may also arise, whether the sib co-exists or not.

My theory does not involve the dogma that all Dakota terminologies are the result of these two forms of marriage. In special cases quite different principles of interpretation are admissible and indeed necessary. For example, the Hopi practise neither the sororate nor the levirate, yet they have both the sib institution and an interesting variant of the Dakota kinship nomenclature, characterized by the frequent overriding of the difference of generation. Thus, a father's sister's son is not distinguished from the father, and the father's sister's daughter and her daughter's daughter are classed with the father's sister. But these deviations from the Dakota norm and the norm itself are deducible from those antecedent conditions of Hopi life that gave rise to the sib. Matrilocal residence and the female tenure of dwellings amply account for the phenomena. The father's sister's son comes from the same house as the father; the father's brothers are one and all original inmates of the same household. Similarly, all sisters are house-mates; and so are the father's sister, her daughters, and their female descendants through females. The terminological equations of the Hopi are thus based on common tenancy and are intelligible without the levirate and sororate. The principal point is that in every case we must look for some correlated usage, whether it be a rule of marriage or of residence, that may have consummated the observed nomenclature so far as it is at all dependent on social custom.

There is an important point that becomes intelligible

in the light of the principles expounded above. It can be readily understood why marriage between parallel cousins should frequently be tabooed. Given the classification of fathers' brothers with fathers and of mothers' sisters with mothers, parallel cousins logically call one another siblings and with primitive exaggeration of the meaning of names they generally eschew intermarriage. But except in a dual division of society only half of the parallel cousins are prevented from marrying by the rule of the sib. As Morgan clearly showed, in a matrilineal society only the children of sisters belong necessarily to the same unit, yet all parallel cousins are called siblings. This indicates that after the levirate and sororate or other conditions had brought about the kinship nomenclature found with sib organizations there must have been a sifting of parallel cousins by which only half of them were segregated to form part of the sib. But this process has already been explained in the discussion of the origin of the sib. The Amazons case is typical: by patrilocal residence there is a dichotomy of parallel cousins, the children of brothers are united in one house, those of sisters are not. Here we even find the marriage rules profoundly affected by the fact of physical contiguity; brothers' children may not marry, while those of sisters may. However, whether this effect be produced or not, the separation of parallel cousins into two groups of sib-mates and members of different sibs, respectively, is abundantly accounted for by the Hupa, Northeast Algonkian, and Pueblo phenomena.

To sum up. The sib grows out of the older family by a number of processes that naturally lead to the characteristic classification and unilateral segregation of kin. The associated Dakota nomenclature is probably in large measure due to the prior action of the levirate and sororate. But this would not suffice to produce the differentiation of parallel cousins that accompanies a multiple sib organization. This does, however, naturally result from those facts of residence and transmission of property rights which establish unilateral lines of kin.[3]

Mother-Sibs and Father-Sibs

There is still another historical problem of the utmost theoretical importance to be considered. What is the chronological relationship between matrilineal and patrilineal descent? A number of abstract possibilities suggest themselves. Mother-sibs may have grown out of father-sibs or vice versa; either type of sib may be of later origin than the other without developing from the earlier form; or there may be no regular sequence whatsoever.

This last possibility is one naturally repugnant to those who seek the establishment of sociological laws; and accordingly Morgan and his followers postulate an invariable order of development. According to them, the archaic sib was necessarily always matrilineal because marriage between single pairs was unknown in ancient times, rendering paternity doubtful. Affiliation was thus with the mother's group and such property as existed was transmitted within the maternal sib, from brother to brother or from maternal uncle to sister's son, but never from father to son. But with the increase of property a natural antagonism arose against this form of inheritance that excluded the owner's children from the legacy, and this motive together with the increasing certainty of fatherhood sufficed to overthrow matrilineal descent and to establish the father-sib. It is an essential part of this theory not merely to assume that matrilineal passes into patrilineal descent but that all father-sibs without exception have grown out of mother-sibs. For example, the historic genos of the Greeks and the gens of the Romans were patrilineal; but applying the principle of uniform chronological succession, Morgan infers that these institutions were anciently mother-sibs.

Everyone of the basic points in this line of argumentation

may be dismissed as contrary to ethnological evidence. In the first place, marriage between single pairs is not absent but common among the simplest tribes and no ground whatsoever exists for assuming a condition of ancient promiscuity. Indeed, on the very lowest cultural plane we frequently encounter matrimonial relations that would be rated exemplary by a mid-Victorian moralist. Among the Andaman Islanders "conjugal fidelity till death is not the exception, but the rule" and corresponding reports are extant for other extremely rude tribes. But even were paternity doubtful, it would prove nothing as to the necessity of matrilineal descent. Biological paternity is one thing, sociological fatherhood another. The polyandrous Toda do not trouble themselves about the former but establish the latter by a purely conventional rite (p. 47). Where adoption plays the part it does in the Andamans and Torres Straits Islands, biological paternity counts for little and the foster-father fulfills all the obligations of a progenitor. The connection between sexual intercourse and conception is, according to competent authority, unknown to various Australian groups, yet at least some of these are patrilineal like the Toda and Torres Straits Islanders.

Further, *some* correlation assuredly exists between the rule of inheritance and the rule of descent, as follows from the part the transmission of property played in establishing a unilateral group of kin. But this correlation is a partial one. On the whole it is more likely that matrilineal not filial inheritance will be found in a matrilineal society, and filial succession with paternal descent; but the exceptions are too numerous to be ignored. There are matronymic tribes like the Crow and Hidatsa, where some kinds of property are transmitted matrilineally, others patrilineally; there are patronymic tribes like the Warramunga among whom the legacy goes to the maternal uncles and daughters' husbands of the deceased, i.e., to his mother's moiety, not his own. These data can of course be twisted into concordance with the traditional scheme by assuming that in the former case there is a nascent father-sib, in the latter a survival of the pristine matrilineal condition. But ugly facts can always be swept aside by making a sufficient number of auxiliary hypotheses. The alternative explanation is just as reasonable that the paternal traits of the Crow persist from a previous patrilineal stage and that the Warramunga are in a nascent stage of matrilineal organization.

Finally, what evidence is there that the development of property may cause not merely the establishment of patrilineal descent substituted for a sibless organization, as I myself have contended, but the *change* from matrilineal to patrilineal descent? The possibility exists no doubt, but a number of historically known cases show that there is no automatic necessity. For example, the Navaho of northern Arizona profited by the introduction of sheep into the Southwest some time in the seventeenth century so as to develop into a prosperous pastoral people, yet in spite of their thriving flocks, tended by the men, they have remained obstinately matrilineal. Similarly, the introduction of the horse surely revolutionized the property concepts of the Hidatsa and Crow, but they still reckon descent through the mother, and it was not a spontaneous evolution but Government edicts that effected patrilineal transmission of real estate when I first visited the latter tribe. Indeed, the possessions of some primitive tribes are so meager that Morgan himself shrank from attributing all change of descent to the father's solicitude for his children's patrimony and invoked the power of recent Caucasian influences. However, this suggestion seems little short of absurd when we recall that peoples like the Hopi and Iroquois, who have been subjected to Caucasian contact for centuries, are among the most typical of matronymic tribes in existence, while the Blackfoot, whose relations have been both less intensive and more recent, are predominantly patrilineal.

In short, Morgan's theory is untenable from various points of view. For its demolition it suffices to show that, as among the Crow and Hidatsa, it is quite feasible to transmit certain kinds of property from father to son without any change of descent.

Nevertheless to refute Morgan's scheme is not yet to refute the sequence it is meant to establish. His conclusions might be right for all the weakness of his evidence; and other arguments must be subjected to examination.

In an article that remains one of the classics of anthropological literature Tylor, among other things, essayed to show that patrilineal tribes had passed through a matrilineal stage. Advancing what he himself designated as a geological argument, he maintained that "the institutions of man are as distinctly stratified as the earth on which he lives. They succeed each other in series substantially uniform over the globe, independent of what seem the comparatively superficial differences of race and language, but shaped by similar human nature acting through successively changed conditions in savage, barbaric, and civilized life." This principle he applies to the case under discussion.

Tylor begins by postulating three layers corresponding respectively to the maternal, the maternal-paternal and the paternal system. In the first "descent . . . is reckoned from the mother; authority is mainly on her side, the mother's brother being habitually guardian of the children; succession to rank and office, and inheritance of property, follow the same line passing to the brother or to the sister's son." In the paternal stage "descent is from the father; he has the power over wife and children; succession and inheritance are from him to his offspring." Connecting these two there is a "transitional stage in which their characteristics are variously combined." Tylor cautiously admits the vagueness of the classification and at the same time boldly proceeds to build upon it as though it provided a firm foundation for historical inference. Before expounding his argument it will be well to regard this point somewhat more closely.

From a logical point of view Tylor's classification is impeccable. The question is merely whether historical verities correspond to his logical categories, and this can only be admitted with such qualifications as to render the whole scheme of little value. Tylor, it should be noted, substitutes for the simple, unmistakable, discrete difference between matrilineal and patrilineal descent the complex, admittedly vague and fluctuating difference between a matrilineal and a patrilineal complex. He assumes, that is to say, that inevitably or at least usually linked with the rule of descent there are certain correlated customs, all of which jointly form an organic whole; and where only some of the features occur, he postulates an intermediate condition. Now it may be admitted that there are some instances of peoples with a genuinely paternal system, e.g., the ancient Romans and the Chinese. But by far the majority of the known peoples of the world are clearly in what Tylor calls the maternal-paternal stage, as might be expected from the coexistence of the bilateral family with the unilateral sib unit. The Khasi father is respected even during his temporary residence in his wife's household and later gains an undisputed ascendancy; the Tsimshian father is found actively promoting his son's interests regardless of matrilineal descent; the Pueblo father is recognized as the provider, and it is his kin that bestow a name on his child, reflecting their and not the child's sib affiliation. Yet these are extreme cases of 'maternal' status; a fortiori we may infer that virtually no purely maternal tribes exist.

There is another and even more fundamental question that obtrudes itself. How does Tylor derive his matrilineal complex? Is it an empirical fact that the phenomena he cites as characteristic of maternal societies are regularly united or is this merely a logical deduction, plausible but not based on the concrete data? The truth is that both motives are at work. There *are* some tribes in which, say, avuncular authority is linked with matrilineal descent, and from the point of view of abstract logic this seems in harmony with the eternal fitness of things. Accordingly these particular tribes are selected as maternal tribes *par excellence,* as norms of what a self-respecting matrilineal tribe should be. But, as I have shown elsewhere, this is an inadmissible procedure. When matrilineal descent was first discovered by Bachofen, it seemed very plausible that such a usage implied the former sovereignty of the female sex, yet this notion is now gracing the refuse heaps of anthropological science. Consequently we must not rely too much on abstract probability; if we desire to determine whether, or to what extent, the avunculate and matrilineal descent cohere, we must take either custom as the pivotal one and ascertain to what extent the other occurs in conjunction with it. But such an investigation is fatal to the assumption that the avunculate is a safe criterion of matrilineal descent: first, because there are matrilineal tribes without the custom; secondly, because there are patrilineal tribes which practise it.

It has been customary on the part of the older school of anthropologists to treat all of the second group of cases as survivals from a prior matrilineal condition; and recently Dr. Hartland has again advocated this interpretation with much skill and learning. Adherents of this view thus convert what at first seems a fatal objection into an argument favorable to their theory. Of course, they will say, the Omaha are patrilineal now; but their having the avunculate proves that they once traced descent through the mother, for on no other hypothesis can such a usage be explained. It is this last assumption that delivers them into their opponents' hands, for the avunculate can be readily conceived as due to other than matrilineal conditions. First of all, we have to reckon with the possibility of diffusion. Grant that the avunculate arises naturally in conjunction with a matrilineal organization; it may nevertheless subsequently be adopted by a patrilineal people, and in that case its occurrence there could not be cited as proof of former matrilineal descent in the borrowing tribe. To take an actual example: the neighboring Pawnee and Omaha share avuncular usages, the former being matrilineal, the latter patrilineal. We may assume with Tylor and his followers that the customs arose with the Pawnee, but on that hypothesis their presence in Omaha society is proof that the Omaha borrowed a Pawnee institution, not that they themselves ever passed through a corresponding matrilineal stage. As to the influence of borrowing on uniform sequences generally, more will be said below.

Secondly, the avunculate is sometimes coupled with cross-cousin marriage of the more common variety. In that case it is by no means certain that the relevant customs are directly due to the relationship of nephew and uncle: they may just as well be the result of the prospective relationship by marriage. For example, among the patrilineal Kariera a young man owes certain duties to his fiancée's father and in lesser degree to all men standing in the same relationship to him, to wit, that of mother's brother. Mr. Brown's language leaves little doubt that it is the marriage connection rather than the blood tie that determines kinship usages in this case, and this may well hold for a number of other instances. The avunculate may thus turn out on occasion to have no direct association with the maternal kin at all.

This brings us to a more general point. In discussing kinship usages we found that primitive tribes assign definite functions to relatives, both maternal and paternal, both by blood and by affinity. From a wider point of view the avunculate is simply a specific type of kinship usage. That the mother's brother should exercise a certain amount of authority over his sister's children is no more remarkable than that the father's sister should be able to veto her nephew's matrimonial plans or that the father's sib-mates

HISTORY OF THE SIB

should be entitled to gifts in a matrilineal community. If the avunculate among the Omaha is a survival of a matrilineal stage, then the prominence of the father's kin among the Melanesians and the Crow may be urged as a survival of a one-time patrilineal reckoning of descent prior to the observed matrilineal condition. This is of course a purely dialectic thrust. In truth neither argument can be recognized as cogent: both sets of usages are exactly on the same plane, exemplifying the range of kinship rules on either side of the family and bearing no necessary relation to descent.

In short, it is not permissible to treat a given example of avuncular customs in a patrilineal society as evidence of an antecedent matrilineal stage because their existence may have a quite different origin. On the other hand, it is a fact that the avunculate is fairly often lacking in matrilineal tribes. The Australians with maternal descent do not practise it in a typical form, and in such distinctively matrilineal tribes as the Crow and Hidatsa there is no trace of it. It may ultimately turn out that additional conditions besides maternal descent are required for the origin of the avunculate; its highest development seems often to be coupled with a sedentary existence and with definite matrilocal residence, and possibly this latter feature or all these favoring conditions jointly are required to produce it. At all events, Tylor's assumption that avuncular authority is a mark of matrilineal society rests on an unwarrantable selection of data. Not that we need deny all correlation whatsoever, but it is clearly of a more involved kind. Perhaps the safest way to formulate the facts would be to say that certain conditions favoring the origin of maternal descent are also favorable to avuncular prominence, but that the result is not inevitable and may also come about through other channels.

Now what holds for the avunculate as an ingredient of the matrilineal complex applies likewise to inheritance rules, though possibly in lesser degree. They, too, cannot be regarded as absolutely correlated with the rule of descent when we find on the one hand patrilineal tribes recognizing the rights of the sister's son and on the other side matrilineal tribes in which, as at Buin, office is inherited in the male line, or where as among the Crow some kinds of property are transmitted from father to son. In short, the classification into maternal, maternal-paternal and paternal systems, while not devoid of an empirical foundation, represents far more nearly a series of abstract logical possibilities than the normal actualities of primitive society.

But let us return to Tylor's geological argument. Applying his triple stratification, he collates with these layers certain primitive usages and draws from their presence in some and absence in others the far-reaching conclusion of matrilineal priority. Two examples will suffice to explain his method. Tylor finds that the levirate occurs in all three of his strata, but in the maternal-paternal a new feature is superadded, viz. the son's inheritance of widows except for his own mother. That is, filial widow-inheritance as an accompaniment of the levirate is limited to the mixed and the purely paternal stratum. Hence, argues Tylor, the maternal must have preceded both, for otherwise there would be found vestiges of filial succession in the maternal layer. Another custom to which the same argument is applied is the couvade,—the strange fashion observed in some countries of confining the father rather than the mother on the birth of a child and subjecting him to a series of rigorous taboos in order to safeguard the infant's welfare. The couvade, also, fails to appear in the maternal layer; it is most strongly developed in the maternal-paternal, and dwindles considerably in the paternal. From this distribution Tylor draws a conclusion identical with that based on the previous case. Summing up, he writes: "Just as the forms of life, and even the actual fossils of the Carboniferous formation, may be traced on into the

Permian, but Permian types and fossils are absent from the Carboniferous strata formed before they came into existence, so here widow-inheritance and couvade, which, if the maternal system had been later than the paternal, would have lasted on into it, prove by their absence, the priority of the maternal."

It is hardly unfair to object that for an adequate proof of Tylor's proposition a somewhat wider basis for induction would have been desirable. The inheritance of widows and the couvade are only two of an indefinite number of usages that might be selected to test the theoretical sequence, and what warrant is there that other features would not yield contradictory results? But this consideration may be waived in favor of another. What, after all, are Tylor's immediate data? Not a chronological succession, not a stratification in the sense of the geologist's observed superimposition of layers, but merely a positive and a negative correlation. The paternal features are linked with filial widow-inheritance or the couvade; the maternal are not. Direct observation does not extend beyond the perception of a simultaneous relationship. The dwindling of the couvade in the purely paternal stage might be taken as direct indication of the course of social evolution, but erroneously so. If the couvade is more common in the intermediate status, this directly suggests no more than that *certain* features of the full paternal system tend to counteract the influence of certain other paternal features that favored the evolution of the custom. There are functional relations between the phenomena but nowhere is a chronological order to be discerned. That order is injected only if we accept as an axiom Tylor's and Morgan's belief in uniform laws of social evolution. Only on that assumption is every difference at once invested with a sequential significance. Obviously if all peoples pass through the same stages, then a matrilineal people has either left the patrilineal stage behind, or is developing toward it. Tylor's evidence thus merely tends to demonstrate that *if* there be a definite sequence the matrilineal stage is the earlier one.

Now in regard to this basic postulate we may first urge Maitland's caution that the extensive spread of cultural traits by borrowing is bound to play havoc with any hypothetical tendency of communities to traverse certain stages in fixed succession. Under a powerful alien influence a people with cultural elements naturally promoting the evolution of patrilineal descent may be led to adopt matrilineal descent; and vice versa. A number of striking ethnographic instances lie at hand. By far the majority of the Northern Athabaskan tribes are sibless, but so far as authority and inheritance go they conform to Tylor's paternal pattern. However, those Athabaskans in immediate contiguity to the coastal tribes have modeled their organization on their neighbors', borrowing the rule of matrilineal descent. The Hopi are known to be of the same linguistic stock as the Shoshoneans of Utah and Nevada, all of whom are sibless and all of whom lack even the germs of a matrilineal scheme. Accordingly, the ancestors of the present Hopi probably derived their present organization by borrowing either matrilineal descent or the conditions favoring it from their predecessors in the Southwest. The Gros Ventre as a recent and numerically weak offshoot of the sibless Arapaho came into contact with the Blackfoot and by assimilation and further development of Blackfoot ideas evolved father-sibs. Thus foreign influences will sometimes produce a change from sibless to matrilineal and in others from sibless to patrilineal status *without either condition being antecedent to the other*. The history of a people's social organization will vary with its intertribal relations.

The suggestions made as to the origin of sibs likewise indicate that apart from borrowing either matrilineal or patrilineal sibs may evolve directly from a sibless condition.

This view obviates a serious difficulty, viz., that of accounting for the hypothetical change from one rule of descent to the other. As already shown, Morgan himself balked at applying the property principle to tribes among which property is infinitesimal. Moreover, it is not easy to see why a traditionally sanctioned inheritance rule should suddenly rouse antagonism, especially since a man is as likely to benefit as to suffer by inheriting from a maternal uncle rather than from his father. If certain Algonkian tribes actually developed patrilineal sibs from the patrilineal transmission of hunting-prerogatives, while the Zuñi evolved mother-sibs from the mode of matrilocal residence with feminine house-tenancy, the difficulty vanishes since neither rule of descent then appears as a necessary antecedent of the other. I am strongly of opinion that in a large number of cases, whether through borrowing or spontaneous evolution, both mother-sibs and father-sibs have grown directly out of a sibless organization.

Siberia is now so well known that it supplies an ideal field for the testing of any sociological doctrines. What, then, does this region suggest as to the history of sib organization? It is remarkable that throughout this vast area there is not a single tribe that is matrilineally organized. The Chukchi and Koryak, who represent the simplest culture, are sibless; so far as inheritance rules may be taken as indicative of potential development in either direction, they suggest the germs of a paternal organization. We may assume that the introduction of reindeer as a highly prized form of property strengthened the importance of patrilineal kin but this was not carried to the creation of definite father-sibs. The history of Chukchi and Koryak society is thus an extremely simple one, representing throughout a sibless status with paternal bias.

At the other end of the cultural scale in Siberia are peoples like the Kirgiz and Yakut, expert cattle and horse-breeders distinguished for their metallurgic skill. These tribes, like the Tungus, Ostyak and Samoyed, are organized into definite exogamous paternal sibs. Furthermore we find among all these populations the functionally related customs of clear-cut bride-purchase and patrilocal residence, further correlated with extremely uniform treatment of women, who are everywhere regarded as inferior. That this complex should have developed over and over again in a continuous area is unthinkable. In other words, the paternal and indeed definitely patrilineal features evolved and spread over their present range of distribution. Of anything even remotely suggesting maternal traits there is no trace here. We shall not go far wrong in inferring that the father-sibs of this group of aborigines developed directly from a sibless condition of the Chukchi-Koryak pattern.

But intermediate between the Chukchi-Koryak and the Yakut and Tungus are the Yukaghir, who are surrounded on all sides by the latter tribe. The Yukaghir differ from all other peoples of the region in being matrilocal. The Koryak serve for the bride and in exceptional instances settle permanently in her household, and these practices seem to have culminated among the Yukaghir in normal matrilocal residence. Nevertheless, this feature has not created a matrilineal kin-group; property is transmitted from father to son and the blood-feud is waged by the paternal kindred. Indeed, the Yukaghir, doubtless owing to Tungus influence, have developed father-sibs, though without the exogamous rule. What is most interesting, however, is the assimilation of Tungus customs by some Yukaghir bands, and vice versa. The Yukaghirized Tungus no longer practise exogamy; the Tungusized Yukaghir have adopted the custom of purchasing the bride with patrilocal residence and greater recognition of the sib. Thus, the development of society instead of following the same stages among all peoples may even within the same area pursue its course in opposite directions; in one band contact with a non-exogamous people will loosen the sib bonds, while in another contact with patrilineal sibs will foster inchoate germs of a paternal organization.

In short, Siberian data lend no support to the doctrine of inherent laws of social progress. They show that matrilocal residence may fail to produce matrilineal descent; they show sibless tribes with no vestige of a former sib system, whether maternal or paternal, and no apparent haste to develop a definite patrilineal system by spontaneous development. Above all, they show the extraordinary leveling influence of contact with alien cultures.

Of course, it would be dogmatic to deny that a change of descent according to Tylor's and Morgan's scheme is possible. For example, a fair case can be made out for the relative priority of mother-sibs in at least parts of Oceania. First of all, there is no question that in various Melanesian tribes matrilineal sibs are observed phenomena; accordingly, the assumption that related peoples now patrilineal may at one time have been matrilineal is admissible as a working hypothesis, which gains in plausibility in view of certain conditions of Melanesian life. The Melanesians like many matrilineal groups, are horticultural and gardening often devolves on the women,—a situation previously recognized as favorable for the development of mother-sibs. The avunculate, though not by itself decisive for reasons explained, can be used as corroboratory evidence in this case because *some* correlation may be assumed to exist between it and a matrilineal system and also because in certain Oceanian tribes the avuncular power appears in exaggerated form. Thus, among the patrilineal Western Torres Straits Islanders a man would instantly cease fighting at his maternal uncle's behest while he might override the wishes of his own father. Further, when we pass in review the matrilineal tribes of the area, we find a series of conditions precisely of that type which would tend to establish patrilineal descent in a sibless community.

Patrilocal residence is universal; and while the ancient hereditary gardens are transmitted to the sister's son the land cleared by a man's individual efforts is inherited by his children, as are also his trees, which rank as a distinct form of property. The Kai data are especially noteworthy. Here the children belong unequivocally to the mother's kin and inheritance is within the maternal line; however, succession to the chieftaincy is from father to son and only secondarily from uncle to sister's son. Residence is indeed patrilocal in the sense that the bride follows her bridegroom to his home; but, as pointed out, the Kai wife, though living in her husband's house, is not permitted by her kin to move to a distant village because they wish to retain part of her services. Given such facts, I see no reason for rejecting as impossible the theory countenanced by Dr. Rivers that in parts of Oceania a change from matrilineal to patrilineal descent has taken place. What I maintain is that this does not prove the priority of matrilineal descent anywhere else, say, in Australia or Siberia or America; and even in Oceania the matrilineal condition may in turn have been superimposed on an earlier paternal one.

Hitherto the question has not been broached whether matrilineal or patrilineal descent is generally coupled with a higher form of civilization. The traditional view naturally assigns mother-sibs to a lower plane, and even so sane a writer as Professor Hobhouse, who declines to accept the universality of a matrilineal stage, finds that broadly speaking maternal descent occurs among the uncivilized, and paternal descent among the civilized stocks of mankind; and that within the range of the uncivilized races maternal descent is coupled most frequently with the lower cultures. It is of course a fact that the highest known civilizations, while devoid of sibs, are essentially paternal in type; and we know that the ancient Greeks and Romans were at one time organized into father-sibs. Nevertheless it does not follow that patrilineal descent is the uniform symptom of a higher civilization. In Australia there is not the slightest indication that matrilineal peoples like the Dieri enjoy a poorer culture than the patrilineal Arunta. Negro tribes with mother-sibs match their patrilineal congeners in industrial activity and political organization. In America north of Mexico, as Swanton has pointed out, the tribes with mother-sibs are on a generally higher level than those with father-sibs. A decade before Swanton, Herr Cunow, whose puerile pugnacity must not blind us to his merits as a painstaking scholar and independent thinker, had already shown that the North American natives who cultivate the soil intensively are mainly matrilineal, while the tribes reckoning descent from the father represent a lower economic condition. Further, if we embrace in our survey not only communities with definitely organized sibs but also sibless tribes, which have been shown to possess a simpler culture, we find that in the vast majority of cases such germs of unilateral descent as exist are of the patrilineal variety. That is to say, the lowest sibless cultures, so far as they tend to segregate one line of kindred by the processes previously noted, segregate the paternal kin. Thus, the Bushmen had the site of settlement descend from father to son and son's son; not only the reindeer-breeding Chukchi but also the maritime division representing the pristine condition of this people practise filial inheritance of property; the Thompson River Indians of British Columbia and the Shasta of California recognize patrilineal descent of the title to fishing-stations; and the influence of patrilocal residence on Hupa and Northeastern Algonkian life has been sufficiently discussed. No doubt instances of matrilocal residence occur among sibless tribes; but they either alternate with patrilocal residence or are restricted to the commencement of matrimony, so that they fail to lay the basis of a unilateral sib, whence the rarity of mother-sibs among hunting tribes.

In short, Professor Hobhouse's generalization is by no

means in accord with the facts. It is true that the highest known civilizations, like those of the Chinese, the ancient Greeks, and our own, are predominantly patrilineal. But this also holds for the lowest known cultures so far as either side is stressed at all, while the position of matrilineal peoples is intermediate. Contrary to my intention and previous declaration, this statement might be misinterpreted as favoring a fixed sequence of stages. I therefore hasten to dispel this possibility by sketching what I conceive a possible line of evolution in a concrete hypothetical case and then showing that the accepted correlation between certain economic and sociological phenomena is quite consistent with the view that maternal descent does not represent a universal stage in the history of mankind.

I can imagine the Andaman Islanders, a sibless people without any noticeable partiality for either side of the family, rising by successive borrowings to any stage of civilization without necessarily developing either father-sibs or mother-sibs. Whether under the assumed circumstances they would evolve such units, would depend very largely on the nature, intensity and prolongation of alien contacts. I do not mean to assert that such industrial advancement as I am assuming would have no effect on the social organization, but simply that it need not produce unilateral kin groups. If, e.g., the Andaman Islanders borrowed the blacksmith's art, this industrial advancement would imply or at least favor the social evolution of a professional guild. This might develop into an hereditary caste, as has actually happened among the Masai, but there is no necessity for such a development. There might be simply a segregation of those having an individual aptitude in this direction, producing indeed a trade guild and consequent complication of society, but not an hereditary sib. Besides, even if the profession became hereditary, it would not need to create a sib organization so long as the entire remainder of the population failed to organize along similar lines. In other words, the Andaman Islanders could make the leap from the Stone Age to the Iron Age not indeed without some social readjustment but without adopting the principle of unilateral kinship.

In picturing the social history of mankind as a whole it is well constantly to keep in mind the phenomena connected with the sexual division of labor. I have already shown how matrilineal descent might evolve in a sedentary community where women till the soil with the hoe. It should be noted, however, that where tillage is practised intensively, though still with primitive implements as in the higher American cultures, man usually assumes at least the major part of the work. Accordingly it is quite intelligible that under such conditions father-sibs should have developed. The matrilineal descent of the Pueblo Indians cannot possibly be explained on the same principles as that of the Hidatsa because the male Pueblo plants and tends the corn; it is based on the very different factor of matrilocal residence with feminine landlordship. Without this element the Hopi would presumably either have remained without unilateral kinship groups or would have organized into father-sibs. That is to say, the gardening stage does not necessarily imply maternal descent; for since men may share or perform altogether the labor of cultivation (as they do in parts of America and of Melanesia), the conditions for the segregation of matrilineal kin may be lacking.

Now, as Hahn has taught us, the agriculture of advanced civilizations rests on the use of the plough with the domesticated ox (or its equivalent) and these cultural possessions are certainly linked with the male sex. Domestication is undoubtedly a masculine achievement and it is interesting to note the rigid taboos which sometimes separate women from the herds and the still more important fact that in the most highly developed pastoral tribes woman occupies a position of definite inferiority. That agriculture and domestication appeared at a later period than horticulture is unquestionable and if they grew out of horticulture we should again have a fixed sequence of stages to which there would presumably correspond a parallel sequence of maternal and paternal descent according to the time-honored scheme. But the assumption is not essential. Apart from the fact that intensive gardening, as noted above, sometimes constitutes man's share of work, there is no proof that agriculture, so different in its methods from horticulture, developed out of the latter. It is entirely possible that the agricultural complex as evolved in Western Asia evolved independently of the horticultural complex through male effort; and accordingly there is no reason to suppose that the bearers of the great historic cultures ever passed through a maternal stage. This is not a dogmatic denial that any of them ever reckoned descent from the mother, which might in special instances have occurred as a result of foreign influences, but merely a denial of the dogma that they *must* once have traced descent from the mother. For example, I see no reason why the ancestral Greeks should not have passed directly from a sibless condition with paternal bias into the definite patrilineal condition represented by the genos and the phratria.

In viewing the phenomena from all parts of the world we cannot fail to note that while definite patrilineal descent is often lacking an asymmetrical stressing of paternal influences is extremely common. In comparison the hypertrophy of matrilineal factors appears as a highly specialized event superadded to rather than substituted for the paternal traits. That is why even in distinctly matrilineal societies the father and his kin usually figure more prominently than do the mother and her kin in such distinctly paternal societies as those of China and of the Turkic nomads. From this point of view we can also comprehend the instability of matrilineal institutions in specific cases, e.g., in Oceania. It is not so much that the maternal factors have an inherent tendency to vanish in favor of the paternal ones, but rather that the paternal factors, never suppressed but merely in abeyance under specific conditions, reassert themselves when those conditions no longer hold sway. This development, however, like all others, is not an inevitable one and will be affected by the influence of neighboring cultures.

To sum up. There is no fixed succession of maternal and paternal descent; sibless tribes may pass directly into the matrilineal or the patrilineal condition; if the highest civilizations emphasize the paternal side of the family, so do many of the lowest; and the social history of a particular people cannot be reconstructed from any generally valid scheme of evolution but only in the light of its known and probable cultural relations with neighboring peoples. [4]

REFERENCES

[1] Morgan, 1871: 484, 490; id., 1877. Swanton, 1905 (b): 663; id., 1906: 166. Martin: 861. Skeat and Blagden: 1, 65; II, 62, 258. Man: 58 seq., 202. Schultze: 305. Rivers, 1914 (a): 67-70. Lowie, 1915: 231. Bogoras: 538. Jochelson, 1908: 759. Brown: 157.

[2] Whiffen: 63, 66. Speck, 1918: 143; id., 1915 (a) and (b). Tylor, 1889: 258; id., 1896: 81. Wilson: 9 seq., 113 seq.

[3] Lowie, 1919 (b): 28. Morgan, 1871: 475.

[4] Morgan, 1877: Pt. II, Chaps. 2 and 14. Man: 67 seq. Spencer and Gillen, 1904: 524. Tylor, 1889: 245. Lowie, 1919 (a): 29. Hartland: 1 seq. Reports, V: 144. Rivers, 1914 (b): 1, 55; II, 126. Keysser: 42, 85, 100. Hobhouse: 162. Cunow, 1894: 138 seq. Bleek and Lloyd: 305. Bogoras: 679. Teit, 1900: 293. Dixon, 1907: 452.

CHAPTER VIII

THE POSITION OF WOMEN

DIAMETRICALLY opposite views are current among the educated laity regarding woman's place in primitive society. On the one hand, she is conceived as little better than a slave or beast of burden, condemned to perform the hardest drudgery, bought as a commodity, and without redress against her master's brutalities. But those who have read of tribes reckoning descent from the mother and have imbibed the shopworn anthropological doctrines of half a century ago are likely to view primitive woman as undisputed mistress of the family, if not of communal life as well. Both conceptions, so far as the overwhelming majority of peoples are concerned, fall ludicrously wide of the mark. However, there is so much variability in the relations of woman to society that any general statement must be taken with caution. It will be best to approach the subject through a number of different avenues before venturing on even a qualified dictum.

THEORY AND PRACTICE

First of all, it should be noted that the treatment of woman is one thing, her legal status another, her opportunities for public activity still another, while the character and extent of her labors belong again to a distinct category. Whatever correlations exist between any two of these aspects are empirical; conceptually they are diverse, and only confusion can result from ignoring the fact. This is at once made clear when we consider certain well-known phenomena. The harem beauty is not compelled to perform the drudgery of a menial, yet her position is not consistent with our ideals of human dignity, and the same applies in only slightly lesser degree to the European lady of quality in the age of chivalry. In a very different environment the Toda women, while well-treated, rank as inferior and are excluded from the ritualistic observances that occupy the foremost place in Toda culture; they are indeed left with very little employment on their hands, being prevented even from cooking, at least whenever the food contains milk as an ingredient. On the other hand, the Andaman Island woman is virtually on a plane of equality with her husband, though a somewhat larger share of the work may fall upon her shoulders. In Central Asia a comparison of Kirgiz and Altaian conditions is especially instructive. Both tribes assign to woman a position of distinct inferiority. The Kirgiz, moreover, possibly under the influence of Islam, treat their wives with much greater severity than the Altaian Turks. A superficial reading of Radloff might readily suggest that the legal status of woman is approximately the same among both peoples, but that among the Altaians her lot is a decidedly easier one. Closer scrutiny, however, reveals the fact that in spite of legal conceptions reinforced by religious sanction, the Kirgiz woman is decidedly better off. Her Altaian sister is at work from early in the morning till late at night, being employed not only about the house but tending the cattle, bringing fuel, milking cows, sheep and goats, manufacturing all utensils, nay, even cultivating the barley plots. The men do little but chop firewood, milk mares, and give subsidiary help in the manufacture of household articles. Among the Kirgiz the division of labor is a far more equitable one, for men tend the cattle, secure fuel, make containers, and till the soil. Possibly in consequence of this very fact the Kirgiz women enjoy a much greater freedom than is granted to their sex in the Altai: they participate at festive occasions, visit back and forth at pleasure, attend games and public assemblies, and take part in competitive singing contests. In short, there is ample compensation for the reported harshness of treatment.

This case illustrates the great caution required in summing up the status of the female sex in a given society. The conditions involved in the relations of men and women are many-sided and it is dangerous to overweight one particular phase of them. Least of all should excessive significance be attached to theory. Theory may and does affect practice, but often only in moderate degree. Theoretically the Mohammedan Kirgiz may divorce his wife at will, practically he very rarely does so. Chinese metaphysics associates the female principle of the universe with evil, and the legal status of woman is one of abject inferiority. This has neither prevented a fairly large number of women from establishing their supremacy in the household by sheer strength of personality nor from playing an appreciable part in literature and affairs. If instead of taking so extreme a case we revert merely to recent periods of Caucasian civilization, we find that American women were not maltreated prior to suffrage amendments; that disabilities as to holding or administering property have not involved subjection to a husband's will; that at a time in which little was heard of emancipation the leaders of the Parisian salons exerted a social influence hardly to be overestimated. In other words, it is important to ascertain what customary or written law and philosophic theory have to say on feminine rights and obligations. But it is more important to know whether social practice conforms to theory or leaves it halting in the rear, as it so frequently does. The exaggerated weight often ascribed to abstract propositions and legal enactments is part of that perverse

THE POSITION OF WOMEN

rationalism which has so often befuddled the understanding of students of human institutions and human psychology.[1]

THE 'MATRIARCHATE

As noted, matrilineal descent was at one time interpreted to mean that women govern not merely the family but also the primitive equivalent of the state. Probably there is not a single theoretical problem on which modern anthropologists are so thoroughly in accord as with respect to the utter worthlessness of that inference. The testimony of the ethnographic data is too clear to be swept aside by a priori speculation. Of the Australians some tribes are matrilineal, others patrilineal, but the lot of woman is not one jot better or more dignified among the former. The same holds for Melanesia. In British Columbia the Tlingit and their neighbors trace descent through the mother, but such authority as her side exert over the children is wielded not by her but by her brothers. Here property of certain types is highly prized; however, it is not held by the women but transmitted with automatic regularity from maternal uncle to nephew. In Africa we hear of female rulers but their occurrence seems independent of the rule of descent and no more affects the status of the average Negress than the reign of Catherine the Great affected the position of Russian peasant women.

There are a few instances of matrilineal communities, so rare that they can be counted on the fingers of one hand, in which women either exercise unusual property rights or play a remarkable part in public life. Probably the best-known illustrations are furnished by the Khasi of Assam, the Iroquois, and the Pueblo Indians.

Among the Khasi there is a well-nigh unique combination of female prerogatives. Here houses, real estate and the prized family jewels are not only transmitted in the maternal line, as is also the case in British Columbia, but are held by the *women* of the maternal line, i.e., they descend from mother to daughter. In one locality even the position of pontiff is held by a woman, her successor being chosen from a group of her female kin. Yet it would be a grievous error to infer that man counts for nought in Khasi communities. In the household, in spite of feminine ownership, the woman's elder brother ranks as the head, and when the husband after initially matrilocal residence establishes an independent domicile he is its undisputed lord; moreover, the husband's right to kill an adulteress taken *in flagrante delicto* is recognized by customary law. Politically, the sovereignty is transmitted in the maternal line but from male to male member; only where male heirs are wanting does a woman succeed, and she in turn is succeeded by her son not her daughter. This system is assuredly called matriarchal only by courtesy.

It is probably the Iroquois that furnish the closest approximation to a matriarchal condition. Here the women arranged marriage and probably owned both houses and land. Some of the most important ceremonial organizations were largely constituted and managed by women, from whose numbers there were also taken three of the six ceremonial officials of each sib. Women nominated a candidate for a vacancy in the council of chiefs and had the right of admonishing and impeaching an unworthy chief-elect. Nevertheless it remains a fact that even among the Iroquois no woman had a place in the supreme council of the league.

In Pueblo villages the status of woman is decidedly less important than among the Iroquois. As Professor Kroeber has well put the case, "it is in the woman's ownership of the house that the so-called matriarchate of the Zuñi centers and rests." Women have no voice in governmental affairs; they play a part, but a subsidiary one, in ritualism; and even within the houses men, so long as they are inmates, are the real masters. These observations coincide very largely with my own among the Hopi.

The foregoing cases supply the a fortiori basis of the conclusion that a genuine matriarchate is nowhere to be found, though in a few places feminine prerogatives have evolved to a marked degree in certain directions. Surely the fact that such privileges are in a handful of cases linked with maternal descent does not warrant the inference that maternal descent is the efficient cause, for the phenomena from Australia, Melanesia and British Columbia are decisive on that point. Since we have recognized maternal descent itself as the result of more fundamental conditions, such as residence and economic perfomance it will be desirable to examine whether these, rather than descent, have influenced feminine activity and rank. In other words, if there is any causal relationship, the sequence is likely to be not maternal descent, hence matrilocal residence and a certain improvement in woman's juridical status, but rather: matrilocal residence, hence improved status and possibly also maternal descent; and similarly with the other basic phenomena. [2]

MATRILOCAL RESIDENCE

The effects of matrilocal residence on woman's position have already been briefly expounded. Here, as everywhere, we must not allow ourselves to be dazzled by catchwords or to draw extreme conclusions from a slender basis of fact. The immediate result of matrilocal residence is not feminine superiority but only the superiority of the wife's kin. There is a great difference between the Central Eskimo households in which a wife settles with her husband's family and those where the bridegroom goes to his wife's parents; but the difference does not affect the status of woman as woman. In the former case she becomes the subordinate of her mother-in-law, in the latter she remains the subordinate of her own mother; and in both cases, the supreme ruler is a man, her father or her father-in-law. Naturally, when not surrounded by her own relatives, she is potentially more liable to abuse than where the husband is obliged to consider the sentiments of his parents-in-law and hosts. Among the Kai the consistency of matrilocal residence with decided female inferiority appears clearly. While the Kai are patrilocal in form inasmuch as the bride goes to her groom's dwelling, they have been shown to be substantially matrilocal since the wife's kin resist any effort to remove her beyond their sphere of influence. The result is that a man is responsible to them for excessive maltreatment of his spouse or for destruction of her belongings; but in any event she remains a ward under the tutelage of some male, whether it be her brother or maternal uncle or grandfather. It is further clear that matrilocal residence by limiting polygynous unions also tends to eliminate those difficulties to which a woman is sometimes exposed through conjugal favoritism in a polygynous household. Altogether, then, there can be no question that practically woman profits from continued residence under her parents' roof; but this need not in the least emancipate her from the thraldom of an alien will; and where, as among the Yukaghir, the husband may ultimately gain the mastery over the household, she will then be in exactly the same position as though she had settled with him from the start.

The situation must be radically different where the house is owned by the women. Under such conditions matrilocal residence veritably gives to woman the whiphand insofar as she may then banish her husband from the home, as happens among the Pueblo tribes. This assuredly is an advantage in marital relations but it does not affect man so seriously as might be supposed at first blush since he is always certain of a welcome from his mother or one of his sisters, i.e., he always finds shelter through a recognized claim on his house-owning female kin.

The Economic Interpretation

Economic factors have palpably moulded some aspects of latter-day civilization and in some schemes of interpretation they have come to play an exaggerated part. The problem how and how far they have fashioned the status of woman is one of extraordinary intricacy, and here we must be particularly careful to specify our precise meaning. A far-reaching economic change seems bound to produce a modification of some sort in woman's life, in her share of work if in nothing else as an immediate consequence. Yet the Amur River fishermen, the Chinese agriculturists, the Turkic horsemen and cattle-breeders, and the Ostyak reindeer nomads, all share essentially the same conception of the female sex. If it be objected that these peoples, however diverse in their mode of life, are at one in the important feature that woman does not materially add to the food-supply, we turn to regions like South Africa and South America and find that while there women plant and harvest they are not indeed in a humiliating but still in a decidedly subordinate position. On the other hand, there are hunting tribes, like the Vedda and the Andaman Islanders, where woman contributes only moderately to the commissary department yet ranks as man's equal in society.

There is one gross correlation, nevertheless, that has considerable empirical support and has been repeatedly emphasized. Among stock-raising populations the status of woman is almost uniformly one of decided and absolute inferiority. Thus Professor Hobhouse finds that the percentage of cases in which woman occupies a low rung in the social scale is 73 among cultivators of the soil, but rises to 87.5 among pastoral tribes. On economic grounds the matter is readily explained. The domestication of animals was undoubtedly a masculine achievement and practically everywhere the care of the herds has remained a masculine occupation. But such complete dissociation of woman from productive toil is bound, according to the argument, to lead to her social degradation. In my opinion this consideration should be extended to agricultural (as distinguished from horticultural) tribes. For, as Hahn has taught, it is not merely domestication but also plough-culture that is linked with masculine effort in the history of civilization. We thus find a very plausible explanation of the relation of the sexes throughout those centers of Old World civilization which supplied the basis for our own. We see why the economically dependent women of China, of Central Asia, and India should be on an unequivocally lower plane than man.

Nevertheless I do not feel that the case for a necessary causal connection is so strong as it at first appears. No one doubts that the cultivation of barley, millet and wheat, the domestication of the ox and the horse, the use of the plough and the wheel, are features which have originated once and have been diffused over wide areas. It is accordingly possible to assume that the sociological correlate of this economic development, viz., woman's lower status, was only an historical accident. That is to say, it so happened that at a certain period and in a certain region the economic dependence of woman led to her being assigned to a low status, that this, however, was not a necessary consequence but one that might have been precluded by an appropriate complex of ethical or other ideological conceptions. These happened to be lacking and accordingly the empirical association of inferior status with non-participation in an advanced economic system could evolve *once*, was disseminated as a unit, and has persisted from sheer conservatism.

I myself believe that the forces of suggestibility and mental inertia are shown to be so powerful by anthropological evidence that the propagation and preservation of an accidental complex is entirely possible. It may be contended that the very fact of extended diffusion and prolonged re-

THE POSITION OF WOMEN

tention argues an inherent fitness in the combination diffused and retained. That much may be conceded. On the other hand we find that among the Hottentot pastoral life goes amicably hand in hand with sexual equality, while among the neighboring Bantu where the women till the soil they occupy a lower position. These facts are certainly favorable neither to the doctrine that economic activity automatically raises woman's status, nor to the theory that pastoral life as such prejudices her status. The economic factor is perhaps an efficient cause but at best it is only one of a series of determinants, so that its effects may be minimized and even obliterated by others. For example, a well-defined religious tenet might retard or even prevent Hottentot acceptance of the sociological inferiority of woman though the people might willingly adopt the utilitarian essentials of the stock-raising complex.

We have here touched the important principle that a people may adopt part of a diffused complex. But it is the sociological as well as the utilitarian constituent that may spread independently of the residue, and I am firmly convinced that this has taken place so as to obscure the causal nexus between economic life and feminine status. Whatever ultimate fitness there may be in the observed phenomena, the immediate reason for the views held with regard to women in a great part of Asia is that the people entertaining those views have been in contact with other peoples holding the same views. This becomes obvious on discovering that we are not dealing with a vague but with a perfectly defined notion as to feminine inferiority. As the Kirgiz case indicates, that notion does not involve seclusion as in some other parts of the world. It does involve the principle that woman is a dependent, a chattel that may be sold to the highest bidder, may be inherited by her husband's kin, and being property is incapable of holding property. When these identical notions occur among the Syryan, Ostyak, Altaian, Kirgiz and other tribes occupying a continuous area, it is manifest that we are dealing with a definite ethnographic trait that has been diffused over the territory in question. This becomes a certainty when we find that among the palaeo-Asiatic tribes of eastern Siberia woman, while still on a lower level than man, does not approximate the West Siberian woman in the humility of her station. Thus the Chukchi woman is not bought by her husband, may leave him on provocation, and is not debarred from owning property. *Some* changes have been brought about in her lot by the introduction of reindeer, as will be seen later, but she has not by any means been reduced to the level of her Ostyak sister because her status is fixed to a predominant extent by the past culture of the Chukchi and their neighbors, and that status a new economic factor cannot simply blot out of existence.

That woman's position in a particular tribe is indeed a function of the historical relations of the people under examination, becomes clear when we turn to Oceania and Australia. The outstanding characteristics of feminine inferiority in this area are very different from those which impress us in Siberia. Throughout most of Australia, as well as in parts of Melanesia and New Guinea, we find a strong tendency to separate the sexes, sometimes even at meals and most emphatically on ceremonial occasions. The consequent exclusion of women from public life stands in striking contrast to her participation in Kirgiz festivities and shows how variable may be the content of the catchword 'inferiority.' But it cannot be mere accident that so sharply defined a conception is spread over the South Seas; the occurrence of the phenomenon in any specific locality of that area is undoubtedly due to the circumstance that the locality forms part of a geographical region over which the trait has been diffused. Whatever may be the origin of the custom, its secondary cause and accordingly its scientific explanation lies not in any economic factor but in historical and geographical relations.

THE POSITION OF WOMEN

North American data furnish corroborative testimony. In by far the greater part of the continent the Indians, whatever may be woman's position, do not maintain the sedulous separation of the sexes so conspicuous in the South Seas. The importance of the Iroquois women in ritualism has already been noted. Even in tribes where their status is much less exalted, they take part in ceremonial performances, and among some of the Plains Indians the notion that husband and wife are one person ceremonially appears clearly in the transfer and care of sacred objects. It cannot be an accident that all suggestions of a sexual dichotomy of society are reported from the vicinity of the Pacific coast. Only in Alaska have the Eskimo men a house from which women are excluded; only among the Northern Athabaskans are girls segregated from boys and women barred from attendance at any dances; only in California do we encounter men's societies comparable in the jealous exclusion of the female sex to the organizations of Melanesia. The reason why the Hupa men sleep apart from the women is probably that they have had cultural relations with other Californian populations which favored that arrangement. For all tribes except the one which evolved the diffused phenomenon its efficient cause is not this or that economic factor but simply borrowing. In the usually unknown place of origin economic factors may conceivably have been at work; everywhere else their function must have been at most selective, i.e., they may have favored or arrested diffusion without acting as a creative force. This view explains at once why tribes utterly diverse in their means of sustenance have come to share the identical view of woman, a fact that remains quite mystifying on the economic theory.

A gross consideration of the economic data thus fails to indicate a particularly close correlation between them and woman's position. To repeat some of the more significant facts. In horticultural communities of Melanesia and

South America where women hoe the plots their prestige is less than in such hunting tribes as the Vedda or Andaman Islanders. Pastoral life has not degraded the Hottentot woman. Everywhere the influence of intertribal cultural relations is shown to have been enormous.

Nevertheless it is highly desirable to make a more precise study of the possible influence of economic usages. A number of significant problems suggest themselves to the ethnographer, but generally the concrete information is lacking for their solution. Thus, of all the Bantu the Herero are the only purely stock-raising people. Accordingly it would be interesting to compare the status of their women with that of the neighboring Ovambo, where breeding goes hand in hand with gardening. But I am not acquainted with any adequate source of enlightenment for this subject. Again, the Navaho have developed into a prosperous pastoral people since the coming of the Spaniards, but we are ignorant of the social condition of their women in the sixteenth century. The Plains Indians furnish instances of purely hunting tribes and of closely related tribes combining corn-planting with the chase; but it may reasonably be objected that since all of them depended very largely on the buffalo, the presence or absence of crops could not produce any profound social transformation. Certainly there is no sensible difference between the status of woman among the semi-sedentary Hidatsa and among the nomadic Crow, their next of kin. In Melanesia local differences have been recorded as to the sexual division of horticultural labor, but adequate data with special reference to correlated sociological customs are not available.

Probably the most satisfactory case for our purpose is that of the Chukchi, being fully described in Bogoras' ethnographical masterpiece. The Chukchi were originally a maritime hunting people resembling the Eskimo in their general mode of life. Part of the tribe adopted reindeer-breeding with the result that there are now living side by side two branches of the same stock with identical cultural traditions and differing solely in point of economic life. Hence the economic factor can here be isolated from other causes with as close an approximation to completeness as possible. How, then, does the status of woman compare in Maritime and Reindeer Chukchi society? If we are willing to cover a wide range of facts with vague catchwords, we shall detect no difference, for in both groups woman assuredly ranks as subordinate to man. The differences are nevertheless interesting. The sea-expeditions of the Maritime hunters are arduous and full of danger; naturally women undertake these masculine pursuits only under extreme necessity. Among the Reindeer Chukchi it happens more frequently that girls take the place of men as herders, being thus able to lead an independent existence, and the wife normally assists in tending the animals besides doing all the skinning and butchering. To the Reindeer nomad marriage is a necessity: "no man can live a tolerable life without having a separate house of his own and a woman to take care of it." A man needs some one to mend and dry his clothes, he requires assistance with the herd, and unlike his sedentary brother he must have a woman to take care of his traveling-tent. Hence it is not surprising to learn that celibacy is somewhat more common among the sea-hunters, but woman's indispensableness in the nomadic bands is coupled with a remarkable increase of her work. Her household duties have multiplied and economic labors have been superadded. The Maritime hunter is hardly ever able to support more than one wife; among the nomads polygynous families occur with relative frequency, indeed, a wealthy breeder will aspire to have one woman for each of his herds. Among the Maritime Chukchi a woman is almost bound to be a dependent; with the Reindeer people a widow has an opportunity of administering her husband's herds during her children's minority and, failing issue, she may even lord it over a second husband by virtue of her legacy.

The alterations produced among the Chukchi by the introduction of reindeer are thus none the less significant because they cannot be pigeonholed as either lowering or exalting woman's position. In a Maritime community she is a non-producer living a fairly easy life but uniformly supported by man; with the Reindeer Chukchi she is economically active, is subject to a far harder lot on the average, but has a better chance to achieve independence. The Chukchi case thus proves that economic phenomena can be efficient causes in the development of feminine status.

But in view of the current tendency to overestimate economic motives it is worth while insisting that they merely constitute a co-determinant. If we compare the Reindeer Chukchi with the Ostyak, there are differences inexplicable through economic conditions since those conditions are alike. The Reindeer Chukchi does not buy his wife and he acquires none of the absolute rights of an Ostyak husband; his wife may leave him or be carried off by her family notwithstanding his services before marriage. Again, under Ostyak custom a widow cannot inherit a herd of reindeer because no woman can hold property, hence all women are necessarily life-long dependents. In other words, it is the pre-existing culture that largely determines how a new economic factor shall affect woman's status. Since the Chukchi held no anterior conception as to woman's inability to hold property, it was possible for the new factor to bring about a result that is barred by Ostyak ideology. If the Chukchi had conceived woman as a purchasable commodity, they would have substituted reindeer for bride-service; but their cultural traditions precluded that result. It might be objected that the time element must be considered; that if the Chukchi had owned reindeer for a sufficiently long period, the results due to reindeer-breeding would be far more intensive. But this is an idle assertion until it is supported by some evidence; and if the Chukchi women were some time reduced to the level of their Ostyak sisters, it would be a serious question whether the cause is to be sought in the common economic factor or rather, as would be my first assumption, in the gradual extension by borrowing of sociological notions found in the more western parts of Siberia.

To sum up. The economic factor appears to have potency, but potency of a strictly limited kind, liable to be offset and even negatived by other determinants.[3]

Correlation with Stages of Civilization

Hitherto nothing has been said explicitly as to the correlation of a higher status of woman with a higher stage of civilization. However, from facts cited it is already clear what attitude the ethnologist must assume toward the popular opinion that woman's status is a sure index of cultural advancement. That proposition is utterly at variance with the ethnographic data. In the very simplest hunting communities, among the Andaman Islanders and the Vedda, woman is to all intents and purposes man's peer. This does not hold for most of the higher primitive levels, say, for the average Bantu village, where woman, though hardly a mere slave, does not at all events rank as man's equal. Finally, on the still higher plane of Central Asia and China woman is definitely conceived as an inferior being. Or, to look at the matter from another angle, George Eliot and Mme. Récamier, in spite of their social influence, did not even remotely approach the legal position of the average Iroquois matron.

This leads us back to the original proposition that the codified, or at least rationalized, customary law is not a uniformly trustworthy criterion of social phenomena. It is true that in by far the majority of both primitive and more complex cultures woman enjoys, if we apply our most advanced ethical standards, a less desirable position than man. But the frequent assumption that she is generally abused or enslaved as compared with her Caucasian sister is a travesty of the facts. In some regions, as among the Northern Athabaskans, women were undoubtedly obliged to perform the heaviest tasks and in addition were brutally maltreated by their masters. But it cannot be too vehemently stated that well-authenticated instances of this sort are of extreme rarity. Much nearer to what may be considered the average primitive condition is that reported by Spencer and Gillen for Central Australia: "Taking everything into account, . . . the life of one of these savage women, judged from the point of view of her requirements in order to make life more or less comfortable, is far from being the miserable one that is so often pictured." Usually the division of labor is an equitable one. Often, to be sure, the wife appears constantly occupied, while her husband enjoys prolonged periods of rest; but by way of compensation his work, as among the Eskimo, is of a more strenuous character and subjects him to frequent jeopardy of life and limb. As to property rights, even among bride-buying tribes the logical consequences of purchase have been seldom drawn in rigorous fashion. Except in rare instances woman holds property and disposes of it at will. In buying ethnographic specimens in North America I never encountered an Indian who would part with one of his wife's possessions or set a price for them prior to consultation with her, and South American travelers recount similar experiences. Apart from theory, primitive woman by force of her personality is probably as often the ruling spirit of her home as with us. This, as noted above, is equally true in the sophisticated civilization of China, despite the abstract propositions as to feminine depravity concocted by native philosophers.

Regarding feminine disabilities, it is necessary to allude to one feature of primitive psychology,—the widespread horror of menstruation. This has often led to the segregation of women in separate huts during the period of illness,—a usage so persistent that I was able to observe it in full vigor among the Idaho Shoshoni as late as 1906. I have little doubt that it is the fear of pollution from this cause that accounts for much of the debarment of women from activities invested with an atmosphere of sanctity. It is indeed sometimes avowedly the reason for dissociating women from certain sacred objects. Even educated Indians have been known to remain under the sway of this sentiment, and its influence in moulding savage conceptions of the female sex as a whole should not be underrated. The monthly seclusion of women has been accepted as a proof of their degradation in primitive communities, but it is far more likely that the causal sequence is to be reversed and that her exclusion from certain spheres of activity and consequently lesser freedom is the consequence of the awe inspired by the phenomena of periodicity.

That neither this superstitious sentiment nor man's physical superiority has produced a far greater debarment of primitive woman, that she is generally well treated and able to influence masculine decision regardless of all theory as to her inferiority or impurity, that it is precisely among some of the rudest peoples that she enjoys practical equality with her mate,—these are the general conclusions which an unbiased survey of the data seem to establish. If contrary statements have been sometimes made with much vehemence, they relate either to exceptional tribes like the Chipewyan, or they are the result of misunderstanding,—most commonly of the observation that primitive man does not practise that sentimental gallantry which comes to us as a heritage of the middle ages and which progressive women themselves repudiate as prejudicial to their dignity as human beings.[4]

References

[1] Radloff: 295, 313, 462, 484.
[2] Gurdon: 66 seq., 76 seq. 82, 93. Goldenweiser, 1912: 468. Kroeber, 1917 (a): 89.
[3] Seligmann: 88. Man: 107. Hobhouse: 177. Theal: 1, 49, 117. Castrén: 297 seq.
[4] Spencer and Gillen, 1904: 33.

CHAPTER IX

Property

NOTIONS of property tinge every phase of social life. Marriage is in part consummated by the transfer of commodities and the woman acquired as a mate may herself be regarded as a chattel, a conception that reacts on her status in the family. Polygyny was seen to depend on the husband's fortune; and at least among the Wahuma temporary polyandry results from the lack of property for the purchase of an individual spouse. If the theory advanced in this book is valid, the transmission of property has been a potent factor in the creation of the sib organization; and in a subsequent chapter will be traced the influence that wealth exerts on the development of rank and castes. So a volume might easily be written solely on the functions of property in society. In the present chapter we are concerned more particularly with the manner in which it is held and inherited, and in the forms it assumes among primitive peoples; and above all must be attacked a moot-problem of long standing, the question in how far primitive tribes recognize individual ownership at all or merely practise communism.

Primitive Communism

Those who set out with the evolutionary dogma that every social condition now found in civilization must have developed from some condition far removed from it through a series of transitional stages, will consistently embrace the hypothesis that the property sense so highly developed with us was wholly or largely wanting in primitive society, that it must have evolved from its direct antithesis, communism in goods of every kind. This assumption is demonstrably false; nevertheless something may be urged in extenuation of those who deny to savages and to early man the notion of private ownership.

In the first place, while full-fledged communism, to the exclusion of all personal rights, probably never occurs, collective ownership, not necessarily by the entire community but possibly by some other group, is common. As marriage was seen to be in certain respects an arrangement between groups of kindred, so property is often associated with a group rather than with an individual. That profound and in the highest sense historically-minded thinker, Sir Henry Maine, was so powerfully impressed with certain phenomena he had observed in India that he set forth the theory of collective ownership as the ancient condition generally preceding personal property rights. "It is more than likely," he writes in *Ancient Law*, "that joint-ownership and not separate ownership is the really archaic institution, and that the forms of property which will afford us instruction will be those which are associated with the rights of families and of groups of kindred." Joint-ownership, as already stated, is by no means necessarily communal ownership. The co-proprietors may be a pair of partners, an individual household, a club, a religious fraternity, a sib or that fraction of a sib comprising only close kindred through either father or mother. But there are conditions where an entire village is settled by men of one father-sib who jointly own the arable and waste. In such a case the landowning corporation and the commune coincide and there is accordingly veritable communism within the precincts of the village.

Secondly, a *legal* state of communism is often simulated by phenomena belonging to quite a different category of social thought. Even in our highly sophisticated civilization the law sometimes fails to prevail because jurors are swayed by ethical conceptions which public opinion exalts above the decrees of jurisprudence. Where law is uncodified and possibly every tribesman is linked with every other by some personal bond, the practical effect of such sentiments is proportionately greater. Nevertheless, though the juridical point of view may become blurred, it is rarely effaced; and in many instances the line of demarcation is drawn with unmistakable clearness. Thus hospitality is a primary element of Plains Indian etiquette. A host who should not regale a visitor at any hour of the day or night with such provisions as were at his command would be set down as a churl and lose his standing in the community. But it is a far cry from this generosity enforced by standards of ethics and good breeding to a communistic theory that would permit the guest to appropriate food unbidden. No such theory is maintained or put into practice, hence the rights of private ownership remain unchallenged. It is true that many primitive societies assume an attitude toward the necessities of life which puts them into a distinct category of possessions, the theory being that in circumstances of stress no one shall go hungry so long as any one holds supplies of edibles. But that is a point of view intelligible from the precarious existence led by many of these peoples, and doubly intelligible since the European War has familiarized us with the issuance of ration cards.

Another example may be cited to illustrate the reality of the difference between ethics and law among the same group of Indians. A Crow warrior who had organized a martial expedition and returned covered with glory was in strict theory sole master of the booty captured, just as he was wholly responsible for any loss of men. A man who exercised his legal prerogatives to the limit of actually retaining everything for his own use would certainly be flouted for his greed and would hardly succeed in recruiting followers for a second venture. To hoard the spoils in miserly fashion is so repugnant to Crow sentiment that probably no captain ever thus laid himself open to universal reprobation. But it is quite clear from native statements that if he had chosen to do so, his soldiers would have been without redress. These men jeopardized their lives under the captain's leadership, yet there was so little recognition of communistic privilege that they were bound to put up with their leader's disposition of the wealth their joint efforts had accumulated.

The reality of private ownership among ruder peoples is far too important to be established by a pair of random illustrations. Indeed, the longer portion of this chapter will be devoted to this subject. For a preliminary orientation a few additional examples will prove serviceable.

An excellent missionary observer mentions the Kai of New Guinea as a communistic people. Yet on the next page he writes that a thief caught in the act on another man's field may be put to death at once without fear of revenge by the slain culprit's kin, that men who have stolen such valuables as boar's tusks or dog's teeth must flee for their lives, that every fruit-tree has its owner. A native may indeed plant a fruit-tree on a stranger's soil but he is not permitted to erect his hut there without leave. Proprietary rights to game are established by the hunter who first sights it; similarly a man who discovers a bird's nest is reckoned its rightful owner. When a Kai desires to cut a tree and is interrupted in his task, he may establish title to it by a property mark and no one seeing this will touch it. Add to these illustrations instances of intangible possessions to be described later, and it is obvious that the Kai have well-defined notions of private ownership. Their alleged communism is reduced simply to a sense not of communal but of *family* solidarity that prompts relatives to assist one another in the purchase of wives and to coöperate in labors transcending the powers of a single individual.

A still better case for critical scrutiny is furnished by the Arctic populations precisely because many of their usages really smack of communism. In Greenland a large whale is not considered the exclusive property of the harpooners but is shared by passive spectators though they number a hundred. A man was privileged to use a trap not for some time set by its owner and the latter had no claim to the catch. In Baffinland when food is scarce a seal's flesh and blubber are distributed by the hunter among all the inhabitants of the settlement. This indifference to individual property rights is also well exemplified by the Eskimo about Bering Strait: ". . . if a man borrows from another and fails to return the article he is not held to account for it. This is done under the general feeling that if a person has enough property to enable him to lend some of it, he has more than he needs. The one who makes the loan under the circumstances does not feel justified in asking a return of the article and waits for it to be given back voluntarily."

The conceptions underlying such usages recur in almost identical form among those Asiatic tribes whose mode of life most closely approximates that of the Eskimo. The ideal hunter of ancient Koryak times "heaps the results of the chase on the shore, and bids the inhabitants of the settlement divide among themselves, and he takes for himself only what is left." With the Chukchi a man who has killed a walrus does not appropriate to himself the product of his labor but shares it with all passive bystanders.

But a closer reading of the sources shows that even in these unusually communistic societies the individualistic motive, while submerged, is not wholly lacking, and at the same time it supplies us with an explanation of the predominant communism. From superstitious or other reasons individual rights are in some cases acknowledged without challenge. When a whale has drifted to the Chukchi shore, the meat is indeed shared by all present, but the whalebone belongs wholly to the person, whether child or adult, who first sighted the whale: appropriation by anyone else would be sinful and cause the death of the transgressor. Analogous notions have been recorded among the Central Eskimo and South Greenlanders. West of Hudson Bay the hunter who first strikes a walrus receives the tusks and one of the fore-quarters. The Koryak and Yukaghir recognize private ownership at least of clothing and ornaments, while certain other possessions are neither personal nor communal but bound up with the household. A Chukchi custom brings us to the core of the matter. A man with an extra boat allows his neighbors to use it: "It is contrary to the sense of justice of the natives to allow a good boat to lie idle on shore, when near by are hunters in need of one." Nothing is paid for the use of such a boat even in cases of extraordinary good luck. In other words, Arctic society recognizes two axioms, the altruistic sharing of food supplies and the necessity for effective use of extant means of economic production. Arctic communism thus centers in purely economic considerations. Apart from them there is room for the assertion of individualistic motives.

It follows from the foregoing that we cannot content ourselves with a blunt alternative: communism versus individualism. A people may be communistic as regards one type of goods, yet recognize separate ownership with respect to other forms of property. Further, the communistic principle may hold not for the entire political unit of however high or low an order but only within the confines of a much smaller or differently constituted class of individuals, in which case there will be indeed collectivism but not communism in the proper sense of the term. These points must be kept in mind when surveying successively the primitive law of immovable and movable property, of immaterial wealth and of inheritance.[1]

Tenure of Land

Primitive real estate law is affected by a variety of cir-

PROPERTY

cumstances. It is often correlated with the political condition of a people and the conception of chieftaincy in vogue among them. The economic status is naturally of great importance, and geographical factors, impotent by themselves, may in combination with the culture of the occupants exert a considerable influence. It will be convenient to group tribes according to their means of sustenance and to examine briefly the regulation of land ownership among typical hunters, stock-raisers, and tillers.

It is often assumed that when peoples support themselves by the chase there is of necessity communal ownership of the hunting-grounds. This proposition, however, has been not only seriously shaken but invalidated by testimony from a number of distinct regions. It holds for such areas as the North American Plains and for such tribes as the Maidu of California and the Thompson River Indians of British Columbia, but not generally. The last two instances are instructive because virtual communism for members of the tribe was coupled by these peoples with jealous exclusion of all aliens. That is to say, the tribe regarded a certain area as its hereditary grounds open to exploitation by any native, but resented trespasses by others. An intruder on Thompson River territory forfeited his life, and the Maidu safeguarded their boundary lines by an elaborate system of sentry service. Tribal socialism was qualified only as regards certain improvements on the land; if a Thompson River Indian or Maidu had constructed a deer-fence or fishing-station, he was entitled to the exclusive use of what his individual efforts had produced and the right descended to his heirs. Thanks to Professor Speck's capital investigation of northeastern Algonkian groups, it must now be regarded as an established fact that in parts of North America not only such improvements but the hunting-grounds themselves were the property of individual families. "The whole territory claimed by each tribe was subdivided into tracts owned from time immemorial by the same families and handed down from generation to generation. The almost exact bounds of these territories were known and recognized, and trespass, which, indeed, was of rare occurrence, was summarily punishable." Among the Timiskaming the penalty might be death, though more commonly witchcraft was resorted to. As a matter of courtesy the privilege of hunting over a domain might be granted to another family, but it was understood to be temporary. If dire necessity had prompted trespass, the poacher at least felt obliged to transmit the pelts to the injured landowner. Only when all the male claimants to a tract had died off, it was parceled out among the surviving families. The boundaries were so definitely established that Dr. Speck succeeded in mapping the districts held by each family. Quotations from older travelers are rightly interpreted by Professor Speck to indicate a rather widespread recognition of individual hunting privileges among the Eastern and Central Canadian Indians. Similar evidence may be adduced from the coast of British Columbia, where each house group owned its salmon creek or portion thereof, while individual families held their own halibut and shellfish banks, berrying and root-digging patches.

A word of caution is here required. When speaking of individual families, our authorities often fail to define their precise meaning. An individual family in the sense in which I have hitherto used the term would include both parents, but at least Professor Speck shows clearly that the titles he is discussing are not associated with the bilateral unit but with its male head and his male descendants. This is quite natural, because hunting is a masculine employment and primitive societies tend to connect effective utilization with ownership, which in this case automatically excludes women. Another question arises as to the possibly joint ownership of a tract by several brothers. To what extent did such sharing of proprietary rights conflict with individual ownership? While our data are not altogether conclusive on this point, so much appears clearly: territorial rights were at most vested in a body of close blood-kindred through the father, never in a more inclusive body of real or putative kin, never in a larger political group. Communal ownership in any legitimate sense of the term is thus excluded. The only point that remains doubtful is whether the hereditary land belonged to one man individually or was shared with his sons or his brothers. My personal interpretation of Professor Speck's data is that both conditions arose at different times, that joint ownership was simply due to joint inheritance from the father, but that there was at least a tendency to adjust matters on a purely individualistic basis by occasionally assigning to each son a special domain.

The attitude of the Australian aborigines toward their land is extremely interesting. A local group, not necessarily the whole tribe but possibly the localized male portion of the father-sib, as among the Kariera, occupied a certain tract and was indissolubly connected with it. Wars occurred but the notion of expropriating the vanquished never even dawned upon the mind of the conquerors. It is not surprising, then, to learn that naturalization in some other group was likewise inconceivable. "Just as the country belonged to him (the Kariera), so he belonged to it." Trespass was extremely rare and the white settlers in West Australia found it difficult to make black shepherds herd sheep anywhere but on their ancestral territories. Information on some of the tribes suggests that the intensity of this attachment to a particular tract of country may be due to mystical reasons, more especially, to the localization of the individual's totemic ancestors; removal to another region would destroy contact with these mythical beings. Apart from the association of definite groups with special localities, there are important regional differences. The Kariera exploited each tract of land in common, so that any member of a father-sib might at any time hunt over the common territory or use any of its products without limitation by special proprietary claims. Not so in Queensland, where individual families, in Dr. Speck's sense, hold the right of gathering roots or seeds and of hunting in particular spots. Poaching is rare, though not regarded as a serious offence if committed by a fellow-tribesman. Generally, the prerogatives mentioned descend to brothers and sons but in one district patches of edible plants are apportioned among the women and inherited by their daughters.

Finally, the Vedda of Ceylon may be cited as a hunting people with a remarkably keen sense of ownership, which attracted the notice of the white observers as early as the seventeenth century. Each group, like the Maidu, meticulously guarded its boundaries by means of archers, and trespassing led to serious bloodshed. But unlike the Maidu the Vedda also recognized holdings of lesser scope, so that Dr. Seligmann was able to map the territories of distinct Henebedda families. A man would not hunt even on his brother's land without permission; and if game ran into an alien region the owner of the soil was entitled to a portion of its flesh. The conditions of transferring land give us an insight into the true nature of Vedda ownership. Such transfers of hills or pools were normally made only to children and sons-in-law, but not without the consent of every adult male member of the family. Whether this means merely every adult son or also includes the brothers whose birthright to hunt on the owner's land is denied, does not appear. At all events, there was a non-communal, though collective, interest in real estate on the part of close blood-kindred. To symbolize and ratify conveyance the donor gave to the new owner a stone or two, to which one of his teeth might be added. Usually the boundary of an estate was defined by natural features, otherwise a mark representing a man with drawn bow was cut upon tree trunks along the line of demarcation.

We thus find incontestable evidence that hunting tribes

not infrequently recognize non-communal, inheritable claims to particular portions of the tribal territory.

Among pastoral peoples, there is usually a highly developed sense of private ownership as regards their livestock but in the matter of land, which alone concerns us at present, there is frequently complete or nearly complete communism. A Masai shares pasturage with all the other inhabitants of his district and when the grass is exhausted there is a general exodus. In this region the steppe is admirably adapted for grazing so that the herders have an abundance of territory at their command. Among the Toda likewise the local group, which here coincides with the sib, owns the pasture land collectively. The Hottentot practised tribal communism with regard to grazing land, but formerly intertribal warfare was often waged for the possession of suitable grounds. Nevertheless one form of immovable property was associated with individual families,— the bushes from which the people derive the *nara* gourd. Trespassing on *nara* patches led to complaints before the headman if fellow-tribesmen were at fault, while poaching strangers were mercilessly shot down.

Far more complicated arrangements obtain among the Kirgiz, who own immense herds of sheep, goats, cattle, and horses. Camels are raised only on a small scale and in pasturing them the communal principle is generally observed. But the natural requirements of the other species under the existing geographical conditions necessitate a careful partition of available territory. In the summer the herds need well-irrigated plains not infested by an excess of insect pests; the winter resort must afford shelter against the rigors of the weather, an abundance of water and wood, and pastures free from heavy snowfalls. Since the prerequisites for favorable winter quarters are far less readily secured, the earlier history of the Kirgiz hordes consisted largely in squabbles over the best winter territories. These bickerings have long since ceased, and in the sixties of the last century each family was found in possession of an hereditary winter domain. Since the necessity for land varies with the size of one's herds, this system is inevitably connected with a transfer of territory in accordance with exigency. A breeder whose stock multiplies must purchase additional pasturage; if his herds diminish his land becomes partly useless and is to that extent sold. The winter quarters are usually marked off by natural boundaries, such as streams, hills or lakes; failing these, their confines are indicated by posts or rocks. The limits of each preserve are generally known, and every individual is assisted by his sib in warding off trespasses. In marked contrast to this apportionment of winter domains is Kirgiz practice relating to the summer pasturage, which is not owned privately at all but shared by the whole community (*aul*). Here is once more a striking illustration of the futility of tossing about convenient but meaningless catchwords. The Kirgiz are neither communists nor individualists in an absolute sense as regards the ownership of land: they are the former in one season of the year, the latter in another.[2]

Regarding the real estate law of tribes depending on tillage our information is often both scanty and, what is worse, vitiated by time-honored preconceptions. This applies with special force to North America, where our ignorance is deplorable. This is partly due to the extinction of primitive usage over large portions of the continent but far more to the befuddling agency of the sib dogma. Any statement in the literature mentioning the sib as the proprietary unit should be subjected to the closest scrutiny, for this is frequently not an observed fact but an unjustifiable inference from observed facts. Thus the retention of property within the sib must not be confounded with ownership *by* the sib. When a Hopi woman dies, her house is inherited by her daughters, members of her sib by matrilineal descent; it does not become, as it never has been, the property of the sib. First of all, by Hopi law the men are excluded from house ownership so that roughly half of the sib cannot possibly figure as owners. Secondly, there is no collective ownership of a house by all the women of the sib but at best by all the actual female descendants through females of the deceased. The law of inheritance may, as I have myself argued, lead to the notion of the sib, but that is very different from assuming that the fully developed sib including not only remote but also merely putative kin holds property as a corporate body.

For the Zuñi there is uncontroverted evidence that the land was never held by the sib. Communal property exists inasmuch as the unused soil, the streets and wells are free to all the Zuñi; but the fields, corrals, houses and chattels belonged to individuals or household groups of blood kindred. This view of Kroeber's only corroborates Mrs. Stevenson's earlier statement: "The fields are not owned by clans [sibs], and the Zuñis claim that they never were so owned." Title is acquired by simple appropriation and tillage, and it is important to note that alienation may occur The little gardens tended exclusively by women are transmitted to their daughters; this evidently has nothing to do with sib ownership but merely with the same principle that makes hunting territories descend from father to son.

Where ancient conditions have suffered to a greater extent from the influences of civilization positive statements cannot be safely made. Thus Dr. Speck leaves us in doubt whether particular portions of the arable Yuchi territory belonged to individuals or to sibs. Nevertheless, when he speaks of occupation and utilization establishing ownership and of corner stones with optional designs serving as property marks, the presumption is in favor of private proprietorship.

For by far the most precise data on horticultural holdings in America north of Mexico we are indebted to Dr. G. L. Wilson's researches among the Hidatsa. His data have already been used to show how the notion of a mother-sib might naturally develop from the assignment of all horticultural labors and holdings to the women. There is no question that the sisters and their descendants who jointly cultivated a plot also shared the produce, and in this sense collective proprietorship may be ascribed to the Hidatsa. But Wilson's informants leave no doubt that it was invariably the actual blood kindred through the mother not the larger mother-sib that cultivated and owned the plot. In the rich bottom lands of the Missouri the women of a family, i.e., the grandmother, her daughters and daughters' daughters, made a clearing, which was subsequently bounded with wooden stakes, stones or little mounds. Difficulties sometimes arose through conflicting claims, but there was a strong sentiment against quarreling about land and usually an amicable settlement was arrived at by offering compensation for a ceded strip. There was, however, probably no sale of entire gardens. When a woman died, her relatives sometimes failed to appropriate her plot. In that case some other woman might use it but not before asking permission of the deceased owner's family.

With regard to ancient Mexico Bandelier has lavished all the resources of his vast erudition on an attempt to interpret the historical sources in a sense favorable to Morgan's sib scheme. Rejecting completely the notion of a Mexican feudal monarchy that had been popularized by early Spanish annalists, he conceived central Mexico as a confederacy of independent tribes which had indeed subjugated other populations but never to a condition of vassalage. That is to say, instead of acquiring dominion over the soil of the vanquished, the conquerors contented themselves with exacting tribute, certain plots being segregated for crops to be surrendered to them. As for the hereditary territory of the dominant tribes, or indeed of any other native peoples, the father-sib (for Bandelier identified the aboriginal term *calpulli* as a designation for the sib) formed the proprietary unit quite independently of other tribal subdivisions. Alienation was impossible. If a sib became extinct, its lands were added to those of another with inadequate territory or were distributed among the remaining sibs. The sib tract was parceled out among male members, who were obliged to cultivate their allotment or at least to provide substitutes if other duties interfered with horticultural labors. Otherwise their plots reverted to the sib at the close of a two-year period and were re-allotted. The function of supervising the distribution of land belonged to the chief of the sib, assisted by a council of its elders. Bandelier strongly insists that even the tribal chiefs had no territorial domains in a feudal sense but merely held certain plots as sib members, while certain other plots were reserved for their official requirements without any notion of ownership by the chiefs. In short, Bandelier's view is that the abstract notion of ownership by either chief or nation was foreign to the Mexican natives; that the sib had an inalienable possessory right in its territory; while the individual families merely enjoyed the hereditary usufruct of plots within the sib area.

Unfortunately none of Bandelier's successors has reexamined the Spanish chronicles with equal thoroughness and accordingly the discussion cannot be considered closed. Bandelier's contention that feudal overlords were unknown in Mexico will probably stand, and the collective tenancy of land by the *calpulli* with mere usufruct by individual families is accepted by the latest writer on the subject. On the other hand, there is serious doubt whether the *calpulli* were father-sibs; Dr. Spinden interprets them rather as "military organizations taking into their membership all the men of the tribe." A complete reinvestigation of all the older sources without theoretical prepossession is thus indispensable for a satisfactory understanding of ancient Mexican land tenure.

Precise statements as to South American conditions are not abundant. In a country practising a form of state socialism like ancient Peru individual land ownership would hardly be expected. By a tripartite division lands were set aside for priestly and governmental uses, the residue remaining for the support of the population at large. Tracts were possessed by the father-sib (*ayllu*), and within each of them the several families received an adequate allotment for utilization. For the Chibcha we have an over-summary declaration that real estate was individually owned: *"La propiedad individual de las tierras existía entre los Chibchas, y los bienes raíces se transmitían par herencia á las mujeres y á los hijos del difunto."* Somewhat greater detail would certainly be welcome. From the ruder tribes, both individual and communal ownership are reported. In the northwest Amazons the tribal plantations belong to the chief, apparently not because he exercises any abstract dominion over the soil but from the practical reason that since all the unattached females in the communal dwelling belong to him he is best able to cultivate the fields. This in no way prevents individual Indians who have private lodgings in the bush from having their special patches of manioc. Tribal boundaries are often carefully maintained. Within them the Bakairi plant communally, though Schmidt observed that on the Kulisehu communal labor created a usufructuary and possessory right for an individual by making a clearing for him.

Thus, so far as the scanty data permit any generalization, it appears that the New World aborigines followed a variety of systems as to land tenure. Communal ownership certainly occurs, especially in the south, non-communal though collective sib ownership has at least been vigorously asserted, while ownership by close blood-kin through the mother occurs among the Hidatsa and individual ownership in Zuñi.[3]

With relatively few exceptions American society was organized on a democratic basis. As we pass to the remaining continents, the effect of other polities on land ownership often appears with great clearness, especially where as in Africa and Oceania greater and lesser degrees of monarchical power are found side by side.

As a result of their political conceptions the African aborigines frequently consider the land the king's or chief's property. It follows that purchase of land becomes impossible. Nevertheless apart from restraint on alienation the man to whom territory has been allotted may become its absolute master. The method pursued by the Thonga may be used for illustration. A headman, having obtained from the king a considerable tract of land, apportions it among his fellow-villagers, who begin to till the most fertile sections of their allotments. When a newcomer wishes to settle on the territory, he is taken to an uncultivated plot, of which the boundaries are fixed by natural landmarks, such as trees, lakes or ant-hills. Henceforth he is rightful occupant of the premises, but if he leaves either because of dissatisfaction with the soil or some personal difficulty with his neighbors, the property cannot be sold, but escheats to the grantor. On the other hand, in the normal course of events possessory rights descend to the grantee's heirs. The headman's title would similarly be invalidated if he left the country, irrespective of the period of his occupancy. But so long as the tenant remains in possession, his control is undisputed and he may in turn parcel out his territory among his kinsmen. Strangely enough, the grantor surrenders his interest to such an extent that he must obtain the tenant's leave for so much as picking up rotting fruit from the assigned tract. In this and other details there is naturally local variation among the Bantu, and much doubtless depended on the powers of individual headmen and rulers, yet on the whole one derives the impression that tenure was relatively secure. Thus, among some of the southern tribes a chief might indeed expel a commoner from his estate and seize his standing crops on behalf of another chief, but it was illegal to dispossess the cultivator in **favor** of another commoner. An interesting deviation from Thonga practice is also noted for their southern congeners in case of abandonment. This did not void the title: the former occupant might recover the arable formerly used by him, though he had no claim to the grounds broken up and brought under cultivation by the newcomer.

Among the Southern Bantu, then, the cultivator remains a tenant, though generally one in secure occupancy of his land, effective use of the soil by a grantee depriving the grantor or any one else of the right to interfere, except sometimes for political offences. So far as I am able to see, the possessory rights are held individually.

Among the Ewe of Togoland chiefs are of rather less consequence than among the Zulu and their relatives. On the other hand, the individual seems to count for less as compared with the group of his patrilineal kindred. These two conditions give a different coloring to Ewe real estate law. Each tribe and each village has its distinctive domain carefully demarcated from that of neighboring units of like order by boundary lines marked with a species of shrub generally used for this purpose. Within the village area each paternal family has its own land, which is again properly bounded. Theoretically the title is based on ancestral appropriation and prescription. So far as the tribal and village land is concerned, ownership is public. The subdivisions of the village area are owned by groups of patrilineal blood-kindred with the heads of families acting as administrators. The head of a group is obliged to assist other members in times of stress, and any kinsman is permitted to till a portion of the hereditary soil. A family of diminishing numbers may cultivate only a relatively small portion of the land they own, nevertheless their title does not lapse through non-use. Other families are permitted to occupy plots in such cases without the necessity of paying rent but they are required to observe local customs as to rest-days and to plant palm-seeds so that the owner may some day have a palm grove on his property. Within the paternal family group there is hardly individual ownership: occupation of a definite plot by one member is neither prejudicial to the interests of fellow-members in the land he tills nor does it interfere with the cultivator's rights to the hereditary land outside his plot. So far as personal titles are recognized, they seem to hold only for the palm-trees planted.

Since the very existence of the Ewe rests on the possession of their fields, a sale of the ancestral property as a whole is out of the question and formerly it was deemed preferable in case of debt to sell or pawn members of the family who had contracted the obligation. It happens, however, that special patches are sold with the consent of the administering head of the group. In such cases, there is a strong likelihood that the fellow-members will strain every effort to retrieve possession of the hereditary plot by re-purchase. Otherwise the transferred property is transmitted to the buyer's heirs according to customary rules of inheritance. Conveyance is not without its formalities. The purchaser pays the price agreed upon, then the seller brings a fixed amount of cowrie shells to be divided between him and the buyer. Next a string of cowries is divided into halves and torn in the middle, whereupon each party ties his half of the string with the shells to his stool or carrying-basket as documentary evidence of legal purchase. Finally both buyer and seller, accompanied by witnesses, repair to the transferred property, where three shots must be discharged. This counts as a public ratification of the sale and is the first point ascertained by judges in cases of subsequent litigation. If it can be shown that the customary shots were fired on the field, the title is established. Dissensions concerning land ownership have always been common and were formerly adjudicated by the chief and a commission of two expert advisers, before whom each litigant was obliged to recite the names of all the preceding owners and to indicate the boundary lines of the estate in dispute. Failure in either respect led to an adverse decision. Sometimes an ordeal was resorted to and the disputant who first died was regarded as the wrongful claimant.

The real estate law as outlined above did not hold for the kingdom of Dahomi, where the autocratic ruler was in theory absolute owner of all the land, of which he merely permitted or specially granted the usufruct to individual cultivators. Accordingly it was his prerogative, though it was not normally exercised, to oust the possessor at will and invest whom he pleased with the rights of occupancy.

In the highly organized state of Uganda the theory of tenure approaches, as in Dahomi, that of the feudal system. The king is owner of all land and disposes of it at will with the exception of sib burial grounds of long standing, which are liable to taxation but not to a shifting of proprietorship. The king grants land to the chiefs, and the chiefs allot lesser tracts to the peasants, who in return are obliged to work for them and render military services. No sale of land is possible since that would be an encroachment on the king's ownership, even the burial grounds remaining inalienable.

Thus in Africa the whole question of land tenure assumes a distinct aspect. It is inextricably bound up with the nature and extent of royal dominion, which sometimes dwarfs the possessory rights of the occupant into those of a mere tenant at the master's will. Additional factors undoubtedly enter, as in the case of the Ewe, where kinship solidarity largely conflicts with separate ownership of the soil. Considering that horticultural work devolves so largely on the women, we might expect to find women more prominently associated with territorial rights. As a matter of fact, a Kikuyu woman owns the patch she cultivates, and though Bakuba soil is the chief's its produce belongs to the female planters. But such references are rare; in Africa the chattel conception of woman has generally prejudiced her proprietary status.[4]

In Oceania the Melanesians, except where influenced by Polynesian example, approach a democratic condition; the Polynesians everywhere prized nobility of descent but except in certain groups lived rather in a commonwealth of gentlemen than in an autocratically ruled state; in Hawaii, however, and part of Micronesia a large body of the population groveled in the dust before the patrician caste. These differences inevitably affected the law of land.

In Melanesia generally there is little indication of feudal tenure; nay, Codrington cites an interesting case of landless chiefs. Even in Fiji, where under Polynesian influence chiefs attained an exalted position, responsibility to the ruler as an individual seems to have arisen only through special conditions. According to Mr. Thomson, the chief as tribal representative would assign plots to fugitives asking for protection, and the tribute presented to him was at first divided up among his people. But by usurpation of prerogatives not originally vested in him he was able to make special levies and even to obscure the original form of tenure to the extent of figuring as an overlord to whom the tenants were personally subject.

Speaking again in a general way, the waste lands were tribal property in the sense that any tribesman was permitted to possess, clear and cultivate an unappropriated part of the area. An important distinction is drawn in the Banks Islands and neighboring sections of Melanesia between the ancient hereditary land and that recently reclaimed. The former belonged to the mother-sibs or at least to the constituent maternal families, so that when a man died his gardens became the possession of his sister's sons, all of whom jointly owned the property and each of whom chose a plot within the inherited estate. On the other hand, plots recently brought under cultivation by a man's individual labor were his and descended to his sons.

who did not hold in common, each becoming owner of a distinct part of the field.

A very interesting detail of Oceanian real estate law is the proprietorship of fruit trees apart from the soil on which they grow, a circumstance that has led to much confusion on the part of colonial administrators. In Fiji, in the Banks Islands, and part of New Guinea the planter has an indefeasible claim on cocoanuts or other valuable trees even if he has not obtained leave to plant them on another man's soil, though permission is usually asked and granted. European settlers are accordingly obliged to indemnify not only the landowner but every native who has fruit trees standing on the property they are acquiring.

Alienation of land was decidedly uncommon. In the Fijian state of Rewa there were nine methods of transfer but in six of them there was definite provision for redemption by a special ceremony, though not for a spontaneous reversion of the property to the line of original owners. Thus, an estate might be given by the bride's family as her dowry to be used by her husband and her male children. Failing male issue, the donors could redeem it with a suitable present, but until this formality was gone through the husband and his representatives could till or lease the land, though without rights of transfer. There was no specified statute of limitations, but if the donors' kin allowed the matter to lapse for three or four generations the descendants of the grantee would be upheld by public sentiment in rejecting a subsequent offer of redemption gifts.

Fijian land tenure varied enormously in different localities and the statements of our authority, possibly reflecting tribal differences, are not wholly consistent as to the matter of communism. It is, however, clear that at least in certain regions individual ownership was recognized. This was noticeably the case in Rewa, where every plot had to be reclaimed from the river or sea by individual effort, which established personal proprietary rights. Indeed, it would seem that the so-called communism of Fiji dwindles into the dominance of moral over legal conceptions: the land cultivated by a man and the trees he planted were his by legal right but the ethical claims of his kindred in practice went far to level the benefits accruing to the holder of an estate with those derived by his kin.

Probably, there is no part of Oceania in which individual property rights as conceived by us are better developed than in the Torres Straits Islands. Every rock and waterhole had its owner, the only piece of common land being the village street. Gardens were leased, the first fruits constituting a sort of rent payment. Contrary to widespread primitive usage, alienation and testamentary disposition were allowable. An irate father might disinherit his children or apportion his property among them at will, which proves that there was no inalienable birthright to land nor joint ownership even by blood-kindred.

In sharp contrast to the democratic polity of Melanesia stands the caste system of the Marshall Islands. Here the upper and lower nobility held undisputed sway, looking down with supreme scorn upon their plebeian serfs and only granting to a middle-class of 'professional men' a sort of feudal tenure of lands in return for distinguished services. It is thus merely the limited patrician caste that exercises proprietorship of the soil and its control is an absolute one. A nobleman's title is based on inheritance or conquest; he may give away or sell his territory at will though the lesser chiefs yield tribute to those of higher rank. The estates are cultivated by serfs who are completely subject to their master's caprice. Some of these plebeian families are allowed to remain in the same spot for generations but such association establishes no claim to safe tenure. The serfs toil for their master, who is wholly supported by them and in addition exacts an annual tribute.

In New Zealand, on the other hand, a general equality of political status proved consistent with high veneration for noble lineage. The mass of the population may be described as landed gentry, whose position in their tribe could never descend to the level of degradation characteristic of the Micronesian serfs. The precise prerogatives as to land accorded to chiefs and reserved to individual tribesmen are not clear. Individual and collective rights, too, coexisted in a manner at times puzzling. Generally it seems that communal claims related to the tribal area not yet definitely occupied; but as soon as a man marked as his property a tree which he designed for a canoe his title would not be disputed. Unlike the Australians, the Maori put into practice the principle that the territory of the vanquished belongs to the victor; it was in fact regarded as an indemnity for the lives lost by the conquering host. Whether tenure conformed to the feudal pattern remains a question. The esteem in which chiefs were held, and indeed the specific statement that unappropriated tracts were parceled out by them as they saw fit, would indicate that conquered land too would be divided up according to this system. On the other hand, we are informed that in settling land secured in warfare any one might acquire proprietary privileges by active possession and would come to own as much territory as he could travel round before meeting a rival prospector. The setting up of his spear would then suffice as an emblem of occupancy. It is of course possible that these prospecting tours were among the prerogatives of higher rank.

Title was allowed on a variety of contentions in addition to those of conquest and inheritance. For example, claims could be advanced on the ground that the litigant's ancestors had been buried on the disputed property, that his umbilical cord had been cut on it, that he had been wounded or cursed there, and so forth. Thus purely religious or even fanciful notions obtruded themselves into the real estate law of this complex culture. Though the Maori were predominantly tillers of the soil, land represented a variety of economic values, and accordingly specific privileges were owned by individuals or families. One might gather shellfish here or berries there, another had the exclusive right of hunting birds in certain localities. It is especially interesting to note the occurrence of multiple seisin; sometimes one family had the right of digging fern-roots in a certain place, while another hunted rats in the same area.

In Samoa political conditions roughly resembled those of New Zealand. The information on land tenure, though meager, presents the points at issue with greater clarity. Each district guarded its boundaries against the encroachments of neighboring settlers. Within the district the individual families, each represented by its head, owned the estates in severalty. The headmen, in spite of their honorable position, could not alienate the land without consulting their kinsmen, who would otherwise depose an arbitrary administrator of what was evidently regarded as a family estate.

Joint ownership by the family is also highly characteristic of the real estate law of the Ifugao of northern Luzon, who may serve as a final illustration of land tenure among ruder peoples. To them, if to any people, may be applied Sir Henry Maine's notion that primitive individuality is swallowed up in the family,—the family in this case apparently including kinsfolk from both the father's and the mother's side. Rice fields and in some measure forest lands are here held rather by trustees than by absolute owners. "Present holders," says Mr. Barton, "possess only a transient and fleeting possession, or better occupation, insignificant in duration in comparison with the decades and perhaps centuries that have usually elapsed since the field or heirloom came into the possession of the family." When there is one field and a multiplicity of heirs, the first-born takes it because apart from practical difficulties it is deemed better to have one powerful representative of the family to whom the rest of the group may repair for aid than to divide the estate into diminutive holdings occupied by men of little consequence in the community. As trustee the holder is by no means free to dispose of the property at will, but may do so only after proper consultation with his kinsmen. No transfer is ever attempted without urgent necessity, such as the need for sacrifices to secure the recovery of some member of the family whose life is endangered by sickness; and conveyance is solemnized in a manner to which there is no parallel in the sale of personal possessions.

Two forms of transfer outside the family occur, pawning and sale. If a landholder requires a loan, say, to defray the expenses of a funeral, he may give his rice field as security to the creditor, who then plants and harvests the field until the amount is refunded. Whenever the borrowed sum, usually equivalent to about half the value of the field, is restored, the estate reverts to the pawner, with the qualification that the creditor remains in possession until the crop is harvested. The transferee may in turn pawn the property, but never for a greater amount than that advanced by himself, so that payment of the debt will restore the field to the original holder without undue friction, which might otherwise result. All pawning is witnessed by an agent through whom the loan is negotiated; his fee is advanced by the creditor but it must be refunded with the debt.

Far greater solemnity is observed when a sale takes place. The price is divided into ten parts, each represented by a notch cut in a stick or a knot in a string. The first two payments are the heaviest and must be rendered within a set period while the time of the residuary payments remains unfixed. Possession is yielded after the receipt of the initial amount. The witnesses include the seller's remote kin and the indispensable go-betweens who have arranged the whole transaction and are entitled to a fee. The transfer of ownership is not possible without a ceremonial feast, and on the other hand the commencement of the eating nullifies all obligations on the buyer's part to render further payments, so that he sometimes resorts to trickery to beguile the seller into premature banqueting.

If the landholder abandons a field and it is taken up, prepared and planted by another man without interference on the part of the hereditary occupant, the latter forfeits all right to the land for a length of time equal to that of his neglect to utilize it. At the end of that period the field reverts to its former possessor, but if he desires to regain it at an earlier date he is obliged to repurchase possession.[5]

A review of the systems of land tenure described in the preceding pages establishes beyond doubt the reality of that primitive joint ownership which so strongly impressed Sir Henry Maine. But it is by no means a fact that the co-proprietors always constitute a social unit of the same type. Communal ownership, apart from the general tribal area, we have encountered only in that highly special case where a father-sib is localized and thus becomes coextensive with the commune. Far more frequently proprietary privileges are shared by corporations of another type, groups of close blood-kindred, unilateral as among the Ewe or bilateral as apparently among the Ifugao. That is to say, there is no communism in land so far as the territorial body goes but only within a strictly limited body of actual kindred. Further, joint ownership, while frequent, is not universal. We also find individual property rights as in the Torres Straits and in Rewa; nay, communism and individualism sometimes coexist; as in the case of the Kirgiz pastures. The burden of the proof surely rests with those who believe in a universal stage of communal ownership antecedent to individual tenure of land. Let them advance evidence to show that land was once communally owned in the Torres Straits; that the Algonkians at some definite period failed to recognize the individual hunter's domain; that separate ownership was unknown to the Vedda of some specified period.

Fortunately it is not necessary to assume altogether the attitude of a passive skeptic. Baden-Powell's researches in India permit us to take the offensive and to show that in all probability this region has witnessed an evolution of real estate law diametrically opposite to that rashly assumed by speculative anthropologists. Baden-Powell points out that the area in which joint villages prevail is considerably less than half of that in which separate ownership of land predominates. Moreover, this latter condition occurs precisely among the populations possessing a ruder civilization. The Kandh of Orissa furnish a capital illustration. Here the head of the family alone owns the homestead and the land attached to it. The sons live with him after marriage but hold no property rights until their father's death, when the estate is divided equally among them. There is no trace of common ownership nor of the allotment of fractional shares of the village area to the several families. Each family clears and occupies a portion of the ample waste according to exigency. Once occupied in this fashion, land becomes heritable property that may be bought and sold. Upon this type of individual tenure by agricultural aborigines there was superimposed, in certain localities, the principle of the joint-village,—often in the form of a conquering non-agricultural group assuming the dominion of the soil and degrading the native proprietors into mere tenants. In such cases the landlords formed a brotherhood owning the village area inclusive of the waste land as a unit estate. Shares might be assigned either on a per capita basis, each household receiving a number proportionate to its members; or the ancestral shares were calculated according to the pedigree table, so that the sole heir of one of the original assignees would hold a larger territory than, say, one of three heirs. In a strict sense, Baden-Powell finds, there is never a holding of the soil in common by any major group, though there is a sense of kinship and obligation to mutual assistance; beyond a certain limit of blood-kinship the joint holding never goes. Equally important is the conclusion that in so far as the joint condition obtains, it is "not original, but consequent on a prior *single* title of the founder, grantee, etc., of the village; the joint holding was the result of the joint-succession (on ancestral shares) to that one founder."

Thus the intensive study of a single, though vast area, leads to an historical reconstruction that directly contravenes the sociological dogma of a primeval communistic tenure. This condition appears not as a universal but as a highly specialized case, as a late rather than an early development.[6]

Chattels

The primitive law as to movable property is much simpler than that of real estate and may accordingly be treated in more summary fashion. Generally speaking, purely personal titles are more clearly established than in the case of land. Communism with respect to plantations may go hand in hand with complete individualism in point of chattels. This applies e.g., to the Bakairi where every man and woman has personal property. It is particularly noteworthy that the right of women to such possessions is not challenged even where their status is one of definite inferiority. An Ewe woman is bought by her husband and regarded as incapable of inheriting land, but she may hold movable property, such as goats and poultry, and the cotton grown by her efforts is given to her husband only in return for compensation. It is not less remarkable that sometimes even the child's individual property rights are regarded as inviolable. On a Paviotso reservation in Nevada I once offered to purchase a little boy's blanket. His parents not only referred the request to him as the rightful owner but were willing to abide by the ridiculously low price he set, which in fairness I felt obliged to raise. In Brazil Dr.

Schmidt had a similar experience in attempting to purchase the mat of an eleven-year-old boy, which his father refused to sell without the boy's consent.

Often the title to movable property rests on individual effort; this is why women so commonly own the pottery they have manufactured. Another principle relates to what might be called effective utilization. Each Yukaghir owns his clothing, the hunter owns his gun, the woman her sewing implements. Nevertheless this very notion may lead to a collective rather than personal ownership: the Yukaghir consider boats, houses and nets as the joint property of the entire family. But these widespread principles may be completely overridden by the structure of political society. Where the caste system attains the rigidity characteristic of the Marshall Islands, the laborer is utterly at the mercy of a chief, who may appropriate not only the produce of his horticultural labor, but also all his movables. The organization of society in this case introduces a specific type of property in the form of serfs or slaves, whose status will be discussed elsewhere. On the west coast of Africa servitude may be merely temporary, the slave functioning as a pawn or security for the payment of debts.

Another category of chattels is represented by live stock. Among pastoral peoples flocks and herds constitute the only or at least the most conspicuous form of wealth, the ready means to matrimony and prestige. There is accordingly a tremendous accentuation of the sense of individual property rights, attested by the branding systems current among such tribes as the Chukchi, the Kirgiz and the Masai. Among peoples who are predominantly stock-breeders individual ownership is often vehemently asserted even against the claims of family ties. A Masai elder will assign some of his cattle to each of his wives, who must care for them in return for usufructuary possession, but they remain the husband's property. Only when she has a son of ten or twelve whose services are not required for the paternal herds, the boy becomes owner of the cattle hitherto entrusted to his mother's care, but she and her son must forthwith leave the kraal and establish a small one of their own at a distance of several kilometers lest the father's and the son's herds intermingle to the former's detriment. The Chukchi who has become impoverished by the loss of his herds may indeed look to his brother or cousin for assistance that shall enable him to resume reindeer-breeding, but he has merely an ethical, no legal, claim against his kinsmen; and an old herder jealously guards his full property rights against his own sons.[7]

In short, with regard to chattels separate proprietorship is seen to predominate.

Incorporeal Property

Contrary to what might be supposed, the notion of patents or copyrights is well-developed in the lower reaches of civilization, and its prominence among certain peoples reduces the dogma of a universal primitive communism to a manifest absurdity. That this fact has not been adequately grasped by earlier writers is in part due to that rationalistic prejudice which is the bane of all historical inquiry. To minds steeped in the spirit of an industrial era it is difficult to conceive that privileges without obvious utilitarian benefits may be highly prized and sometimes distinctly rank as wealth.

Even in so humble an environment as that of the Andaman Islands 'choses in action,' to use our legal phraseology, are not wanting. This is all the more remarkable because with reference to utensils, such as cooking-vessels, the aborigines display a large-mindedness actually approaching communism: "the rights of private property are only so far recognized that no one would without permission appropriate or remove to a distance anything belonging to a friend or neighbor." But no such latitude holds with regard to the songs composed for the occasion of a tribal gathering. A song that has been received with applause may be repeated by request at lesser gatherings, but irrespective of its popularity no one dare sing it except the composer himself.

The Koryak believe that the course of events may be shaped by magic formulas, which serve to banish disease, lure game, consecrate charms, and exorcise evil spirits. All incantations originated from the Creator. They are now held by elderly women, who treasure them as trade secrets; indeed, there is a belief that to divulge the formula is to destroy its efficacy. For chanting a formula the owner receives from her client cakes of pressed tea, or several packages of tobacco, or a reindeer. "When a woman sells an incantation, she must promise that she gives it up entirely, and that the buyer will become the only possessor of its mysterious power."

On one of the Eastern Torres Straits Islands Professor Haddon discovered distinct ideas of proprietorship in local legends, for an informant never liked to tell a story connected with another locality. This type of experience has been shared by many investigators of the North American Indians. Additional examples of copyright are furnished by the Kai. Among them, as in the Andamans, a poet is the absolute owner of his composition. No one else may sing it without his consent, and usually he exacts a fee for granting it. Similarly, there is ownership of magical formulas, the instructor being entitled to compensation. Certain carvings, too, must not be copied without special leave. Even personal names are in a sense a form of patented property, so that a young man adopting a name already held presents his elder namesake with a gift by way of conciliation.

Among the natives of British Columbia the Nootka are conspicuous for the number and variety of their intangible goods. From data kindly supplied by Dr. Sapir it appears that the patent rights of these people are divisible into two categories, those called *topati* which are necessarily transmitted from father to eldest son and those which a father normally surrenders to his son but is not obliged to transmit. That is, such a privilege as the knowledge of the family legend could not be withheld from the eldest son since it is his birthright. On the other hand, a father may exercise some discretion in regard to such a secret as the ritual for spearing fish; if he consider his son unworthy, he will refuse to give him the requisite instructions. The *topati* are exceedingly numerous. They include names,— not only those designating the owner himself, but also those he has an exclusive right to apply to his slaves, his houses, canoes or harpoons; the right to certain carvings on grave posts or totem poles; the prerogative of singing certain songs, including even lullabies, and of executing certain dances; and many other privileges. Some of these are of an amazingly special character. For example, in the Wolf ritual the particular coloring and decoration of certain performers are the inherited patents of the man who arranges the festival; the right to set a trap to capture the wolf-impersonators is associated with a particular lineage; one actor who limps and howls in a peculiar way does so by virtue of inherited prerogative. The same applies to solemn chants sung at particular junctures, to the lassoing of novices, the loud and rapid beating of a drum at one point of the drama, the wearing of bear skins at another, the blackening of all the spectators' faces. Other ceremonies are marked by corresponding exhibitions of *topati;* thus, in the girls' puberty festival the right to receive a ceremonial torch was a jealously guarded hereditary privilege.

While the Nootka stress the hereditary character of their immaterial forms of property, which is tantamount to making the privileges the joint property of a group, the individualistic character of incorporeal property is on the whole strongly marked among the Indians of the Plains. In order to understand the phenomena found in this region we are obliged to transcend for a moment the sphere of purely sociological data and enter the domain of religious belief. The center of Plains Indian religion is occupied by the conceptions and practices connected with visionary experiences. These sometimes come unsought to the fortunate man favored by supernatural beings but were far more commonly stimulated by a several days' fast on a lonely hilltop. The tenor of the revelation would often determine the course of the successful visionary's future career. If he saw a buffalo recommending the use of a certain mixture of roots for the treatment of wounds, he would set up as a practitioner and success would gain for him fame and riches. If he was instructed to organize a new dancing society with a definite set of songs and regalia, he would forthwith become the founder of such an organization with a probable rise of prestige and possibly other benefits. If he saw a horseman carrying a peculiarly ornamented shield and escaping unscathed from a hostile onslaught, he would henceforth feel secure in any encounter and establish a reputation for reckless bravery.

But the visionary experience might extend its beneficent influences to other individuals who had never ventured in quest of a revelation or had tried and failed to obtain supernatural favors; and they might come to share the benefits not merely in a subsidiary fashion, as patients cured by a visionary or as participants in the dance he founded, but in the fullest sense, as though they themselves had enjoyed the spiritual blessing. This was rendered possible by the notion that privileges conferred by a spirit are transferable; and this conception became a source of gain to the visionary through the additional conception that they were alienable only through sale. Why certain rights should have come to be prized by the people of this or that tribe is not always obvious any more than in the case of the Nootka; the important fact is that they are highly esteemed and thus add to the social standing of the possessor; that no one ventures to infringe his patent; and that any one desirous of sharing it or buying it outright will sacrifice property to what we should consider an absurd amount. Transfer by gift is excluded even where the relationship of the negotiating parties is as close as possible: I know of a Crow who bought the right of using a special kind of ceremonial paint from his own mother, and the Hidatsa medicine bundles, uniformly derived from ancestral visions and hereditary in certain families, must nevertheless be bought by sons from their own fathers. In many instances, as in the one last mentioned, tangible commodities too may be transferred, but the principal thing is not the corporeal object—the pipe or feather or rattle—but invariably the immaterial privilege with instructions about correlated songs and methods of handling the sacred object or warnings as to taboos indissolubly bound up with the visionary prerogative. Because of the comparative insignificance of the visible object a replica may readily be substituted for the visionary's own emblem, nay, may be supplied by the purchaser himself. It does not matter whether he takes the seller's rabbit foot, ermine skin and eagle feather or secures them by his own efforts: what he is buying is the right to use this particular combination of objects together with the right to the associated songs and activities, but also with any coexistent duties and restrictions on conduct.

The rules as to different ceremonial privileges naturally vary somewhat. Sometimes the seller does not alienate his ownership completely but merely permits the buyer to share in its benefits in return; but sometimes there is the qualification that the owner may not dispose of his rights more than four times, the fourth partial sale terminating his own proprietary rights. In other cases the buyer purchases the privileges in question outright, a single transfer completely divesting the seller of ownership.

These general principles are best driven home by concrete illustrations. I will select two examples, the right to plant the sacred Tobacco of the Crow and the purchase of membership in the military organizations of the Hidatsa.

In order to secure the right to join in the planting of the sacred Tobacco, it is necessary to be initiated by a member of the Tobacco society, to be adopted as his 'son.' This feature emphasizes the individual character of the proceeding. No man can be taken in by the society as a whole; he is fathered by his individual sponsor as he in turn was fathered by the person who introduced *him,* and as the founder of the society was fathered by the supernatural being that bade him plant Tobacco for his own and the tribal welfare. The fact that the planting privilege is shared by a group is from the Crow point of view incidental: it has merely happened that in the case of the Tobacco those purchasing the same medicine have shown greater solidarity than those buying, say, the same war medicine, and that consequently they have come to form a society instead of a mere series of unassociated individuals with similar privileges. In addition to the generic right to plant Tobacco, each novice acquires specific medicines, which he is allowed to choose from those unfolded before him by the adopting section of the society. Further, there is a multiplicity of specific privileges recalling those of the Nootka but differing in their non-hereditary character. For each medicine object and each privilege separate payment must be made. Thus, a woman named Cuts-the-picketed-mule paid a horse for a Tobacco bag, another horse with otterskins for a breast ornament, a horse for the privilege of sitting next to the door. These payments were over and above the initiation fee given to the 'father' and were yielded to such members of his section as held the prerogatives. Since the novice is aided by friends and relatives and because the main privilege he seeks is held jointly, an appearance of collective purchase is produced that is quite foreign to the essence of the transaction. Inasmuch as it is a matter of pride to do things handsomely at an initiation, the candidate is more or less liberally aided by his kin, his friends, and his club. On the other hand, the 'father' who receives, say, fifty horses would incur the reproach of avarice if he retained the fee without making adequate deductions on behalf of fellow-members of his section. These are, however, merely personal or ethical motives intruding on a strictly legal procedure, by which an individual A yields a share in his planting privilege to an individual B, who is obliged to furnish compensation.

A remarkable blending of the collective and the individualistic element appears in the Hidatsa military clubs. Other features of these organizations will be noticed in a later chapter; here it is the conception of membership as property that alone requires attention. According to Hidatsa theory, these societies with their songs, regalia and functions were revealed to visionaries who subsequently founded them in obedience to supernatural instructors; when an Hidatsa does not know the legendary vision on which a society is based, he at once suspects its alien origin. In other words, we meet again the notion of an individual revelation bestowing on the beneficiary transferable prerogatives. Since the visionary was instructed to found a society, the collective feature is inevitable under normal conditions. Yet in principle we are merely dealing with a proprietary right that may be shared by a group but may also be held by a single person. This is proved by the fact that at one time when all the owners of a certain society with a solitary exception had been carried off by disease, this survivor actually was sole proprietor and sold his membership to a group of young men eager to acquire it. As compared with the Tobacco-planting privilege, the membership in a military club differs in that it is sold outright, so that the 'father' wholly abdicates his place in favor of the 'son.'

Normally the collective feature appeared in that a group of buyers jointly purchased membership from a group of sellers. A reason for the collective procedure will be suggested later. What concerns us here is that the transfer of property was essentially individual. There was an initial accumulation of goods by the 'sons' in a body, and through this property they sought to induce the owners to consider selling their membership rights. But with the commencement of the sale itself each buyer selected a seller belonging to his own father's sib as his individual 'father,' and henceforth the affair was an individual transfer. In purchasing certain of the societies it was customary to surrender one's wife; but there was never a wholesale surrender of wives by the buyers to the sellers as a group: each man took his wife to his individual 'father.' Again, if the 'father' held some special office and regalia in the society, then they were automatically transferred to his 'son.' The entire transaction was at bottom not the transfer of proprietary rights from one corporation to another but resolves itself into a multiple simultaneous transfer of individual ownership rights.

Thus the individual character of proprietary rights founded on visionary experiences asserts itself even where the rights are shared by a company of individuals. A fortiori, it will have to be accepted as unquestioned where, as in the case of many war medicines and medicine bundles, there is a negotiation between only two individuals, the buyer and the seller. Certain incorporeal forms of property thus support beyond cavil the possibility of personal ownership at a rude stage of civilization. This is certainly quite unequivocal where a father cannot transmit a mode of painting the face nor even an hereditary set of rituals to his own son without receipt of compensation. Of course we must not forget that incorporeal property, as among the Nootka, may also descend automatically and in that sense be joint property. The point is that among the Andaman Islanders, the Kai, the Koryak and the Plains Indians, regardless of any laws relating to material possessions, there are also patents and reserved rights which are held personally and upon which no one not duly qualified dare encroach.[8]

Incorporeal property, however, should not be considered merely from this angle. Its very existence among the simpler peoples is of the highest interest; and not less remarkable are the Protean forms it assumes under favorable conditions.

Inheritance

Nothing brings out more clearly the difference between individual and collective control of property than the varying degrees of liberty accorded to the individual by different societies as to testamentary disposition. The contrast is marked between a Torres Straits Islander who may deprive any of his children from a share in his estate and the Kai whose possessions are automatically disposed of by customary law,—whose pigs are slaughtered for the funeral feast, whose boar's tusks and dog's teeth bags pass into the hands of his brothers or maternal uncles, and whose sons inherit the fruit-trees he has personally planted.

This last-mentioned case illustrates an important principle already envisaged by the penetrating intelligence of Maine. Archaic law often establishes a differentiation between hereditary and acquired possessions, as has already been pointed out for Melanesia. Where this classification occurs, the tendency is to assign greater freedom with regard to the acquired belongings, a man being reckoned master of what his personal efforts have produced. This consideration may naturally be overruled by factors of a different order. A Plains Indian cannot simply transmit the rights acquired through fasting for a vision because of the principle that such rights can be acquired only by like visions or by purchase; and, as shown for the Hidatsa bundles, the feeling on this subject may be so strong that even an hereditary privilege can be validated only by formally buying it from one's father.

Rules of inheritance are sometimes greatly simplified by the custom of burying or otherwise destroying all of the decedent's effects. Thus the Maidu burn practically all of the dead person's belongings, the meager residue being apportioned among the eldest son as chief heir and other children and relatives, and the right to fishing-holes and deer-drives descending in the direct male line. Among the Assiniboin the weapons, clothes and utensils of the dead were deposited with the corpse, as were sacred shields and pipes. Here and in other parts of the Plains area the dead man's best horses were sometimes turned loose or killed, leaving a very small remnant for distribution among the survivors. In addition we sometimes learn of the abandonment or destruction of the lodge in which the demise occurred, a custom resting on a morbid fear of death. Thus the Pima of Arizona not only kill and eat what live stock may remain and destroy personal belongings, but also burn down the householder's hut.

Certain principles already described in connection with the titles to ownership necessarily apply to inheritance. Thus, a woman's articles of dress or artifacts made and used by women, such as earthenware vessels, generally pass into the hands of her daughters or other female kin because only they could make effective use of them, while a man's weapons are inheritable only by men. It is this principle, doubtless often in conjunction with others, that accounts for one of the most frequent rules of inheritance, viz., the exclusion of the widow from the number of her husband's heirs. Her disabilities cannot be wholly explained by her lowly status, for they obtain also in regions where women occupy a fair position in society, and they are paralleled by the husband's inability to inherit from the wife. When therefore, an Ostyak widow is described as incapable of owning her deceased husband's reindeer, the matter may be conceived as follows. The domestication and care of reindeer by the male sex established an empirical association between men and this form of chattel so that it appeared as unnatural for a woman to hold property of this type as for a man to inherit feminine apparel. Accordingly, the herds went to a man's nearest male relatives and women were barred from any share. This in itself need not affect their status since a priori they might have property rights offsetting their disabilities. Empirically, however, no such compensatory privileges exist in pastoral tribes, hence the relative degradation of women among them.

Another factor that must be considered in this connection is the conception of marriage as a contract between distinct groups of kindred: husband and wife are allies whose individuality remains separate, i.e., merged in that of the groups they respectively represent, hence their property reverts to the group of their origin. Thus it happens that while a Kai man's heirs are his brothers and maternal uncles his wife's valuables are appropriated by *her* brothers and mother's brothers. This factor may appear very prominently where the groups are sibs, in other words, where the kindred group is defined with perfect precision. Among the Altaian Turks property is inherited by the sons or, failing male issue, by the father's brothers or male kinsmen; only when all of these are lacking can a daughter become the heiress.

But in recognizing the potency of the sib factor in moulding inheritance rules we must be careful not to exaggerate its importance. In the first place, while a sib system once firmly established often reacts on property law, we have found reasons for assuming that fundamentally it is often the rules of inheritance that lie at the bottom of the sib notion. What the sib organization can do is to make a remote relative who belongs to the dead person's sib take precedence of a close relative outside the sib, but probably it is never strictly correct to describe the sib as the proprietary unit. For the sib embraces both men and women, yet by the ever-present division of sexual function whatever proprietary rights occur are usually not held by both male and female members but either by one sex or the other. The Hopi furnish a favorable illustration. Houses invariably belong to women and consequently descend from mother to daughter; the position of Snake priest likewise remains within the sib but it is transmitted from brother to brother, or from uncle to sister's son. It is somewhat misleading to say that the sib owns the dwellings and the ceremonial office; the real co-proprietors are female sib-mates in one case and male sib-mates in the other. Further, frequently it cannot even be asserted that all the male or female sib-mates are co-proprietors since the real owners are the blood-kin within the sib. Just as with the levirate so in the case of other proprietary rights descent is to the nearest kinsman of the sib, not to any sib-mate without distinction. The sib organization, in short, involves the exclusion of certain close kindred from inheritance and the inclusion of remote or putative kindred, but it acts in conjunction with existing notions as to sexual functions and the precedence of relatives on the basis of propinquity.

Equally important is the circumstance that in communities organized into sibs property is not all necessarily transmitted within the sib. The Crow when in recent years confronted with a new type of property in the form of real estate, applied their matrilineal scheme to the inheritance of land; but a different principle usually obtained with regard to inheritable sacred possessions, which were transmitted from parent to son and from brother to brother. In this respect they resemble the Hidatsa, who transmitted gardens matrilineally and sacred bundles patrilineally. It can of course be argued that such instances exemplify a transitional stage from one uniform rule of inheritance to another. But that is to assume that rules of inheritance must follow a consistent plan for all forms of property. The trouble is that historical processes are not shaped with such logical nicety. Granted that a fixed rule of descent were followed by a people regarding one form of property, the borrowing of a new form of wealth might produce an entirely new set of laws for its transmission. This new code could either originate spontaneously or be simply borrowed together with the property itself. Accordingly, I am not inclined to accept the theory, unless supported by concrete data, that mixed rules of inheritance are a sign of a change in the rule of descent, either from the maternal to the paternal or vice versa. For example, the Melanesian custom of transmitting fruit-trees patrilineally and land matrilineally may be due to the distinct history of these forms of property; and no unification has taken place simply because the concrete mind of the savage jurist does not develop an abstract conception of real estate property, under which are subsumed both trees and land, but conceives trees as one thing and land as another. This mode of thinking was forcibly impressed on me when in an heroic attempt to render a nursery tale into classical Crow I spoke of a little girl who owned nothing but a loaf of bread in her hand and the clothes she wore. I was at once informed that the two possessions could not be coupled; between food and raiment there was no connecting link for the Crow mind. It was not possible, accordingly, to express the English thought in a single sentence, which had to be resolved into two distinct predications, the one relating to the limitation in the food supply, the other to the category of movables represented by dress.

In other words, if we substitute a psychological and historical for the irrelevant logical point of view, the coëxistence of different rules of inheritance for different classes of property is quite intelligible. Those inheritance laws which give rise to the sib concept will of course often persist in accord with the fully developed sib system; but other laws of equal or greater antiquity may continue to apply to special types of property, and still other laws may be added in connection with novel possessions.

I will now discuss more particularly certain rules of inheritance, merely mentioning the avunculate here because its implications have already been discussed.

Primogeniture occurs but is relatively rare in primitive society even where the eldest child enjoys a certain ascendancy over his siblings. Sometimes there is no discrimination on the basis of seniority; the Vedda distribute property fairly among the adult children, the daughters' shares being often nominally given to their husbands. The Kandh of Orissa also have an equal division of land among the sons, though the office of headman descends to the eldest. The Ifugao allot to the first-born the major portion of the estate, yet we have seen that he is virtually not more than its administrator for the benefit of the entire group of kinsmen. Among the Maritime Chukchi the eldest son has the best share of his father's weapons and implements, but all the brothers receive their portion, even the house being frequently divided into parts. Primogeniture is further qualified in polygynous communities by the superior status of one of the wives, usually but not always the first one, regardless of the age of the sons. Among the Masai it is the eldest son of the principal wife who inherits the largest portion of his father's stock and assumes control of the girls in the family. However, all the other sons inherit that share of the herds which has been previously assigned to their respective mothers for usufructuary possession. In practice all sorts of complications may arise. The testamentary powers yielded to a decedent will modify the customary disposition of property. A dying Kikuyu may allot larger and smaller herds to his several sons according to their place in his affections. While the eldest adult son takes possession of the legacy, he is merely an executor administering the estate according to the testator's bequest. If there are only infant children, the property goes to one or several of the dead person's younger brothers according to his will. But they, too, are merely trustees carefully watched by the wives of the deceased, whose sons claim their legacy on reaching maturity. Among some of the Kafir tribes of South Africa two wives were formally appointed as taking precedence over other consorts,—"the great one" and the "right-hand one." The eldest son of the great wife inherited his father's rank and all the property that had not been specially assigned to the son of the right-hand wife. A father could set aside some portions for the eldest sons of his minor wives, but if undue preference was shown to them his settlements were invalidated after his death. In the absence of issue, brothers inherited the estate; failing brothers, it was appropriated by the chief, daughters being barred from the legacy.

The Kikuyu and Kafir tribes introduce us to the rule of collateral inheritance, which in some other parts of the world attains a far greater importance, brothers being the principal heirs, at least in a possessory sense, to the exclusion or disadvantage of sons. This custom is clearly brought out in the Thonga law regulating succession to office, which seeks to reconcile two disparate principles, the preëminence of one branch of the family and the collective ownership of property by brothers. When a headman or chief dies, the oldest son of the principal wife is viewed as the rightful heir, but he cannot succeed until all the deceased ruler's younger brothers have in turn held office and died. This system likewise regulated the succession of Aztec war chiefs in Tenochtitlan. The Maori case is likewise of interest. As regards rank, primogeniture held sway: the priest-chief was the eldest son of the eldest son of the eldest son, etc., of the line claiming descent from the gods. But in the inheritance of land primogeniture was tempered with collateral privileges: "If a father had sons named A, B, C, D, on the death of the father the property passed to A, but not on the death of A to A's son. It went to B, and on B's death to C, and so on to D, but at D's death it reverted to the son of A." Sometimes the claims of collateral heirs were still stronger. Among the Arapaho Indians the bulk of the property, which in recent times consisted largely of horses, was appropriated by the siblings of the deceased, the adult sons being to all intents and purposes disinherited. Similar practices obtained among the Crow as regards both land and horses.

Where a matrilineal organization affects the rules of inheritance both estate and office may descend by preference to a brother and only secondarily to the sister's son, either method of course assuring the retention of the property within the sib. From this fact some writers have drawn the conclusion that fraternal inheritance in a given tribe constitutes a survival from a former matrilineal scheme. The Arapaho, who are described as sibless, would by this school be classed as at one time matrilineal. It is difficult to advance a weaker argument in support of a hopeless case. Of course, brothers are members of the same mother-sib if descent is matrilineal, but it is equally true that they are members of the same father-sib where descent is patrilineal. The mere fact of fraternal inheritance is thus utterly inconclusive as to either maternal or paternal descent. On the other hand, the collateral rule has much to commend it on grounds of equity, in which respect it is certainly far superior to primogeniture. If a title is established on the basis of effective utilization, the mature brother must certainly take precedence of the adolescent or juvenile son. Again, if a unit estate is founded by a father with four sons and partition is impracticable, it is assuredly one of the fairest of conceivable plans to transmit the superintendency to the eldest son and then successively to each of the others. Collateral inheritance is consequently not in the least mysterious when found within a patrilineal society.

The antithesis of primogeniture is represented by a custom that held sway in parts of Britain under the name of 'borough-english' and is ethnologically known as *junior-right* because it makes the youngest child the principal, or at least the preferential, heir. India forms one center for this usage. The Badaga, neighbors of the Toda, have the sons of a family leave the parental roof on marriage and set up households of their own; only the youngest remains with his parents, supports them in their old age, and automatically acquires possession of their home when they die. To a lesser extent junior-right occurs among the Toda themselves. The father's buffaloes often remain the joint property of all the sons, but if the need for partition arises there is an equal division except that one additional animal falls to the share of the eldest and one to that of the youngest son. If there are only two sons, each would take half of the herd. With four sons and sixteen buffaloes the eldest and the youngest take four each, the second and third brothers take three apiece, and the remaining animals are either sold, the purchase money being equally divided, or taken by one of the brothers who indemnifies the others, dividing three-quarters of the value of the buffalo among them. The Naga of Manipur, while on the whole inclining to limited primogeniture, practise junior-right in certain localities, the youngest son inheriting both the father's house and the most valuable of his movable belongings. Most interesting are the inheritance rules of the Khasi, who blend feminine prerogatives and junior-right. Here the youngest daughter performs the family ritual in propitiation of ancestors, inherits possession of the house and contents, and receives the lion's share of the family jewelry; however, she may not dispose of the house without the unanimous consent of her sisters. On her death she is succeeded by the next youngest daughter, and so on. Failing daughters, the inheritance passes to the sister's youngest daughter, who in turn is succeeded by her youngest daughters. Failing sister's daughters, the estate reverts to the mother's sisters. But the laws regulating succession to office rest on a different principle. A chief is succeeded by his eldest uterine sister's sons in order of seniority, and, failing issue, by the sons of the next oldest sister. In one district where the pontifical position is held by a woman, she is succeeded by her eldest daughter. A trace of junior-right has likewise been noted in the higher levels of Hindu civilization, for the Laws of Manu, while assigning a larger share to the first-born, also mention a special allotment in favor of the youngest son.

This usage, so contrary to current legal notions, also appears farther north. During his lifetime a Kirgiz father seeks to establish his sons as independent stock-breeders. He will assign to his first-born a large portion of his herds; if necessary, he buys new winter-quarters for him, otherwise he assigns to him a section of his own grounds. In similar fashion other sons are provided for, and the youngest remains heir of the paternal pastures and other possessions. If several sons remain, there is an equitable division of the herds and the winter quarters are used by them jointly or are divided up by common agreement; a division, however, rarely occurs as it would be to the disadvantage of the youngest son. For by Kirgiz law it is the eldest brother's duty to acquire new winter pastures as soon as the herds multiply beyond the capacity of the inherited or assigned territory, and if the increase continues after his separation the obligation still rests with the eldest of the remaining brothers to find new grazing-land, until finally only the youngest remains in possession of his father's land. Among the Yukaghir a like result is accomplished by another cause. The prevalence of matrilocal residence brings it about that the elder brothers leave the father's house, which accordingly together with other property is inherited by the youngest son. It is doubtless an extension of this basic custom that junior-right is applied to distinctly feminine articles, which pass from the mother to the youngest daughter. Those tundra-dwelling Yukaghir who have borrowed the Tungus custom of bride-purchase are naturally patrilocal and in their case the bulk of the property is shared by all the brothers, their surviving mother administering the household and the eldest son controlling the reindeer herds. But ancient usage is sufficiently strong to preserve for the youngest son's share his father's gun and clothing.

Eskimo inheritance rules are illuminating both as to junior-right and primitive property conceptions in general. At first blush a profound difference of principle seems to divide the practice of the Alaskans about Bering Strait, where the father's rifle and most valuable heirlooms descend to the youngest son, and that of the Greenlanders, who generally transmit property to the eldest. But a closer reading of the sources clarifies the situation. The Greenlanders in reality modify the rule cited by the principle of ownership based on effective utilization. Now since no one can take care of two tents or two boats under Arctic conditions, the eldest son, if he already owns such property, will not take possession of his useless legacy. If his brothers are minors, he may abandon it to an utter stranger, and the sons growing up to maturity will have no claims on it. Accordingly, Greenland primogeniture, so far as it exists, does not imply any mystical exaltation of the first-born, and we are not surprised to meet with the explicit statement that among the Central Eskimo it is the eldest son *living with his parents* that figures as the principal heir, while sons and daughters with households of their own are excluded. We need only assume that the Alaskans of Bering Strait observed the Yukaghir or Kirgiz custom with respect to the separation of adult sons and the devolution of the paternal estate on the youngest follows as a natural consequence.

Junior-right, like so many other cultural phenomena, suggests once more the problem of diffusion versus independent origin. It is impossible to avoid the conclusion that to some extent borrowing has taken place. The sporadic occurrence of junior-right among the Naga living in a country where the usage attains fuller development indicates that it is merely with them the weak reflection of an institution characteristic of neighboring tribes. Again, the dual preference for the eldest *and* the youngest son found in the Laws of Manu and in the Toda inheritance law suggests an historical connection. On the other hand, there is not the slightest evidence that the Asiatic custom is connected with borough-english; and since junior-right is so commonly associated with the departure of the elder brothers from the paternal roof any condition favoring such separation would tend to establish this mode of inheritance. That is to say, there is no necessity for deriving the Alaskan from the Yukaghir, or the Yukaghir from the Kirgiz practice.

The data are theoretically interesting from another point of view. Departure of elder sons as an antecedent condition may produce junior-right as a result in remote regions. To that extent, then, there is parallel evolution. But this parallelism is strictly limited. We need merely go back a single step in comparing the evolution of Kirgiz and Yukaghir junior-right in order to encounter quite different phenomena. Preceding and effecting the breaking up of the Yukaghir family is matrilocal residence, while no such cause operates among the Kirgiz. Thus, back of the partial parallelism the lines of evolution lead to the distinct determinants, in other words, we are once more dealing with a case of convergence.

In this extremely sketchy treatment of primitive rules of inheritance it has been impossible to do more than allude to some of the ramifications and intricacies of the subject. In conclusion I must remind the reader that the operation of the customary laws may be far more variable and complex than this brief description would suggest. An unscrupulous Thonga regent may seek to divert the succession from his elder brother's to his own line. Elsewhere failure of issue and extinction of the entire lineage in the presence of a valuable inheritance may stimulate the aboriginal jurists into novel arrangements, establishing original precedents. Finally, the examples quoted suffice to show that inheritance of different kinds of property may follow distinct principles, that sacred objects may be transmitted from father to son while horses are appropriated by the decedent's brothers, that the chieftaincy may descend in the paternal line while real estate is inherited by the sister's son, that office may go to the eldest born while movables and immovables may be passed on by junior-right. Here, as everywhere in ethnology, the obstacles to a clear understanding of reality lie in the bewitching simplicity of catchwords.[9]

References

[1] Keysser: 92 seq. Cranz: 1, 234. Boas, 1888: 582. Nelson: 294. Jochelson, 1908: 769. Bogoras: 633.

[2] Teit, 1900: 293. Dixon, 1905: 224. Speck, 1915 (a); id., 1915 (b): 289. Swanton, 1908: 425. Malinowski: 150. Spencer and Gillen, 1899: 590; ei., 1904: 13. Fraser, J.: 36. Brown: 146. Roth, 1906: 8 seq. Seligmann: 106-115. Merker: 28, 176, 212. Rivers, 1906: 557. Schultze: 197, 318. Radloff: 414-420, 452.

[3] Stevenson: 290. Kroeber, 1917: 178. Speck, 1909: 18. Wilson: 9, 10, 108-114. Bandelier, 1878: 385. Spinden, 1917: 184. Markham: 35. Restrepo: 121. Von den Steinen: 285. Schmidt: 439. Whiffen: 103.

[4] Junod: 11, 6 seq. Maclean: 149. Spieth: 111-115. Ellis, A. B.: 162, 216. Roscoe: 14, 133, 238, 268, 424. Routledge: 121. Torday and Joyce: 91.

[5] Codrington: 60. Thomson: 70, 354-386. Reports, v: 284-291; vi: 162-168. Erdland: 99-113. Tregear: 127-136. Turner: 177. Stair: 83. Barton: 39-60.

[6] Maine: Chap. viii. Baden-Powell: 1-37, 171 seq, 398-423.

[7] Spieth: 116, 191. Von den Steinen: 285. Schmidt: 316. Merker: 28. Bogoras: 677.

[8] Man: 120, 169. Jochelson, 1908: 59. Reports, VI: 167. Keysser: 100. Sapir, 1911: 15; id., 1913: 67; id., 1915: 355. Lowie, 1913: 225 seq.

[9] Dixon, 1905: 226. Russell: 194. Merker: 200. Seligmann: 118. Baden-Powell: 172, 305. Routledge: 143. Maclean: 11, 116. Junod: 1, 303, 383. Spinden, 1917: 185. Tregear: 122-129. Kroeber, 1904: 11. Lowie, 1912: 188. Rivers, 1906: 559 seq. Hodson: 103. Gurdon: 68, 83. Radloff: 416. Jochelson, 1910: 109. Cranz: 1, 247. Boas, 1888: 580. Nelson: 307.

CHAPTER X

ASSOCIATIONS

PRIMITIVE society as pictured by Morgan and his followers is an atomistic aggregate. The tribe consists of units fashioned on a single pattern, the sib concept, all sibs being generally similar in function and of equal dignity; and within each sib the constituent members are on one level of democratic equality. In other words, if Morgan were right, individuals in lower cultures would differ from one another socially only as members of this or that sib. We have already seen that this scheme is inadequate because it ignores the bilateral family; but it suffers from an equally vital deficiency in failing to take into account principles of classification in no way dependent on kinship, whether unilateral or bilateral. Primitive tribes are stratified by age distinctions, by differences of sex and of matrimonial status, and affiliation with one of the resulting groups may affect the individual's life far more powerfully than his sib membership. Herr Cunow was perhaps the first theorist to recognize the part played by age discriminations in savage society, but it is to the late Dr. Schurtz that we are indebted for a systematic treatise on all *associations,* as I propose to call the social units not based on the kinship factor. Somewhat later Professor Hutton Webster in a meritorious compilation described practically the same range of data, but to Schurtz above all others belongs the glory of having saved ethnologists from absorption in the sib organization and stirred them to a contemplation of phenomena that threatened to elude their purblind vision.

Though like other pioneers he erred and erred grievously in many of his interpretations, his insistence on the theoretical significance of associations must rank as one of the most important points of departure in the study of primitive sociology.

In trying to give some notion of the types of association it would be easy to group the facts in a series of separate compartments. But these categories would hinder rather than promote a synthetic understanding of social organization. For example, we might deal with sex dichotomy under one head and with age-classes under another; yet such treatment would lead to all sorts of artificiality. It is true that in Australia the sexes are often rigidly divided in ceremonies, but feminine disabilities are shared by the younger males, so that in one sense the real division at a particular moment is into initiated males and the remainder of the tribe. Elsewhere there is a tripartite division into the married couples, the bachelors, and the spinsters, so that sex dichotomy applies only to the unmarried. Again, there is little doubt that the bachelors' dormitory and the men's clubhouse are often genetically connected; the men after marriage continue to resort for pastime or work to the dwelling they occupied before wedlock. Yet a logical classification might easily lead to a separation of these related institutions. In the present chapter, then, I will rather select a number of tribes from different geographical areas and will describe in each case their social organization apart from sibs and families. In this selection I shall be guided partly by the quality of available literature, partly by the desirability of presenting at least all the main varieties of associational units. In the following chapter the treatment will be topical, embracing a number of points of theoretical interest.[1]

Andaman Islands

Since the Andaman Islanders are sibless, each of their

communities should, on Morgan's theory, resolve itself into an unorganized horde of individuals, but they perversely insist on dividing themselves into groups independent of the sib concept or indeed of relationship in any sense. In every encampment there is a triple arrangement of huts for bachelors, spinsters and married couples, the last-mentioned group intervening between the single men and the single women; and even at the homes care is taken to segregate the unmarried of opposite sex and to have the married couples occupy the intervening space. This classification by matrimonial status and sex is not equivalent to a simple grading by age such as will be encountered elsewhere, since even elderly widows will dwell in one of the huts dedicated for the use of spinsters. Nevertheless, indirectly an appreciable correlation with the age factor is effected since among primitive tribes marriage as a rule is rarely deferred long beyond the girl's physiological maturity, while in the Andaman Islands the economic obstacles to early marriage for the men do not seem to exist. Indeed, the part played in native consciousness by age together with its correlates, conjugal and parental status, appears clearly from the fullness of the relevant vocabulary, which permits an unambiguous definition of any individual of either sex with reference to age and matrimonial condition. Thus, an infant is designated by one term during the first year, by another during its second, by still another during the third and fourth years, while special words define the period from the fourth till the tenth, and from the eleventh to the twelfth years. The husband of a few months' standing is distinguished from the man who has been married for only a few days, and the prospective is differentiated from the actual father of a child, corresponding refinement of nomenclature obtaining for wives and mothers. Among the socially most significant status terms, however, are those relating to the initiation of boys and girls into the status of full-fledged members of the tribe, and the relevant ceremonies demand special notice.

Beginning approximately with the eleventh year both boys and girls are subjected to a probationary period of fasting, during which turtle, honey, pork, and other delicacies are forbidden food. Abstention from these luxuries is regarded as a test of the neophyte's self-denial and the period terminates only at the chief's suggestion. The total period is trisected, each lesser division closing with a formal ceremony that absolves from specific restrictions; in this way the taboos against eating turtle, honey, and kidney-fat of pig are successively removed.

When a lad is permitted to break his turtle fast, the chief boils a large piece of turtle-fat, allows it to cool, and then pours it over the novice's head, those present rubbing the grease into his person, which he may not wash off until the close of the next day. He is then fed with turtle flesh, led to his hut and ordered to sit cross-legged in silence, a group of friends supplying his wants and keeping him awake by chanting. It is believed that he is now entering on an important epoch of his life with its incident trials, hence there is great lamentation by his mother and female relatives generally. These paint and otherwise decorate his person, and with broom-like bundles of leaves in his hands he rises to dance vehemently to the accompaniment of the women's time-beating, while the men look on or participate in his performance. When worn out by his efforts, the youth ceases dancing and mingles with his friends as a member of what might be called the first grade of majority. A similar ceremony raises girls to an equivalent rank in society.

After this performance, subsidiary taboos, say, as to the eating of ray-fish kidney-fat, may be removed by the chief without further ceremony than the necessity of strict silence on the part of the neophyte when first breaking his fast. It is otherwise with abstention from honey, which can again be terminated only by formal procedure. The chief helps the novice to a large portion of the hitherto tabooed delicacy and anoints him with honey, which, however, is washed off in order to guard against the aggression of ants. Silence is again enjoined, but no other prohibitions are recorded. On the following morning the boy, adorned with leaves, wades into the sea and splashes water on himself and the spectators, also ducking his head, the whole performance being considered a magical protection against snakes. Young women passed through a similar procedure, but only after the birth of their first child.

Generally a year after the breaking of the turtle fast comes the final ceremony removing the taboo on pig kidney-fat. The novice's friends organize a pig hunt, a boar being killed for a youth and a sow for a young woman. The candidate receives of the hitherto forbidden food, the melted fat of the pig is poured over him, and he is obliged to hold his tongue, sit still, and remain awake. The next morning he dances as on the first occasion.

For comparative purposes certain facts relating to these performances require attention. First of all, it is clear that in a rough way the beginning of initiation coincides with puberty. More accurately the maturity of a girl is indicated by her assuming a 'flower name,' i.e., a name derived from a flower blossoming at the time of her first menses, this designation remaining in vogue till the birth of a child. Secondly, while it is not obligatory for a boy to undergo the three ceremonies before marriage, many postpone wedlock until they have passed through the several grades and it is a matter of honor to do so at an early opportunity after marriage.

In viewing Andaman society as a whole, we find its members classed in a number of varying ways. The most conspicuous grouping is that into married people, bachelors, and spinsters, since it has an objective equivalent in the spatial arrangement of the camp. Apart from this, it would be exaggeration to speak of sexual dichotomy of the tribe. Though such occupations as shaving, procuring water and fetching wood are reckoned as distinctively feminine, while hunting, fishing, and canoe-building devolve on the men, this division of labor does not imply the separation into practically distinct castes found in some other regions. On the other hand, the assumption of a flower name by mature girls creates a definite demarcation between the members of the female sex who have and who have not reached the age of puberty. The abundance of status terms yields evidence of a further classification of the community none the less real because men or women of the same category are not necessarily bound together by a common purpose but merely share the same more or less honorific appellation. Retrospectively, punctilio in this regard furnishes a plausible partial explanation of teknonymy, as has been previously suggested by Dr. Elsie Clews Parsons. Where the status of a person is appraised differently on his becoming a parent, designation in terms of parenthood ceases to puzzle. The probationary fasting period is of course correlated with the status classification. Roughly it has been found to coincide with the age of adolescence, but the subdivisions of the initiatory period are manifestly no longer correlated with any physiological condition.

On the whole, the Andaman Islanders are less rigorously organized than many other peoples will be found to be; nevertheless, the segmentation of their communities according to definite principles not connected with kinship is an undeniable fact.[2]

Australia

While the Andaman Islanders exhibit associational groups in a sibless society, Australia furnishes one instance after another of the coëxistence of associations and sibs, the former frequently playing at least as important a rôle as the latter. Since Australian conditions have been repeatedly described in popular or semi-popular books, a summary treatment seems permissible. Several features recorded for the Andamans are equally characteristic of the Australians, and in connection with certain additional principles, such as the hegemony of old men and a sense of feminine disabilities, they have produced a more conspicuous division of society along associational lines.

First of all, the matter of sex dominates social activity in a distinctive way among nearly all Australian tribes. To be born a girl not merely determines industrial and economic employment, nor is the import of womanhood exhausted by the theory of feminine inferiority. The Kirgiz women, as already shown, are both practically subordinate and theoretically inferior to men, yet that does not bar them from tribal festivities, where they participate on practically equal terms. But to the Australian woman the public activities of the male are largely forbidden mysteries shrouded in fabulous tales *ad mulierem*. It is true that her disabilities are shared by the uninitiated lads, but since initiation is each male's birthright there is after all genuine sex dichotomy: the men form a secret society for which every woman is ineligible. This fact must be collated with the data on sib affiliation. Sex dichotomy is bound to rend asunder the bond that might conceivably unite all male and female members of the sib, for by grouping all the men in a tribal association it supplants sib solidarity with what Professor Webster properly calls 'sexual solidarity.' An Emu man who constantly associates in ritualistic performances and political assemblies with Eagle-hawk, Bat, Crow and Frog men will develop for men of all sibs a sentiment of class consciousness that is simply impossible under the circumstances between men and women of the Emu sib. True, all Emu individuals must abstain wholly or largely from the flesh of their totem, but parallel dietary restrictions hold for women as women. The Yualaroi, according to Howitt, prevent females from eating emu and their eggs; and among the central tribes no woman, irrespective of her sib, may eat a brown hawk. Thus, even in matters of food, sex figures as a rival of the sib motive; the fact that an individual is a woman is not less significant than that she belongs to a certain totem group.

But while sex is socially far more important in Australia than among the Andaman Islanders, age and status also play their part. The Kariera and Kurnai are typical in segregating the bachelors from the rest of the camp, though there is no corresponding separation of spinsters. Generally, too, there is great nicety in distinguishing the stages of social progress. The Kurnai infant is called by one term, the boy of eight or nine by another, while the uninitiated youth living with his parents, the novice, the bachelor, and the mature paterfamilias are each designated by a distinct term. Elsewhere the several steps of the initiation are carefully discriminated. A noteworthy trait is the relaxation of the food taboos for old women.

The initiation ceremonies of the Australians resemble those of the Andaman Islanders in being performed about the time of puberty, but otherwise the differences are rather remarkable. Among the Andaman Islanders every one undergoes the period of probationary fasting with its successive grades of freedom from dietary taboos, but the performances are not reckoned an essential preliminary to marriage. In Australia, however, no one is allowed to have a wife until he has passed through the corresponding rites; and in the central region there is even an analogous nubility rite for the females. Among the Andaman Islanders the initiation rites are not conceived as mysteries never to be revealed to women, as they are in most Australian tribes. In other words, the Australian initiation is definitely a rite preparatory for matrimony and assertive of masculine ascendancy; even where the nubility ceremony occurs it is conducted by men in the presence of male spectators, while women are almost always barred from the more important proceedings of the boys' initiation. Finally, the character of the initiation itself is different. There are tribes like the Kariera who content themselves with decorating the neophyte in a conventional manner, say, by tying a string tightly round each biceps. But far more commonly the Australians promote lads to the status of manhood by an infinitely more severe ordeal, the knocking out of a tooth being characteristic of one area, circumcision and subincision (additional operation on the genital organ) of another. In still another region the youths ready for initiation are segregated in a lonely spot, where they receive inadequate food and are severely cuffed and kicked by the old men, a trial to be borne without wincing; besides which they are compelled to cut and roll heavy logs or perform other kinds of hard labor. When they have passed their examination satisfactorily, the old men in charge give to each novice a sacred stick ('bull-roarer') to be secreted in a safe place. In short, formally the Australian initiation is a severe test of the adolescent's self-control. But substantially, too, it is a far more solemn affair than that of the Andamans. It is a genuine propaedeutic course in tribal knowledge and ethics: the neophyte is exhorted to obey implicitly the teachings of his elders and to keep mum in the presence of the uninitiate on the arcana divulged to him; he is told what food is tabooed to him and also gets practice in finding a living by his own efforts.

One detail associated with the Australian initiation merits special mention. Among the secrets imparted to the neophyte is the real cause of a curious buzzing noise that has alarmed him prior to initiation and which the women and children are taught to regard as the voice of a spirit presiding over the ritual of initiation. He now learns that it is produced simply by whirling a bull-roarer, i.e., a flat stick or stone slab, through the air at the end of a string. Strangely enough, the greatest stress is laid on the necessity of keeping the women in ignorance of the true nature of the bull-roarer, which they are never permitted to view. Indeed, formerly some tribes had the rule that if a man showed a bull-roarer to a woman, both must be punished by death. The reason for now singling out this feature will appear later. In exceptional tribes the bull-roarer is indeed associated with initiation but no attempt is made to conceal it from the female sex.

Initiation, while qualifying a youth for marriage and other social functions, by no means raises him to a status of equality with the older men. His place in society is indeed a distinctly humble one for many years to come; he has nothing to say in affairs of political moment and even in the matter of food he will be well along in years before he is freed from the last restrictions. These are the facts which Schurtz and, before him, Cunow rightly insisted upon as proving that apart from the sib organization the Australians are subdivided into social units not less significant in the individual's life. Every person belongs from birth to the male or the female sex moiety, to the caste of prerogative or of disabilities; every person in the course of his life progresses through a series of social steps, at each of which his behavior must conform to a conventional pattern. A Warramunga man may belong to the Wild-cat sib and be free to eat emu flesh so far as any sib regulation goes; he must nevertheless abstain from emu food till he is at least a middle-aged man. He may be of either moiety and of any sib or family whatsoever, but if he is an initiated bachelor he will live divorced from his family, sib and moiety in the company of the other bachelors of the encampment. Thus, in everyday activity the joint influence of sex and age may well outweigh that of the kinship groups.

There is one feature of Australian organization which I have advisedly refrained from mentioning until the present. Over a large section of the island continent there holds sway what is known as the *class* system, which appears in a four-class and an eight-class variety. For our purposes consideration of the former will suffice. I have already mentioned the occurrence of the dual organization in Australia. Frequently the moieties are subdivided each into two classes, making four altogether in the tribe. Until recently our authorities generally represented the four classes as matrimonial groups, the principle on which they regulated marriage being as follows. Taking the patrilineal Kariera for illustration, we may designate their exogamous moieties as A and B, the former composed of classes 1 and 2, the latter of classes 3 and 4, numbers being substituted for the phonetically difficult native names. Then according to Kariera law a member of 1 cannot marry into either his own class or into 2 because both are divisions of his moiety. But neither may he marry into 3; he is restricted by the four-class system to one and only one class in the choice of a mate, viz., 4. However, it may be asked by what method an individual's class affiliation is determined, and here develops the most curious part of the scheme. The child of a man of class 1 must belong to its father's moiety because descent among the Kariera is patrilineal; nevertheless it cannot belong to his *class,* but must enter the complementary class, to wit, 2. Correspondingly, when a man of 4 marries a woman of 1, the child is 3 since it must belong to his moiety and cannot belong to his class. If instead of the Kariera some matrilineal four-class tribe were taken, a corresponding principle would apply; every child there belongs to the mother's moiety and to that class in her moiety which is complementary to her own. An interesting trait of this system is the fellowship of grandparent and grandchild in the same class. Taking the Kariera, a man of class 1 not only has children of class 2 but also a father of that class since father and son belong to the same moiety, though never to the same class. Thus, father's father and son's son are fellow-members.

I said above that this scheme of Australian marriage systems is the one followed until recent years because at present Mr. Brown's researches indicate that while the four-class scheme is formally correct it does not penetrate to the core of the phenomena. For, as had already been clear from earlier accounts, though any one class might marry only into one of the three remaining classes it is not permissible for *any* member of class 1 to marry *any* individual of 4, there being still further restrictions. Mr. Brown showed that the essence of the arrangement was simply that a man must marry a maternal uncle's daughter (or a woman so designated in the aboriginal nomenclature) and no one else. The four-class scheme fits the data merely because the possible mates as just defined are bound to belong to the opposite moiety and to the class different from the prepotent parent's. But in reality marriage is regulated by consanguinity alone, by a particular kind of cross-cousin relationship, and it is for this reason that I have mentioned the relevant facts merely under the caption of preferential mating.

Mr. Brown's interpretation explains admirably why the supposedly marriage-regulating classes really fail to determine the union of individuals since these depend on the cross-cousin relationship. But with their matrimonial occupation gone it is not easy to understand what may be the functions of the classes. That they exist as social units of some sort, is attested by a dozen observers, and often they have definite appellations where the moieties have none. Some scholars have suggested that they are merely halves of moieties, but this is an utterly ridiculous assumption, for in that case they would follow the same rule of descent instead of the curiously indirect one they do.

Although I am not acquainted with any fully satisfactory theory of the Australian classes, Cunow's contribution must be cited as a suggestive addition to the far from ample stock of original ideas relating to the theory of social organization. Cunow assumes that the classes represent agestrata and are associated with the rule that only members of the same stratum are potential mates, while the moieties were originally two distinct but intermarrying local groups. Then, since a child cannot belong to the same age-group as its parents it is intelligible why the rule of class descent is of the observed anomalous type: the child is of the parent's moiety but not of his (or her) class because the class scheme is at bottom precisely a method for differentiating age.

Cunow's theory suffers from a number of difficulties. If the classes are age-grades, class affiliation should of course vary with age, yet as a matter of fact each Australian belongs to his class from birth until death. Cunow assumes that affiliation was made immutable to prevent a man's being married to two wives of distinct grades. According to his scheme there are three grades, that of childhood, that of an initiate, and that of an old person, i.e., of one who has a child in the group of initiates. When Cunow insists that only age-mates were permitted to marry, he means that husband and wife must both belong either to the grade of initiates or to that of elders. Now on this assumption it may evidently happen that a man after ten or fifteen years of wedlock takes a second wife who will be of his own and the first wife's grade but who will remain in that grade after her husband and her fellow-wife have attained higher status. That is, she will be of like status with her fellow-wife's eldest son. In order to prevent this condition, Cunow argues, it was necessary to render the class names permanent like the sib designations. It cannot be denied that the reasoning is ingenious, but nothing indicates that it rests on more than sheer conjecture.

Furthermore, since there are only four class names instead of the six demanded by the tripartite organization of each moiety, Cunow is driven to assume that the members of alternate generations designated by the same class name are not really members of the same class but of distinct classes which merely for convenience' sake are similarly named. This again seems an arbitrary interpretation. Cunow himself calls attention to the fact that in many Australian kinship nomenclatures grandparent and grandchild are designated by one term used reciprocally; to him this is an inexplicable phenomenon, which, however, readily suggested the application of the same class name to grandparent and grandchild. But another interpretation is possible. Grandparent and grandchild may be designated by one term precisely because by the four-class scheme they are what they are ostensibly, members of one and the same class, in which case classes and age-grades would not coincide. Nevertheless, in spite of its drawbacks Cunow's theory furnishes so simple an interpretation of the enigmatical feature of class descent that we may cling to its core in the hope that some day the difficulties in the way of accepting it will be removed.

Summing up the Australian situation irrespective of all hypotheses, we find that in most tribes every individual is simultaneously a member of a variety of social units. He is born into a sex, a moiety, a totem sib and a class, with all of which his affiliation is permanent; he is also born into a certain status from which he advances through a special ceremony into that of maturity, and by less perceptible stages into that of a full-fledged elder. At any one period of his life his duties and privileges may depend as much on his associational as on his kinship connections.[3]

MASAI

While among the Australians sibs and associations are perhaps of equal importance, the former are definitely less significant in Masai society. Not that it is possible to ignore them. In earlier times they regulated marriage, and at present religious functions and specific cattle brands are connected with the major or lesser kinship groups. Moreover, chiefs and medicinemen are recruited exclusively from the paramount section of a single sib. Nevertheless the activities dependent on affiliation with the sib are meager compared with those affected by membership in other units.

First of all, there is a spatial separation of the bachelors and their paramours, the immature girls, from the rest of the community (see p. 50). This condition is strikingly different from that of the Andaman Islanders, where bachelors and spinsters are sedulously segregated by the interposition of married couples.

Secondly, males and females are definitely grouped according to status. As among the Australians, every male is subjected to a puberty ordeal (circumcision), through which he attains the position of a warrior. During the period of initiation and until the wound is healed he ranks no longer as a boy but as a neophyte (literally, 'recluse'), while for the first two years following he is designated as an apprentice ('shaved one'). Until 28 or 30 he figures as a full-fledged brave, whereupon he marries, leaving the bachelors' kraal and assuming for the remainder of his life the dignity of an elder. Since the initiation and recruiting periods are obviously preparatory, we need recognize only three stages for males, that of boy, of warrior, and of elder, the bachelor braves playing the most prominent rôle among this warlike people. As an equivalent of the boys' circumcision the girls undergo clitoridectomy after the first menses and are subsequently known as novices until the healing of the wound. Then they maintain a distinct rank until the menopause, whereupon a new word defines their status, which only alters with the blanching of the hair. Unrelated persons of either sex address each other by terms dependent on their relative status.

With these stages there are linked definite usages. Married women are distinguished from girls by iron necklaces and ear-rings; indeed, without the latter no wife would dare confront her husband. They are also recognizable by their long garments. Boys and girls put increasingly large blocks of wood into their ears, while the bachelors and elders wear chain ear-rings and bracelets. After circumcision the bachelors carry the sword, spear, club and shield distinctive of their rank, also donning a special cap, ostrich-feather headdress, cape, anklets, arm-clamp, calfskin garment, and a piece of goat's skin for the waist. They plait their hair, subsist entirely on meat, milk and blood, and must abstain from intoxicants. Before recovery from circumcision the novices mimic women as to dress and earrings, and if they have stood the ordeal without flinching they are permitted to shoot small birds and wear them on the head.

In addition to the dichotomous division of society into the inmates of the warriors' kraal and the rest of the settlement and the essential trisection of the male population by status there are still other groupings. It is obvious that the tripartite organization of the males links together in a single grade the benedict of thirty and of eighty. A suggestive subdivision of this step has taken place, those elders having circumcised children being distinguished by the privilege of wearing a certain kind of ear-ring. However, it does not appear that elders of this type are united by any feeling of solidarity. There is distinction among elders, inasmuch as owners of large herds who have many children may wear an arm-ring of elephant's tusk or buffalo horn as a badge of affluence. This ill-defined criterion, however, has also failed to produce a determinate social group and remains interesting mainly as demonstrating the variety of classificatory devices to which the natives resort. On the other hand, there is a division based on the period of initiation that is of far-reaching significance. The circumcision rite not merely separates the categories of boy and warrior but underlies a far more refined classification of society.

ASSOCIATIONS

All boys circumcised during the same quadrennium belong to the same 'age.' There follows a period of three and a half years during which no initiation takes place. After this interval comes another quadrennium during which boys are circumcised. Reckoning from an apparently arbitrary or at least unknown starting-point, the Masai designate the individuals circumcised during one quadrennium as of the 'right-handed' circumcision, those of the subsequent quadrennium being 'left-handed.' That is, the age-classes are not dextral or sinistral relatively to each other, but absolutely so by virtue of their position with reference to the point of departure. A right-handed age and the immediately following left-handed age are said to constitute a 'generation.' The processes by which one age-class relieves its predecessor as representative of the warrior grade and by which correlated classes are welded into a generation must be described in some detail.

Immediately after initiation and restoration to health the apprentices find themselves in a peculiar position with reference to the full-fledged warriors. In order to figure as genuine braves the tyros must first secure a name for their class, a distinctive design for the decoration of their shields, and a separate kraal. About the former there is no special difficulty since an appellation is bestowed by the headman of the tribe in return for a herd of cattle; but the shield pattern is not so readily acquired. Black figures for the purpose are selected by the most eminent elder, but it is the red coloring of the shield that is held as really characteristic of a warrior's dignity. No sooner, however, have the novices attempted to paint their shields red and to construct a camp than the warriors swoop down upon them, attacking the new establishment, and if possible efface the paint. If the older men are victorious, the recruits must bide their chance, improving the meantime with raids against hostile tribes. If they exhibit conspicuous prowess in such enterprises, the warriors may gracefully assent to recognize them as their peers; otherwise the youths must conquer opposition by force. When they finally succeed, there are then two distinct bachelors' kraals in the district, though united in all martial undertakings. But this is an anomalous and transitional condition according to native standards. Soon the older warriors decide on their departure, leave singly after an appropriate feast, marry, and settle down in individual homes. When all members of the age-class have married and discarded the bachelors' kraal, they collectively assume the rank of elders, leaving their successors in sole possession of the warrior's estate.

The significant thing in all this is that simultaneous initiation creates ties transcending the bonds due to equal status. Though two age-classes may temporarily share the degree of bachelor, they remain distinct units. Similarly, the new group of married men is by no means simply merged in a society of elders. The only close tie, formed at a much later period, is between the dextral and sinistral classes of a couple, which are formally united into a 'generation,' receive a common name and adopt a distinctive arrow brand. But before and after this union the age-class preserves its name and individuality and determines its members' actions. It is, above all, an agency regulating sex relations. Girls initiated during a certain quadrennium are reckoned as belonging to the age-class of the boys circumcised during that period; and no Masai is permitted to have sexual relations with a woman of his father's class. On the other hand, fornication with a woman of one's own class is not considered an offense, so that widows or divorced women may consort with their husband's fellow-members. A visitor from another district at once enters the kraal of an age-mate, who withdraws from the hut, leaving his guest to sleep with his wife. In this there is no choice, for an unobliging host incurs the curse of his age-mates. A wife beaten by her husband may seek refuge with one of his age-mates, and thereafter the husband will let her in peace lest he be cursed by his class.

On the strength of our data it is fair to say that the group of elders does not form a firmly knit unit but that all the social solidarity within that status is attached to the smaller associations described, the generation and particularly the age-class. Reverting in conclusion to a comparison of the Masai associations with their sib organization, the initial appraisal of their relative importance seems fully vindicated. Even a feature so peculiarly typical of the sib as its marriage-regulating function is here more prominently connected with the age-class. If from Masai communities the division into sibs were eliminated, an ample residue of social relations would still obtrude itself on our notice; but without the bachelors' kraal, the initiatory subgrades, and the age-classes, Masai society would assume an aspect of baldness and drab monotony.[4]

Banks Islands

In the Banks Islands, as among the Masai, there is a sib structure that is overshadowed by associational units but these vary fundamentally in the two areas; indeed, the Melanesians introduce us to entirely novel principles of aggregation. Nevertheless, one feature that arrested our attention in surveying the Australian field recurs in the Banks Islands in a still more conspicuous form. The cleavage of society into sex moieties here attains its maximum intensity. Not only are women debarred from public solemnities, but even in everyday life there is a well-nigh complete dichotomy. Men neither eat nor sleep with their wives but in a separate establishment, which boys try to enter at the earliest opportunity. Hence the males, as in Australia, constitute a sort of tribal secret organization. Yet there is an all-important difference: admission in no way depends on puberty, but may occur at any age; and it is secured not through an ordeal involving personal disfigurement or bodily mortification but by the payment of a fee. Further, the men's society is not a single body or at best one in which the older men are set off from the younger initiates by more or less imperceptible degrees of dignity, but comprises an hierarchically graded series of divisions.

The tangible manifestation of masculine exclusiveness is the village clubhouse, a lounging-place and refectory by day and a dormitory by night. The house is subdivided into a varying number of compartments of successively higher rank, each with its own oven as a rallying-place for members of equal degree. Failure to join means remaining a nonentity in point of social estimation; hence, while admission may be deferred, it always occurs sooner or later. "If a man cannot enter the *Sukwe* (club) he has to feed with women and this may sometimes so excite the pity of a friend that he may undertake to act as introducer, knowing that he will thereby have to spend a large sum of money." In the lower ranks the introducer, often the candidate's maternal uncle, defrays most of the expenses; in the higher degrees the charges devolve on the novice, his kindred and friends. The act of initiation consists in the ceremonial eating of food by the tyro's new messmates; but all the club members regardless of rank seem to profit by his payments.

As a respectable place in the community is impossible without club affiliation, so a gain in prestige is directly proportionate to advancement in the society, which invariably demands increasingly greater pecuniary sacrifices. Hence the man who has climbed to the highest rung of the ladder is quite exceptional, ranks as a chief in real life, and figures as the hero of legend. He is then in a position to retrieve with interest the fortune spent in achieving eminence, for he can wring exorbitant fees from subsequent aspirants to honor. The common herd never dream of such eminence; though they enter the club as boys, they will be lucky to rise to the middle degrees of the organization. It is true that though the divisions are definitely localized in the clubhouse, each invested with a clearly defined relative rank, there is an abstract possibility of leaping at once to a high station in the society. But practically the fees would be too extravagant to convert theory into reality, and all that is ever attempted is to dispense with entrance into some of the very lowest compartments, which have accordingly fallen into decay in some of the villages. Besides, even the theoretical chance has one limitation: in order to progress beyond a certain point in the club a man must belong to another organization of a related though distinct order that will be treated below.

The club of the Banks Islander is seen to be bound up with property rights. It is only the man of wealth who can reach the highest degrees and thus acquire prestige. Yet the aboriginal conception is not that of avariciously hoarding wealth but rather of displaying one's greatness by exhibiting contempt for property. So a man of the loftiest status in the club may still promote his renown by providing the lavish entertainment associated with certain festivals; nay, a suggestion of niggardliness on these occasions would go far to destroy his influence.

The several grades of the club were anciently marked off with such rigor that to enter a compartment higher than one's own was to incur certain death. Yet there is very little individuality about the various steps. They have their distinctive masks or hats, some use peculiar pudding-knives, and only in the higher degrees are members allowed to drink the native stimulant, kava. But it is difficult to say in what way the functions and privileges of adjoining degrees differed. The essential idea seems to have been simply that by making an additional sacrifice for a new initiation a member was entitled to higher honor, which fact was expressed in visible terms by the assignment of a spatially distinct compartment.

The significant traits of the Banks Island system at once stand out in relief when we compare it with that of the Masai. The East African scheme is thoroughly democratic, that of Melanesia is an essentially timocratic one. Every Masai is bound to advance from boyhood to bachelorhood and from bachelorhood to the elder's estate, and the differentiation of age-classes among elders carries with it no suggestion of superior and inferior caste; an outward emblem for prolific and wealthy elders has been reported, but the practical consequences of this distinction are negligible. It is of course part of this generally democratic conception that status should be attained collectively by a group of approximate coëvals. In the Banks Islands the exaction of increasingly prohibitive admission fees inevitably prevents the steps from being gained with equal rapidity by age-mates. At every stage beyond the very lowest perhaps we must be prepared to encounter a commensality of varying years and vastly different social prospects. Seated round one oven and for the time being on a par in the public eye are the elderly laggard whose straitened circumstances will keep him from transcending the plane to which he has just struggled by his utmost efforts, and the soaring youth for whom family connections have gained precocious preferment, bidding fair to raise him in course of time to the pinnacle of native aspirations.

So far, however, only one phase of the complicated associational life of the Banks Islands has been described. Its complement is represented by a host of secret organizations, 'Ghost' societies, as the aborigines call them, of which the diminutive island of Mota boasts not less than seventy-seven. Unlike the clubhouse the equivalent meeting-place of the Ghost associations, whether a lodge or mere clearing, is not situated in the village but in the relative seclusion of the bush, and the path leading to it is tabooed to all non-members. Notwithstanding Codrington's and Rivers' noteworthy contributions to the subject, the intricacies of these organizations have been by no means completely unraveled and in this chapter the merest sketch of what seems fairly certain must suffice.

The secret organizations vary enormously in character, but ordinarily they figure as so many additional clubs. With one another and with the men's club they share the feature that entrance is dependent on an initiation and the payment of a fee. But some of the societies may be entered even by boys who have not yet joined the club, while for others that would be simply unthinkable. In certain organizations several men may enter together and jointly pay the amount requisite for an initiation; but no such economizing is permitted by the more important societies.

Practically all the societies have distinctive masks or objects to be carried in the hand. These objects are exhibited to the uninitiated only when the members stalk about the island on certain solemn occasions and not even then at close range. At all other times non-members, and especially women, must under no condition see or come near the sacred articles. Most of the societies also possess badges of a totally different nature, with which the desirability of entrance is largely bound up. These emblems consist of the leaves of croton plants; when they are stuck into the ground by a member, they protect his property against the inroads of all tribesmen who are not fellow-members of his fraternity. Any one who should transgress the taboo must pay a pig to the affronted society, and a similar fine is required if a non-member cuts down or uses the particular species of croton serving as a badge for some organization. Since women are ineligible to all fraternities, they are obliged to refrain from destroying any of these plants. Joining a particular organization is thus in a measure equivalent to taking up a policy in an insurance company against loss of property. Since protection is secured only against non-members, the smallest organizations are naturally the most effective from this point of view, which results in an amusing cycle of vicissitudes. One of them becomes popular because of its protective value, automatically loses its efficacy as the membership increases, hence sinks in general estimation, dwindles in numbers, and may then again be revived. Certain of the fraternities are not liable to these fluctuations because the motives for seeking admission are quite independent of those connected with property insurance. For example, entrance to the *Tamate liwoa* organization would be sought as an indispensable preliminary to gaining the higher degrees in the club.

A feature characteristic of the secret societies is the attempt to terrorize the uninitiated. A man will blacken his face and body to irrecognizability and sally forth, a cane in the left hand and a club in the right. He hits people who do not get out of the way with the club and continually moves about his stick so that no one can see it distinctly. Occasionally there also occurs the wanton destruction or spoliation of a luckless individual's property by an organized band of fraternity members. Thus, when a candidate is admitted to the *Tamate liwoa,* it is necessary to pull down a house, which is chosen by the novice's father. The members, partly in disguise, rush out, scare off women and the uninitiated, and destroy the dwelling selected. At a later stage in the ritual of admission not only the candidate but any person met by the fraternity who has not yet attained high rank in the club receives a beating.

Certain proceedings connected with entrance into the *Tamate liwoa* recall the tribal initiation of Australia. The one secret learned by admission into the Melanesian fraternity is how to produce a curious sound by rubbing a stick on a stone. Though the details are not alike, this strongly suggests the Australian attitude toward the bullroarer. Again, though no mutilation is inflicted, the tyro must undergo all sorts of trials during a probationary period of a hundred days. People come to throw his food into the fire, break his knives and fine him if he voices a complaint; difficult tasks are set, and when he offers the product of his labor, it is spurned. Here again the analogy is general rather than specific, yet it is illuminating as an example of the notions commonly underlying a formal acceptance into the fold in the cruder levels of culture.

If we now pass in review the position of an individual Banks Islander with reference to his various social relations, their potential multitude is startling. The significance of sex has already been sufficiently commented upon. Another affiliation follows from the occurrence of the dual organization. Every person is thus born into an exogamous moiety, and since the moieties are subdivided into sections with specific taboos he automatically enters still another group. Sooner or later he will join the men's club, belonging successively it may be to nine or ten of its grades. But concomitantly he is likely to hold membership in half a dozen of the secret fraternities, either in order to safeguard his possessions or to enhance his social status. It hardly requires proof that to reduce the social organization to the sib divisions would obliterate all that is genuinely distinctive of the Banks Islands scheme of society.[5]

PUEBLO INDIANS

The multiplicity of ceremonial organizations among the Pueblo Indians converts their social scheme into a bewildering maze. Fortunately since the publication of Kroeber's guide-book there is fair promise of seeing the light of day as a sequel to much labyrinthine wandering.

The religious corporations of the Zuñi may be listed under two heads. On the one hand, there is a Masked Dancer society comprising by necessity all the males and no females; secondly, there is a series of fraternities into which entrance is optional and open to both sexes. The function of the Masked Dancer society centers in the magical production of rain under the direction of Rain priests;

the fraternities cure the sick and give demonstrations of magical power.

From the constitution of the Masked Dancer society it appears that we must conceive it as the equivalent of the tribal club of other areas. But though there is a supreme director of the club it is strictly speaking not a single men's organization as in Australia, but a series of half a dozen units, each associated with a distinct ceremonial chamber. These six subdivisions symbolize the cardinal directions, zenith and nadir being classed in this category. This arrangement of spatially separate lodges would suggest the Melanesian grouping of messmates were it not for the absence of grades in the Southwest: the Zuñi groups appear as coördinate social units. Membership in a particular one is settled at birth; the infant is allotted to the lodge of the husband of the obstetrician who first touches him. It is this man who acts as sponsor for the child both at the earlier involuntary and subsequent voluntary initiation, the latter taking place at the age of twelve or thirteen. At the second initiation the boy is severely whipped by members who impersonate gods. Each novice, for several boys are admitted jointly, receives a rain-maker's mask, which becomes his individual property and is buried at death. On this occasion the boys learn for the first time that the supposed gods, who have removed their masks, are only men. The god-impersonators put their masks on the neophytes and surrender their whips to them, and the boys thereupon lash their former tormentors. Finally the mummers replace the masks on their own heads, and the novices are warned not to divulge the initiatory mysteries lest their heads be cut off with a stone knife. It happens, but very rarely, that a man in later life alters his lodge affiliation from choice, though in such a case he may at any time return to that of his boyhood. Further, a man convicted of adultery with a fellow-member's wife may be expelled and driven to seek admittance into another chapter; yet

ASSOCIATIONS

there seems to be a strong sentiment against expulsion even in extreme cases.

Since the Pueblo Indians have a remarkably well-developed sib organization, the question arises whether and to what extent sib affiliation affects membership in the several ceremonial units. From the mode of entering a club lodge, it is clear that mere membership in a subdivision of the men's club has nothing to do with the sib. But there are special offices in the Masked Dancers' ritual which are more or less associated with the sib. Thus, the director-general of the club is invariably of the Deer sib, certain masks are in the custody of an Eagle man, and the rain songs at the close of a quadrennial ceremony must be chanted by a Frog man. Yet there are numerous deviations from this rule of determining ceremonial office, which fairly often alternates between the member of a certain sib and a son of that sib, who with maternal descent and exogamy can of course belong to any sib whatsoever except his father's. The rain priests of the tribal club are theoretically associated with definite sibs, yet in the actual personnel of the priesthood the same departure is noted as in the case of other positions of dignity. The heir-apparent and other associates of a ranking priest may be his sons, who cannot possibly be of the same sib; sometimes they are brothers or sister's sons, in other words, sib-mates; and sometimes they may not even be kindred of any sort. On the other hand, there are fetiches manipulated by each set of priests, and these are stored in specified houses and are definitely linked with the sib units.

In general, then, the rank and file of the club are not grouped according to sib membership, but association with the sib principle occurs for ceremonial club offices, being especially conspicuous in the case of the priesthoods and their fetiches.

Far less prominent are the bonds between the fraternity and the sib organization, as becomes at once obvious from the mode of entrance. The usual basis for joining is a cure effected by the fraternity; the patient is not compelled to enter if he pays adequate compensation to the acting practitioner, but commonly he prefers to enter the society. In a typical fraternity 34 of 42 members had entered in this fashion. Another method is compulsory initiation when a person has stumbled into an executive session of the fraternity. With one or two exceptions there is a possibility for the member of one fraternity to shift his allegiance to any other, in which case a purely perfunctory ceremony takes the place of regular initiation. The independence of the sib implied in the regulations of entrance applies in virtually equal degree to the ritualistic offices; in an important fraternity Professor Kroeber found that only a single function was necessarily executed by members of a specified sib.

Professor Kroeber has fortunately not confined his attention to the Zuñi, but furnished an analysis of the Hopi fraternities as well. These are theoretically of special significance because previous writers treated the fraternities as a natural outgrowth of the sib, as basically representing the ritualistic aspect of the sib concept. This view seemed to derive support from the fact that Hopi fraternities frequently bear the same names as sibs and that native speculation ascribed the founding of a society to its namesake or some other particular sib. By tabulating the concrete material available as to the sib membership of Hopi fraternities, Kroeber shows conclusively that in most cases the alleged bond does not exist. Of 35 Snake fraternity members only 7 belong to the Snake sib; only 3 of the 10 Antelope fraternity members are of the Horn sib; not more than 6 Rabbit sib people are found in the supposedly associated fraternity. My personal census in the field largely corroborates Kroeber's conclusions, though with the qualification that ritualistic office commonly descends in the sib. Thus, in the village of Mishongnovi the Snake dance is performed by members of the Corn, Parrot, Bear, Badger,

Eagle, Cloud and Masiqwai sibs, but the Lizard sib, which represents the Snake sib of other villages, holds the leader's position. The mode of entering the Snake fraternity is quite like that generally followed by the Zuñi in joining any of their fraternities: a man cured by a Snake member joins in lieu of paying a fee. It is clear that very little importance attaches to the coincidence of name. In the village of Shipaulovi there is no Snake sib and the directorship of the Snake fraternity is vested in a Bear man, from whom it will descend to his sister's son, i.e., another Bear man. In one respect Kroeber may have overstated the case inasmuch as one or two of the societies seem to recognize a birthright of members of a certain sib to fraternity membership. Nevertheless, generally speaking, the validity of his interpretation is sustained.

In other words, Pueblo society no more than that of other regions can be regarded as an atomistic structure of sib blocks. A dual division on sex lines is created by the compulsory initiation of all men into a club, and within this tribal organization affiliation with a special lodge is again independent of the sib, whatever may be the rule of succession to ritualistic service. The curative fraternities of the Zuñi are even more largely free from the sib influence, and the same may be stated for the comparable societies of the Hopi. Thus, the importance of the associational as a concomitant of the kinship grouping is manifest. As Kroeber points out, an individual of sib A may belong to family B, have a father of sib C, join fraternity D, priesthood E and lodge F; his sib mate may be of family D, have a father of sib E, and join fraternity F, priesthood A and lodge B. There is no reason to suppose that the one bond represented by the sib must at all costs take precedence over all other social connections. It is as though we assumed that a man who votes the Republican ticket is bound to act as a Republican at the meeting of his church, in an assembly of his labor union, and in the privacy of his home

Manifestly there is no need to assign to any one social tie a predominant position; the individual normally acts as a member of the group with which he is at the time linked and these several groups need not come into contact at all, whether by way of coincidence or collision.[6]

CROW

In the chapter on Property mention was made of the Tobacco society of the Crow into which individuals of either sex gain entrance by payment of a fee to their adopter. The novice is properly trained during a preliminary period, learning certain songs selected for him by his 'father,' i.e., sponsor, and gains the status of complete membership with the privilege of henceforth planting the sacred Tobacco in the course of a public solemnity. There are numerous chapters of the Tobacco order and the tyro naturally joins that of his 'father,' but there is a considerable *esprit de corps* among the several subdivisions, so that members of any and all chapters may participate in the proceedings, though only those of the adopting group are morally entitled to a share in the initiation fee and give the novice the choice of their sacred objects. The Tobacco initiation is quite devoid of attempts at chastisement or mutilation of the candidate; it centers in his receiving appropriate instruction, ceremonial songs, regalia and prerogatives in return for the heavy payments demanded. Formerly it was usual to apply for admission but latterly members pique themselves on the number of their adoptive children and are likely to urge individuals to join. It has also been customary for a person in a position of hardship, say, when his own or a beloved relative's life seemed in danger, to pledge entrance provided that things turned out in accordance with his desires. Another difference divides ancient from modern usage. At an earlier stage membership was restricted to a relatively small number of elderly couples and the religious features were predominant; more recently it has become a matter of social prestige to belong to the order, so that almost all adults are members and even young children have been adopted. Nevertheless, the ceremonial character of the society has not by any means been obliterated. The preservation of the tribe is still believed to hinge on the continued planting of the sacred Tobacco, which symbolically represents the stars. From a strictly social point of view the Tobacco organizations are important since an altogether special bond unites the persons standing to each other in the ceremonial relationship of father and child, who will treat each other with the loving-kindness of genuine kindred. Another feature that merits notice is the tendency to initiate husband and wife at the same time.

At the present day there is also a quartet of secular clubs that figures prominently in tribal life,—the Night Hot Dancers, Big Ear-Holes, Last Hot Dancers and Sioux Dancers. These share the same performance, the Hot Dance, which was introduced by the Hidatsa in the 'seventies of the last century. Practically all of the men now living belong to one of these clubs. Unlike the Tobacco chapters, these do not exact an entrance fee, nor is there any suggestion of formal initiation. Each club aspires to have a large membership, and consequently so far from extorting payment the members will present substantial gifts to clubable men in order to make them join, individuals of known liberality who are likely to entertain members being specially sought. It even happens that persons of renown in this regard are enticed to transfer their membership by a tempting offer of property. These clubs must be conceived as in large measure mutual benefit associations. If a member of the Big Ear-Holes is required to perform a certain amount of labor, all his comrades in the society will coöperate. When one man seeks initiation into the Tobacco order, every club member helps accumulate the amount requisite for going through the performance in due style. On such occasions the candidate's club acts in precisely the same fashion as his sib. From time to time feasts are celebrated by the club, which has no special assembly lodge but meets in the tent of one of the comrades.

These clubs, however, represent merely the bowdlerized edition of an earlier form of association that still flourished in the second half of the nineteenth century. In 1833 Prince Maximilian of Wied-Neuwied had found no fewer than eight of these organizations; somewhat later they dwindled down to four,—the Muddy Hands, Big Dogs, Foxes, and Lumpwoods; and about the 'seventies only the two last-mentioned were in full vigor. These clubs were in part military associations seeking to gain renown on the battlefield, and they were accordingly confined to male membership, which, however, did not lead to a rigid exclusion of the women. On the contrary, women commonly participated in the feasts and excursions of the clubs. There was a public function assigned by the tribal chief each year to one of the clubs,—the preservation of order during the communal buffalo hunt. Further, each society had its dance and song, but religious features were absent to a surprising extent in view of the well-known tendency of Plains Indians to invest all sorts of phenomena with a religious glamor.

The method of joining a military club was as informal as that noted for the clubs of today, that is, there was no adoption, no solemn procedure of any sort, no purchase. If a member died, his comrades sought to replace him by a brother or close kinsman and would offer gifts to this person in order to gain his consent. But there was no obligation for the several brothers of a family to belong to the same society, and in any of the clubs all sorts of families and sibs were represented. Even when there was no vacancy the members might offer presents to a renowned warrior inducing him to join their band, whether he already belonged to another club or not. A personal grievance likewise would lead to an occasional change of affiliation, but on the whole membership was for life. Some persons joined a club simply because they liked its songs and dances.

Like the modern clubs, the military associations are coördinate units. Each embraced young and old men, each might in rotation execute the civic duties of a police force, each had an equivalent set of songs and performances, and all modeled their internal organization on a single pattern. Of course, equality of status did not extend to an imitation of the adult clubs by the boys, who under the name of a Hammer society mimicked the activities of their elders.

Impossible as it is to give in this chapter a complete account of the Crow scheme of military associations, even a moderately vivid picture of their spirit is out of the question unless one of them is described in some detail. Accordingly, I will select for this purpose the Fox organization.

The Foxes were subdivided into several minor groups according to age, but in point of dress, songs and eligibility to posts of honor there was no differentiation. There was little in the way of distinctive badges for the rank and file except for a foxskin cape worn by the members. Some of the officers, however, were distinguished by special emblems. Their dignity, it is essential to note, had nothing to do with any such status as attaches to the presidency or secretaryship of one of our organizations. The functions corresponding to such offices were executed rather informally by the older members. As for the Crow officers, their eminence rested on prospective or tried prowess in battle. In the spring of every year the older men of the club summoned the others to assemble in a lodge and choose the eight or ten braves who were to shed lustre on their association. Of these, the four standard-bearers had the most clearly defined duties. Two of them were presented with curved and two with straight staffs; in sight of the enemy they were expected to plant these emblems into the ground and defend their standards without budging, even at the risk of their lives. To abide by the rule, whether for survival or death, meant achieving fame in the society and the tribe; to retreat was to lose caste and be despised as "a menstruating woman." Owing to the danger incurred by acceptance of office, many would decline the peril-fraught honor but in case of necessity the elders could force a mandate on a particular person by stealthily touching his lips with a pipe. Even close relatives thus compelled a young warrior to become an officer, not because they wished him ill but because they were eager to have him gain distinction. With the first snowfall of the year the arduous duties of the position ceased, and the following spring a new incumbent would receive the fatal lance.

One of the most remarkable phenomena linked with this society is the spirit of rivalry that animated the Foxes and the Lumpwoods, i.e., the two clubs which ultimately gained the ascendancy among Crow military organizations. There was no trace of personal hostility in this relationship, which was sharply defined. In certain games the Foxes with their wives were pitted against the Lumpwoods and their wives; in war each club tried to score the first blow struck against the enemy; and in the beginning of spring there was a brief period during which a Fox might abduct the wife of a Lumpwood if she had at some previous time been his mistress, and vice versa.

The last-mentioned custom was remarkable in several ways. As soon as the kidnapping season had been announced by mutual signals of defiance, the men of both clubs sallied forth to seize former mistresses now wedded to members of the rival society. Resistance was in vain, for if necessary there was recourse to force. Least of all might the husband offer the slightest sign of resentment or he would completely lose his social standing in the tribe and become the common laughing-stock. The only way for a woman to evade abduction was to throw herself on her former lover's generosity. For the husband the ideal behavior was to assume a brazen face and encourage the abductor in his enterprise. As soon as the Foxes had kidnapped a Lumpwood woman, they took her to one of their lodges, where she received from her paramour's kin all the finery customarily bestowed on a bride. The next day there was a solemn procession in which the members exhibited their captive to the public gaze. However, she must ride double only with a Fox of conspicuous war record, otherwise the Lumpwoods would throw her and her companion from the horse they rode. Apart from this the Lumpwoods attended merely as interested bystanders, making an ostentatious display of feigned indifference. Usually the kidnapped mistress was soon abandoned by her lover, but under no condition might she return to her former husband's tent. A man who took back a kidnapped wife not only utterly disgraced himself but brought ignominy on his society as well and the rival club was at liberty to cut up the blankets of all the members.

Almost equally curious was the custom connected with martial competition. If a Fox struck the first blow of the season, the Lumpwoods thereby forfeited the right to sing their songs, which became for that year the property of their rivals. All this emulation was confined to the period from early spring till the first snowfall, when it automatically ceased, the two organizations thenceforth living together in perfect amity.

To sum up. The classification into sibs constituted but one type of social grouping, which was criss-crossed by other divisions of equal and perhaps even greater significance.[7]

Hidatsa

The Hidatsa, too, had a series of military organizations, many of which closely resembled those of the Crow, as might be expected from the partial identity of names. Thus, the Fox and the Lumpwood, Hammer and Dog societies are common to both tribes, and often the similarities are of the most detailed kind. The hooked-spear officers of the Crow Foxes reappear in the Hidatsa equivalent with precisely the same duties; and in both tribes the Dog men carry peculiar rattles of dewclaws tied to a stick, while certain officers wear slit sashes. But while corresponding clubs were fundamentally alike and doubtless served similar social needs of the members, the mode of entrance was wholly different. As already explained (p. 242), the Hidatsa were not invited to join individually and gratuitously, let alone, were tempted by desirable presents, but were obliged collectively to buy membership, which was henceforth renounced by the previous holders, so that the whole transaction was tantamount to a transfer of property rights.

But there was another basic difference between the two schemes in addition to the differences as to mode of acquiring membership. The adult men's clubs of the Crow were coördinate organizations with which men were as a rule permanently associated. Among the Hidatsa the military societies formed a graded series, and in the course of their lives the men passed from one grade to another. Since purchase played so decided a part in the arrangement, it might be conjectured that this is merely a replica of the Banks Island scheme. Yet there is a profound distinction between these systems. Among the Melanesians there is individual promotion, so that the affluent youth may soon stride past the indigent dotard; with the Hidatsa advancement is uniformly collective, and the buyers are all agemates. In other words, the Hidatsa recognize a dual basis for membership, purchase *and* age. No group of persons can automatically become Foxes or Dogs when they have attained a certain age; they can only become members by paying the fees exacted. On the other hand, no man can become a Fox or Dog alone but only in conjunction with a whole body of novices all about his own age.

An interpretation of this dualism will be given in the next chapter; at present our concern is with the stratification of society consummated by the Hidatsa scheme. Since there was variation in detail at different periods, I will take a definite point of Hidatsa history for illustration. In 1833 Prince Maximilian found all the male population beyond very young boys grouped into ten societies. The youngest were the Stone Hammers, aged from ten to eleven; lads of fourteen or fifteen formed the Lumpwoods; youths of seventeen and eighteen owned the next higher society; and so it went on to the Raven club, which united the oldest men in the tribe. Strictly speaking, it is not true that the males of the tribe were divided up among ten societies but rather into ten *age-classes*. The societies really correspond to degrees, and according to the Hidatsa scheme, which precluded automatic promotion, certain degrees would be vacant whenever an age-class had sold its membership since its members might have to wait a long time before being able to buy the next higher degree. In other words, each age-class was a permanent unit but it was not always possessed of a definite place in the series. In speaking of age-classes, however, we must recollect that these Indians never knew their ages by years and that the grouping found was only an approximate one. In this as well as in other respects a comparison with the Masai age-classes is illuminating. In both tribes there is a certain latitude from the point of view of a strict age-grouping. Some Masai are initiated at a rather earlier age than others either because of economic reasons or because circumcision occurs only during certain periods; the age-class is thus indeed constituted of approximate coëvals but arbitrarily includes some and excludes others who might just as well be otherwise classified. Among the Hidatsa the age-class is likewise founded on rough-and-ready principles: a group of playmates decide to buy their first society together, but as soon as they have been united in the purchase this joint experience converts them into a definite social unit. Thereafter the Masai or Hidatsa individual's age-class affiliation is immutable like his sib relationship.

There was a somewhat amusing alliance between alternate Hidatsa age-classes. When age-class 2 attempted to buy the membership then held by age-class 3, it could depend on the assistance of class 4, and indeed of the other even classes, while a similar bond united the odd classes. The reason for this alternation may be sought in the mutual relations of adjoining classes. Between these there was necessarily a 'class struggle' since the sellers would always extort the highest payments possible; hence alternate classes would be united by their common antagonism to the intermediate class, which was the prospective flayer of the lower group and the future victim of the higher one.

While the Crow women had no societies of their own, their Hidatsa sisters had a smaller but parallel series slightly enlarged by borrowings from the neighboring Mandan. The mode of purchase was identical with that of the men's clubs, and there was even a direct affiliation with the male series, inasmuch as certain groups of women aided the odd and even male classes, respectively. Naturally these organizations were not distinctively military, but indirect martial associations are recorded. The Skunk women would celebrate the slaying of an enemy, while the Enemy women performed a dance in commemoration of braves who had fallen in a recent engagement. In the higher units of the series, notably the Goose and the White Buffalo Cow organizations, the secular aspect practically vanishes, the most significant activities being of a magico-religious nature. The Goose women were expected to promote the growth of the corn, while on the white Buffalo Cows devolved the duty of luring buffalo herds to the village in times of scarcity. These societies were accordingly invested with an atmosphere of holiness quite absent both from the lower members of the series and the majority of the military clubs. In the women's societies the age factor was not wanting, but it was less clearly marked. On the one hand, it was customary to admit one or two infants to the older groups of White Buffalo Cows and Goose women. Secondly, it is doubtful whether all the women were grouped into these societies; it is quite possible to infer from the data that while fellow-members were generally approximate age-mates many women belonged to no definite age-class, in other words, that the sex as a whole was not stratified by age.

In addition to the age-classes, which will have to be discussed later from still another angle, the Hidatsa had distinctly sacrosanct bodies linked with bundles of holy objects and performing the correlated rituals. Every Hidatsa had a birthright to his father's bundle and ceremonial prerogatives, but before the potential privilege could become an actual one it had to be validated by purchase from the parent, siblings usually combining in the transaction. This would not create an association but would merely fortify a kinship group were it not for the fact that the same bundle and ritual were shared by distinct families, so that individuals totally unrelated were brought together by identical ceremonial prerogatives and ritualistic performances. Thus, despite their hereditary character, the Hidatsa bundles led to the formation of still another type of social unit. In these ritualistic associations women played a part, notably as custodians of the bundles bought by their husbands.

Thus, a typical Hidatsa individual would be born into a sib, but would in boyhood help in the formation of an age-class, passing with his comrades from one degree or society to another through successive joint purchases; and independently of these affiliations, he would by purchase of the patrimonial bundle become a member of one of the ritualistic associations of his village. A woman, while perhaps not necessarily connected with an age-class, was often so affiliated, and also held a definite relation to her husband's bundle.[8]

Summary

Brief as is the preceding survey, it demonstrates the importance and variety of associations both in sibless communities and those organized into sibs. Sex moieties, divisions on the basis of matrimonial status, social clubs, secret fraternities, all crisscross the bonds of the family and the sib, creating new units of incalculable significance for the individual's social existence. So far, then, Schurtz's view of primitive society is wholly justified, and the description of the Morgan school must be recognized as inadequate.

References

[1] Schurtz: 1-82. Webster.
[2] Man: 40, 60 seq, 108, 207. Parsons: 282.
[3] Cunow, 1894: 25 seq., 144 seq. Spencer and Gillen, 1904: 257, 328, 498, 611. Howitt: 509 seq.
[4] Hollis, 1905: xvi, 260 seq., 280 seq. Merker: 16, 67 seq.
[5] Rivers, 1914 (b): 1, 60-143. Codrington: 101 seq.
[6] Kroeber, 1917 (a): 150-188. Stevenson: 62-107.
[7] Lowie, 1913: 147-211.
[8] Lowie, 1913: 225-354.

CHAPTER XI

THEORY OF ASSOCIATIONS

IN the preceding chapter I have merely pointed out the important position of associational groups in primitive social organization. No attempt was made to grapple with the problems, historical and sociological, that develop from these data. In examining these it will be well to begin with an exposition of Schurtz's scheme, which furnishes a convenient set of pegs for the attachment of theoretical considerations.

SCHURTZ'S SCHEME

According to Schurtz's theory, a profound difference in the psychology of the sexes underlies the differentiation between kinship and associational groups. Contrary to received notions, woman is an eminently unsociable being and refrains from forming unions on the basis of like interests, remaining centered in the kinship group based on sexual relations and the reproductive function. Associations created or even joined by women on equal terms with the men are rare and must be considered weak imitations of the exclusively male associations. Man, on the other hand, tends to view sexual relations in the light of episodes and fosters the purely social factor that makes "birds of a feather flock together." Thus the psychological differences between men and women lead to a sociological separation. There is another form of cleavage within the family circle, but one that not merely destroys but also creates social ties. The antagonism between the older and the younger generation that separates parent and child forms the germ of a classification by age, which Schurtz accordingly regards as the oldest type of associated grouping.

Schurtz does not contend that the kind of age-grouping found in the simpler cultures has a purely natural basis. It rather represents a blending of physiological and conventional factors. The typical condition is the tripartite division of a community into children, marriageable youths and girls, and married couples. Here the separation of the first two groups depends on a natural difference, while that of the second and third is an artificial one. Schurtz sees its *raison d'être* in an effort to regulate sex relations on the Masai plan of permitting free love to the young and establishing firm conjugal bonds in later life. In such a society the bachelors form the best-marked and organized group, the spinsters representing merely a degenerate reflection of it on account of the feminine inaptitude for comradeship. Entrance into the important body of bachelors at the time of puberty is properly signalized by complicated solemnities, while the girls' initiation into the status of maturity is of relatively insignificant character in correspondence with the less definite organization of the spinster class.

Schurtz assumes that wherever a greater number of age-classes occurs this is the effect of secondary elaboration of the tripartite division. Thus he recognizes the possibility that simultaneous initiation may establish a bond of union; but he holds that the resulting classes have been superimposed upon the simpler scheme. In the case of the Hidatsa and related systems, which he specifically deals with, he derives their secondary origin not only from the great number of the age-classes but also from the qualifications for entrance. For it is one of his axioms that the grouping by physiological age and matrimonial status preceded all others, purchase as a factor for the admission into a social unit representing a later stage of evolution.

In intimate connection with the age-classes and more particularly with the dominant rôle played by the organized bachelors there develops the men's house. It is characterized as a structure in which the adult but single men cook their meals, work, play, and sleep, while the married men dwell apart with their families. Women and children are usually barred from the premises, while the mature young girls may freely consort with the inmates. Though he regards this as the archetype of the institution, Schurtz recognizes that its observed representatives deviate widely from the assumed norm. Such divergences he interprets invariably as later differentiations and he admits that several lines of evolution have been pursued. For one thing, the bachelors' dwelling may retain its hold upon the married men and thus be transformed into a general club and even become a dormitory for all the adult males. On the other hand, the bachelors' house loses its original character if its facilities for convivial assemblage and dancing are accentuated, which may even lead to the admission of women. Still other lines of development will convert it into a sweathouse, a council chamber, an armory, an inn or a workshop, to mention only some of the possibilities. Schurtz does not ignore the objection that the men's house may be characteristic only of certain related stocks of mankind and that its distribution could be explained as the effect of historical connection rather than of a sociological law. Indeed, he admits that the most typical forms are restricted to the Malaysian family. Nevertheless, the ethnographic evidence as a whole leads him to the conclusion that societies have an inherent tendency to develop the men's house, which is merely "the external phase of a simple, extremely obvious (*nahe liegenden*) division into age-classes and in this sense an almost inevitable transitional stage in the evolution of higher social structures."

But sex and age do not remain the only socializing agencies. At a more developed stage of society the tendency to exclusiveness makes itself felt and clubs arise, supplanting the earlier age-classes. This trend is fostered by a differentiation according to rank and wealth. Slaves and paupers are barred from the age-classes, which thus naturally acquire a club-like character. Where entrance fees are required, the age-qualification and with it the age-stratification of society vanishes, and instead there appears a system of grades such as characterizes the organization of the Banks Islands. Clubs may follow either of two lines of development: they will grow into ceremonial associations, representing distinctively religious orders; or they will stress the strain of conviviality peculiar to male groups from the start and become groups of banqueters whose symposia have no more serious aim than the promotion of good-fellowship.

Secret societies represent the last form of association founded by masculine gregariousness. They are not a necessary stage in the social evolution of associations from the primeval age-grouping, nor can all the secret societies be traced directly back to age-classes, though an indirect relationship may be assumed. Their activities are manifold. One prominent trait is the attempt to keep women and slaves in subjection, a feature not unintelligible from the basic nature of associations as conceived by Schurtz. As for the formal side of secret organizations, that is also traceable to phenomena in the older age-divisions with their trying initiation solemnities. The beginnings of an ancestral cult, such as many secret societies practise, is likewise discoverable in the tribal initiation rites, which are often linked with corresponding notions. The secret societies have developed this germ, together with such special elements as the wearing of masks, skull-worship, and the use of taboo rules for the safeguarding of property. Deriving support from their supposedly mystic powers, these organizations sometimes degenerate into gangs terrorizing and robbing the uninitiated. But they are also likely to assume at least the forms of a body dispensing justice. They will punish the membership for breach of confidence or like transgressions and inflict penalties on outsiders for antagonizing their interests; they may develop into the one body wielding political power and as such they have even been utilized by British colonial administrators. Though the potentiality for secret organizations is ever present, particular representatives of the type are eminently unstable units. For one thing, Schurtz believes that in the long run it is impossible to preserve the secrecy of the watchwords or other arcana. He considers as typical the development noted in Central Brazil, where one people excludes women from all dances, while another tribe admits them to ceremonies of lesser dignity; where in one region the bullroarers must never be seen by a member of the female sex and are carefully concealed in the men's house, while in a neighboring section of the country they are coolly exposed to the public gaze. Elsewhere the atmosphere of secrecy is dispelled and the society persists as a mere club, and in still other parts of the globe the secret organizations are transmuted into a constabulary force serving the chief or into ecclesiastical orders that may even come to admit women.

This brief sketch suffices to indicate the character of Schurtz's thinking. In comparing his system with Morgan's a fundamental likeness is revealed by closer scrutiny. Schurtz envisages phenomena wholly ignored by Morgan, but like Morgan he imposes upon his data an evolutionary scheme that purports to possess general validity and thus seeks to formulate sociological laws. It is true that Schurtz has a keener sense of the intricacy of social arrangements, so that he makes allowance for a multitude of developments from the same standard condition, as in the case of the men's house. But this does not prevent him from adhering rigidly to his chronological sequence so far as it relates to the main stages of evolution. He is as certain of the uniform priority of age-classes when compared with clubs or secret organizations as Morgan is of the necessary priority of matrilineal descent. To be sure, Schurtz frequently makes obeisance to the principle of transmission, but at bottom he yields to it little more than lip-service; indeed, he expressly states that for sociological inquiries the problem of diffusion is insignificant.

Now, as has been previously pointed out, the question of diffusion is never insignificant. Though it may be conceded that the mere knowledge of how one people borrowed a given trait from another does not itself furnish the key to its comprehension, proof of borrowing has a most important bearing on interpretation since it involves the proof that in the borrowing society the feature has not arisen spontaneously, that its occurrence there does not rest on the operation of a sociological law by which it was inevitably bound to evolve. Of course it may be contended that it would have evolved independently, but that is mere allegation. So it might be contended that the aboriginal Britons would have developed the art of writing, that the Alaskan Eskimo would ultimately have hit upon the notion of domesticating reindeer, by their own unaided efforts. Such assertions are indeed readily made but not so readily demonstrated. To apply this principle to the case under discussion, it is by no means a matter of slight moment whether the men's house in Assam and in the Banks Islands developed separately, or whether they and the comparable institutions of Indonesia all originated in a single spot. On the former assumption it is hard to deny some tendency on the part of human societies to segregate the male population in a distinctive structure. On the latter hypothesis the strength of that tendency shrinks considerably and the question inevitably obtrudes itself whether a phenomenon that has traveled over so great a distance may not have gone still further, in short, whether all samples of the men's house, no matter where found, are not traceable to one fountain-head. Were this inference established, the argument on behalf of a sociological force impelling the creation of a men's house would have not a leg to stand upon; the utmost that could be contended for would be a tendency to copy the institution when it had once been presented for imitation.

Schurtz blinks at these rather obvious facts and accordingly his marginal remarks on historical connection, while indicating that he has heard of diffusion as an active principle in culture history, do not imply its efficient use by himself and cannot be taken to divide his method logically from that of Morgan. This holds more especially since Morgan's own occasional rodomontades about historical connection put to shame the most swashbuckling of recent diffusionists: not only has the sib in his opinion a unitary origin but for the systems of relationship even diffusion will not do and nothing short of racial affinity is made to account for a like classification of kin by the Zulu and Hawaiians! All of which in no way interferes with the essentially unilineal evolutionism of his system. In substance, then, Morgan and Schurtz stand on the same plane and employ the same conceptual machinery; and Schurtz's distinction lies in having very materially expanded the field of sociological inquiry rather than in the suggestion of new methods of cultivation. Pioneer husbandmen in science, to borrow Turgenev's telling phrase, lightly skim the surface of the virgin soil with the hoe, and deep-ploughing comes later.

After these introductory comments I will now discuss the more important general problems connected with associations.[1]

Sex Dichotomy

With fulsome iteration Schurtz insists on the basic mental

difference that leads men to aggregate in associations, while the unsociable females of the species rarely so much as timidly copy the masculine prototypes or join in the societies of the other sex. One need hardly be a perfervid feminist to repudiate this sort of reasoning. In order to enter a society something more is required than the will to membership. Considering that women who should venture near an Australian initiation ground were mercilessly killed, it is not remarkable that relatively few exposed themselves to so perilous a form of blackballing. Nor is it by any means certain that the organization of independent societies would always be permitted by the men; in some regions at least the total absence of women's clubs may be due largely to the discountenancing attitude assumed by men. But even this factor is not required to explain the empirical facts. The Altaian and Kirgiz data have already been cited in another chapter but are especially illuminating in the present connection. The Altaian household drudge has simply no time for sociability, whether her husband would grant his consent for such indulgence or not. Given a different division of labor and her Kirgiz sister, laughing to scorn the abstract tenets of Islam, mingles freely in the company of other women and men, even engaging in spirited singing contests with members of the other sex. Whatever psychological differences may divide the sexes—and I am not prepared to deny them—the lesser gregariousness of women can hardly be reckoned an innate feminine failing so long as fairly definite alternative explanations suggest themselves for her limited associational activity.

One of the most convincing of these interpretations has been suggested by Professor Karl von den Steinen and Dr. Paul Radin. The former conceives the Bakairi mysteries as an outgrowth of the chase, as hunters' festivals, from which women would naturally be barred. Similarly, Radin remarks that a soldiers' society would not be likely to admit women, nor a sewing circle men. The exclusion is in these cases almost automatic. We may add that the activities of women are frequently not of a nature that calls for concerted effort in the same sense as, say, a warlike enterprise. A potter can execute her earthenware just as well without a crowd of fellow-workers. On the other hand, Mooney found that among the Cheyenne the women were organized into a variety of guilds devoted to the higher reaches of the various feminine crafts, such as tent-cutting, quill embroidery, moccasin decoration, and rawhide painting. Entrance was granted only on payment of heavy fees, and altogether these organizations are plausibly likened by their discoverer to our trade unions. Here the necessity for gaining expert advice and recognition in a chosen field of endeavor has caused an exuberance of societies that puts to shame the dogma of woman's unsociability.

Indeed, the North American data amply illustrate the baselessness of Schurtz's cardinal principle. In the Crow Tobacco society women figure at least as conspicuously as men and are commonly admitted with their husbands, a married couple almost representing a fixed unit. A similar notion is found among the Hidatsa, where the medicine bundles are usually transferred to a buyer through his wife, who is first expected to touch the fetiches with her body. The presence of distinctively feminine organizations in this tribe has already been noted, and if they are less numerous than the comparable men's societies they are also more sacred in character. As Radin points out, the Midewiwin, the great secret society of the Central Algonkians, admits both male and female shamans. In a number of Omaha organizations a communication from a definite supernatural being, such as Thunder or the Buffalo, was the prerequisite to membership, and female as well as male visionaries were eligible. In the Southwest men are certainly more active ceremonially than women, yet women too have their separate societies and dances. The Shoshoneans of the Great Basin have nothing that can properly be classed as a society but in the various dances and festivities men and women engage on equal terms.

Not less instructive than the many instances of feminine gregariousness in North America are the reported analogies to the men's house or tribal society of other continents. These, as shown in a previous chapter, are confined to the vicinity of the Pacific coast, a circumstance suggesting the possibility of transmission from a common center. What interests us more especially in the present connection, however, is that the implications of the American institutions are as a rule quite different from their apparent parallels in Australia and Melanesia. In the Banks Islands there is a genuine dual organization on the basis of sex, by which all the initiated males eat, live and sleep apart from the females. The Australians do not carry the separation so far but at least make it apply to religious and public life. In both areas all the men are initiated and none of the women can be. Now it is precisely this basic view of woman's status, functions, and disabilities that strikes the Americanist as essentially un-Indian and to which there is hardly any parallel in North America.

For example, in the northern half of California there is a men's house and also a men's secret society, but the underlying conceptions seem very different from those recorded for other continents. In the winter the Hupa men sleep apart from the women, occupying the village sweathouse, but they eat with their wives throughout the year and live with them in brush shelters during the summer. The segregation of the men is thus only a partial one. Moreover, it does not involve the exclusion of women from ceremonial activity: there are female shamans and at the time of Dr. Goddard's sojourn the Brush dance was conducted by an old woman, the only person conversant with the 'medicine' required. In the same general region the Shasta have men's winter dormitories and clubhouses where the men sweat, lounge and gamble. Shasta ritualism is almost wholly restricted to shamanistic performances, and here we are astonished to find that shamanism is largely a feminine profession. That is to say, in spite of the men's house ceremonial activity is to a considerable extent in the hands of women, which would certainly strike an Oceanian as the acme of topsy-turvydom. Passing on to the Maidu, we discover a somewhat different condition of affairs. The large structures corresponding outwardly to the Shasta men's house coincide only partly in function; they are sudatories but not so much clubs as ceremonial chambers. Furthermore, the women are not barred from these dance lodges on all occasions but actively participate in a number of the ceremonials; female shamans occur, though fewer in number than among the Shasta, and attend the annual shamanistic festival in the sweathouse.

So far, then, the Californian data do not indicate a rigid separation of the sexes on Oceanian principles. Segregation of the men during part of the year is quite consistent with common meals and in a measure with common ceremonies. However, the Yuki, Pomo and Maidu have a secret organization that at first strongly suggests the tribal society of other continents since there is a rigid exclusion of all women. Indeed, the somewhat journalistic report of Powers on the two former tribes invests their societies with a distinctly West African and Melanesian atmosphere in its description of mummers impersonating evil spirits to cow women into submission and chastity. But in appraising the significance of the Californian phenomena we must not forget one all-important fact. The secret society was not a group comprising *all* men; initiation was not an indispensable stage in the individual's life, was not a prerequisite to matrimonial status. This feature suffices to distinguish it from the tribal society of the Australians. It may be compared with the Ghost organizations of the Banks Islands, but such parallelism as exists is not significant in the present connection, i.e., as regards the existence of sex moieties. These cannot be ascribed even to the Pomo because, as Dr. Barrett's report demonstrates, in most of the dances an indefinite number of both men and women might participate, while in two others the number of each sex was prescribed. In addition there were five dances in which only men took part, though at least two of these were witnessed by women; and two women's dances from which, however, men were not barred. Accordingly, the exclusion of women (together with uninitiated men) from one esoteric ceremonial cannot be subsumed under the caption of sexual dichotomy. Similar considerations apply to the Maidu case. The position of the female shamans of that tribe is especially interesting when we contrast it with that of corresponding practitioners in Queensland. The Australian woman doctor practises certain tricks, yet she must never handle or look upon the charms that constitute the regular physician's stock-in-trade and "on no account is she ostensibly allowed to join in the secret deliberations of the other medical practitioners."

What holds for California applies likewise to the Pueblo region. The subterranean ceremonial chambers ordinarily used as men's workshops and lounging-places are known to have once served also as the bachelors' dormitories and as sweathouses; but their existence does not interfere with the free association of both sexes in daily life. Even the additional feature of a men's tribal organization has failed to compass that end or to prevent women from participating in ceremonial activity. In the extreme north the Alaskans differ from the other Eskimo in having a men's, especially bachelors', dormitory combining the features of a clubhouse, town hall, dancing pavilion, and tavern. Women are indeed excluded at certain times, but there is no general prohibition against their admission. On the contrary, they bring food to the men's house twice or three times a day, sitting by their relatives during the repast, and frequently not only attend performances but take an active part in them. In the light of all these facts Hearne's observation that the Chipewyan of the Mackenzie River region excluded women from all dances and took pains to segregate even young boys and girls with the vigilance of an English governess must stand as anomalous. This point of view represents a 'sport,' a deviation from the typical attitude not only of North American Indians generally but of the Northern Athabaskans as well, since other members of that family, such as the Dogribs, are known to permit the joint participation of both sexes in dancing.

To sum up, the North American Indians neither display that masculine exclusiveness which would divide a tribe into sex moieties, nor are their women devoid of gregariousness since they join men socially when they are allowed to do so and also by no means rarely have founded associations of their own. That these are fewer in number than the men's can be readily accounted for in the manner suggested above without recourse to the mystical absence of an instinct of sociability.

The African phenomena, on the whole, fall in line with those from North America. Notwithstanding the usually inferior status of women, there is generally free intermingling of the sexes in social intercourse. It is true that, especially on the West Coast, there are secret societies to which women are not admitted but, as Radin has pointed out, the number of parallel women societies is considerable. Some of the men's organizations are charged with military and juridical functions, others devote themselves largely to the chastisement of adulterous wives, so that the exclusion of women is natural. Far more significant is the positive fact that the women's societies are not only fairly numerous but of social importance. Thus the men's Poro society of the Mendi in Sierra Leone is balanced by the women's Bundu; and while it might be an exaggeration to claim equal rank for the latter, its sacred character is acknowledged by the male population. "No man would under any consideration venture to approach the 'Bundu bush,' for the mystic workings of the 'Bundu medicine' upon any delinquent are believed to be exceedingly severe; and this belief is so firmly rooted in the minds of all men that Bundu girls when under the protection of the Bundu medicine can walk about unattended within bounds, knowing that they are perfectly secure from the smallest molestation." For a region somewhat farther south Miss Kingsley reports that a man who should penetrate into the female mysteries would be killed just as a woman would be put to death if she encroached on the privacy of a men's secret gathering. The women's organizations are at least often connected with the initiation of girls at the age of puberty, and it is worth noting that the African girls' introduction to the status of maturity is often conducted with as much solemnity as the equivalent rites for the boys. This certainly does not hold true for Australia nor, so far as I know, for Melanesia.

Altogether there is no rigid separation of the sexes in Africa; and while ceremonial segregation occurs, it differs *toto coelo* from that reported for Australia and Melanesia since the women do not always form an unorganized congeries of individuals but often constitute tribal or more restricted societies of their own. Considering that for a very large portion of Asia Schurtz himself could discover no male tribal society nor indeed any other association, we must repudiate as unwarranted the doctrine of virtually absolute unsociability as a secondary sexual trait of womankind. Schurtz has mistaken a phenomenon of restricted geographical distribution for one of universal range; and even within the area favorable to his view he has ignored the difference between an institutional result and an organic disability. When the influence of the division of labor combined with that of the male gerontocracy in Australia or of the male club in the Banks Islands are shown to be favorable or at least not antagonistic to the formation of women's associations, then and only then it will be possible to interpret the paucity of sororities in direct psychological terms implying greater or lesser gregariousness.

Before leaving the subject of sex in relation to associations, I must briefly deal with a subject of apparent triviality but of the utmost ethnographic interest. In the sketch of Australian initiation rites mention was made of the bull-roarer, the buzzing musical implement tabooed to women. The care taken to prevent the uninitiated from learning that this simple device lies at the bottom of the weird sounds heard by them is extremely ludicrous; it appears as though the essence of all the mysteries centers in the production of the whirring noise, as if all the pother and pain of a protracted ritual came to a climax from the native point of view when the boys were told how to make a little slat boom through the air. It is sufficiently remarkable that the death penalty was inflicted on a woman who discovered the secret and on the man who divulged it. But far more striking is the occurrence of the same association of ideas in different regions of the globe. The following samples will suffice for illustration.

Among the Central Australian Urabunna the uninitiated are taught to believe that the sound is the voice of a spirit "who takes the boy away, cuts out all his insides, provides him with a new set, and brings him back an initiated youth. The boy is told that he must on no account allow a woman or child to see the stick, or else he and his mother and sisters will tumble down as dead as stones." Farther north the Anula of the Gulf of Carpentaria tell their women that the whirring of the bull-roarer is made by a spirit who swallows and afterwards disgorges the boy in the form of an initiated youth. At the initiation of the Bukaua, who live about Huon Gulf, New Guinea, the novices' mothers are told that the booming of the leaf-shaped slats is the voice of an insatiable ogre that swallows and then spews out young lads. In the Solomons and the French Islands the bull-roarer is likewise kept secret from women, who believe that the strange noise represents the voice of a spirit, and the Sulka of New Britain impress upon them the additional fact that this being occasionally devours the uninitiated. The foregoing illustrations are culled from the Australian and Oceanian literature. But what shall we say when similar conceptions appear in various parts of Africa? The Ekoi of South Nigeria allow no woman to see the bull-roarers or to know the cause of the sounds they produce, and similar regulations are reported from the far-off Nandi in East Africa. Among the Yoruba the women are indeed permitted to view and even handle the bull-roarers, but under no condition must they see one in motion. A jocular gesture of Dr. Frobenius' suggesting that he was about to whirl it through the air sufficed to throw the females into fits, and it is reported that in ancient times women who appeared during a procession of the men's society when these implements were swung through the air were mercilessly put to death. Finally must be cited a South American instance. The Bororo of central Brazil have mortuary rites at which bull-roarers are swung, this being the signal for all the women to run into the woods or hide at home lest they die. Here the belief is shared by the men that the mere sight of a bull-roarer would automatically cause a woman's death and Dr. von den Steinen was cautioned to avoid fatalities by never showing a purchased specimen to the women or children.

These resemblances are hardly of a character to be ignored. They aroused the interest of Andrew Lang, who explained them as the result of "similar minds, working with simple means towards similar ends" and expressly repudiated the "need for a hypothesis of common origin, or of borrowing, to account for this widely diffused sacred object." In this interpretation he has been followed by Professor von der Steinen, who remarks that so simple a contrivance as a board attached to a string can hardly be regarded as so severe a tax on human ingenuity as to require the hypothesis of a single invention throughout the history of civilization. But this is to mistake the problem. The question is not whether the bull-roarer has been invented once or a dozen times, nor even whether this simple toy has once or frequently entered ceremonial associations. I have myself seen priests of the Hopi Flute fraternity whirl bull-roarers on extremely solemn occasions, but the thought of a connection with Australian or African mysteries never obtruded itself because there was no suggestion that women must be excluded from the range of the instrument. There lies the crux of the matter. Why do Brazilians and Central Australians deem it death for a woman to see the bull-roarer? Why this punctilious insistence on keeping her in the dark on this subject in West and East Africa and Oceania? I know of no psychological principle that would urge the Ekoi and the Bororo mind to bar women from knowledge about bull-roarers and until such a principle is brought to light I do not hesitate to accept diffusion from a common center as the more probable assumption. This would involve historical connection between the rituals of initiation into the male tribal societies of Australia, New Guinea, Melanesia, and Africa and would still further confirm the conclusion that sex dichotomy is not a universal phenomenon springing spontaneously from the demands of human nature but an ethnographical feature originating in a single center and thence transmitted to other regions.[2]

Age-Classes

Coördinate in Schurtz's system with the doctrine of a sexual difference that leads men to form associations and women to cling to kinship units is the principle that the associations created by male solidarity are one and all derived from age-classes. But the value of these two complementary tenets must be very differently estimated. The former proved an unacceptable generalization caused by the theorist's submersion in a special set of ethnographic data. On the other hand, the conception of society as a structure segmented into age-layers, while developed by Schurtz with one-sided emphasis on a particular type of age-stratification, reveals genuine insight into sociological dynamics. If, disregarding at first his special formulation of the age factor, we attach ourselves solely to the general principle, its importance must be acknowledged as overwhelming. In the family itself, as Schurtz insisted, there is that opposition between the older and the younger generation to which Turgenev has given classical expression in *Fathers and Sons*. To transcend the limitations of one's years requires an effort of imagination almost beyond the reach of genius. The old people piquing themselves on their fund of experience never learn the wisdom of not giving advice that will not and cannot be heeded and remain unconscious of the fathomless boredom into which their futile prolixities of reminiscence plunge the impatient listener. The young, inclined to brush aside their elders as at best well-intentioned dotards, have not the prophetic gift to divine that all need not be senility that is not grist to their mill. Often rupture may indeed be avoided but there is ever the latent possibility of discord and the manifest incompatibility of thoughts, tastes, and modes of living. Of course the estrangement is not limited to the confines of the family because in essence it is not a personal but a class struggle. Hence any mixed assemblage will reveal the same cleavage, the same clash of temperaments that divides fathers and sons, mothers and daughters. What gathering might be supposed to be freer from the imperfections of human frailty than a meeting of scientific men? Yet on such occasions it requires little penetration to sense the ill-suppressed contempt the youthful knight-errant of truth entertains for the old-fogyism of his elders, while the patronizing cynicism with which some of these flout his high-flown notions is only surpassed by the supreme indifference with which others greet suggestions not emanating from their own ranks. Now this grouping and differentiation is far too deeply rooted in human nature not to loom largely amidst all the flux of cultural variation, though the class of greatest prominence will vary, as will the ideals of the age-classes. In Australian public life the absolute dominance of the elders is the most conspicuous phenomenon; among the warlike Masai the fighting bachelor braves hold the social hegemony; and in some Plains Indian communities there was a constant antagonism between the young men eager to distinguish themselves in raids against hostile tribes and the prudent chiefs seeking to prevent a hazardous warparty.

So far, then, Schurtz is eminently on the right track. Where he errs is in taking it for granted that this inveterate tendency must always be *formally* organized, that where it is so recognized it invariably goes back to a tripartite organization of society into boys, bachelors, and married men, and that this scheme represents the oldest form of association. This is again an unwarrantable generalization, probably founded on the picturesque aspects of Masai and Bororo life. Approaching without prepossession the facts concerning the graded club of Melanesia, we do not detect any evidence of discrimination between single and married men; indeed, such a distinction would be alien to the plan of the club. It is true that in other parts of Oceania the division of males is at least partly on this basis since the bachelors have their separate dormitory while the benedicts sleep with their wives. But this constitutes a very imperfect division of classes, because the married men often spend most of the daytime in the single men's dormitory and on special occasions even sleep there, as in Fiji. Schurtz, as was pointed out, holds that the dormitory was first of all a bachelors' hall, which only secondarily assumed the additional character of a general club for males. But by what process does he arrive at this conclusion? If we pass in review a narrowly circumscribed section of New Guinea, the following variations of custom confront us: The Bukaua have council-chambers serving as bachelors' and guests' halls, but where the married men of the village also occasionally sleep, while the deliberations of all the men are conducted on the platforms of these public structures; the Kai have public houses only for the circumcision ritual, guests being entertained by the chief and each family occupying a separate hut; farther inland there is complete separation of the sexes, the men living in houses of their own. Now, what criterion is there for determining the relative priority of these several conditions? Considering the undoubted tendency to sex dichotomy in this region, would it not be quite defensible to say that the last-mentioned stage was chronologically the first, that married men subsequently came to live with their wives, leaving the bachelors in possession of the dormitory which formerly had sheltered married and single men alike? On this assumption there would be first a dual division of the tribe into initiated and uninitiated, and only for the specific purpose of sleeping there would be a secondary segmentation of the initiated. The hypothesis is not one whit more arbitrary than Schurtz's and seems more plausible in the light of relevant information.

In Africa there are peoples among whom the difference in connubial status established a basic classification. The Masai customs have been described and the Zulu under King Chaka may be cited as an additional example, since their ruler segregated his warriors as a bachelors' group from the ranks of the married. But in many other tribes the distinction produces no division of society; the initiates form one class irrespective of conjugal condition.

Asia is admitted by Schurtz to be meagerly provided with tripartite schemes of organization except in the extreme south, that is, within the pale of Malaysian influences. The Andaman Islanders, though of Negrito race, were evidently not beyond the reach of this cultural stream. It is significant that they segregate not only the bachelors but the spinsters as well. Now this double segregation has a relatively limited distribution in the world. It does occur, however, among such Philippine tribes as the Bontoc Igorot, also in Sumatra, among the Naga of Assam and the Dravidians of southern India. That the Andaman Negrito share so characteristic a variant of the institution under discussion with tribes so close at hand, cannot be considered an accident: we must assume that they borrowed the custom, as they presumably borrowed other elements of their culture, such as the outrigger canoe, from more advanced populations with which they came into contact. This point is an important one, for the spontaneous evolution of a bachelors' group among the Andaman Islanders would not only support Schurtz's theory that the tripartite scheme is a natural social construct, but would also go far to prop up his chronology since so rude a people as the Andaman Islanders might be expected to preserve a primeval plan of organization.

It is, however, North America that supplies the most crushing refutation of Schurtz's theory. Apart from the faint suggestions of a bachelors' group in the Southwest and in Alaskan Eskimo territory, the difference between the single and married men has failed to leave any impress on social structure. Even where bachelors' dormitories are reported there is no evidence that the implied grouping was fundamental. Certainly all initiated males irrespective of matrimonial status were united in the tribal society of the Zuñi or Hopi, and a host of other bonds were quite independent of this factor. Schurtz conjectures that the North Californian sweathouse formed only the bachelors' sleeping-quarters, but this is contrary to the facts.

However meager may be the North American evidence for a separation of the married from the single men, that for a formal distinction between initiated youths and uninitiated boys is practically lacking except for the Pueblo phenomenon already cited. In his desire to establish essentially uniform lines of development for distinct regions Schurtz postulates the equivalence of the American boy's puberty fast and the Australian or African boy's initiation festival. But this is perhaps the most infelicitous of his conceptions, though it has unfortunately been adopted by Professor Webster. The initiation ritual of, say, the Arunta or the Masai is *tribal* business, is an indispensable stage in the individual's life since not to be initiated is not to marry. But whether an Hidatsa or Crow youth retires to the seclusion of a bald hilltop, mortifying his flesh in supplication of supernatural beings, is no concern of the community at all, is a personal or at best a family affair. If he succeeds in gaining a vision, so much the better for him; but if he fails, there is no communal reproach. As a matter of fact, far from all Plains Indians obtained a revelation. This would exclude them from certain Omaha organizations founded on particular types of supernatural blessing, but in general it did not affect their social position, certainly it had nothing to do with their matrimonial chances. Moreover, the quest of a vision was not necessarily coincident even with approximate puberty. Among the Arapaho, indeed, it was usually the middle-aged who attempted to secure guardian spirits. To be sure, this is rather anomalous, but the reason for courting divine favor at an earlier age is plain. The ambitious young Plains Indian desired distinction on the battlefield. He had before him the precedent of men who had fasted and perhaps tortured themselves, who had seen a vision in consequence and subsequently won renown, which they ascribed to their revelation. Hence nothing was more natural than for the aspirant to tribal glory to emulate the example set by these men at a fairly early opportunity, though often rather later than the age of physiological maturity. The mortification he underwent was not compulsory but voluntarily inflicted by himself and solely in the hope of arousing the commiseration of the powers of the universe. There was thus no resemblance with the tortures to which an Arunta or Masai lad was obliged to submit. In short, the North American puberty fast was not a tribal initiation ceremony, led to no bachelors' group as distinguished from uninitiated boys, and often was not even a puberty rite.

As though the North American data were bound to fly in the face of Schurtz's system, the very region of the globe where adolescent ceremonies for males are remarkable for their rarity is conspicuous for girls' puberty festivals or at least for a definite procedure at the time of the first menses. Fairly elaborate celebrations of this type took place among such diverse tribes as the Apache, the Dakota, and the Shasta. This, it is true, did not lead to the organization of a definite social unit, but it remains noteworthy that while the existence of formalities furnished the basis for a possible classification of females, the general lack of boys' puberty rites was unfavorable to an equivalent grouping of males.

Thus, while the age factor must be recognized as a real determinant of social life, as will be further illustrated below, the particular conception of a triple classification of males based on the age factor as modified by the conventional usages of initiation and matrimony must be rejected as inadequate.

Varieties of Associations

It would be possible to continue an analysis of Schurtz's system along the lines hitherto followed, but another avenue of approach seems more profitable. Let us shift the center of interest from the operation of his several principles throughout the world to a consideration of the associational instrumentalities of a single restricted cultural province. I will select for this purpose the Plains area of North America. I intend first to summarize the main varieties of associations that confront the observer there; and shall then proceed to study the history of that particular type already described under the head of age-societies.

As a diminutive association of altogether peculiar character may be cited the union of two unrelated friends pledged to mutual support and life-long comradeship. This Damon-Pythias relationship flourished especially among the Dakota and their congeners. The moral obligations involved are well illustrated in an Assiniboin tale, where a father disowns his son for having been a disloyal comrade, while the deceived friend is so overwhelmed with shame that he retires into voluntary exile. In the formation of these friendships the age factor undoubtedly played a dominant part; but the exclusiveness of the bond established a type of association very different from that contemplated by Schurtz. There were created an indefinite number of friendly couples, representing so many independent social units without forming a complete cross-section of society along lines of age cleavage.

Of a wholly different cast are associations based on a common supernatural experience. This type of society might be expected to flourish throughout the entire area since all the Plains Indians seek visions and nothing seems more natural than that persons with like guardian spirits should develop a sense of social solidarity. Yet empirically this result has been effected only in the south and among such intermediate tribes as the Dakota. An unusual efflorescence has been recorded among the Omaha, where persons with visions of the Buffalo, the Thunder, and so forth, congregate in shamanistic organizations, sometimes charged with surgical functions and of course always of distinctly religious character. These groups, as might be supposed, embraced persons of various ages and as a rule did not exclude women. They thus deviated as widely as possible from Schurtz's primeval type of association; yet their importance in Omaha life indicates that they represent a very old cultural possession of the tribe. On the other hand, certain feasting societies of the Omaha roughly representative of age-classes are of hardly any significance. There are three of these, the mature men, the young men, and youths, each group meeting as a distinct set of messmates. Schurtz does not fail to impress this fact into the service of his tripartite scheme and contends that it represents the relic of a primeval three-class system, which of course must have antedated all other forms of association. What there is in Omaha history to suggest the priority of these commensalities, he does not deign to inform us. Devoid of any serious function, they played so subordinate a part as not even to be mentioned in Miss Fletcher's and Mr. La Flesche's bulky monograph. To us the case is nevertheless important as showing that the age factor tends to assert itself in manifold and even trivial ways, not necessarily in a basic classification of an entire community. Given the restricted distribution of the commensalities and their lack of importance in Omaha society, there can be little doubt that they represent an incidental development, later than the religious corporations which rest on one of the most essential features of their culture.

Even more suggestive is the case of two Omaha dance organizations corresponding to the Dogs and the Foxes of northern tribes. Among the Omaha the former included exclusively aged and mature men, the latter being composed of boys. Here, then, there is a clear-cut age-stratification. The only question is how far it dates back. Fortunately the history of these societies is known. The Omaha derived both of them in recent years from the Ponca, who in turn borrowed them from a Dakota band. Now the Ponca do not grade these associations at all; indeed, among them the societies which for simplicity's sake I will simply call the Dogs and the Foxes are rivals stealing each other's wives on equal terms. The Dakota likewise treat both organizations as coördinate yet have the germ of an age-classification. Their Foxes comprised middle-aged men as well as young boys, while the Dogs had on the average an older membership, though promising youths were not positively barred. The theoretical implications of these facts are exceedingly interesting. Since the Ponca organizations were not graded by age and at best retained in submerged form the rudiments of an age-classification from their Dakota prototype, the application of the age principle represents an independent Omaha addition. That is to say, age enters at a late stage in the history of these societies; and from the Omaha point of view it also enters in recent times; moreover, not in the ancient and most characteristic organizations, but in those of demonstrably alien origin. This beautifully attests the vigor of the age factor, and we certainly cannot deny that it may have manifested itself sporadically at earlier periods as well. Of that, however, we have no evidence. We know only that among the Omaha it is not the basis of the old societies and has been recently imposed on borrowed organizations.

The Foxes and the Dogs introduce us to the category of military societies so-called. But since from the present point of view mode of admission is more significant than function, we must subdivide them into at least two disparate types, those conforming to the Crow pattern and those following the Hidatsa model. The former, it will be remembered, are ungraded and either invite members or permit joining at will; the latter are graded by age and can be entered only on payment of a fee. Here, then, we have one type that rests on a blending of age and purchase; another that is independent of age. But since the evolution of the ungraded from the graded societies is conceivable, a special consideration of this case will be given below.

However, there are societies of various functions with membership unrelated with age and dependent on payments. The Tobacco order of the Crow falls into this category, and so do the Cheyenne women's craft guilds, which have already been described from another angle. In the Hidatsa bundle fraternities, correlated with the most sacred ceremonials of the tribe, membership is hereditary but must be validated by appropriate fees.

It is not necessary to exhaust the assortment of Plains Indian associations. Enough has been cited by way of illustration to show that the qualifications for entrance vary, that age appears as one of two factors in some of the military societies, but simply on the face value of the findings it is not obvious that it is the fundamental one. The tripartite scheme, moreover, occurs only in the insignificant trio of Omaha feasting groups. Certainly it is the height of arbitrariness to decree that a feature of relatively restricted range within the area, and virtually absent in what Schurtz considers the typical form, must have been the most ancient, the one on which all the others have been superimposed. How, it might be asked, could such a notion as that of a common vision as the basis of association evolve out of the quite different notion of an age grouping, let alone, a congregation of bachelors or of married men? Where is the *tertium quid?* And if it did not evolve, if its origin is independent, why could it not have antedated the age factor as a formal mode of classification? These are questions a disciple of Schurtz might find it difficult to answer. And if we embraced in our survey the entire globe, we should of course encounter still other principles of solidarity, rendering a monistic reduction of the entire series of associations still less plausible. But it is more satisfactory to take the bull by the horns, to examine somewhat more carefully the history of an ostensible age-grouping and to determine in how far it bears out Schurtz's position or sheds light on the general theoretical problems involved. The amount of material accumulated on the Plains Indian age-societies suggests them as the most suitable subject for critical scrutiny.

The Plains Indian Age-Societies

The Hidatsa system of age-societies has been shown to involve an age-classification by which the male population is divided into approximately ten classes of successively higher degree, each with its distinctive dance, songs, paraphernalia and privileges. At the same time promotion to these ranks was not automatic on attainment to a certain age but had to be purchased by the entire class of coëvals. This scheme, instead of being confined to the Hidatsa, was shared by their next-door neighbors, the Mandan, and three other tribes, the Blackfoot, the Arapaho and the Gros Ventre; hence in an historical reconstruction the five variants must be considered in conjunction. But even this does not suffice. Though the *scheme* of organization, a blend of the age and purchase factors, is limited to the five tribes mentioned, the complexes and elements characteristic of the degrees are far more widely distributed.

For example, the Dog degree of the Hidatsa, held by mature or even old men, has among its badges a peculiar slit sash, a dewclaw rattle, and an owl-feather headdress. The identical emblems are used by the Dog society of the Crow, which comprises men of varying ages. That the two complexes have sprung from one source, is incontestable, but who borrowed from whom? Indeed, the case is not nearly so simple as I have stated it, for the features are shared by all the five graded tribes and by several peoples having an ungraded series, such as the Cheyenne and Dakota. Hence on the basis solely of the facts so far cited any one of possibly ten tribes might have evolved the Dog dance and it might have traveled back and forth in a great number of ways. Corresponding questions arise for Hidatsa complexes associated with other degrees, and accordingly specific problems develop by the score. From a broader point of view it is of course not the historical minutiae that interest us. We want to know whether a given dance common to the graded and ungraded systems was originally affiliated with an age group or not. If not, there is a further case in which Schurtz's sequence is simply inverted: i.e., where a grouping first occurred on some other basis and subsequently became an age-grouping. If, on the other hand, the Dog or Fox or Lumpwood society began as a society of age-mates, Schurtz's theory would to that extent find corroboration. However, another question would arise. What does the correlation between age and a certain dance signify? Does it mean that the latter is linked with men of a particular age, say, married men, or young men, or men from sixty to seventy? Or does it mean that the particular age is irrelevant and that it is simply essential for all members to be coëvals? Finally, if we are dealing with age-classes, why does the purchase factor obtrude itself on our notice?

This last feature, indeed, provides us with an entering wedge. It is not merely the positive correlation of purchase and age that arrests our attention but the equally important negative correlation between purchase and the ungraded military societies. In a real age-stratification promotion should be automatic. Schurtz asserts that this was originally the case here but that later the idea of payment was superimposed. The sequence, then, would be: first, automatic advancement with age; later, the introduction of some other qualification. Very well. Lack of the age factor and purchase would then both belong to the later epoch. But, if so, why do they never coincide in military societies? The allegedly late feature of purchase clings tenaciously to the one postulated as the earliest feature of all associations; and it is never found united with notions more or less contemporaneous on Schurtz's scheme. This is certainly mysterious. It rather suggests that something is wrong with the hypothetical chronology, that the bland assumption that the age-societies of the Plains are at bottom genuine age-classes may be without foundation.

Let us begin with the problem whether the complexes or degrees in the age series represent essentially a definite age or a definite rank in the series. For this purpose we can compare equivalent complexes in the several tribes; and also the same complex at different periods in the same tribe. The Dog complex, widely spread and almost always linked with an important society, furnishes a favorable instance. In 1833 Prince Maximilian found that the Blackfoot Dogs were decidedly young men, while those of the Hidatsa and Mandan were middle-aged. The latter conforms to their status in the Arapaho and Gros Ventre series as determined by Professor Kroeber. Judging not merely by a counting of noses but by the great importance of this organization throughout the Plains, we must certainly regard the early Blackfoot condition as atypical. Yet it is impossible to say categorically that the Dog dance belongs essentially to the middle-aged or is associated with any other particular age for the simple reason that its age connection is known to have varied with time even within the same tribe. The Blackfoot of forty years ago assigned to the Dogs a much higher rank than they had done in the 'thirties of the last century, and in Hidatsa society they represented at one time the status of very old men. Other complexes suggest the same conclusion. The equally common Fox society was a young men's company among the Hidatsa, with the Gros Ventre it represented a rather older group, while among the Blackfoot they ranked superior to the Dogs in 1833 and more recently all but reached the highest place in the series. The Ravens of the Blackfoot were middle-aged in Prince Maximilian's day, but in the same year they were recruited from the very oldest Hidatsa. Obviously, then, there was no essential connection of a certain complex with a special age even for a particular people. Since a complex formed a member of an hierarchical series, it was inevitable that at any one point of time it must hold a definite ordinal rank, involving a more or less definite age association because age-mates always made a joint purchase, but that was all. A shifting of position, whatever may have been the cause, was evidently not felt as an outrage on the eternal fitness of things; so long as the masters of a complex belonged to the same age-class it mattered little whether they were fifteen or seventy.

This inference is even more conclusively demonstrated by the autobiographical statements of Indian informants. With the breakdown of ancient Hidatsa and Mandan custom under modern conditions degrees ceased to be bought. The men who normally would have become Bulls or Ravens lacked a chance to make the requisite purchase, and so on down the entire scale. Thus, the older men not only found it impossible to buy advancement but also to dispose of their membership prerogatives because no younger group presented itself for their acquisition. Now the startling truth is that a man never outgrew the membership privileges acquired in youth, as would be the case if the age factor were the dominant one. To take a single instance, a man named Poor-wolf considered himself at 90 the master of a complex bought at 7; of another obtained at 20; of a third held since he was about 27; and of a fourth purchased at about 45. The principle, manifest from the objective circumstances and definitely formulated by the natives themselves, is simply that a man owns any and all complexes he has ever bought provided he has never sold them. A man cannot at 90 class himself a contemporary with boys of 7 and it is a monstrous absurdity for any one to be counted a member of three or four distinct age-classes at the same time; but he can very well hold property he has secured at any and all preceding periods of his life. In other words, the basic notion connected with a degree in the series is ownership of purchased property rights and the age element is wholly subsidiary.

This conclusion is also supported by certain peculiarities of the Gros Ventre scheme. Here the age-mates do not supersede the group immediately superior to their own but buy the coveted ceremonial privileges from a heterogeneous assemblage comprising men of any or all groups that at one time had acquired these rights. The immediate occasion for a purchase was always a vow by one member of the group that on recovery from illness or on extrication from some difficulty he would inaugurate the transaction. In these conditions there was nothing to prevent several age-classes from simultaneously holding the same ceremonial complex, and as a matter of fact the Gros Ventre had several times as many age-classes as dances, each dance being the property of several classes. It was these classes that were the social units involved. There was no bond of union allying the three or four classes owning the same complex; each exercised its privileges apart from the rest and their distinctness was emphasized by distinct designations, which, unlike their dance names, were not altered with time but persisted through life. Thus, a man shared with all his class-mates and only with them the permanent and exclusive designation of 'Holding-to-a-dog's-tail,' but he was a Dog or Fox only for a limited period and shared the title with men of his own and of several other age-classes as well. In other tribes a certain complex of immaterial rights was held exclusively by *one* corporation; the Gros Ventre permitted several corporations simultaneously to exercise ownership over the same complex, but this of course did not imply abandonment of their separate identities. It was simply as though several firms, say, in England, France, and America had the prerogative of publishing a certain book. In other words, while the Hidatsa classes could simultaneously hold complexes of the most varying degree, the same degree or complex was simultaneously held by a number of distinct Gros Ventre classes. The complexes, then, were simply negotiable commodities, which a priori might be associated with different ages or different degrees. The only problem is how they came to be graded in a series associated with age differences. Now this problem resolves itself into the problem of the ultimate origin of grades, and into a set of special questions as to how specific complexes were added as such and such degrees. Schurtz is not very much concerned about the later growth of the system, which as a matter of course he simply treats as an elaborated form of the tripartite division of the tribes. We, however, consider positive historical knowledge as to recent developments the foundation for all speculation about earlier processes and shall accordingly attach more weight to how complexes have actually been graded within the historical period.

The factor that has clearly had the deepest influence on the later growth of the graded system is the imitation or purchase of foreign societies. We know that in 1833 the Mandan lacked the Fox society and that subsequently they borrowed it from the Hidatsa and incorporated it into their own scheme. Similarly, the Hidatsa adopted the Mandan Crazy Dog society, and the Mandan the Hidatsa Little Dog organization. The Hidatsa Stone Hammers of Maximilian's time had acquired the Arikara Hot Dance, by which process an ungraded complex came to be linked with a definite degree. It was subsequently possible for the Stone Hammers either to merge the new features completely in the old or to keep the two complexes dissociated and sell them independently of each other. Though the matter is not absolutely certain, the second of these contingencies was apparently realized, and it meant that a new degree was added to the series. The owners when approached by the next younger age-class would sell them either only the Hot Dance or only the old Stone Hammer complex. In the former case the newly bought dance would become the lowest degree, in the latter the second lowest. There is not the slightest doubt that this type of process went on long before we have any documentary evidence of it. For example, the Arapaho and Gros Ventre are closely related tribes with very similar graded schemes, and the Gros Ventre after their separation lived with the Blackfoot. One of the Gros Ventre deviations from the Arapaho scheme is the possession of a Fly dance at the bottom of the series. Such a dance also occurs among the Blackfoot, whence it was first reported, and among one of the neighboring tribes of the Blackfoot, but nowhere else. The only possible inference is that the Gros Ventre borrowed it from the Blackfoot and assimilated it to their system. Now this incorporation is bound to affect the other members of the series, all of which are dislocated in relative rank; and wherever a system has had several accretions of this type it is manifest that an extensive shifting of status must have taken place. Everything indicates that this is precisely what occurred, and from this point of view the strange anomalies as to the rank of the same society in different tribes become intelligible. If the Blackfoot adopted the Dog complex at a later time than the Fox complex, then we can understand why with characteristically primitive fondness for antiquity they placed the novel acquisition farther down the scale. In other cases a newly purchased society may have been of so sacred a character as to be placed at the top, whereby all the older degrees would be correspondingly degraded. Since every one of the five systems has demonstrably developed piecemeal by such accretions, it follows of course that the several complexes *could* not have more than a haphazard connection with a special rank or age.

But diffusion was probably not the only agency in the elaboration of the graded series. Given such a scheme, there would be a natural tendency to bring other complexes of possibly native origin into relation with it. This is what happened in the case of the Hidatsa Notched-Stick ritual. So far as it is possible to judge, this was an indigenous performance standing apart from the age-societies. But in one of the Hidatsa villages the notion arose of integrating it with the popular scheme and accordingly it was added as the lowest degree. The further consequences for the other degrees would of course be identical with those due to the adoption of an alien complex.

So far a disciple of Schurtz might assent, turning the historical data into so much grist for his mill. Quite so, he would say; the amplification of the series must be relatively recent, for originally there could have been only the three fundamental age-classes of boys, bachelors, and elders. *That,* however, he would contend, is not due to borrowing nor to any subsequent internal evolution but is a primeval grouping as the result of an immutable social law. We, however, shall not readily admit that principles which have been established for the known period of history suddenly sprang into being and were inoperative in the period immediately preceding. And as a matter of fact, the data are such as to prove beyond the shadow of a doubt that the scheme of graded societies was borrowed as a scheme from one source. Comparing, say, the Hidatsa and the Blackfoot series, we find the identical conception of purchase joined with the characteristic feature that wives are ceremonially surrendered to the seller, and no fewer than four of the complexes, the Fox, Dog, Raven, and Bull societies occur in both. Even to think of independent evolution in this case would be madness. One of the two tribes certainly borrowed its system from the other or from a common source; and when comparison is extended to the three other peoples with graded societies the observed resemblances deepen the conviction that there were not five spontaneous evolutions of a graded system but that a single basic scheme has been locally modified in so many distinct tribes. Even if we grant, then, that the degrees or dances originally represented the tripartite division, this could apply only to the one people who transmitted the scheme. All the others came to possess that feature not through the action of an inherent law of progress but because they came into contact with a people who did produce that phenomenon. So far as *they* are concerned, there is no evidence that male society automatically groups itself into three or for that matter any other number of age-classes.

In truth, the case against Schurtz is even stronger. For he has no right to assume that the people who first had graded societies, say, the Hidatsa, originated the societies themselves in addition to the notion of grading them. While only five Plains Indian tribes share the age-societies, a considerable number of other tribes have the same complexes without any age connection. It is, therefore, possible and indeed probable that even among the Hidatsa the grading was a secondary phenomenon: they copied some ungraded organizations of their neighbors and somehow came to range them in an hierarchical series. The importance of this development is manifest. It strikes at the very root of Schurtz's philosophy. Not a classification by age but some other socializing instrumentality underlies the military organizations of the Plains, the age factor only appearing at a relatively late period and in a specialized variant of these societies.

What the original socializing agencies may have been, has already been partly indicated in the account of the varieties of associational types. The influence of visions, than which no more fundamental cultural element occurs in the area, makes itself felt in several ways. There may be a grouping of persons according to their visions, as among the Omaha; or the visionary may initiate others and with them organize a distinct society, as in the Tobacco dance of the Crow; or he may drill a company of men to perform a ceremony he has dreamt, the temporary union of participants becoming fixed, as probably happened among the Eastern Dakota. An equally important trait of the culture of this region is the undertaking of a war expedition, and there is good evidence that among the Dakota the comrades in arms became permanently associated. Several causes were thus at work that could and doubtless did produce associations of men long before there came into being that extremely localized and specialized phenomenon of grading associations by age.

The argument has been of necessity somewhat complex, so that a brief recapitulation will not come amiss. Confronted with a chronological scheme that derived clubs, secret societies and all other associations from three age-classes, we undertook to examine the hypothetical sequence in the light of data from a single area. A rapid survey of Plains Indian associations made it appear that age-classes formed by no means the predominant type of grouping and that in certain cases the age grouping is demonstrably a secondary feature. Narrowing the discussion to those systems of societies that most clearly indicate an age-stratification, we discovered a number of significant facts. The supposed degrees were shuffled about by the natives with the utmost abandon, so that the same society which represented a young men's club in one tribe was composed of mature or even old men in another. The subjective attitude of the Indians showed that they were essentially not grading themselves by age but buying certain prized ceremonial prerogatives, so that one individual could simultaneously claim several degrees,—a sheer impossibility if they represented differences in age or conjugal condition. There remained the problem of the historical growth of the graded series. Preferring to pass from the known to the unknown, we found that in the period of which we have definite knowledge the great factor has been diffusion, that the complexity of the observed systems is due to piecemeal additions through borrowing. Still it would be conceivable that at an earlier stage a simpler tripartite grouping underlay the scheme of these societies, in which case there would be harmony with the supposedly basic law of social evolution expounded by Schurtz. But since the five tribes undoubtedly derived their graded series from one source, that law could have found expression in only one of them;

in the other four tribes the hypothetical tripartite scheme would be the result not of any inherent social force but of borrowing, hence the 'law' would not be a law at all. And even taking the people who first graded societies by age, it would be rash to assume that they were the first to originate military societies because these are far more commonly found in ungraded form. Finally, the basic phenomena of Plains Indian existence offer a number of means by which men could have been and actually were united into associations. Schurtz's unilinear scheme resting on the theory of a tripartite age-division is thus wholly inapplicable to a type of associations that ostensibly gives evidence of an age-grouping. In an area abounding in associations the age-classes appear as a local and late type, not corresponding, moreover, with the tripartite division.

Yet when we have smitten Schurtz's chronology hip and thigh, the fact remains that age has played its part, though not as he imagined, in the history of the military organizations. Among the Crow, Dakota and Kiowa, all of whom had coördinate societies, one genuine age-class arose in the most natural manner in the world, by boys imitating the organizations of their elders. This seemingly trivial fact gives us a clue to the possible inception of grading. Let us assume that among the originators of degrees, say, the Hidatsa, this juvenile mimicry was in vogue. Suppose further that there was a single society into which many or most of the adult men purchased entrance, joining in order to enhance their prestige, a constant motive in primitive communities. All that was then required was for the boys in their eagerness to own a *real* complex of dancing and other privileges to buy membership jointly, the collective character of the transaction constituting its revolutionary feature since thereby the informal group of playmates became as definite an age-class as the Masai boys undergoing joint circumcision. The dispossessed sellers would then lack a dance but their former bond was likely to keep them together and at the first opportunity they would dream, that is, invent a new one or buy it from a foreign tribe. The new dance would then become the next goal of the boys' ambition and accordingly a second degree. It should be noted that the original adults' group was not necessarily a definite age-class. On the one hand, it might have embraced any man from 20 to 80; on the other, it need not have included more than, say, sixty per cent of the adults. But the mimicking youngsters did constitute an approximate age-class, and when they had once in a body bought a higher society they had set in motion the machinery required to found such a system as was characteristic of the Hidatsa and the four other tribes with grades. A new generation of boys would buy the lowest degree from the originators of the practice, the latter would advance collectively, gradually the amorphous group of original adults would die out, and leave behind successive groups of younger men approximately graded by age. The fact that young boys flock together, itself an illustration of the associative power of age in a general way, might thus have led to that incidental affiliation of age-distinctions with societies described above. The age factor thus remains a reality, though it is neither the only nor necessarily the predominant feature in the history of associations, nor yet the earliest one in the Plains area.[3]

General Conclusions

From the actual history of the Plains Indian associations certain general conclusions can be drawn. For one thing, the baneful effect of catchwords has once more become manifest. A division of all male society into groups of uninitiated boys, bachelors, and elders is one thing; a division into age-classes on the Hidatsa pattern represents something utterly different; the division of the Crow Foxes into young, middle-aged and old members is again a disparate phenomenon since it involves no tribal partition but merely a grouping within a single association out of many. We must, accordingly, be on our guard when other equally broad and equally vague terms are used to designate phenomena in disconnected areas. The probability is that the identity of nomenclature simulates a likeness that does not exist. If, for example, we compare the secret societies of Melanesia with those of the Pueblo Indians, there is no analogy whatsoever either in constitution, function or anything else but the exclusion of non-members. Entrance into the secret societies of the Banks Islands is by purchase, in the Southwest it is by virtue of being cured by a member or being received at birth by a member's wife or by heredity, never by payment. The Banks Islanders never admit women; some of the Pueblo societies do, and some of them are even constituted wholly by women. The activities of the Melanesian societies center in the production of a queer noise and the protection of members' property, together with occasional terrorizing of the uninitiated and wanton destruction of their belongings. To all this there is no parallel in the curative fraternities of the Zuñi or the rain-making ceremonial associations of the Hopi. There is thus neither an historical nor a psychological affinity between these organizations.

All this has a most important bearing on the problem of unilinear evolution. An intensive consideration of the Plains Indian societies certainly goes far to show that as regards phenomena of this type history does not tend to repeat itself except in the most general way or for a very limited span of time. It might be said that in all sorts of communities the gregarious instinct asserts itself in one way or another; and I have myself admitted that the age factor ever and anon tends to effect a sub-grouping if not a primary grouping of individuals. These, however, are sociological rather than historical generalizations; they express no formulation of any fixed sequence of events. Now let us consider the number of principles whose confluence is requisite to form something comparable to the Hidatsa age-societies. There must be the notion of dances associated with insignia, good-fellowship of the participants, military obligations, and the purchasability of such complexes; and the last trait rests on the native theory of visionary experiences. No wonder that with such a multiplicity of essential factors, this type of association has not been duplicated. The Masai are as warlike as the Hidatsa but this general similarity cannot produce specific resemblances in the absence of identical cultural traditions. With a quite different conception of ceremonialism, with no such theory of individual visions as was held by the Hidatsa, the Masai could not possibly evolve a corresponding system. If this is so, it follows that the search for all-embracing laws of evolution on the model of Morgan's or Schurtz's schemes is a wild-goose chase and that only an intensive ethnographic study in each cultural province can establish the actual sequence of stages.

REFERENCES

[1] Schurtz: 83-109, 125-128, 202-213, 318-333, 347-367.
[2] Von den Steinen: 268. Radin, 1911: 198-207. Mooney: 415. Goddard, 1903: 15, 50, 67. Dixon, 1905: 269, 272; id., 1907: 420, 471. Barrett: 397. Powers: 141, 158, 305. Roth, 1903: 31. Nelson: 285, 347. Hawkes, 1913. Annual Archaeological Report: 213. Alldridge: 220. Kingsley: 376. Spencer and Gillen, 1904: 498-501. Lehner: 404 seq. Parkinson: 636, 640, 658. Hollis, 1909: 40, 56. Talbot: 284. Frobenius: 170. Von den Steinen: 384. Lang: 29-44.
[3] Lowie, 1916.

CHAPTER XII

RANK

AS I have already pointed out, Morgan's conception of society was an atomistic one. Perhaps it was the traditional American bias in favor of democratic institutions that caused him to blink at evidences of social discrimination in the ruder civilizations. He paid little attention to the differences between sibs of the same people or to those between different individuals of the same community; and privileged orders he assigned to a far later epoch of evolution. Yet, even restricting his survey to North America, he might have detected schemes of social organization in which the differentiation of upper and lower classes was fundamental; and what is still more important, he might have found that the absence of hereditary castes by no means excludes vital distinctions on the basis of personal desert. Primitive man is no imbecile; he is quick to perceive and to appraise those individual differences which as an inevitable biological phenomenon mark every group, even the lowest, as Dr. Marett has rightly insisted. Primitive man knows that X, though a dullard at spinning a yarn, is a crack shot with the bow and arrow; that Y, for all his eloquence in the council, has proved a poltroon in sight of the enemy; that Z is an amiable all-round mediocrity. Imperceptibly he grades them, imperceptibly their influence on his own deeds and thoughts depends on his evaluation. That in turn is not wholly nor largely an individual affair but a social matter, affected by the tribal standards. The man who in one milieu is esteemed as a hero will be considered no better than a ruffianly brute in another; mechanical skill may be rated highly by one people and accord no distinction whatsoever elsewhere. In our own civilization the stigma of effeminacy still clings to the musician, and the professional scholar has a far less enviable position than he occupies in continental Europe. It is precisely part of ethnology's task to show how societies differ in their canons of personal appreciation. Aboriginal North America is an unusually favorable field for demonstrating the power of individual differences because with a few exceptions to be noted later the greater part of this continent was occupied by democratically-minded tribes. We may profitably begin by considering some Plains groups.[1]

Bravery

With the Plains Indians the quest of military renown was as hypertrophied as ever has been the lust for gold in our most money-mad centers of high finance. It was in order that he might gain a vision assuring distinction in battle that a young brave fasted and dragged buffalo skulls fastened to his punctured shoulder muscles; and to gain the coveted glory he would throw caution to the wind, risking life and limb in senseless deeds of derring-do. These, moreover, had to conform to a conventional pattern in order to count as heroic, and they differed in some measure from tribe to tribe. In the normal course of Crow events four exploits were considered honorable and jointly conferred on their achiever the title of chief, which was usually quite devoid of political significance. In order to acquire such distinction it was necessary for a warrior to cut loose and steal a horse picketed within the hostile camp; to take an enemy's bow or gun in a hand-to-hand encounter; to strike a 'coup,' i.e., touch an enemy with a weapon or even the bare hand; and to lead a victorious war expedition.

Naturally only a limited number of men ever scored on each of these counts; but even though he might not rank as a chief, a brave who had accomplished one or more of these deeds of valor acquired to that extent favorable notice in the tribe, indeed, his standing was altogether proportionate to his war record. At all tribal gatherings he was privileged to recite a list of his experiences; he might have them painted on his robes or on the windbreak of his lodge; parents would come to him, requesting that he name their children; ambitious youths paid him for part of his war medicine; on every public occasion he would be selected for some post of honor, say, to act as herald; his father's sib-mates would chant his praises through the camp; and even in ceremonial life precedence would be yielded to the successful warrior with regard to honorific services.

Sometimes this point of view found extravagant expression in current songs and adages. "It is proper to die young" was the *dulce et decorum* of Crow and Hidatsa sages. "Eternal are the heavens and the earth; old people are bad; be not afraid" is the burden of a Crow song. Hence an elder brother might force a younger to assume the unusual obligations of bravery associated with special office in a military society, not from malice but in order that the youth might acquire glory. On the basis of this attitude we find warriors not only pledged to intrepidity but deliberately courting death in foolhardy ventures, e.g., by rushing single-handed against a hostile troop.

Naturally a coward was the object of supreme contempt, jeered at by his joking-relatives and compared with a menstruating woman. The one-sided accentuation of martial valor naturally led to inadequate recognition of men whose parts in communities with different standards would have assured them an enviable prestige. Thus, I found that one of my ablest Crow informants, a man remarkably well-posted in tribal lore, was universally pooh-poohed as a nobody. It developed that he had never won distinction on the battlefield and had made matters worse by reciting meritorious deeds to which he had no claim. In other words, a highly endowed individual may receive no recognition in his social setting simply because the rigidity of the native canons renders any merit in the direction of his capacities irrelevant.

Certain other qualities were prized by the Crow not as substitutes for valor but as additional embellishments of the warrior's character. Foremost among these was liberality and there was corresponding contempt for the miser. The estimation of women was just as definitely on the basis of individual merit, though the set of values inevitably differed. Despite the general looseness of morals, a chaste woman was held in high esteem and for certain ceremonial offices immaculate virtue was a prerequisite. Skill in feminine crafts and kindliness also were conducive to a woman's prestige. Thus, it appears that in a relatively simple culture and in a markedly democratic community individual differences nevertheless produced enormous differences in social rating.

From the nature of the case warlike peoples might be expected to develop somewhat similar schemes of an aristocracy based on individual merit. To be sure, the Maori of New Zealand furnish the example of a martial people among whom the caste spirit was too deep-rooted to be minced with any Napoleonic principle of a general's baton in the recruit's knapsack. But more frequently the soldier's life is in primitive conditions coupled with notions following the Crow pattern. In the bachelors' kraal of the Masai there is virtual equality of status, but those who have distinguished themselves by munificence and valor, respectively, take precedence as the Generous People and the Bulls, and are permitted to assume special ornaments. Cowards are mocked in the presence of the girls, and a man who absents himself from a raid solemnly agreed upon may be slain with impunity. And as the Plains Indian brave might pledge himself to extravagantly reckless conduct, so the Masai will implant a pompon on the head of his spear, vowing never to remove it till he has run the point through a foeman's body. A similar frame of mind is evinced by the Bagobo of far-away Mindanao, whose chief aim in life is to wear the distinctive attire that rewards the man who has at least twice slain a human being. After the second killing he is permitted to don a chocolate-colored headband, the fourth entitles him to wear blood-red trousers, and when he has scored six he may use a complete suit of that color and a red bag to boot. Every additional life taken, while no longer resulting in a change of costume, brings additional credit. Those who have never killed a person are nobodies, while the acknowledged braves fill positions of importance and are deemed under the special tutelage of two powerful spirits, between whom and the common herd they are the intermediaries. Not only the status but even the garments of the brave are uninheritable, and the latter should be buried with the owner.[2]

Shamanism; Wealth

Radically different notions as to eminence occur in other parts of the world. The Northern Maidu may serve as an example. Here there was an elective chieftaincy based on wealth and generosity, but in reality the shaman, especially if leader of the secret society, completely overshadowed the headman. It was indeed through the shaman, who revealed the will of the spirits, that the chief was chosen; and a similar communication led to his degradation. The shaman himself did not inherit his office but became a professional by mysterious visitations and by passing a satisfactory examination imposed by the older practitioners. In other words, an aptitude for religious experiences was the stepping-stone to social prominence. To all intents and purposes, the shamanistic leader of the secret organization was the most eminent person in the community. He regulated the ceremonial life of his people, adjusted disputes, insured a good corn crop, warded off disease and by his magical powers inflicted condign punishment on the enemy; indeed, he himself often led war parties in person. Over and above all these things, he was the authority on tribal mythology and lore, and it was his duty to instruct the people on these lofty topics.

In northern California a motive already discernible in minor degree among the Maidu gains the ascendancy: distinction is founded primarily on wealth. The Hupa headman was the man of greatest affluence; the villagers looked to him for the necessaries of life in time of scarcity or for assistance with money in case of disputes. His power descended to his son *provided* his property also descended; but if some unusually able or industrious rival acquired greater wealth, he won with it the dignity of office. Exactly the same conception prevailed in Shasta society.

The place of wealth in the polity of primitive tribes generally is a matter of great comparative interest. In the pastoral stage a new form of property is introduced that might result in far-reaching differences of status were it not for the leveling force of natural conditions, which may debase the nabob of yesterday to the position of a pauper. Hence the basic frame of mind may still be democratic. The poor Altaian asserts all the pride of shabby gentility in his relations with wealthier tribesmen; he enters the household of a rich cattle-breeder as a member of the family, brooking no suggestion of menial servitude, and would rather starve than obey a peremptory command. With the Reindeer Chukchi the assistant's status is less favorable, for the master may abuse and even beat his helper. Nevertheless, this privilege is limited both by the native ideal, which requires generous treatment, and also by the relative prowess of the men concerned, for a powerful assistant may turn the tables on an abusive master. A peculiar conception of wealth occurs in Melanesia. As explained in the description of the club of the Banks Islanders, advancement in the organization and consequent promotion in the social scale was dependent on wealth, yet it was not the hoarding of money or property that conferred distinction but its lavish disposal. Precisely the same notion is characteristic of the Indians of British Columbia, though there the matter is complicated by the coëxistence of hereditary castes to be noticed presently. "Possession of wealth," writes Boas, who has graphically pictured the Kwakiutl point of view, "is considered honorable, and it is the endeavor of each Indian to acquire a fortune. But it is not as much the possession of wealth as the ability to give great festivals which make wealth a desirable object to the Indian." The more property a man distributes at these festivals or potlatches, as they are called, the higher he rises in social estimation. Boys, chiefs and whole communities are pitted against each other in a competition of extravagance. The challenger gives his opponent a large number of blankets, which cannot be refused and which must be returned in the future with 100 per cent interest unless the recipient is willing to undergo the humiliation of insolvency. Sometimes, to show his contempt for pelf, a chief will wantonly destroy valuable property and in former times slaves were killed from sheer bravado. The stress placed on this feature has even in exceptional cases affected the otherwise rigid lines of caste. Sapir notes "cases in which men of lower rank have by dint of reckless potlatching gained the ascendancy over their betters, gradually displacing them in one or more of the privileges belonging to their rank. Among the West Coast Indians, as in Europe, there is, then, opportunity for the unsettling activities of the parvenu."

Thus martial valor, a bent for mystical experiences, and in one way or another wealth, are all motives in primitive communities by which men otherwise equal come to be differentiated in position. To this we may add as a common feature in the lower levels dexterity as a provider of food. Among the Maritime Chukchi the family that has lived in a village for the longest period and gained an intimate knowledge of the economic conditions takes precedence; and the organizer of a sealing expedition has a position of some distinction. The Yukaghir recognize a specific post of chief hunter; it is an onerous one since he has to procure sustenance for the entire community and there is little if any emolument save the honor attached to the office. Less formally many American Indians, such as the Chipewyan and the Plateau Shoshoneans, attested their respect for the skilful hunter.[3]

Caste

The factors hitherto examined are based on individual differences independent of rank due to pedigree. However, the cases are fairly numerous in which distinction, however subsequently affected by personal competence, is primarily a matter of inheritance. Where a full-fledged caste system exists it generally moulds political conditions, but at present our concern is solely with the matter of social rank.

In Polynesia the family pride of the aboriginal bluebloods rivals the superciliousness of Gilbert and Sullivan's Pooh-Bah. This sentiment derives its sustenance from the belief in the divine descent of the nobility. The chiefs are descendants, representatives and in a sense incarnations of the gods, as Mr. Hocart has explained. Among the typical Maori social precedence depended on directness of descent through primogeniture from the highest gods. Every man of distinction was obliged for his own sake to memorize his pedigree, partly historical and partly legendary, so that he might establish his status when challenged. Thus, a famous Maori soldier of recent times traced his lineage from Heaven and Earth through sixty-five intervening generations. The intricacies of native heraldry were labyrinthine, for both parental lines counted and the balance between contending rivals would have to be struck with not a little nicety. A chief's children would naturally differ in status according to their respective mothers' families. A child born of a noble mother would outrank its parents because it united the honors of both lines; on the other hand, the chief's first-born by a slave wife might exercise many privileges but was never regarded as a full-fledged chief, nor could personal merit completely compensate for a flaw in the genealogy. Those without a single blot on the family escutcheon were naturally few and their preëminence might become uncomfortable when no maiden of adequate quality could be found for a suitable mate. Sometimes, too, the legitimate priest-chief by primogeniture was reckoned too exalted a person actually to execute the duties of office, which were accordingly delegated to his next younger brother. One of the prerogatives of the prospective lord-pontiff was admission to the sacred college, where he learned the legendary history of his people and acquired a knowledge of dread incantations. From this institution of learning women were barred, but if a girl appeared as the first-born in the sacred line, she possessed privileges of a quite unusual character; she alone of all women might taste of human flesh and eat sacred offerings; she was permitted to learn something of the ancient lore; and no person was allowed to eat in her company. Some of the other characteristics of lofty nobility will be treated under the head of Government. Next in rank after the sacerdotal chiefs came the chiefs of lesser tribal divisions and their kin in the order of relationship. Then came the professional classes, to wit, the wizards and skilled artisans, while the bulk of the population was made up of gentlemen remotely affiliated with a chief's house and possessing little property.

Last of all came the slaves recruited mainly from captives in war. Ordinarily their lot was not one of material degradation, and owing to the superstitious dread of certain indispensable tasks as defiling a person of quality the slave's estate really formed one of the pillars of the Maori state. Menial labors, such as cooking or burden-bearing, might contaminate a warrior but not the slave whose spiritual and temporal status was negligible. Sometimes a bond of friendship developed between the slave and his master, and abuse was rarely to be feared since it was reckoned inconsistent with the code of the upper classes. It sometimes happened that a slave was permitted to work for some other person and to keep the payment received. In short, his position was tolerable and attempt was never made to escape because his own people would have disowned him as a person whose capture was proof of divine disfavor. However, there was the ever present danger of execution when a ceremonial sacrifice was needed, say, at the erection of a building, or even at a mere caprice of the owner's. The poorer men of the tribe often married slave women and their progeny soon became merged in the ranks of freemen but their low origin was always likely to make them the target of disdainful comment. Sometimes, though rarely, a man with a strain of slave blood might gain eminence by his valor, yet he was always viewed as an upstart incapable of vying with the aristocracy. It mattered not that prior to captivity the enslaved ancestor might have been the peer of the noblest, the mere fact of capture obliterated all trace of his blue blood and formed an ineffaceable stain on the escutcheon of his lineage.

The social fabric of the Samoans bears a generic resemblance to that of the New Zealanders, but naturally with some local variations. Stair distinguishes five classes of freemen—the chiefs, priests, landed gentry, large landowners, and commoners. However, the gradations of rank were far more numerous than this list would imply. Chiefs were by no means of uniform status and the precise degree of deference to be paid to each of them in terms of address or otherwise was adjusted with much punctilio. Then there were the attendants of the great chiefs, who, while in a sense members of one of the five ranks mentioned, derived special kudos from exercising the functions of barber, cup-bearer, trumpeter or buffoon. Skilled artisans, such as canoe-builders, architects and tattooers, corresponded to our professional class. By their control of essential industries and class-conscious organization they were able to impose their will on the community at large, as Stair has vividly described. When an influential man desired to have a canoe built, he first amassed as much property as possible with the aid of his neighbors and repaired to the workmen, formally requesting the chief boat-wright's services in a complimentary speech and offering a valuable mat or axe as an inducement. Consent might not always be readily granted since the builders were greatly in demand and possibly were too busy to accept new orders, but if disposed to undertake the job the master carpenter replied in a set speech, received the initial payment and made arrangements for the beginning of his labors. On the day appointed the canoe-builder and all his assistants with the families of each and every man engaged in the work appeared, it being understood as a matter of course that the customer must provide for their maintenance, which meant entertainment for possibly three months and possibly the impoverishment of the host. However, every effort was made to keep the numerous visitors in the best of humor, and some important representative of the household daily attended to the wants of the laborers, who were sheltered in a special shed protected from all interference by passers-by. No definite fee was agreed upon, but it was customary for five ceremonious payments to be made at proper intervals, and if the first two or three seemed niggardly, the workmen coolly struck until their employer apologized or yielded compensation. This was, indeed, the only way out of the dilemma, for no other party of builders would continue the work lest they be excommunicated by the remainder of their guild and deprived of their tools and their livelihood during the pleasure of this domineering trade union. Corresponding scenes occurred during the construction of a house since the architects formed an equally powerful organization. These two guilds might of course be considered under the caption of associations but it seemed preferable to view them in connection with the strata of the society of which they form part and in which they occupied a fairly definite place.

One rather important difference divides Samoan from Maori usage, the absence of primogeniture in the case of the loftier titles. These neither descended automatically to the eldest son of the chief nor was it in his power to appoint a successor. It was indeed his privilege to make a nomination, but this would have to be ratified by the influential men of the locality with which the title was associated and these leaders of public opinion were able to set his wishes at naught. There was not so much ceremony in the case of the title held by a landed gentleman, which could be bequeathed by the dying owner, but it was by no means necessarily allotted to the eldest-born son, another of better appearance or superior qualities, nay, even an adoptive favorite being frequently substituted.

This sketchy description of Polynesian conditions suffices to indicate the importance attached to hereditary titles and other class distinctions, and it merely remains to add that patrician and plebeian were assigned to separate afterworlds in order to afford some comprehension of what part these differences of caste assumed in the aboriginal consciousness.

Africa, like Polynesia, is a region of marked social distinctions, but these bear a totally different character. There are often potentates treated in the most reverential and indeed abject manner by their subjects and surrounded by a host of hierarchically graded functionaries that would have done honor to a mediaeval European court. But the dignitaries derive their station not from their lofty ancestry, they are not blue-bloods with endless pedigrees connecting them with some traditional figure, but political officials and as such usually the creatures of the king. The sovereign and his kin stand apart; the rest of the population are on a plane of equality. The example of Uganda is typical. The king traced his lineage from a legendary hero; all other officials of the state owed their distinction to competent and faithful conduct in the royal service, and every position in the realm save royalty was open to any tribesman. A patrician caste with its members bandying genealogies is an utterly un-African conception. A remarkable feature that may be noted in this place is the frequent preëminence of the queen dowager, who may reign in a court of her own. Among the Bakuba, though the king is an incarnation of the supreme deity, he yields precedence to his mother in conversation, it being her prerogative to address him first, which constitutes the badge of superiority according to native etiquette.

The slaves of course occupy the status of inferiors, but here some discrimination must be exercised. There were indeed captives enslaved in war who could be sold like cattle and executed at their master's will. But there was another class of native slaves pawned for debt and these enjoyed far milder treatment, suffering no particular loss of prestige since their servitude was often undergone to rescue an impoverished kinsman. In Uganda a slave girl who bore children to a freeman became free together with her progeny, and sometimes, though not generally, her sons were permitted to inherit property.

The preceding remarks apply to Negro territories. Where a mixture of stocks occurs, conditions are complicated. For example, the cattle-breeding Wahuma in East Africa occupy a station varying locally. In Ruanda they constitute the governing caste looking down upon the horticultural Bantu, while elsewhere they are simply professional herdsmen in a land of tillers.

A curious phenomenon occurs among the Masai and their neighbors. Though generally democratic, these tribes segregate as unclean pariahs the guilds or sibs of blacksmiths upon whom they are dependent for their weapons and whom one would a priori imagine to rank high in a warlike community. Since there is no suggestion of any racial difference, the reason for this attitude remains enigmatical.

North America, as already noted, was largely the scene of both social and political democracies. This fact is thrown into relief when we turn from the narratives of early explorers of our continent to the corresponding accounts of African or Oceanian travelers. It is not altogether unintelligible that Morgan should have hailed "liberty, equality, and fraternity" as the "cardinal principles" of the American sib organization and, accordingly from his point of view, of Indian society as a whole; and that he should thence have derived "that sense of independence and personal dignity universally an attribute of Indian character." But very few ethnographical propositions can be laid down without qualification, and to the generalization cited there are two remarkable exceptions—the Natchez of the lower Mississippi and the natives of the coast of British Columbia.

The Natchez evidently had a most interesting caste system, but unfortunately known to us only from the records of eighteenth century observers, which, however, have been carefully brought together by Dr. Swanton. The common herd were designated by the unflattering term of Stinkards and were sharply set off from the nobility. This was subdivided into the three ranks of Honored People, Nobles and Suns, the ruler standing at the head of the scale as Great Sun. Status descended primarily through the mother. The position of a Sun man (and of the nobility generally) was not wholly without effect on that of his descendants but it suffered progressive debasement in successive generations. His children were only Nobles, his grandsons Honored People, and his great-grandsons sank to the rank of commoners. This system was in some measure alloyed with democratic notions inasmuch as a Stinkard might advance himself by bravery to the lowest rank of nobility, while an Honored man could in corresponding fashion gain the next higher rung.

What was perhaps the most remarkable among the correlated Natchez customs was the rule underlying marriage arrangements. While the presence of rigid class distinctions almost everywhere else involves endogamous laws, the Natchez not only permitted but prescribed the marriage of Suns with commoners, the regulation affecting both sexes. When a Sun woman espoused a Stinkard, the customary patriarchal arrangements of the tribe were suspended, the husband occupying the status of a domestic not privileged to eat in his wife's company and being liable to execution for infidelity. The working of the scheme has been thus summarized by Swanton: The Suns comprised children of Sun mothers and Stinkard fathers; the Nobles were children of Noble mothers and Stinkard fathers, or of Sun fathers and Stinkard mothers; the Honored People included children of Honored women and Stinkard fathers, and of Noble fathers and Stinkard mothers; finally, the large class of Stinkards was recruited from plebeian inter-marriages or from the unions of Stinkard mothers and Honored men.

Rather more amazing than the caste system itself are its outward manifestations, which are utterly un-American if judged from the point of view of the other Indians of the continent and reveal little of that personal dignity ascribed to the noble Red man in Morgan's characterization. The descriptions of court etiquette by the French chroniclers rather suggest the atmosphere surrounding an Oriental potentate than the position of an Indian chief. "The veneration which these savages have for the great chief and for his family goes so far that whether he speaks good or evil, they thank him by genuflections and reverences marked by howls." This attitude had a religious foundation since the Suns were reckoned descendants of the Sun, the supreme deity, and capable of averting evil by their intercession. The Great Sun towered above the rest of his kin in grandeur and was hedged about with special prohibitions. No one but his wife might eat with him, and when he gave the leavings to his own brothers he would push the dishes toward them with his feet. The Stinkards were treated as so much dirt, and on the death of a Sun his servants were obliged to die with him. The intermediate grades were clearly of some consequence, especially did a council of the older warriors serve as a check on the authority of the sovereign.

Thanks to the labors of Boas, Swanton, Sapir, Barbeau, and others, our data on the Northwest Coast suffice to afford a clear idea of their caste system. Both as to its existence and as to the intensity of the correlated sentiments there is no doubt; endogamy was strongly fostered; and even a few years ago Barbeau was able to observe the abject servility with which the plebeian children at a Government school treated the royal bratlings. Three classes are recognized—the nobles, the commoners, and the slaves. The last-mentioned group may be briefly dismissed. It was recruited from captives, who after the Maori fashion were not ill-treated but were at any time liable to be put to death, whether as a ritualistic sacrifice or to gratify a mere whim of their master's. For example, at one of those public festivals where each grand seignior sought to excel his peers in his magnificent scorn of property a slave would be killed to enhance his master's display of magnificence; and an indignity, even from natural causes, could be properly wiped out only by the slaying of a slave. The commoners are a group of lowly freemen or of very remote and hence unprivileged kinsmen and in a way retainers of the nobles.

Among the slaves and the commoners there are no further gradations of rank; not so in the nobility, where notions of precedence are developed with all the nicety of the Polynesians. Status depends mainly on the ownership of those principally incorporeal forms of property outlined in a previous chapter. Its clearest outward manifestation is in the seating arrangement at public celebrations, where the seats are carefully graded as to rank. But owing to the variety of privileges there is not necessarily any one noble who is reckoned preëminent in an absolute sense. One will rank the other in seating and yield the priority to another when the order of being invited to a feast is at stake, and so on. However, a correlation does obtain, so that usually many high prerogatives are linked under the ownership of the same person.

The theoretical independence of multiple prerogatives is at least partly connected, as Sapir suggests, with the strong sentiment that each privilege originated in a definite locality of which the memory is retained long after place and prerogative have become dissociated. Thus it may come about that an individual has inherited rights associated with distinct villages, and in that case he may split his patrimony, transmitting one set to an elder son and another to a younger one, who may be established in the proper community under his father's tutelage. This form of succession would of course hold only for the patrilineal tribes; the Coastal tribes farther north have matrilineal descent and by the avunculate transmit privileges to the sister's sons.

Sapir strongly emphasizes the fact that in spite of the stressing of rank it is the lineage, the group rather than the individual, that counts. "Among the Nootka Indians, for instance, an old man, his oldest son say, the oldest son of the son, and, finally, the infant child of the latter, say a daughter, form, to all intents and purposes, a single sociological personality. Titularly the highest rank is accorded.

among the Nootka, to the little child, for it is always the last generation that in theory bears the highest honors. In practice, of course, the oldest members of the group get the real credit and do the business, as it were, of the inherited patrimony; but it would be difficult in such a case to say where the great-grandfather's privileges and standing are marked off against those of his son, or grandson, or great-granddaughter." This is, of course, a point already illustrated with respect to other social phenomena, viz., the tendency of primitive man to merge the individual in the group, as in the arrangement of matrimonial unions.

It cannot be denied that there is something about the caste organization of the Northwest Indians that suggests Polynesian arrangements. Nootka primogeniture furnishes a parallel to Maori usage; the slaying of a slave at the erection of a house represents a rather specific resemblance; and above all the atypical nature, from an American point of view, of any caste system, joined to its occurrence on the Pacific side of the continent might arouse suspicions of an Oceanian origin. However, these circumstances are hardly to be judged conclusive. The Natchez furnish an example of an interior tribe that has developed a radically different scheme of hereditary class distinctions, showing that such divisions may arise spontaneously. Further, the Polynesian and the Columbian systems have, after all, a different character: The Indians lack the exuberant sense for genealogy, while the Polynesians evince no taste for that type of privileges which serves to distinguish the nobles of the Northwest Coast. We may, therefore, assume an independent evolution of castes in these two regions.[4]

Conclusion

The foregoing summary of American, African and Oceanian conditions conclusively refutes the view that primitive society was uniformly averse to the aristocratic spirit.

Slavery did not commence, as Morgan fancied, in communities conversant with the smelting of iron, the domestication of cattle, or the use of irrigation and stone architecture. It occurs in the far ruder stage represented by the Neolithic Polynesians and the non-agricultural Nootka, as does the segmentation of society into castes and gradations of rank. But even in genuinely democratic communities where children are sociologically equal at birth their psychological differences produce inevitable differences in social estimation that make of society an aggregate of individuals rather than an agglomeration of undifferentiated automata.

Still another point merits attention. How far do the facts cited harmonize with that economic interpretation of history which we have had occasion to scrutinize once before? It must be confessed, very indifferently. When a Tsimshian chief murders a slave to retrieve the prestige his daughter has lost by a wound or when a Kwakiutl in a paroxysm of vainglory confounds a social rival by destroying a canoe and breaking a copper plate valued at a thousand blankets, the motive is manifestly as far removed from the economic as it can well be. So the Plains Indian fought not for territorial aggrandizement nor for the victor's spoils, but above all because fighting was a game worth while because of the social recognition it brought when played according to the rules. True, the stealing of horses was one of the principal factors in warfare. But why did a Crow risk his neck to cut loose a picketed horse in the midst of the hostile camp when he could easily have driven off a whole herd from the outskirts? And what was the point in granting distinction not to the warrior who had killed or wounded the foeman but to him who, however lightly, touched his body? Why, finally, that Polynesian punctilio about precedence? Were it a matter of setting off the dominant from a subject people, a utilitarian reason might be given. But that was not the case. Between the blue-blood and the plebeian bickering as to priority was inconceivable; it was solely a question of superiority among the patricians, and of a kind of superiority linked with no temporal advantage but constituting its own reward. Thus, the utilitarian doctrine completely breaks down in the interpretation of aboriginal consciousness. Primitive man is not a miser nor a sage nor a beast of prey but, in Tarde's happy phrase, a peacock.

References

[1] Marett.
[2] Lowie, 1912: 230; id., 1917 (a): 82. Merker: 92, 216. Hollis, 1905: 289, 298, 353 seq. Cole: 96.
[3] Dixon, 1905: 223, 267, 323; id., 1907: 451. Goddard, 1903: 58. Radloff: 1, 312. Bogoras, 614, 639. Boas, 1897: 341 seq. Sapir, 1915: 355 seq.
[4] Tregear: 123, 146, 163, 383. Stair: 65 seq., 147. Turner: 173. Krämer: 1, 31. Roscoe, 1911: 14, 187, 269. Torday and Joyce: 60. Merker: 111. Swanton, 1911: 93, 100 seq. Sapir, 1915: 355 seq.

CHAPTER XIII

GOVERNMENT

COMPARED to the effort expended on the elucidation of the family and sib organization, the theoretical work devoted to the political institutions of primitive tribes has been almost negligible in quantity. Indeed, as we shall see later, there has been a rather persistent attempt to deny the very existence of such a thing as political organization properly so called in the ruder cultures. That is, of course, a point of primary importance, to which we must revert. For the present, however, it will be best to view the facts without theoretical prepossession of any sort and to inquire merely what governmental agencies exist in different areas and how they are correlated with features of aboriginal life already sketched in previous chapters. Though I shall employ the word 'political' for convenience' sake, for the present I do so merely to denote legislative, executive and judicial functions and its use in no way prejudges the question to be broached after a survey of the concrete data. These several functions, as has sometimes been pointed out, are often merged. The Australian council issues ordinances, directs their execution, and passes judgment on criminal offences, and the same is true of corresponding governing agencies elsewhere. But it should be noted that the legislative function in most primitive communities seems strangely curtailed when compared with that exercised in the more complex civilizations. All the exigencies of normal social intercourse are covered by customary law, and the business of such governmental machinery as exists is rather to exact obedience to traditional usage than to create new precedents. Under the despotic rule of some of the African or Oceanian autocrats this principle naturally does not hold to nearly the same degree. A Zulu monarch was able to abrogate the time-honored usage of circumcision by a royal edict and the decrees of a Hawaiian sovereign could absolve men from obedience to established law. Nevertheless, it is probable that even in such extreme cases the transactions of social intercourse were regulated in a far greater measure by the time-honored usages of antiquity than by the sum-total of these autocratic ukases.

In the present chapter we are more particularly concerned with the question of the existence and character of a central governing agency; for practical reasons the administration of justice will be treated separately in the one following.

Australia

The salient feature of Australian public life is the dominance of the aged men. There are local differences as to the powers of the elders' class as a whole, but almost everywhere the women are rigidly excluded from political activity and everywhere young men are reckoned of little if any importance in the tribal deliberations. Nevertheless within the limits of this gerontocracy, to use Dr. Rivers' apt term for the rule of elders, interesting differences have arisen.

The Dieri furnish a favorable example of one of the varieties found. The assembly of full-fledged men, i.e., of men who have passed through the initiation ceremony officially conferring the status of maturity, constituted practically a secret society, for to divulge the acts of this parliament was to court death. The subjects discussed included cases of murder by magic, transgression of the incest rules, and ceremonial arrangements. It was this body that dispatched an armed party to kill a murderous sorcerer and re-allotted concubines on festive occasions. Apparently no vote was taken: "If all were agreed to some course the council separated, if not, then it met at some future time." So far we are dealing merely with the elders as a whole. But their proceedings were directed by the principal headman, who gave instructions for the summoning of the council and led the discussion. In the 'sixties of the last century the chieftaincy belonged to one Jalina-piramurana, who had inherited the position from his father. He is described as "a man of persuasive eloquence, a skilful and brave fighting-man, and a powerful medicine-man." He was universally reverenced and received presents from various local groups, which he generously distributed among his friends. He was able to prevent fighting, his decisions being accepted without murmuring. None of the elders, including his own brothers, dared interfere with his decrees. In short, we here have a case of extraordinary authority due to an unusual personality. Jalina-piramurana eclipsed his father and doubtless was not equaled in importance by his successor. The fact is, however, noteworthy that in this section of Australia there is a frequent tendency toward the evolution of preëminent headmen whose office descended from father to son.

Rather different are the conditions in the central area inhabited by such peoples as the Arunta and the Warramunga. Here there is no single individuality that could be considered the tribal chief; but neither is there anything in the nature of a *general* elders' council. What happens is that each local totem group has a headman whose office descends from father to son, and that from these headmen, whose functions are mainly if not wholly ceremonial, are recruited the members of a governing board. This is a close corporation of a very few of the most important elders. Their number is not fixed, but hovers about five; ten or twelve is mentioned as most unusual. This council meets quite informally and without any regular speeches. All its members are headmen, and if some other headman has commended himself to them through his ability and public spirit they will some day reward him by an invitation to join their deliberations. The oligarchs are implicitly obeyed by the whole tribe and completely control every matter of public concern. On the other hand, the younger men, even though of mature years, are of no importance whatsoever and pay the utmost homage to the leading elders.

The aborigines of North Queensland do not conform strictly to either the Arunta or the Dieri pattern in their camp council. It is evidently a rather larger body than that of the Central Australians, for it includes all the older men of some consequence. But among these there is no single one that rises to a status of supremacy. What gradations of power there are depend on personal factors: a man who has passed through the various stages leading to an elder's status, or one of fighting quality, or with a large following acquired by plural marriage, is likely to exercise more than usual influence. The nature of the discussions closely resembles that noted for the Dieri. Questions of peace and war, the reception of strangers, the shifting of the camp, the punishment of incest, and the prevention of brawls within the settlement all fall within the province of the elders' assembly, while such acts as infanticide or the maiming of an adulterous wife are deemed purely private matters with which the council does not interfere.[1]

Polynesia and Micronesia

That excessive regard to differences of pedigree which is so conspicuous a feature of the Polynesians does not necessarily involve the political ascendancy of the noblest patricians. This is most clearly demonstrated by the example of New Zealand and Samoa, though it is probable that the condition there found represents a later development, as will be indicated below.

It is not easy to define briefly and with precision the polity of the New Zealanders. That there was nowhere a vast realm governed by a supreme liege lord, is clear. But it is not so easy to determine the constitutional powers of those chiefs of exalted lineage but restricted territory who presided over the numerous tribes engaged in constant warfare with one another. On the one hand, we learn that though primogeniture might confer the purple with the mitre, only the latter was an inalienable appendage of birth. The landed gentry who constituted the backbone of the nation could depose an heir-apparent whose cowardice, avarice or incapacity had estranged the people; and they would elect in his place a worthier representative of the kin, say, an uncle or brother. In a sense, then, the prince was only the first gentleman of the tribe. On the other hand, his religious character, if not degraded by especially grievous faults, invested him with an atmosphere of awe that evidently bestowed not a little authority in all the phases of life. Thus, he acted not merely as an intercessor with the gods, consecrating warriors before the fray, blessing the crops and regulating the ritual, but also served as a judge in property disputes, conducted horticultural operations and was entitled to the first-fruits, to wrecked canoes, and to cetaceans caught ashore.

Indissolubly bound up with the temporal powers of a prince or noble was the characteristically Polynesian prerogative of imposing a taboo, which probably attained as high a development in New Zealand as anywhere throughout the region. It is impossible to follow the native concept through all its labyrinthine ramifications since we are here concerned only with its political import. This was sufficiently simple in principle, though most far-reaching in practical results. The noble or chief, partaking of the divine essence of which he was the incarnation, was able to communicate his contagious holiness so that the objects in question could not be appropriated by any one but a superior in rank. He might stop traffic on a river or cause great inconvenience to his people by tabooing a forest. This was generally done by putting up a pole with a bunch of rags or leaves or by erecting some corresponding notice-board. Infringement of a taboo was not merely a crime but spiritual iniquity calling down the wrath of the gods, who would visit the offender with disease or death. Even outside of Polynesia the Oceanians practise the taboo custom in diluted form. The method followed by the Melanesian Ghost societies for safeguarding personal property (p. 279) falls in this category, and though in the Banks Islands it is the offended organization that inflicts condign chastisement Dr. Rivers shows that in the Solomons corresponding transgressions are supposed to be automatically punished by the ghosts, a belief that serves as a connecting link between the Melanesian and the Polynesian notion of taboo. How tremendous a power the taboo prerogative conferred on its possessor when linked with the office of chief, hardly requires exposition, and it is rather remarkable that in spite of its development in New Zealand the chief was nevertheless subject to loss of secular ascendancy.

On the essentials of the Samoan constitution the information is clearer. There was a nominal ruler of the whole group—the lord who had secured all the five regal titles from the electoral districts privileged to dispose of them. But to a very considerable extent each district was autonomous, as appears from the multiplicity of internecine wars and the jealous protection of local boundaries. Within each district there was a dominant settlement, which summoned the local parliament. This met in executive session in an open square tabooed for the time being to all outsiders, whose intrusion was punished with death. The provincial chief, the rustic aristocracy, and the lesser landowners had access to this assembly, which combined legislative and judicial authority. Village chiefs might take the floor, but usually each was represented by a speaker, one of the gentry, who acted as his mouthpiece. The right to address the assembly was highly prized, and in consequence all those entitled to deliver a speech would rise simultaneously and contend for the honor of the first oration, frittering away much time before the point of precedence was settled. The orator permitted to speak was again confronted with a matter of etiquette, being obliged to recite first of all the various honorific designations of all the Samoan districts, the omission of any one of which was regarded as an affront. As he proceeded, his party prompted him, refreshing his memory or urging a choice of topics, and if bored by his eloquence they had the right to bid him be seated. From other groups he suffered no interruption till a moot-question was touched upon, when the orator of another party might take the floor and launch a debate. Refreshments supplied by the surrounding villages were handed about during the minor speeches, and throughout the day the members not actually addressing the assembly were busy plaiting sinnet from cocoanut fiber.

When matters affecting several districts were at stake, the dominant settlement of the district which took the initiative dispatched messengers informing each of the other districts as to the topic for deliberation. Each district then had a separate assembly and came prepared to what may be styled the provincial parliament. Sometimes the principal men of the first settlement would make the rounds of the other districts canvassing the members so as to gain their point ultimately in the formal council. Owing to the absence of a sense for centralized government, there was little coöperation and no power to enforce the decisions outside the minor groups.

Generally speaking, it was the assembly of country squires that had the whip-hand, and among them the speakers stood preëminent. Their influence could award the district chieftaincy to a particular individual among those qualified by virtue of pedigree, and though unusually gifted chiefs exercised great powers the generality were unable to dominate the speakers when these were supported by the other heads of families. Accordingly, unpopular chiefs were not only exiled but beaten and sometimes even killed by their subjects. Their hereditary sacredness, which rendered them taboo like the Maori priest-chiefs, formed an obstacle to such summary treatment, but Samoan ingenuity rose equal to the task. By sprinkling a chief's body with cocoanut water they rendered him profane, formally divested him of the title they had once conferred, and were then at liberty to hack him into pieces if they so chose.

The polity of the Maori and the Samoans may thus be likened to a state of barons granting precedence to the ruler of their choice but without allegiance and reserving to themselves the ultimate voice in matters of government. This differs utterly from the conditions prevalent in Hawaii and the Marshall Islands, where the bulk of the population were not landowning gentlemen but degraded serfs cringing before the select class of the upper Four Hundred. In Hawaii there was even a distinct tendency toward monarchical despotism, though there is evidence that the patrician caste was not without influence on important decisions. The social stratification of the Marshall Islands has already been dealt with in connection with property rights. It was shown that the aristocracy is sharply divided from both the middle-class and the common herd. The middle class comprises the expert navigators and other professionals whose services are prized in this region of the globe; and though their utterances have no legal validity, they enjoy the respect of the nobility and may hold land as feudal tenants. The nobility is subdivided into a higher and lower caste, but both are in an equally absolute sense owners of their hereditary soil, and though the lesser chief is tributary to the greater, his allegiance is voluntary and in case of serious misunderstanding complete independence ensues. With reference to either class of patricians the commoners are a body of pariahs cultivating the chiefs' lands and rendering all manner of menial services. The chiefs are not only supported by their subjects, but have access to their wives and daughters, and could once wantonly destroy the lives of the plebeians. This relationship, doubtless fostered for ages, engendered a servile frame of mind on the part of the oppressed caste, which survived the pressure of necessity. As late as 1905 Father Erdland found commoners willingly jeopardizing their lives to prop up the hurricane-shaken walls of a princely hut. In the same year an aged fisherman sunk in indigence through a natural catastrophe borrowed money from the missionary to fill the well-stocked coffers of his lord with the customary annual tribute. Though the colonial administration would doubtless have protected the supplicant and though Erdland offered to plead with the chief and have him remit the payment, the commoner's mind was not set at rest till his tears had won the loan, in return for which he vowed to furnish his benefactor with fish as long as he lived. It does not readily occur to man to adapt himself to modified social conditions. The Marshall Islander's psychology does not differ notably from that of impoverished gentlemen in our own civilization who anachronistically remain class-conscious members of their natal caste instead of joyously throwing in their lot with their new associates.

The social and political conceptions diffused with many local variations over the whole of Polynesia and Micronesia must have had an intricate history, which it will require the efforts of many specialists to unravel in detail; but the general course of development has been most plausibly traced by Waitz and Gerland. Observations by the earliest travelers and legendary aboriginal accounts of early society suggest that several centuries ago the conditions more recently noted in Hawaii were prevalent over the entire region. This is a conclusion that, moreover, flows logically from the divine descent of the nobility, which is naturally converted into a divine right to rule. From this point of view the punctilio of Maori and Samoans in matters of etiquette and genealogy are relics of an earlier stage at which differences in rank were not nearly so largely questions of academic interest but involved differences in political authority. That so rigid an insistence on caste distinctions, so hypertrophied an elaboration of the theory of taboo, necessitates a very long course of development preceding it, is evident; but what may have preceded the aristocratic and theocratic conception of Polynesian philosophers and statesmen eludes historical scrutiny. We can only surmise that the antecedent condition savored of the simplicity now current in the remainder of Oceania.[2]

Melanesia and New Guinea

Those parts of Melanesia exposed to Polynesian influences, notably New Caledonia and sections of Fiji, share the theory of divine princes; elsewhere the chief's status is of far more modest character. Among the Baining of the Gazelle Peninsula, indeed, there are no chiefs. A brave warrior gains distinction and the title of 'hero,' forming a nucleus for groups of men so long as his prowess is maintained. In the Banks Islands, too, no real chiefs occur, for there the title that might be so translated is inseparable from membership in the highest grade of the men's club. Attainment to that degree was seen to be dependent on wealth, and in that sense we might speak of a plutocratic government. But it is clear that there was no one dominant ruling body, that the men of the highest grade were not so much potentates as persons highly esteemed by the community, and that not a little power was wielded by the several Ghost societies.

Rather more complicated arrangements occur in Buin, Solomon Islands. Here three grades of chiefs are recognized, the lesser chiefs, the hundred chiefs, and the great chiefs. The lesser chiefs are hardly more than influential heads of families. Any one possessed of sufficient shell-money to erect a hall with several wooden drums and to organize entertainments in it can become a lesser chief. The 'hundred chiefs' are not necessarily the leaders of fully a hundred followers; indeed, the number sometimes sinks to but sixty, including servants. These chiefs are generally allied with one another. The great chiefs are recruited from certain prominent families and are always leagued with the hundred chiefs and lesser chiefs of several districts. It is in fact on these alliances that their power rests. All three grades of the chieftaincy are inheritable, but the title is validated only when the claimant has built the assembly hall and entertained his neighbors, whose acceptance of the invitation is equivalent to an acknowledgment of his superiority. Thus, a distinctly timocratic element is associated with the hereditary principle. The assembly hall is a men's clubhouse, council-chamber and ceremonial chapel, from which women are ordinarily excluded.

Alliances are ratified by a solemnity united with a boy's initiation into the tribe. The boy's father pledges his support of a certain chief or boasts of his past deeds on the chief's behalf, urging him in return to protect the novice. There is an exchange of gifts and it is possible to extend the circle of allies by dispatching presents to other chiefs. All those leagued together in this fashion assume the obligation of the blood-feud, but this bond is a purely personal one, that is, it cannot be inherited by the children of the allies, who would have to undergo a similar ceremony in order to perpetuate the relationship. Though a great chief by virtue of his numerous allies can play an important part in warfare, he has no authority beyond that due to his personality. He does not interfere with the privacy of family life and he cannot force one of his followers to obey a command. If one of them takes umbrage and absents himself from the hall, the chief will try to conciliate him with presents. A pouting brave might otherwise desert his district and join another chief, thereby diminishing the forces of his native settlement. On the other hand, a miscreant who transgresses tribal law may be sent into exile.

In New Guinea the chief's rôle is an equally modest one. Among the Kai he has the largest field but then his is the obligation of entertaining all guests and his own people to boot. He is the wealthiest of the villagers, and is expected to supply his helpers liberally with tobacco and betel-nuts, to slaughter pigs for them and regale them with other delicacies. Beyond his general claim on their support, he has little authority. Every tribesman acts as he sees fit, and the chief has no means of coërcion. Similar conditions obtain among the Jabim. Every one helps the chief build a house or plant his field, but it is understood that a lavish entertainment will compensate them for the work. There is no popular assembly, but on important occasions there are sessions with a few prominent men, at which deliberations are conducted in a very low tone of voice. There is no debate pro and con, and as seems the universal custom of the ruder peoples no vote is taken. A common formula of submitting to the will of others is: "Thou hast spoken, and thus it shall be."[3]

Africa

The political institutions of Africa are of peculiar interest. Certain differences between the character of the social gradations found there and that of corresponding features in Polynesia were pointed out in a previous chapter. Politically equally noteworthy differences must be noted in spite of the occurrence of despotic monarchs in both Africa and at least ancient Polynesia. For one thing, the Negro rulers often extended their dominion over an enormous area, so that in comparison the exalted sovereigns of Hawaii or Tahiti appear as petty princelings. This cannot be explained by geographical considerations, for the Polynesians were admirable navigators and could easily have established something of a maritime empire. Yet the strength of centrifugal tendencies prevented any such development. It is especially remarkable that in New Zealand, where the geographical barrier is wholly lacking, there is no evidence of a powerful sovereign uniting dozens of tribes under his scepter. Secondly, the course of political history in Africa seems to have been far more fluctuating and capricious than in Oceania. In Polynesia, if Waitz and Gerland's theory is accepted, there was a general tendency for the large body of landowning gentlemen to possess themselves of an increasing measure of political power. Among the Negroes an inveterate disposition to monarchical rule, though qualified by the influence of elders or other officials, has again and again made it possible for forceful personalities to convert themselves into absolute tyrants; but the structure reared by their individual efforts utterly collapsed under lesser guardians or degenerated into a mere mockery of autocracy with various functionaries representing the real power behind the throne.

The Thonga and Zulu jointly furnish an especially illuminating sample of African political history and accordingly merit a place of honor in our descriptive account.

The territory of the Thonga is split up into a considerable number of petty principalities politically independent of one another, though united by virtual community of speech and custom. In each of these diminutive realms there reigns an hereditary monarch, the eldest son of the preceding ruler's queen (not necessarily the first wife, but the first after his accession). His office is invested with an atmosphere of sacredness; he alone is entitled to the honorific salutation "Bayete!"; his name is taboo except in oaths; he takes precedence in the rites of the first-fruits, of which he partakes after an offering to the spirits; and above all he is in possession of a powerful charm that magically insures the invincibility of the country. The king exacts tribute in kind; he receives a basket of food from each kraal at harvest time and part of the game animals killed in the chase. His subjects must till the royal fields, clean his public square, build and repair his huts. Finally, he appropriates a large portion of the fines imposed by him in court, for legislative, judicial and executive functions are merged in his person and from his judgment there is no appeal.

Although the king thus enjoys great prerogatives and wields considerable authority, he cannot be described as an absolute autocrat. If his actions run counter to received standards of propriety, he is severely criticised by the people and may even be deposed. Secondly, his actual powers are divided with members of his family. By the established system of government the king's kinsmen—sons or brothers—are set up to rule over the provinces of the state. On his accession to the throne a new monarch may find these relatives reluctant to acknowledge his suzerainty, and it has repeatedly happened that they have established independent principalities. Finally, the king is surrounded by a group of councilors, mostly mature men from his own family, who may gain great influence over him, even to the extent of determining his decrees. Many decisions are made by this assembly, for the king, though presiding at the meeting, will frequently take no part in the debate, merely nodding his assent.

Family disputes are fostered not only by the method of ruling provinces but also by the law of succession, which attempts to reconcile two quite distinct principles, primogeniture and fraternal inheritance. The eldest son of the queen is indeed the theoretical heir-apparent, but he can only ascend the throne after the regency of all his father's younger brothers. These are naturally in effect kings and one of them is often loath to surrender the sovereignty to the elder line, attempting to bequeath it to his own son. In this fashion bitter family feuds arise, and men plot to rid themselves of closely related potential rivals with all the callousness of a Borgia. This condition of affairs, however, may tend to throw some authority into the hands of the populace, since a rival needs the support of the warriors in order to gain his ends.

There is little ostentation about Thonga kings as compared with other African rulers. They do not differ in their attire from the subjects, sometimes occupy kraals no larger than those of commoners, and may indulge in so modest an occupation as scaring sparrows from a plantation. Nevertheless each sovereign is surrounded by a court of dignitaries with a characteristically African formality of procedure.

The councilors have already been referred to. In addition to the cabinet composed of the king's kinsmen, there are the leaders of the army; the diplomatic staff, each of whom has one of the adjoining principalities for his special subject; and the minor district magistrates. Another group of courtiers is composed of the king's personal friends and age-mates, his companions in feasts and games, who usually live in a bachelors' house near the royal dwelling. While these favorites are without specific functions, the herald enjoys a peculiar official status. His duty it is to appear before the king's door every morning and to exalt the exploits of the ruler's ancestors, which is followed by vigorous disparagement of the present incumbent. Eloquence seems to be the sole qualification for this office and what is its nature here may be gathered from a few characteristic sentences in a long rhapsody by a distinguished herald:

"Muhlaba Shiluvane (the king's father), you are like the rhinoceros who seizes a man, bites him through and through, rolls him over and cuts him in two! You are like the crocodile which lives in water; it bites a man! You are like its claws; it seizes a man by his arms and legs, it drags him into the deep pool to eat him at sunset; it watches over the entrance to prevent other crocodiles from taking its prey. . . .

"Why do you govern them so mildly! Look at them with terrible eyes! You are a coward! . . . Act with bravery and defend yourself!"

At least equally remarkable is another licensed character, the "public vituperator" or court jester, who may hurl the most offensive insults at anyone in the country, from the king down. He may wantonly accuse his countrymen of incest and snatch food from the hands of the king himself.

The precision of court etiquette is well illustrated by the customs incident to the visit of a stranger. The visitor seats himself outside the central square of the capital and announces to some native that he desires to see the chief. At once the diplomat in charge of relations with the stranger's principality greets him and announces his arrival to the king, who arranges for his entertainment. If the matter to be brought before his majesty is of some moment, the visitor expounds it to the diplomat dealing with the relevant part of foreign affairs. This official repeats the speech, sentence by sentence, to one of the king's councilors and he in turn recounts the whole tale as if his lord had not heard it all before. As Junod points out, this procedure is not without merit among people devoid of written records.

The Zulu are a closely related people living to the south of the Thonga. From a mass of ethnographical material it is clear that their condition, say, a century and a half ago was strikingly similar to that of their northern fellow-Bantu. About the beginning of the nineteenth century they came under the sway of a neighboring ruler, Dingiswayo, who had organized a standing army and by its aid not only conquered various native tribes but also established himself as an autocrat with powers far transcending those of his predecessors. However, he was outdone by a Zulu king, Chaka. Building upon the military suggestions offered by Dingiswayo's system, Chaka developed it into an even more effective engine of militarism and by his far-reaching conquests earned the title of the "Napoleon of South Africa," while the disturbances caused by his career extended as far north as Lake Tanganyika. Two fundamental innovations were introduced by Chaka. For one thing, he substituted for the reed javelins hitherto in vogue a thrusting-spear to be used at close quarters, with the result that the shock tactics thus originated proved quite irresistible. Secondly, he organized subjugated tribes so that they strengthened his own forces. More especially when the conquered people were not immediate neighbors, all but the boys and marriageable girls were put to death, while the survivors were placed on the same level with his former subjects—the girls entering his seraglio, the boys his army.

In this fashion Chaka succeeded in maintaining a standing army of from 12,000 to 15,000 warriors. Each regiment of from 600 to 1,000 men occupied a kraal or barracks of its own. Adolescent boys would volunteer for enlistment, so that new kraals were formed every year. The novices were distinguished by their black shields, those of the veterans being white. As soon as the young warriors had distinguished themselves in battle, their heads were shaved by the king's orders and they assumed the official status of 'men.' But this did not yet entitle them to settle down in marriage. Soldiers were bachelors so far as legitimate matrimony was concerned, though nothing prevented indulgence in love affairs with women of nearby civil kraals. It required a special dispensation of the king for the warriors to marry, and this was granted individually or wholesale to an entire regiment only for special service or when the disabilities of age had become evident. The married men ranked as socially inferior and formed the reserves of the royal host. The soldiers were maintained at the king's expense; as many as twelve head of cattle might be supplied daily to a single barracks. Freedom from economic necessity, participation in the spoils, and the social

GOVERNMENT 375

distinction of warriorhood compensated the soldiers for the rigors of a system that was moulded and wielded with an iron hand. For the life of the Zulu military was not one of ease. Obedience was exacted to the most extravagant commands; pain must be borne without flinching; and retreat in face of the enemy was punished with death, nay, from a policy of terrorism after every battle the officers were obliged to mark out for slaughter 'cowards,' whether there had been such or not.

With such a force ready to do his bidding, Chaka evolved a despotism beside which that of Dingiswayo paled into insignificance. His subjects were to all intents and purposes his slaves, whom he might put to death at the nod of his head. They were not permitted to render services to any one else and he reserved for himself the monopoly of trade with the whites. Chaka had for his advisers two principal ministers superintending his own kraal and a group of twenty lesser councilors; but there is little doubt that at the height of his power the monarch could override their opposition. Yet the type of autocracy founded by Chaka bears within itself the germ of disintegration. In order to be successful it requires a virile, nay, ferocious, personality. The form of government itself furnished no stability, and as it makes a difference whether a Peter the Great or a Nicholas is Autocrat of Russia, so in South Africa it was not the same whether Chaka or Dingaan held the reins, and under a weaker successor the royal power crumbled. While Chaka had ruled his army, the warriors ruled Dingaan, who came to preserve the outward appearance rather than the substance of regal authority.

The history of Zulu government within the brief space of less than a century thus presents a typical picture of African conditions. In the modest confines of a petty state organized on the principle of a benevolent monarch's rule, not without checks and balances, there rises an imperious ruler who organizes the military, terrorizes and subjects to his sway adjoining populations and makes himself an absolute despot. But the realm created by his energy cannot be held together by the epigonoi and it splits once more into smaller units presided over by the patriarchal sovereigns of the earlier type.

A comparison of the Ewe polity with that of the related inhabitants of Dahomi shows practically the same sequence of events among the Sudanese Negroes as we have just traced among the southeastern Bantu.

The rulers of the Ho-Ewe are even farther removed from the status of autocracy than the Thonga kings. Though the element of inheritance enters into the arrangement of succession, the king is chosen from a number of possible candidates. The aspirant to the throne attempts to conciliate influential electors by gifts, but his donations are not all-important since the candidate's character is duly considered. The chiefs nominate the man of their choice for king and the populace ratify the nomination. There follows a formal inauguration in the presence of the chiefs and a limited body representing the commoners, for the rank and file must never view the throne nor some of the other regalia. As the king is elected, so he may be deposed, but such action is most exceptional, being resorted to only when the sovereign has seriously injured the tribal welfare. An ideal king is affable and hospitably entertains his subjects; in court he tempers with kindly phrase the bitterness of an adverse judgment; in private life he is an industrious horticulturist and weaver.

The core of the governing body is formed by the king and two local chiefs, assisted by a speaker and his deputies. Added to these is a group of councilors recruited from the heads of the largest families. But opposed to this more or less aristocratic body are the rank and file of the village community presided over by a headman and his speaker. This headman is the leader in war and acts as intermediary between the populace and the chiefs. The people have the right to protest against the decrees of the ruling body and their objections are transmitted through the headman to the council, whose members are careful to give due consideration to the wishes of the subjects. In unusual times of stress the king summons a popular assembly.

Though the king is thus very much limited in power, he is not without the outward trappings of royalty. The throne, which is preserved from the sight of vulgar eyes, has already been mentioned. More important is the institution of personal attendants, sometimes to the number of twenty-four. Some of them are beadles who summon people to court, others carry the king in a special basketry frame. When acting officially they are privileged to whip anyone in their way and may kill and eat any sheep or goats they encounter. They receive no regular pay but appropriate as their perquisites a large part of the court fees. Accordingly it is to their interest to have large fines imposed, and this obviously may become an ample source of abuses.

The laws which enjoy the greatest respect and of which the transgressions are most severely punished are not the special decrees of the king's council but those rules of customary law which have been in vogue from time immemorial—the laws against murder and theft, for example. In the main the legislative council merely adds ordinances of minor significance. These decrees are first discussed by the chiefs' council, then submitted to the village assemblies, whose members debate among themselves before jointly deliberating on the matter with the chiefs. Only when both bodies have come to an agreement are the laws duly ratified and must then be heralded to the people.

The Coastal Ewe differed from their Ho congeners in that the commoners had no voice in the government but in the limitations of royal power by a council of chiefs they conform closely to the Ho pattern. A fundamentally different condition is encountered among the linguistically and culturally related population of Dahomi. Here the ruler appears as an all but absolute monarch; theoretically he was sole owner of all land and other property, which was held in practice only through his tolerance; and the greatest officials were little better than his slaves, obliged to grovel in abject deference before him. There was, of course, no hereditary aristocracy: the king appointed both the provincial chiefs and the great ministers of state, and of these only one, combining the duties of police commissioner and lord high executioner, might not be beheaded at his master's will. The power over life and death was a distinctive attribute of royalty, for the provincial chiefs were only privileged to imprison and fine, though they could legally compass the death of their subjects by indirect methods, such as starvation in jail.

The great national officials were seven in number. Foremost stood the lord high executioner and the superintendent of public festivals, who also united in his person the functions of a revenue-collector and an intermediary between the sovereign and the people. These two officers between them appointed a successor to the throne from among the king's sons, for though primogeniture was favored they had the power of setting aside the customary rule. They also judged criminal cases and were in a preëminent sense the king's advisers. Next in order of rank came the governor of the coastal town of Whydah, then the chief of the palace interior, a eunuch who was executed on the death of his sovereign. The fifth and sixth officers were the chief military commander and his assistant, both of whom resided near the principal gate of Agbomi, the capital. Finally came the superintendent of the plantations supplying the monarch's household; in addition he served as an assistant to the lord high executioner. These seven great officials were greeted by all inferiors with marked tokens of respect. This organization of male officials was exactly duplicated by a series of female dignitaries in the palace interior, and though their authority did not extend beyond the palace they formally took precedence of the corresponding male officers because of the legal fiction that all women attached to the court were the king's wives.

Of lesser rank than the national dignitaries were the civilian captains; next came the royal attendants; below them the military officers; then the provincial chiefs and officials; and finally the traders. The rest of the population were practically the slaves of their superiors.

All the higher officials were distinguished by insignia of rank, such as a wooden stool, an umbrella canopy, a pipe and tobacco pouch, and ivory clubs. A king's or chief's messenger invariably bore a stick of office, which served as a safe-conduct and was received with the same esteem as the sender. Any disrespect to this badge was reckoned a serious crime.

Ellis presents a sufficiently lurid picture of conditions in Dahomi—commoners plundered and browbeaten by the local authorities, chiefs and ministers in abject subjection to a despotic ruler, an espionage system that threatened the life of every subject, ceremonial sacrifices in honor of deceased monarchs at which hundreds of people were slaughtered to convey messages from the ruler to his ancestors. Tyranny was certainly rampant in Dahomi, yet human nature is such that a really absolute despotism proves insupportable and a close reading of the evidence shows that even the Dahomi despot was not governed solely by his whims. Theoretically omnipotent, he was in practice obliged to act with some degree of circumspection. A sovereign of the early part of the nineteenth century who wallowed in blood and organized gangs of men to plunder his own people finally precipitated a rebellion that led to his dethronement and death. And though the king might condemn to execution individual chiefs and officers, he was generally careful to avoid defying at the same time the priests, the chiefs, and popular prejudice. His exercise of authority was undoubtedly arbitrary in the extreme; but in his confiscation of property and infliction of capital punishment he did not appeal so much to the powers theoretically vested in him as he sought to lend a semblance of justice to high-handed procedure. In a concrete case the individual peasant or chief was pillaged not on the basis of an abstract right of royalty but because he had disobeyed an arbitrary ordinance or had been accused of plotting against his lord. In all this Dahomi autocracy differed little from the despotic governments of more highly civilized nations.

A comparative survey of the several tribes of the Ewe family leaves little doubt as to the course of political development in this area. Underlying the systems of all these peoples we have that differentiation of rank which is so highly developed among both Bantu and Sudanese Negroes. In the Ho territory this characteristic condition remained perfectly compatible with a far-reaching influence not only of official circles but even of the rank and file. Among the Dahomi, on the other hand, the organization of a relatively large standing army maintained by the king gave him a preponderance over the whole remainder of society, which was checked only in cases of exceptional abuse. Nevertheless the precise power of a particular ruler inevitably depended on his personal qualities.

A somewhat different condition of affairs characterizes certain other Negro populations, e.g., the Bakuba of the southwestern Congo. Here political institutions seem to have enjoyed a certain stability. The sovereign, an incarnation of the deity, is theoretically an absolute monarch and is surrounded by a magnificent court comprising male and female dignitaries by the score. He is treated with extreme reverence on public occasions, even his enemies resenting a slight offered to his station. This does not prevent his six ministers from arrogating practically all authority and virtually enslaving him by exacting fastidious observance of traditional court etiquette. Though it is not altogether impossible for an unusually gifted king to assert his theoretical prerogatives, there seems less chance of such an occurrence among the Bakuba than in most countries of Africa. The grandees treat him with great independence since they enjoy a safe tenure of office, and while the sovereign theoretically may fill any vacancy his choice is practically determined by the force of public opinion. He dare not appoint his greatest favorites in the face of staunch opposition and is sometimes obliged to yield a lofty position to persons he heartily dislikes.

In Yorubaland, too, there is merely the shadow of royalty. A king deriving his title from divine descent is treated with all the outward marks of respect but is a mere puppet in the hands of his cabinet. Outside of his capital there is complete local autonomy, and he is obliged to content himself with a purely nominal recognition of his sovereignty over a host of city-states. The actual government of these communities, some of which have a population of over 100,000, is highly interesting because it illustrates once more the necessity of correlating the several aspects of a culture. West Africa is eminently a region of secret organizations, and in Yorubaland it is an association of old men called the Ogboni that has usurped the supreme power. They form, for one thing, an electoral college that elevates a suitable tribesman to the office of burgomaster or governor of the town, who surrounds himself with an impressive array of officials, partly appointed by himself and partly chosen by the people. During his term of office the governor is entitled to assistance from his subjects and may add to his possessions by punitive expeditions against the unruly. But he is wholly dependent on the support of the Ogboni. As soon as his acts are contrary to their interests, they prove by a casting of lots that the deity is unfavorably disposed to his continuance in office and effectively remove him by clandestinely administering a poisonous potion. The reign of the governor is said to have averaged only two years. It is by their manipulation of the divinatory art that the Ogboni terrorize the entire population. An upstart with a limited circle of retainers whose wealth arouses the cupidity of the members is accused of some crime and summoned to an ordeal. The dice are of course loaded against him, he is convicted and summarily executed, and his fortune is divided among the Ogboni and the burgomaster.

Regardless of variations in time and space, it is justifiable to say that the Negroes evince an inveterate proclivity for at least the forms of monarchical government. Apparently this represents essentially an old cultural heritage of both the Bantu and the Sudanese. The fact cannot be impressed into the service of that geographical mysticism which is once more raising its head, because stocks possessing a different set of traditions depart widely from the Negro norm even though they may live surrounded by Negro tribes, that is, in the identical geographical environment. This is demonstrated most clearly by the case of the Masai, which is likewise instructive from another point of view. A priori one would certainly be inclined to conjecture that the head of so martial a people must be some warrior of renown, but this assumption for all its reasonableness does not even approach the truth. Such central power as exists is vested in an hereditary seer who is not so much as permitted to accompany a war expedition, but is expected to prepare a medicine insuring the warriors' success and to foretell future events. He is also empowered to appoint by divination the headmen of the several districts. But though he enjoys the respect due to a holy man, the character of his office is far removed from that of a typical Negro autocrat. He is more of a national saint than a ruler, does not dispose of life and death, indeed, rarely acts as judge at all, and never basks in the splendor of a court. Naturally a man of unusual force like Mbatian, who died in 1890, may exercise great authority, but even then there is nothing approximating the autocracies, real or formal, so common in other sections of the continent.[4]

North America

As has already been pointed out, the Indians of North America generally incline to democracy and thus contrast sharply with the Negroes of Africa. Departures from this norm might be most readily expected among the tribes with a clearly defined caste system, yet only among the Natchez do we find a centralization of authority corresponding to the powers of an African despot. The Natchez ruler was not merely treated reverentially but served with humility. His least wish was blindly obeyed, so that whenever the French required rowers or hunters they merely needed to bribe the chief into requisitioning the services of an adequate number of subjects, who received no compensation for their labor. He had power over life and death, and when he himself died his attendants and others as well deemed it an honor to accompany him to the hereafter. Needless to say, all the best products of the chase, fishing or horticulture were yielded as a tribute. The sovereign, whose prerogatives were in some measure shared by his closest relatives, appointed his ministers, more particularly two war chiefs, two temple officials, and officers regulating peace treaties and the performance of festivals. Though the contemporaneous sources cited by Swanton agree in exalting the chief into an absolutely autocratic ruler, incidental remarks suggest that at times a council and the abler village chiefs, presumably all of the noble caste, could materially restrict his freedom of action. Nevertheless, the Natchez institutions remain the most remarkable example of monarchy north of Mexico.

On the Northwest Coast, in spite of the rigidity of class distinctions, the strictly political powers of a chief were disproportionately small when compared with his social eminence. With the Tlingit he merely presided over collective deliberations; in general the head of every family could act as he chose so far as he did not collide with customary law. A Tsimshian chief possibly wielded greater power: he decided when the tribe was to move or when fishing operations were to begin and he was entitled to a certain tribute. He took precedence at all dances and commanded over messengers and attendants. However, he was not an irresponsible ruler. As leader in war, he had to answer for the losses sustained and to compensate the bereaved kindred. Matters of importance were decided in council, and without its members' consent no chief could announce a potlatch feast.

The democratic individualism not wholly suppressed even in Northwest Coast society gains almost complete ascendancy throughout the remainder of the immense territory under consideration. This is by no means due to the breakdown of ancient chieftaincies through contact with Caucasian civilization. On the contrary, everything goes to show that white officialdom tended to enhance the powers of the native chiefs. There is indeed incontrovertible evidence from early travelers, reporting observations in the most widely separated regions. The great Chipewyan chief Matonabbee, whom Hearne glorifies in an amusing panegyric that would do more than justice to a Lincoln or Pitt, did not have sufficient authority to prevent a muscular Indian from abducting one of his wives. Writing of the Algonkians of eastern Canada in 1612, a Jesuit father says: ". . . each man is his own master and his own protector. They have Sagamores, that is, leaders in war; but their authority is most precarious, if, indeed, that may be called authority to which obedience is in no wise obligatory." And James Adair, who had an intimate knowledge of the Muskoghean Indians of our Southeastern states in the first half of the eighteenth century declares: "The power of their chiefs is an empty sound. They can only persuade or dissuade the people, either by the force of good-nature and clear reasoning or coloring things, so as to suit their prevailing passions." That the Crow 'chiefs' were for the most part simply warriors who had achieved conventionally acknowledged deeds of valor, has already been explained.

Certain qualifications will be made presently; but in general the absence of central authority is one of the most impressive features of North American society. It might be imagined that a chaotic condition was inevitable under these circumstances. But that would be leaving out of account the tremendous, not to say terrific, force of established custom and public opinion. To meet with universal reprobation on the part of one's neighbors; to have derisive songs sung in mockery of one's transgressions; to be publicly twitted with disgraceful conduct by joking-relatives—these were eventualities to which no Indian lightly exposed himself. They made it possible to dispense largely with a powerful executive and with penal institutions; while the customary law sufficed, rendering new legislation unnecessary.

Yet while covering a very considerable portion of the phenomena, this statement does not do justice to all the facts. Circumstances affecting the weal and woe of the community required more concentration of power than was commonly vouchsafed to a more or less honored figurehead. This is illustrated by the Plains Indian police organizations at the time of a communal buffalo hunt, when a single false step might have scared off the entire herd and jeopardized the food supply of the entire camp. Hence the utmost rigor temporarily supplanted the extreme individualism of normal times. Women were not allowed to chop trees, men were not permitted to go hunting by themselves lest their premature efforts imperil the success of the co-operative enterprise. The police not only confiscated an offender's game, but severely beat him, broke up his weapons, and destroyed his tent. If he offered resistance, he was likely to be killed on the spot. The constabulary had other functions, though less conspicuous ones. They would restrain war parties from setting out at an inopportune moment, and it was their duty to effect a reconciliation between tribesmen whose personal hostility might lead to a feud. The constitution of this police force varied in different tribes. Among the Crow one of the titular chiefs would act as camp-chief during the pleasure of the people, that is, so long as they prospered under his guidance. His function then was to direct the movements of the camp and to delegate police authority to one of the military organizations, which took turns, though by no fixed rule, in policing the camp each for one season. The Hidatsa had a corresponding village chief responsible for the welfare of the people, but the police power was permanently associated with the Black-Mouth society, which occupied a rather high but by no means the highest degree in the series of graded organizations.

Given the slight authority that usually accompanied the chief's office, it is natural that important decisions, e.g., as to war and peace, were not made by him on his personal authority but only in consultation with a council of mature men. This senate or cabinet was sometimes indeterminate as among the Northern Maidu, where the conference was attended in a general way by the older members of the secret society. Elsewhere there was a fixed number of councilors. The Cheyenne had a board of forty-four elective chiefs, four of whom ranked as superior and chose a supreme representative of the tribe from their own number. Among the Omaha, too, there was a fixed council of seven chiefs with a life-long tenure of office, based on the achievement of meritorious deeds. Two of them ranked as preëminent by virtue of their record, and the rest were graded on the same principle. There was no popular assembly, so that the Omaha senate seems to partake of the nature of an oligarchy. However, as explained, their status rested wholly on individual merit and the scope of their deliberations was restricted so that it did not interfere with personal liberty in the affairs of ordinary life.

They made peace, determined the time of the annual hunt, and appointed the leader of the hunt; during the hunt itself they were subordinate to the man chosen. A peculiar feature that characterized the discussions not only of the Omaha but apparently all similar Indian assemblies is the absence of majority rule: every decision required the unanimous consent of the debaters.

Indian individualism has its corollary on a larger scale in a strongly developed separatism. The 2,000 Hopi are sprinkled over seven or eight completely autonomous villages; even the tiny hamlet of Shipaulovi, with barely 150 inhabitants, maintains a ceremonial chief and celebrates the whole set of Hopi ceremonials independently of its neighbors. This attitude, as Professor Kroeber has trenchantly demonstrated, is hypertrophied on the Pacific coast. The word 'tribe' there loses all political significance, no unit being recognized beyond the single encampment or village. Maidu villages sometimes united for an attack on a common enemy, but the league was of the frailest, most ephemeral character, and that jealous safeguarding of communally owned land described under another head was directed with equal severity against the neighboring Maidu village and against the intruder of alien speech. The Shasta were somewhat less particularistic, for they grouped their settlements into four main divisions, each embracing a number of communities under a common headman; yet these units were of diminutive size considering that the total population of the Shasta at the time of their discovery is set at only 2,000. Farther east the tendency to disruption into petty groups is less glaring but sufficiently pronounced. The Dakota represent anything but a single political aggregate; the Crow not only remained distinct from the closely related Hidatsa but split into at least two, or possibly even three, independent local divisions; and everything goes to show that the several Hidatsa and Mandan villages were wholly autonomous units.

Nevertheless alliances between distinct tribes, that is, between groups of diverse speech did occur, though generally without any attempt at integration. Only the Creek in the Southeast and the Iroquois of New York State founded something after a more pretentious pattern, and the League of the Iroquois in particular merits closer consideration. It comprised primarily five tribes speaking distinct but mutually intelligible languages. Each preserved complete sovereignty so far as its local affairs were concerned, which were governed by a board of chiefs. There was no one supreme executive magistrate of the league but a federal council of forty-eight sachems, the Mohawk and Oneida having nine, the Onondaga fourteen, the Cayuga ten, and the Seneca eight delegates. This uneven distribution did not involve tribal hegemony since there was no individual balloting, the principle of unanimity being applied so that every tribe had a single expression of opinion. Furthermore, complete concurrence of all the tribal representatives was necessary to give validity to a decision; if this proved impracticable, the whole matter was laid aside as incapable of effective treatment. The federal council was summoned at the initiative of any of the tribal councils; its forum was open for orations by any member of the league, but only the forty-eight senators had the right to render a decision. These councilors represented their respective sibs, though not every sib had a representative. Each was chosen from a single section of the sib on nomination of the women of the sib, but this proposal had to be ratified first by the tribal and then by the federal senate. In corresponding fashion an unworthy incumbent might be deposed. There was thus a blending of the elective and hereditary principle. The investiture of a new sachem on the death or resignation of his predecessor was one of the principal occasions for the summoning of the council. In addition the reception of embassies from other tribes, the ratification of peace and declaration of war fell within its jurisdiction. The development of this confederation doubtless contributed largely to the ascendancy of the Iroquois among the tribes of the northern Atlantic seaboard.[5]

Democracy and Primitive Organizations

Having briefly examined some of the salient ethnographic data, we are now prepared to wrestle with some of the general problems growing out of them. And first of all we must pay our respects to Morgan's view that primitive institutions are invariably bound up with democratic government. Monarchy, he holds, is incompatible with the sib, which it must be remembered he regards as a well-nigh universal feature; "it was impossible in the Lower, in the Middle, or in the Upper Status of barbarism for a kingdom to arise by natural growth in any part of the earth" under a sib organization. Such an evolution belongs to the later period of civilization, to the epoch of phonetic writing and literary records. Even differences of caste, including slavery did not arise before the upper status of barbarism, i.e., before the manufacture of iron.

It may be said categorically that even at his worst Morgan never perpetrated more palpable nonsense, and that is saying a good deal. The African Negroes, being conversant with the iron technique but without a phonetic alphabet, would fall into Morgan's upper status of barbarism; and no feature is more constant among them than a monarchical constitution. On the coast of British Columbia the natives are ignorant of pottery and accordingly represent the upper status of savagery in Morgan's classification, yet this did not prevent them from recognizing fixed castes of noblemen, commoners and slaves. The Polynesians, who rank still lower in his strange scheme, have been found to possess a corresponding classification. As for the alleged incompatibility of sibs with monarchy or aristocracy, the Northwest Coast Indians and many of the Negro tribes are organized into sibs.

In this connection still another point merits notice as bearing on the atomistic theory of primitive society. Morgan assumes that all the sibs in a tribe are on a plane of equality. But this is by no means always borne out by the records. In Uganda, e.g., certain sibs were regarded as of lower rank than the rest, others were at least disqualified from presenting a prince as a candidate for royalty, that is, the sons of the king by women of these sibs were never heirs to the throne. Such discriminations might perhaps be expected in a powerful kingdom, but they occur also among the generally democratic Masai, where the sibs of the blacksmiths are viewed with a strange abhorrence and debarred from marrying into any other sibs. Even in the distinctly democratic areas of North America some sibs take precedence over others, as in the Southeast, and in more than one tribe the chieftaincy, such as it is, is confined to a particular sib. In short, the mutual exclusiveness of a sib organization and distinctions of rank is an untenable proposition based on a restricted range of information.

Tribal and Territorial Organization

According to Morgan's atomistic theory, primitive society differed fundamentally from civilized society in that it lacked *political* organization founded upon territorial contiguity. Primitive tribes, he contended, deal with an individual as a member of a sib, i.e., of a kinship group, and accordingly through his personal relations; the civilized state deals with him through his territorial relations, as a member of a township, county or larger spatial unit. This political organization in the narrower sense is, according to Morgan, a relatively recent development at a very high cultural level. He denies that it was achieved by the Aztec of Mexico and his follower Cunow denies its existence in ancient Peru. Primitive tribes might have combinations of sibs into major sibs, they might even organize confederacies of the Iroquois pattern, yet the duties of the individual remained bound up with his kinship status. This was the original condition of ancient Greece, including Athens, until Cleisthenes about 509 B.C. divided Attica into a hundred demes or townships. Thereafter every citizen was registered as a member of a local unit; he voted and was taxed not as a member of such and such a sib but of such and such a township; and together with his fellow-demotae, not with his sib-mates, he elected representative officials. Similar in principle were the larger units, ten demes being united into a district, and ten districts into the Athenian state.

Sixteen years before Morgan interwove the conceptual differentiation outlined above with his scheme of social evolution, Sir Henry Maine had expressed similar views: "The history of political ideas begins . . . with the assumption that kinship in blood is the sole possible ground of community in political functions, nor is there any of those subversions of feeling which we term emphatically revolutions, so startling and so complete as the change which is accomplished when some other principle—such as that, for instance of *local contiguity*—established itself for the first time as the basis of common political action. It may be affirmed then of early commonwealths that their citizens considered all the groups in which they claimed membership to be founded on common lineage." [6]

The soundness of Maine's and Morgan's position in drawing a sharp distinction between kinship (tribal) and territorial (political) organization is beyond cavil. The question is to what extent it is coterminous with the distinction between rude and advanced cultures. It may at once be admitted that there are primitive tribes which conform admirably to the theory that kinship is the one factor in all governmental relations. An ideal example is furnished by the Ifugao of northern Luzon. Here all the customary law revolves about the kin group as the pivotal unit, and there is absolutely no central authority to render decisions binding on different kins. The group is collectively responsible to another group for a member's misdeeds; every member supports his fellow-members with zeal proportioned to his proximity in kinship, and there is no possibility of one kinsman proceeding against another; land and articles of value are held in trust by individuals but cannot be disposed of except with the consent of the family. And except in so far as an intangible public opinion is concerned, practically no bond unites the inhabitants of a given territory. "One owes no obligation in the matter of procedure to another merely because he is a co-villager or inhabitant of the same district." In cases of dispute between groups there is indeed a go-between to adjust the difficulty but he is chosen *ad hoc* and his authority is nil.

It should be noted that the Ifugao unit is not a sib but a bilateral group but it corresponds sufficiently well to the general concept of a *kinship* group as the governmental organism. The question is as to the frequency of an arrangement that excludes the territorial factor in what are commonly viewed as political relations. It is certainly conceivable that human society even in its ruder manifestations may as a rule be more complex than Maine and Morgan assume, and that it need not be *either* based on personal *or* on spatial relations but may rest on both. There need not even be divided allegiance; kinship may involve one set of obligations, territorial relations another, very much after the fashion of our Church and State. To be sure, the abstract possibility of a clash cannot be denied, but there may be such separation of jurisdiction that conflicts are out of the normal course of events.

The point to be examined first of all, then, is whether in a fair number of instances there is a territorial grouping of individuals over and above any coëxisting kinship classification. A recapitulation of facts already cited in other connections suffices to yield an affirmative answer but some discrimination must be exercised. In Australia Kariera groups are each indissolubly linked with a definite locality by mystical ties, and it is the local group that wages war against other local groups of the same tribe. But we should not be justified in holding this up as an example of a territorial organization because the fellow-inhabitants and co-owners of a tract are kinsmen in the paternal line. Hence their cohesion can be plausibly explained as the result of consanguinity rather than of spatial contiguity. But in Australia there are regions where whole tribes are as closely united with their habitat as the Kariera sibs are with their respective localities, where such a thing, e.g., as divesting a defeated tribe of its ancestral land is not even conceived as a possibility. Here, accordingly, the entire tribe, uniting many kin groups, functions as a territorial unit, as among the Arunta and their congeners. It is, however, the Dieri who present the most favorable case. Here descent is matrilineal, but marriage is patrilocal, consequently the men united in one locality are not members of the same totem sib. While each sib has a headman, to wit, the oldest male totemite, the local group also has a headman who may or may not be likewise the head of a totem group. The ranking totemite will not hold the office of headman in the locality unless he exhibits special merit. Here, then, the territorial unit coëxists with and is independent of the kinship unit. Further, it has been shown that among the Dieri there is what the Kariera completely lack, a paramount head of the entire tribe, embracing under his leadership all the people encamped on Dieri territory.

As an instance in some respects parallel to the Dieri illustration may be cited the disparity between the Melanesian rules of descent and of political organization. The patrilocal natives of Buin derive their sib affiliation from their mothers, so that the settlement embraces members of various maternal kin groups. But from a governmental point of view it is the territorial group that is of importance, e.g., in warlike undertakings; and, significantly enough, the office of chief descends not in the sib but from father to son, i.e., within the territorial unit as fixed by the rule of residence.

Extreme jealousy regarding territorial rights has been noted as characteristic of various tribes, some of them in a very rude state of culture, such as the Vedda, the Maidu, Shasta, and Thompson River Indians, and it occurs on a higher level among the Samoans. In each of these cases the local group exists as a unit independently of kinship bonds. Similarly, among the Maritime Chukchi the village "is founded, not on family connection, but on territorial contiguity," and it is the village as well as the kinship group that functions in the blood-feud. Even when the sentiment for a definite stretch of territory is far vaguer than in any of the instances hitherto cited, the geographical location may exert an influence on political status. The two main bands of the Crow spoke the same language, intermingled freely and included members of the same sibs, but when a man had settled in one division his lot was for certain purposes cast with that group, irrespective of any other affiliations.

The point here is not to ascertain whether the kinship or the local group is more fundamental in its influence on life; or whether the latter is merely a derivative of the former. What matters is that even in very humble cultural levels local contiguity is *one* of the factors determining social solidarity independently of blood-relationship. Now I have designated as associations those social units not based on kinship, and the territorial group may veritably be conceived as a specialized form of association. Its members, or many of them, are in some instances more passive than in clubs or secret societies, but they are none the less united by community of interest.

It is indeed one of Schurtz's most signal services to have explained the early origin of political society in Morgan's sense without recourse to any deliberate legal enactment. A Buin chief who erects a council-house and gathers about him the men of his settlement in a men's club, is in so far forth disrupting the ties of the family or sib, or rather is creating a new bond which by its very existence restricts the dominion of the kinship motive. The nature of that bond is territorial since it unites men of the same locality and of different lineage; and it is invested with political significance as soon as the assemblage of fellow-villagers no longer contents itself with common festivities but undertakes joint expeditions against a neighboring encampment. As already hinted, it is not necessary that all inmates of the settlement should actively participate in the association. The women, of course, are often excluded, and under the Australian gerontocracy solely a few elders or at best the age-class of elders act as the managing board. Nevertheless the women and the younger men of the district, though submissive spectators, are associated with *their* elders in a manner altogether different from possible relations with the elders of another locality and in so far forth are members, though impotent ones, of a territorial association. The same would, of course, apply to the conditions effected by the secret Ogboni of Yorubaland. That is to say, the several types of associations discussed by Schurtz are potential agencies for the creation of a state by uniting the population within a circumscribed area into an aggregate that functions as a definite unit irrespective of any other social affiliations of the inhabitants. When, therefore, a philosophically minded historian, Professor Teggart, complains that Maine and Morgan have defined the difference between kindred and political organization without clearing up the transitional processes, his complaint is warranted against these students, but it leaves out of account Schurtz's memorable contribution. Even at a very early time and in a very lowly environment there was no necessity for disrupting the ties of kinship in order to found a political state.

For concomitantly with the family and the sib there have existed for untold centuries such associations as the men's clubs, age-classes and secret organizations, all of them independent of kinship, moving as it were in a quite different sphere from the kindred groups, and all of them capable of readily acquiring political character if not invested with it from their inception.[7]

REFERENCES

[1] Howitt: 295-326, especially 297 seq., 320 seq. Spencer and Gillen, 1904: 20-30. Roth, 1906: 5 seq.

[2] Rivers, 1914 (b): II, 409. Tregear: 123, 150, 192. Stair: 65-91, 128. Erdland: 99-113. Waitz and Gerland: 165-222, 343 seq.

[3] Thurnwald, 1912: 314-326; id., 1910: 9-15. Keysser: 100. Zahn: 308.

[4] Junod: I, 355-409. Ferguson: 197 seq. Spieth: 98-110. Ellis, A. B.: 161-181. Torday and Joyce: 53 seq. Frobenius: 172 seq. Merker: 18.

[5] Krause: 122. Boas, 1916 (a): 429, 496. Jesuit Relations: II, 73. Adair: 428. Fletcher and La Flesche: 206. Lowie, 1912: 228; id., 1913: 274. Kroeber, 1917 (b): 396. Morgan, 1877: Pt. II, Chap. 5. Goldenweiser, 1912: 468.

[6] Morgan, 1877: Pt. II, Chaps. 2, 8, 10. Maine: Chap. v.

[7] Brown: 144. Spencer and Gillen, 1904: 13. Howitt: 47. Bogoras: 50, 628, 668. Lowie, 1912: 245.

CHAPTER XIV

JUSTICE

PRIMITIVE administration of justice furnishes especially illuminating examples of the relation of the kinship factor to motives of another character. Given the complete absence of central authority as among the Ifugao, the kinship group becomes the judicial body—one that confronts all like bodies in the tribe as one sovereign state confronts the rest. But that is an extreme case; far more commonly there is a central power that intervenes—not to be sure in all cases that would demand governmental interference with us, but in those circumstances which from the native point of view are of collective interest.

In this connection reference may be made to Maine's comparison of rude and mature jurisprudence. The former, he points out, is marked by a strange preponderance of criminal over civil law; "the more archaic the code, the fuller and minuter is its penal legislation." This had been explained by earlier writers as due to the supposed turbulence of barbarian life. With his usual acumen Maine does not rest content with this facile interpretation, but shows that the disproportionately small body of civil law in ancient times is due to the fact that there was little occasion for that part of jurisprudence to come into being under archaic conditions. The regulation of personal relations by the status of the individuals, the administration and inheritance of property within the family according to customary law, and the absence of contracts between individuals adequately account for the diminutive part played by civil jurisprudence as compared with penal law "even if it be hazardous to pronounce that the childhood of nations is always a period of ungoverned violence."

The last remark is emphatically an understatement of the case. It cannot be too often explained that the extreme individualism often found in primitive communities is very far from favoring universal anarchy or anything approaching it. Generally speaking, the unwritten laws of customary usage are obeyed far more willingly than our written codes, or rather they are obeyed spontaneously. Among the Crow personal brawls are looked upon with contempt, and a man will not readily imperil his social position and invite the public derision of his joking-relatives by engaging in fisticuffs with a fellow-tribesman. To become the laughing-stock of his daily associates for minor misdemeanors and to be completely ostracized for graver offenses are terrific punishments for the native and they have a deterrent force of which the infliction of penalties in our sense is often quite devoid. To this should be added the religious motive. Certain crimes are reckoned as sins, they are offenses against the unseen powers of the universe and invite condign punishment regardless of any secular agency. That, e.g., was the conception underlying Polynesian observance of the taboo rules. In short, even in the more individualistic societies of the ruder peoples there are adequate motives for the maintenance of order, though the conception of order will naturally vary in different places and will sometimes differ widely from ours.

After accounting for the predominance of criminal law in early society, Maine qualifies his conception by pointing out that at bottom "the penal law of ancient communities is not the law of Crimes; it is the law of Wrongs, or, to use the English technical word, of Torts." This brings us to the very core of our problem, for what Maine means is that in archaic jurisprudence it is not the state that is regarded as the aggrieved party but the individual sufferer and his kindred. In other words, this is the old question of personal versus territorial relations. I have already indicated that in the generality of instances primitive man recognizes both torts and crimes, but before adducing some of the evidence I must refer to certain widespread principles of primitive law. These may be dispatched with great brevity in view of Professor Hobhouse's lucid exposition in a generally available work.[1]

Collective Responsibility

Given the conception that the individual is merged in his group, it follows logically that his fellow-members are collectively responsible for his misdeeds. Though this is an archaic notion, it persists to the present day in the warfare of civilized nations, which summarily shelves the practice of determining individual guilt or innocence. It should be noted that the facts coming under this head cannot be perverted into evidence in support of the sib dogma, because the group concerned is frequently not the sib but the family, the association, or the tribe. The sibless Hupa were content to kill any member of a murderer's family in order to punish the crime; among the Crow if a Fox had disgraced himself and his society by taking back an abducted wife, the rival Lumpwoods had the right to cut up the blankets of all the Foxes; and in the same tribe the grief of parents mourning the death of a son slain by the Dakota was at once assuaged when vengeance had been wreaked on any member of the hostile people.

As a corollary from this principle, an offense of one group against another resembles an encroachment of one state on another's sovereignty; on the other hand, a crime committed by one individual against a fellow-member concerns no one outside their group. This latter point is constantly demonstrated in Ifugao practice. Thus, two cases of parricide went unpunished because as internal family affairs they were nobody else's business and the kindred concerned regarded the murder as justified since the old man had wrongfully pawned his son's field and thereby imperiled his family's livelihood. These people do not proceed against a fellow-member even for more heinous offenses. Thus, if a father had incestuous relations with his daughter, he might be punished by the girl's mother's family on the ground that he had committed a crime against them, but his own kin would take no measures against him.

From the supreme law of group solidarity it follows that when an individual has injured a member of another group, his own group shield him while the opposing group support the injured man's claims for compensation or revenge. Thence there may develop blood-feuds and civil wars. The stubbornness with which these are waged varies in different regions. The Chukchi generally make peace after the first act of retribution, but among the Ifugao the struggle may go on almost interminably till at last an inter-marriage re-establishes friendly intercourse. An interesting example of how different practices may spring from the same principle is furnished by the two tribes mentioned. While the Ifugao tend to protect a kinsman under almost all circumstances, the Chukchi often avert a feud by killing a member of the family whose spitefulness is likely to embroil them with other kins.

A strange variant of the underlying theory occurs among the Australian Dieri, who deliberately inflict the death penalty on the criminal's elder brother rather than on the offender himself.

Criminal Motive

As might be inferred from the satisfaction of justice by the punishment of any member of the offender's group, criminal intent plays not nearly the same part in primitive law as it does in our own jurisprudence. A Hupa incident narrated by Goddard serves as a classical example. "A child was burned to death in a fire a woman had built for heating wash-water out of doors. Although the woman was in no way at fault, the life of her son was sought as a recompense." Yet this must not be regarded as a universally recognized postulate. The Ifugao are especially remarkable for the care with which they discriminate between voluntary and involuntary deeds, and between those purely accidental and those resulting from carelessness. If a man's knife flies out of his hand and puts out another's eye, no damages are demanded. In the scrimmage over sacrificed carabaos many men are injured and some are killed, yet even in the latter event no payment is assessed by the kin. On the other hand, a man killing a child running in the way while throwing spears at a target must pay half the fine for manslaughter because he has not taken adequate precautions; and an even heavier fine is imposed on a man who slays a neighbor whom he mistakes for an enemy, since the intent to kill is held to aggravate the charge of carelessness. There is one notable exception to the general Ifugao rule: at sumptuous feasts the host and the officiating priest are jointly held responsible for any accidents that may happen —the host because if he had not given the feast there would have been no brawl; the priest because of his inferred remissness in the execution of religious functions. The Southeastern Bantu draw a highly interesting distinction between accidental manslaughter and accidental injury to property. All homicide is criminal since it deprives the ruler of a subject and must be atoned by a compensation paid to the *chief* irrespective of criminal intent. But injury to another man's fields or other possessions is a tort, and if the harm is done without premeditation no indemnities are paid.

These three examples illustrate the danger of premature generalization, but after all qualifications are made it remains true that the ethical motive of an act is more frequently regarded as irrelevant in the ruder cultures than in our courts of justice.

WEREGILD

Feuds between the offender's and the sufferer's group are often averted by composition, that is, by the payment of weregild in compensation for the injury sustained. In many cases there is a traditional tariff schedule defining the payment to be made for any and all possible injuries. It is important to remember, however, that societies differ as to the range of offenses for which payment may be accepted. The Ifugao have a complicated scheme of fines for the adjustment of all sorts of difficulties, but wilful murder can be expiated only by blood. Less rigorous is the practice of the Chukchi, nevertheless they are far more likely to accept weregild in lieu of inflicting personal chastisement for minor transgressions than in cases of murder. But in many regions even felonies are compounded in the interests of the public peace. A few concrete illustrations will serve to render the spirit of the conventional tariffs clearer.

Ifugao customary law recognizes a three-class division of society on the basis of wealth, fines varying with the financial status of the parties concerned. Thus, for adultery after the second marriage ceremony but before the final one the wealthy man pays a fine of ten articles estimated in value at 47 pesos; a middle-class individual an equal number appraised at only 24.20 pesos; and a poor man only six articles worth altogether about 12 pesos. For those cases of homicide which do not require a shedding of blood in return the rich slayer must provide elaborate feasts and supply a variety of articles to be distributed among the dead man's heirs, the total expense sometimes running up to 975 pesos. This, however, depends somewhat on the rank of the slain individual and would be rather less if he were a

JUSTICE

member of the middle-class, let alone, of the caste of the poverty-stricken. On the other hand, if the slayer were of the two lower grades, his fine would not be materially commuted; he would be saddled with it for the remainder of his life and his children would have to pay the balance after his decease.

The ancient Kirgiz likewise recognized class distinctions in the imposition of fines. For a freeman's death the slayer was mulcted one *kun,* i.e., 100 horses or 1,000 sheep, but a nobleman's kindred were entitled to a sevenfold amount, while composition for a woman or slave was effected with half a *kun* plus nine head of sundry domesticated animals, and a third of a *kun* paid for a child. For the loss of an eye or of the right arm a man claimed half a *kun,* a woman one-fourth of a *kun.* A broken upper arm, the loss of the left hand or of one foot are each compensated with three times nine head of cattle, for a broken thumb nine head are paid. In case of a broken tooth or finger or a wound in the head the sufferer receives from the culprit one horse and a coat. Theft is punished with a fine of three times nine head, one camel being reckoned equivalent to three horses or thirty sheep. If an enceinte woman is knocked down and in consequence bears a still-born child, the assaulter must pay a horse for each month if the mother is in her fifth month, but if she has been pregnant for a longer period a camel has to be paid for each month.

These regulations are evidently very circumstantial but in many cases the principle of composition was acknowledged without fixed stipulation as to the amount to be paid. Thus, among the Plains Indians a varying number of horses seem to have been presented to a slain man's kin, and other offenses were blotted out by equally undefined offerings of gifts. A curious substitute for compensation was fairly popular in this region. Instead of awaiting weregild or forcibly seizing some of the culprit's belongings, the injured individual might destroy one or more of his enemy's horses, or other valuables. This practice was especially common in cases of adultery.

The Shasta methods of adjustment depart to some extent from the norm. Blood-money must always be accepted if offered, but if revenge is taken previously on any one but the actual murderer the regular compensation must be offered to the kin of the second person slain, so that their liability for the first killing is largely or wholly wiped out. Adjustment is very simple in this tribe because every individual has a fixed value determined by the bride-price paid for his mother in marriage. Perhaps the most curious feature among these people is the part played by the chief, who not merely tries to effect an agreement between contending parties, but advances or pays outright the requisite property if the aggressor proves insolvent.

Finally may be cited the Samoan treatment of murder and adultery. Frequently the criminal would not only tender valuable mats and other property but would eat humble-pie by bringing likewise firewood, stones and leaves to the wronged party, thus symbolically indicating that they might kill, cook, and eat him, and thereby thrust himself upon their generosity. Generally this combination of gifts and self-degradation did not fail to conciliate the wrath of the aggrieved. The low-born did not undergo this symbolical self-mortification but merely offered payment, which, however, might be declined.

Evidence

As Professor Hobhouse has pointed out, archaic procedure frequently revolves not so much about the exact determination of guilt or innocence as about the prevention of internecine strife. Nevertheless even in the ruder cultures methods are employed to ascertain the truth of an accusation or the merit of a dispute, but usually the means used are shot through with the magico-religious notions prevalent among the people. Under this head two sets of usages demand attention, oaths and ordeals.

Among the Plains Indians oaths were sworn primarily to establish a disputed title to war honors. Thus, it happened among the Crow that two men laid a claim to having first touched the prostrate body of an enemy. In that case solemn oaths were recited before an assemblage of warriors. Two methods were popular. One was for each of the litigants in turn to take a knife, put it in his mouth, point it at the sun, and recite a formula calling upon the sun as a witness and invoking death on the false claimant. In the other case an arrow piercing a slice of meat was laid on a dry buffalo skull, then each contestant would raise the arrow, taste of the meat, and recite a similar formula. Of course no immediate decision could be rendered; but if either of the rivals soon after met with a serious accident or was afflicted in some other manner, the judgment of the tribe was that he had perjured himself and that the other man was entitled to the disputed distinction. In other parts of the world the oath is administered for the general purpose of determining guilt. The Samoyed or Ostyak defendant is made to swear over a bear's nose. While cutting it up with a knife, he declares, "May the bear devour me if I commit perjury!" There is a general belief that the perjuror will be punished, hence any one undergoing the oath is held innocent. But if he should subsequently be killed by a bear or perish in an accident, this is attributed to his having perjured himself. The Kirgiz have the curious rule of not having the defendant take the oath but some other man of known probity who thereby assumes the criminal's sin. On the whole, oaths are eminently characteristic of the Old World, though as pointed out they are by no means lacking in a restricted manner among the natives of America.

The ordeal is likewise an Old World institution. It assumes Protean forms. Among the Chukchi differences are sometimes settled by a wrestling-match, there being a firm conviction that a wronged man will be victorious. The same means is used by the Ifugao to ascertain disputed rice-field boundaries, while various methods serve in other forms of litigation. Thus, in cases of adultery the adversaries hurl eggs at each other, while in settling other disagreements each litigant slowly thrusts his hand into a pot of boiling hot water to extract a pebble, undue haste or a severe scalding being interpreted as a sign of guilt. Additional illustrations will be cited below in dealing with the African data.

Magico-religious means are of course employed in a variety of ways to determine guilt, but without necessarily possessing juridical character. Thus, when an Ifugao divines a thief by balancing an egg on a spear blade, the egg standing on end at the mention of the culprit, the intellectual process may be of the same order as that characterizing the ordeal, but legally the two phenomena are distinct. The divinatory act has purely personal significance. It merely encourages the robbed person to challenge the suspected criminal to a trial that *has* juridical standing.[2]

Having now rapidly touched upon some of the features particularly characteristic of primitive jurisprudence, we had better examine connectedly the juridical culture of several selected peoples, mainly though not wholly in order to ascertain to what extent society takes note of transgressions of customary law.

Australia

The Australians furnish an admirable example of people very low in the scale of material advancement yet with a definite central authority for dealing with crime. It is true that some deeds ranking as felonious in our law are not regarded as falling within the jurisdiction of anyone beyond the family circle immediately involved. A Queens-

JUSTICE

lander may maim or even kill his wife so far as the tribe is concerned, though in the latter case her kindred may call him to account; and a mother may lawfully kill her child within a few hours after birth. It is also true that even for certain transgressions of the native code the punishment is none other than general ridicule and reprobation, though this is often felt far more keenly in primitive communities than one would imagine. Finally, other misdeeds are believed to be punished automatically by magical means; thus, a man's hair will turn prematurely gray if he speaks to his wife's mother. But when all deductions are made, there remains a group of offenses which are neither settled by private arrangement nor allowed to meet with mere mockery or impersonal punishment but where the state in the form of the tribal council intervenes.

Let us first consider typical instances of the private administration of justice. As already indicated, a Queenslander has almost complete control over his wife, and for infidelity he may strike her with a boomerang, spear her in the thigh, or heap hot ashes upon her stomach. Similarly, a father may chastise an uninitiated son in any way he chooses without being in the slightest degree amenable to outside interference. In cases of trespass on individually owned patches of land the proprietor may merely vituperate the poacher or he may spear him in the leg provided he is of the same tribe, but an alien is liable to be killed.

Since collective responsibility is recognized, the murder of a man may lead to a vendetta, but by one of the most remarkable of aboriginal institutions this is often averted through the substitution of a legalized encounter in which the criminal, armed with a shield, confronts the kin or local group of the slain. These hurl spears at him, which he parries as best he can, until his blood flows, which normally closes the proceedings and puts an end to all hostility. These expiatory combats have been styled ordeals but they are obviously nothing of the sort, since they do not determine the defendant's guilt, which is assumed from the start. Such combats also take place in the case of lesser offenses, and then the defendant may be actively aided by some of his kinsmen and permitted not only to protect himself but to throw missiles at his opponents. Formal expiation is in vogue for various misdeeds but seems to have a restricted range of distribution. It is very popular in the Southeast and also in Queensland, where a thief will express contrition and offer his head for a blow, while a gossip will allow his mouth to be struck by the slandered person. In Central Australia atonement of this type does not seem to be customary to the same extent, though after an elopement the abductor may have to submit to maltreatment by the offended husband so as to prevent a fight between the members of the local groups concerned. In this region a death ascribed to evil magic is avenged by an organized party dispatched by the tribal council.

There is doubtless some local variation in the conception of what constitutes a crime against society but throughout the continent a breach of the incest laws would fall under this head. Thus, at a tribal council of the Dieri a young man was charged with mating within the forbidden degrees. The elders examined the matter, sustained the accusation, and almost killed the convict, who escaped death only through the appeal made by an influential tribesman that he was an imbecile. Very different was the adjustment of, say, an elopement of a girl promised in marriage with another man. This was a matter for her kin to deal with. The aggrieved brothers would engage in a fight with the abductor until blood flowed, and the girl was severely beaten by her mother and sisters. But so long as the elopers stood to each other in the potential relationship of mates as recognized by the tribe, this act fell without the jurisdiction of the elders' senate.

Other crimes generally penalized by this governing body are divulgence of the secrets revealed at initiation and murder by evil magic. Regarding other forms of homicide usage probably varied locally. In northern Queensland the settlement of ordinary disputes was a personal matter, but any serious injury to a member of the local group was avenged by the tribal council unless the assault was considered justified by some flagrant provocation.

To sum up, Australian does not differ from advanced jurisprudence in an exclusive recognition of torts but in regarding certain misdeeds as torts which we consider crimes, reserving for the latter category a relatively small number of transgressions.[3]

IFUGAO

Ifugao law presents an extraordinary combination of traits. A society could hardly exist where the separatist tendencies of distinct kins have been carried to a greater extent than among these natives of Luzon. The individual owes allegiance to the kin and the kin owes protection to its members against other kins; no obligation devolves on either in a matter concerning other kins of the same village or district; and there is accordingly no functionary acting as arbitrator by virtue of any authority vested in him. When kins are arrayed against each other, a go-between unrelated to both parties is chosen by common consent but his sole power is that of personal persuasiveness. Theoretically, then, disintegration might reach the point where a community would break up into completely dissociated kins. On the other hand, it would be difficult to find a primitive tribe where customary law has settled with greater particularity what course is proper in any one of a host of possible contingencies. This means that what is lacking in formal cohesion is partly made up by the force of a public opinion covering the main incidents of social intercourse. Thus when an adulterer taken *in delicto* is slain by the irate husband, the kin may indeed prepare to wreak vengeance but in so doing they do not condone the act of adultery; they merely take the stand that the offended mate should have demanded the customary fine, "that if this had not been immediately forthcoming, no one would have questioned the propriety of the killing." In other words, grievances are not solely regarded from the angle of kinship but are appraised according to canons accepted throughout the community, which, of course, would cease to be one if such were not the case. It remains a strange phenomenon, however, that the Ifugao with all their accentuation of the kinship factor have gone so far in standardizing what might be likened to international procedure. To be sure, there are deviations from the norm precisely as in the relations of nations; the strong kin is able to browbeat a poorer or less numerous group. Nevertheless, the overriding of justice seems to be restricted within certain limits. The wealthy adulterer may refuse to pay the high-grade indemnity demanded by an indigent plaintiff, but he throws a sop to morality by offering the lowest possible fine in such a case, that paid when both litigants are of the poverty-stricken caste. Moreover, it happens that the poor sufferer, reckless because he has nothing to lose but his misery, assumes so menacing an attitude that the culprit, counseled to be prudent by his terrified relatives, consents to pay the exorbitant fine. The general acceptance of certain modes of conduct as proper is also strikingly illustrated by the law of seizure. When a debtor refuses to pay the customary fine for some misdeed, the creditor may furtively or by a ruse remove a gong or some other valuable from his opponent's dwelling. Provided the confiscator leaves his knife or some other article identifying him, his act has legal validity, that is, is acknowledged as just, otherwise it constitutes a form of larceny.

The anarchy that on abstract principles follows from the coëxistence of a series of sovereign groups in the same locality is thus seen to be mitigated by common standards, to which at least approximate conformity is yielded by the entire community. Indeed, it may safely be stated that Ifugao society for all its centrifugal character is not lacking in germs that might under favorable conditions develop into a political organization. The very existence of the go-between's office must be viewed in this light. True, he has no authority in the strict sense of the term; but he may acquire a reputation for peace-making that becomes both a source of income and of personal prestige. To maintain his standing he will go to considerable lengths: he will follow the unconciliatory plaintiff or the obdurate culprit, war-knife in hand, and compel him to listen. Secondly, in spite of the neutrality of all kins not immediately concerned there is by no means general indifference as to a quarrel. "Neighbors and co-villagers do not want to see their neighborhood torn by internal dissension and thus weakened as to the conduct of warfare against enemies." That is to say, the territorial motive, completely overshadowed as it is by the kinship ties, nevertheless exists in embryo. At an actual feud skirmish the onlookers shouted: "What kind of way is this for co-villagers to settle a dispute? Go back home and beget some children, and marry them to each other, giving them the two fields, and then it will make no difference where the division line is!" Scattered remarks in Mr. Barton's essay show that this sentiment crops up in various ways. We learn of a tacit understanding that an Ifugao shall so behave as to avoid involving his neighbors in difficulties with natives of inimical or semi-inimical districts. It is also important to note that while collective responsibility applies mainly to the kin it may also extend to the district. A creditor will seize property belonging to the wealthy kinsman of a tardy debtor, but when occasion arises he is also likely to confiscate the carabao of his debtor's fellow-villager. Finally may be cited the distinction drawn between an alien and a fellow-villager as regards punishment: the foreigner caught stealing is almost certain to be slain, the neighbor of another kin merely pays the regular fine. It cannot, accordingly, be denied that a sentiment based on local contiguity exists among the Ifugao, however faint when compared with the rival sentiment of blood-relationship.

The main features of Ifugao jurisprudence, kin solidarity, the functions of the intermediary, the influence of caste, and the arrangement of ordeals have been briefly referred to in this and preceding sections. It remains to point out specifically one feature as to the nature of penalties, and another as to procedure. All punishment falls into either of two categories—the imposition of fines and the infliction of death. Flogging or any other form of personal chastisement such as we encounter in Australia is not in vogue; nor is imprisonment reported as a possible penalty. In procedure it is a noteworthy fact that plaintiff and defendant never confront each other. As soon as the controversy is formally launched, there is complete severance of diplomatic relations, all business being conducted by the go-between, who hears the testimony of each litigant separately and reports the strong points to his opponent. Naturally this principle becomes inoperative when ordeals are resorted to.[4]

Eskimo

Sharply defined as the Eskimo are, both racially and linguistically, there is not the slightest political cohesion among even neighboring districts. "The inhabitants of a settlement," says Holm, "often form a society apart, and indeed are often at variance with the people living in another settlement. Thus the inhabitants of the lower part of the Angmagsalik fjord and those of the upper part abused each other roundly. Similar amenities existed between the inhabitants of the three fjords." Among the Central Eskimo also there is a deep distrust of neighboring

Eskimo tribes, preventing frequent intercourse. A stranger is often challenged to a contest of strength or endurance and if vanquished forfeits his life. In Greenland no one may settle in a winter hamlet without the general consent of the inhabitants.

These facts, of course, tend to show that there is a feeling based on territorial community within a very restricted area rather than that such a feeling is lacking. But since there is no dominant governing agency in an Eskimo settlement, the adjustment of grievances is mainly a matter for the individuals or kins rather than for the community at large. In this respect, then, the Eskimo resemble the Ifugao. But the Eskimo represent a much ruder state of society, and accordingly there is none of that precision so characteristic of the Ifugao. The communistic trend of Eskimo thought alone suffices to render their jurisprudence of a simpler nature since it minimizes property law and is hardly conducive to an elaborate scale of fines. Indeed, we hear nothing concerning such penalties.

On the whole, the Eskimo are not a quarrelsome people and the method of adjudicating a personal difficulty in Greenland is typical of their general spirit. A Greenlander who has suffered some injury, whether by theft, destruction of property or the abduction of his wife, will compose a satirical song in mockery of the culprit and challenge him to a public singing contest. Drumming and chanting, he throws his enemy's misdeeds into his teeth, exaggerating and deriding them and even rattling the family skeletons as well. The accused person receives the mockery with feigned composure and at the close of the challenger's charge returns in kind. Apart from the period of singing, no hostility whatsoever is displayed. The spectators follow proceedings with the greatest interest, egging on the performers to their utmost efforts. Such contests need not be settled in one evening but may be continued for a number of years, the litigants taking turns at inviting each other.

Cases of murder are naturally viewed in a different light, but here, too, there is usually no pretence at a public administration of justice. The nearest relative of the slain person wreaks vengeance on the slayer or one of his kinsmen, through the principle of collective responsibility the quarrel may be handed down to the following generation, and a number of innocent people will suffer death before a formal reconciliation is effected. In connection with the carrying out of the feud curious usages are reported from widely separated sections of the Eskimo habitat. Years may pass before punishment for the misdeed is attempted, and in the meantime the murderer may visit his victim's family, be welcomed and entertained by them, and live in peace for the longest period. Then he may suddenly be dispatched by his companions on a hunting party or challenged to a wrestling match and put to death if vanquished.

There are instances, however, where a murderer or some other offender has made himself obnoxious to the entire community. In such a case he may be killed by anyone simply as a matter of justice. The man who intends to take revenge on him must ask his countrymen singly if each agrees in the opinion that the offender is a bad man deserving death. If all answer in the affirmative, he may kill the man thus condemned and no one is allowed to revenge the murder. Summary punishment is also meted out to people accused of witchcraft supposed to have caused the death of a relative; but then the slaying of the sorcerer may precipitate a feud of the usual character.

There is another category of delinquencies coming under the head of sins. It is a cardinal tenet of Eskimo religion that the transgression of any one of a legion of taboos endangers the food supply: all efforts to hunt seals prove fruitless and the settlement is on the verge of starvation. Only confession by the transgressor will ward off the penalty inflicted by the supernatural powers. Hence a shaman is invoked to discover the cause of the calamity. If the criminal confesses, all is well; "but if he obstinately maintains his innocence, his death alone will soothe the wrath of the offended deity."

It appears accordingly that the community is not uniformly indifferent as to the acts of its members, but that like other societies it interprets in a manner *sui generis* the conditions under which collective interference by the territorial unit is desirable.[5]

Plains Indians

As might be expected from the prevalently individualistic character of Plains Indian culture, most difficulties were settled by individuals and by their kindred. Thus, adultery was not an affair of public concern, and if an indignant husband cruelly beat or maimed his unfaithful wife he was not answerable to any communal authority. Even in cases of homicide the families or sibs of the murderer and the slain person were primarily involved, but in such instances there was generally a definite attempt by the chiefs or other officials to avert a feud. This was often done by thrusting a pipe into the principal mourner's mouth, which morally obliged him to accept such composition for the felony as the slayer and his relatives were only too glad to offer. Peacemaking was generally the duty of the constabulary superintending the buffalo hunt. It has already been pointed out how large the powers of these policemen were at the time of this coöperative enterprise. Indeed, disobedience to their orders on that occasion and consequent imperilment of the food supply may be regarded as the one crime against society recognized by all the Plains tribes. The severe punishment meted out to the culprit has already been described. The police society also restrained men from inopportune raids, preserved order on the march or on ceremonial occasions, and in general exercised authority when the success of collective undertakings was at stake.

The Omaha present typical Plains characteristics in their administration of law, but with some additional traits. The Council of Seven had the power to order the killing of an unruly and rebellious tribesman. The decree was executed by some trustworthy man with the aid of a poisoned staff. Usually it was customary to give the criminal fair warning by first destroying his horses; but if he failed to pay heed to this admonition, he himself would suffer the extreme penalty. The councilors also took note of deliberate murders, which were punished with a four years' banishment. During this period the murderer was obliged to remain on the edge of the camp and hold no intercourse with anyone but his immediate family, who might seek him out and furnish him with provisions. The duration of the penalty was in a measure dependent on the sentiments of the mourning kin, for as soon as they relented the exile was allowed to return. That is to say, homicide despite tribal interference ranked after all as a tort: it was not the tribe that exacted punishment but the suffering family, and the council intervened not to inflict a condign penalty but to satisfy the private feeling of revenge and prevent civil dissension with consequent weakening of the community. The crimes of Omaha law were apparently only twofold—setting at naught the authority of the seven chiefs and premature hunting in the communal chase.[6]

Polynesia

The parliamentary body that governed the Samoan settlements and districts combined judicial functions with legislative and executive powers, but it is not altogether clear to what extent personal wrongs were redressed by the council. That in some instances private arrangements for composition were made, has already been shown, but where the line of demarcation was drawn, what type of offences were reserved for public vengeance, is a matter of some doubt. Thus homicide was evidently at times compounded, but in the case of a particularly atrocious multiple murder reported by Stair the perpetrator was formally tried and executed.

A strange feature of Samoan customary law was the organization of a plundering expedition against the culprit by the local assembly. As soon as a decision had been reached, the leaders of the community proceeded to the household of the offender, formally pronounced sentence, and began to ring a breadfruit-tree on the estate, at which signal their followers at once stripped the taro patches, killed the livestock, set the house on fire, and drove the whole family into exile. Primitive raids of this type were not confined to Samoa but flourished in other parts of Polynesia. Thus, if a Maori had accidentally destroyed collective property by a fire or deprived his tribe of food through an act of carelessness, his neighbors would come in a body and freely appropriate his belongings, possibly thrashing him in addition.

Other penalties display great refinement of cruelty. For theft, for affronting travelers, and for some other forms of misdemeanor the assembly might order the defendant to beat his head and chest with a rock till his blood flowed freely. He was sometimes forced to bite a poisonous root that would cause his mouth to swell, inflicting intense pain for some time to come. Another favorite torture for thieves was to bind their hands and feet and expose them to the broiling sun.

Hawaiian jurisprudence acknowledged the absolute primacy of the king, whose will was law and could absolve from obedience to traditional laws. Though the lesser lords had similar powers over the inhabitants of their domain, it was possible for a subject to appeal from a decision of his chief to the supreme court of the king. In spite of monarchical and feudal institutions, however, some characteristic Polynesian customs continued to obtain in ordinary relations. For example, plundering expeditions were recognized as legal in retaliation for theft, and the malefactor would submit even if commanding a strong force lest the man power of the entire district be hurled against him. A curious ordeal was in vogue in Hawaii. Plaintiff and defendant were ordered to hold their hands above a calabash filled with water, which was supposed to tremble and thus reveal the guilty party.

Evidently the Polynesians must be reckoned among those peoples who, irrespective of their law of torts, also punished as crimes offenses against the community or the ruler.[7]

Africa

Among the Negroes of Africa primitive jurisprudence attains its highest development. In precision and scope their code rivals that of the Ifugao, but unlike the Ifugao the Negroes have almost everywhere an orderly method of procedure before constituted tribunals. They display a remarkable taste for juridical casuistry and a keen enjoyment of forensic eloquence. The notion of collective and consequently vicarious responsibility is by no means lacking, but such is the authority of the courts that vendettas are rare and in the fullest sense of the term probably unknown. When an Ewe had committed murder, the victim's kin sometimes kidnapped members of the criminal's household or destroyed their fields and houses, but that seems as far as the feud went and even in this diluted form it was rather exceptional. There is no one source that adequately describes African jurisprudence; accordingly, it will be well to summarize the mutually complementary data from several areas.

In contemplating the legal institutions of the Ewe, and indeed of all the Negro peoples, we are again reminded of the intimate bond connecting departments of primitive culture that are largely though not wholly separated in our own. Ewe jurisprudence is unintelligible without some knowledge of Ewe philosophy of the universe. More particularly are we concerned with two basic conceptions, the belief in sorcery and the belief in ordeals for the ascertainment of guilt. Opposed to the benevolent magician who cures disease is the evil sorcerer who furtively strews poison on his victim's bowl or furniture, afflicting him with suffering or death. When a man is accused of bewitching a tribesman he attempts to clear himself by undergoing one of the prescribed tests of innocence. These are in charge of a special guild, each member of which has acquired his knowledge by purchase and adoption into the fraternity.

First of all, the test-owner subjects the defendant to a cross-examination. He asks whether the accused has ever bewitched any one or has previously been condemned by an ordeal, which of course is vigorously denied. Next comes the choice of the particular test to be applied. For example, a grain of salt may be cast into a bowl of boiling palm-oil: if it splits in two, this is taken as a sign of guilt; if it remains whole, it indicates the accused man's innocence. This proof is supplemented by another. Boiling oil is poured into the defendant's hand; if he holds it without signs of distress, his innocence is established, otherwise the charge is sustained. The outcome naturally lies in the manipulator's hand; if he favors the defendant, he will merely feign pouring hot oil and substitute oil that is relatively cool. In another test the eyes of the guilty are blinded by a poisonous juice, while those of the innocent remain unscathed.

These, then, are typical methods for the determination of the sorcerer's guilt. If he stands convicted, he may yet escape the extreme penalty provided his supposed victim is still alive. A hoe or pickaxe and a basket are placed before him, and he is himself presented with a chance to select his fate. Pickaxe and hoe symbolize the grave to be dug for him unless he chooses the basket, which signifies merely a heavy fine. But if the sorcerer is guilty of murder, he is bound with a rope, led out of town by several executioners and interred alive or beaten to death.

It is difficult from our modern point of view to regard with anything but abhorrence what seems a farrago of savage brutality and ignorance. Yet the cruelties proceed solely from the notion that the sorcerer is actually or by intention a fiendish murderer; and as for this misconception it remains a fact that even in western Europe a witch was legally executed as late as 1782.

The ordeal is not applied solely to cases of sorcery; the test-owner is also invoked to detect a thief. A man may appeal from the verdict, but if the chiefs decline further examination he has no redress. On the other hand, with the chiefs' consent he is permitted to seek a new trial at the hands of another tester; but since all testers form a brotherhood and keep one another informed as to matters of professional interest, the privilege is of only academic significance. The tester's fees are paid by the guilty party and his kin; they are generally set at a very high figure and reduced only at the earnest solicitation of the unfortunate convict. A certain amount of cowrie-shell money, four chickens, a goat and four bottles of whiskey constitute a typical honorarium.

Obviously by no means all legal action requires or admits of the machinery of the ordeal. Under ordinary circumstances suits are simply tried by the council of chiefs vernacularly designated as "the old woman." Plaintiff and defendant in turn take the floor, the witnesses of both are examined, and at last the judges withdraw and announce their verdict to the speaker. The latter proclaims the decision, rubbing white earth on the arm of the person who has won the case. The loser is obliged to pay all costs and frequently in addition must offer compensation to his opponent. Judges are indemnified for their labors out of the court fees, but the older chiefs receive a disproportionately large share of the proceeds. To convey an idea of the spirit of these court sessions is hardly possible without reproducing in detail the transactions themselves. Both the style of the pleading and of the procedure are remarkable. The utterances of every witness are repeated by the official speaker, through whom alone the judges are apparently expected to take cognizance of testimony. Judgments, as in the case of the ordeals, are not inexorable, so that a fine may on petition be commuted to one-half of the amount originally set. In the deliverances of the witnesses and litigants wise saws, long-drawn-out similes, and parables abound. "Listen!" the speaker exhorts his audience, "we need not quarrel in to-day's assembly. If we calmly discuss one point after the other, we shall discover who is to blame and shall know what to do in the case. If little birds are swarming together and a stone is cast among them, usually none is struck; but if a particular one is aimed at, it is sure to be hit. . . ." A chief complains of being involved in frequent litigation by his opponent in these words: "The mouse boxed the cat's ears; but when the cat was about to box the mouse's ears, the mouse said that the cat was seeking a quarrel." Indeed, whole folk-tales are recited in illustration of a point.

One peculiar feature of Ewe jurisprudence is the character of the oath. There are private, tribal, royal and religious oaths. By swearing them the aggrieved person affirms his innocence and compels an official investigation of the case. Oddly enough, the formula is commonly derived from a calamitous event. Thus, the tribal oath consists of the words, "I swear by the eve of the Ho," the references being to a sort of Bartholomew's night terminating a hostile assault by the Asante. When the king has officially designated some such catastrophic occurrence as the subject of an oath, it must not thereafter be mentioned for any other purpose. Private oaths refer in corresponding fashion to hardships encountered by a private individual.

Turning from Togoland to the Limpopo region, we meet with the same essentials of African jurisprudence. The notion of collective responsibility survives in both areas: as a Ho may have his fields destroyed because his brother has committed murder, so a Thonga is liable for his kinsmen's debts. In both tribes an authoritative tribunal renders decisions, in both witchcraft and the ordeal play a strangely conspicuous part. Only in minor particulars are there interesting variations. Thus, among the Thonga there is a confirmed belief in divination by means of magical bones and shells; hence the diviner casts lots in what may be called the preliminary investigation of a death by evil magic. If the same sorcerer is twice designated by this test, the accusation becomes official and is brought before the tribunal, whereupon the diviner undertakes a new examination by questioning, working himself into a trance-like condition. If the earlier suggestions are still corroborated and the defendant asserts his innocence, he is tried by an ordeal, being obliged to swallow an intoxicating draught. If he falls under its sway, his guilt is certain and under aboriginal law he is condemned to death by hanging, impalement or drowning. In all this there is no new principle involved, and the same applies to civil cases. But details are naturally moulded by specific cultural features. Since Thonga social life largely centers in the conceptions of the marriage contract, ninety per cent of the civil suits revolve about the bride-price and are decided in accordance with its traditional interpretation. When a woman has definitely left her husband, her relatives must restore the amount paid for her, while the children revert to the mother.

Regarding the law of the Kafir tribes to the south of the Thonga much valuable information has been made accessible. Among the Amaxosa and their neighbors a fundamental distinction is drawn between criminal and civil cases. The former include political offenses, sorcery, and crimes against the persons of tribesmen; they are prosecuted by the chiefs and the fines belong to them by inalienable right. All other cases are prosecuted by the plaintiffs and the chiefs have no claim to the award made, though the plaintiffs must pay the sheriffs for execution of the court's sentence, the amount generally consuming one-third the value of the fine. If the case is thrown out of court, there are no expenses to be paid. Civil cases may be settled by agreement before any councilor, but either party may appeal from the decision to the chief. Sometimes a councilor mulcts a subject for assault and retains the fine, but this is an act of usurpation and the chief can at any time demand the amount pocketed by his subordinate.

Kafir criminal law rests primarily on the principle that the persons of individuals belong to the chief. Accordingly, he must be compensated for the loss of a subject. The penalty is seven head of cattle for a male and ten head for a female; this difference is due to the dowry obtained at marriage. Compensation for all kinds of homicide is exacted regardless of the circumstances. If a sorcerer dies under torture or is killed without the chief's explicit sanction, the chief is entitled to compensation though he sometimes renounces his prerogative. In the case of a general brawl the fine for each person slain is imposed on all those engaged in the fight collectively. Previous to about 1820 a husband might with impunity kill an adulterer taken in the act; but the chief Gaika abrogated this law and placed such cases on the same plane with other forms of manslaughter. For assault and battery the fine ranges from one to five head of cattle; generally both parties are fined as nothing is considered to warrant one man in striking another, even in self-defense. For abortion the woman and her accomplices are mulcted four or five head of cattle, and a similar fine was imposed in the solitary case of sodomy that came to Mr. Warner's notice during a residence of twenty-five years.

Adultery is a civil case. The fine ranges from one to four head according to the husband's station in society and is raised to from seven to ten head if pregnancy has demonstrably resulted. The child belongs to the husband, who is obliged to provide for it. A wife cannot proceed against her husband or his paramours for adultery. For the seduction of virgins no fine is imposed, but if pregnancy ensues the father must pay one head of cattle and may subsequently claim his offspring by an additional payment of two or three head to reimburse the mother's kin for the trouble of rearing the child. Without such indemnification it remains in their custody. Theft occurs mainly in the form of stock-raiding. When the property is not recovered, a tenfold compensation was anciently deemed proper; otherwise no fine was imposed. As already set forth in another connection, wilful injury to property calls for complete indemnification, but for accidental injury no damages are granted.

Fines thus constitute the only normal penalty recognized by Kafir law. Only when a subject defies the authority of the ruler, the chief will clandestinely gather an armed force, descend upon the rebellious household, seize all the livestock, and if resistance is made have the outlaws killed without ceremony.

The kingdom of Uganda represents the most highly organized of aboriginal states and its legal institutions naturally display some additional features. Here there was a series of hierarchically graded courts. Even petty chiefs acted as magistrates for their subjects, but these had the privilege of appealing to successively higher authorities until they got to the grandee combining the functions of a prime minister with those of a chief justice. In his court most appeals ended, but exceptional cases were brought before the king himself. The chief justice had a deputy for trying the less important cases, but expected a report from his assistant and himself rendered judgment accordingly. In each of the lower tribunals the plaintiff paid a fee of twenty cowrie-shells when stating his case and a supplementary fee of a goat and a barkcloth before the defendant was summoned; the latter also made an initial payment of a goat and a barkcloth. If the defendant was convicted, he had to pay the plaintiff two goats and a barkcloth over and above the award. In appealing to the prime minister's court the plaintiff was obliged to pay ten goats and five barkcloths as the initial fee. The minister, besides this fee, received one-fourth of the fine imposed, and the loser had to refund all the court fees.

In addition to features common to African tribes such as the ordeal and collective composition for crime Uganda law recognized torture for the purpose of extracting information and as a penalty confinement in the stocks, the culprit usually having his foot thrust into the hole cut through a heavy log. A rope tied to the leg enabled the prisoner to lift it and walk, but the constant rubbing of the wood against his foot and the use of guards made escape impracticable. Sometimes both arms and one leg were put into the stocks. Uganda usage certainly demonstrates once more how little connection there is between elaboration and refinement of social life.[8]

Conclusion

It has now been demonstrated to satiety that the majority of primitive communities recognize not merely wrongs inflicted by individuals upon individuals and precipitating a dispute between their respective kins, but that over and above the law of torts there is generally a law of crimes, of outrages resented not by a restricted group of relatives but by the entire community or its directors. The conclusion reacts upon and strengthens the argument of the preceding chapter, for it shows the reality of the territorial unit for certain specific social aims. Naturally the relative strength of the kinship and the territorial sentiment varies with the tribe; or better, their spheres of dominance differ in different parts of the globe. But even in so exaggerated an instance of discrete kins as that of the Ifugao a latent neighborliness comes to light when the mutual reactions of co-villagers are contrasted with the sentiments evoked by an outsider. The territorial bond must then be considered as one of the social ties occurring concomitantly with others in the simpler stages of civilization.

References

[1] Maine: Chap. x. Hobhouse: Chap. III.
[2] Barton: passim. Bogoras: 662. Goddard, 1903: 59. Maclean: 60, 67. Radloff: 523. Stair: 96. Dixon, 1907: 452. Lowie, 1912: 238.
[3] Roth, 1906. Spencer and Gillen, 1904: 25, 556. Howitt: 183, 254, 296, 326 seq.
[4] Barton.
[5] Thalbitzer: 59, 127. Boas, 1888: 465. 561, 582, 609; id., 1907: 115-121, 467. Cranz: 1, 231, 249. Hawkes, 1916: 109.
[6] Fletcher and La Flesche: 213.
[7] Stair: 91 seq. Tregear: 139. Ellis, Wm.: IV, 419-423.
[8] Spieth: 123-181, 278-283, 535-543. Junod: 1, 410-421. Maclean: 57-75. Roscoe: 260-267.

CHAPTER XV

CONCLUSION

PRIMITIVE society wears a character rather different from that popularized by Morgan's school. Instead of dull uniformity, there is mottled diversity; instead of the single sib pattern multiplied in fulsome profusion we detect a variety of social units, now associated with the sib, now taking its place. Let us visualize the actual aspect of primitive conditions by a concrete example from a by no means unusually complicated social environment.

In the Mountain Crow band, some eighty years ago, a woman of the Thick-lodge sib gives birth to a boy. Her husband summons a renowned warrior of his sib, the Bad-leggings, who dubs the child Strikes-three-men in memory of one of his own exploits. As Strikes-three-men grows up, he learns how to act towards the relatives on either side of his family and what conduct to expect in return. The female Thick-lodges make for him beaded shirts and moccasins, on the male members he can rely for aid in any difficulty. His father he comes to regard as the natural provider and protector of the immediate family circle; to all the other men of the Bad-leggings sib he gives presents when he can and treats them with respect. On their part they become his official eulogists as soon as he distinguishes himself by skill as a hunter or by bravery in battle; and the bond between him and them is so close that when one of them commits an offense against tribal etiquette an appropriate nickname is attached to his own person. With the children of his 'fathers' a curious reciprocal relationship unites him. They are his mentors and he is theirs. They throw in his teeth his foibles and misdemeanors, and he retaliates in kind. To these various relations based on family and sib ties associational ones are soon added. He enters a league of playmates mimicking the warrior societies and tries to gain glory by striking deer and buffalo as the older braves count coup on Dakota or Cheyenne foemen. As he grows older, Albino-bull, one of his companions, becomes a bosom friend. Together they go courting and share each other's mistresses; together they set out on war parties, each shielding the other at the risk of his own life; together they join the Fox society to which Albino-bull has been invited; and together they leave it when the rival Lumpwoods, impressed by the young men's war record, bribe them into their fold. Now a novel set of relations ensues. Strikes-three-men aids his fellow-Lumpwoods as he aids his sib-mates; he and his comrade participate in all of the society's feasts and dances; and they while away leisure hours lounging and smoking in the tents of their new associates and singing Lumpwood songs. When Strikes-three-men buys a wife, still another unit is added to his social groups; added rather than substituted for the old family group because the tie that links him with his brothers and sisters remains not only unsnapped but in full force. About this time a fancy may seize our hero to cast in his lot with the band hunting about the Yellowstone confluence. Henceforth its political relations become his. With his new fellows he pays visits to the friendly Village tribes of the upper Missouri, with them he pursues a gang of Dakota raiders, and when the Mountain Crow decline to join a punitive war party against the hereditary enemy he is as vociferous as any River Crow in denouncing the pusillanimity of the band of his nativity. From the start he has been no stranger in the strange land: there are Thicklodges on the Yellowstone who greet him as a brother, and he mingles without formality with the Lumpwoods there resident. The illness of one of his children may evoke a vow: on its recovery he pledges himself to seek admission into the Tobacco order. Four-bears, of the Weasel chapter, is willing to initiate him, and so Strikes-three-men and his wife become members, privileged to join in the annual planting of the sacred weed and in all other ceremonial activities of their branch. A special bond of intimacy unites them henceforth with their sponsor Four-bears, from whom an occasional horse may be expected as a token of paternal affection.

Thus our Crow comes to be a member of some half-a-dozen well-defined groups. By birth he belongs to a sib, a family and a band. Later a life-long friendship couples him with Albino-bull; he joins the Fox and subsequently the Lumpwood organization; and is finally admitted to the religious Tobacco order. As a mature man he is simultaneously a Thick-lodge, Albino-bull's partner, a Lumpwood, a River Crow, a Weasel, besides forming the center of an individual household. Manifold as are his affiliations, they are hardly above the average in number and complexity. Under special circumstances a variety of others could be added. Through distinguished valor he may become a chief; the purchase of one medicine would establish a ceremonial tie between him and the seller; by buying another he would come to join still another definite organization, the Horse Dancers. On the whole, there is remarkably little collision of interests through this varied allegiance; and an extension of sentimental attachment takes place rather than a clash of emotions associated with diverse groups. Doubtless some obligations sit more lightly than others. If one of two comrades were affronted by their military society, both would leave it and seek entrance into another. It is also safe to infer that regard for one's wife would be readily sacrificed either to one's blood kin or to one's club. Not in the real life of the Crow bourgeois, but by that swashbuckling standard of honor to which he is content to make public obeisance, a woman is only a woman and to show overmuch solicitude on her account would mean a loss of face. But the occasions for such demonstrations are not over-numerous and the average tribesman does not suffer much distress from the variety of his memberships.

The multiplicity of social relations could be as strikingly illustrated by other examples. In the sibless Andamans we should have to reckon with status as determined by dietary restrictions, conjugal and parental position. A Banks Islander would be found to belong at once to a sib, a grade in the club, and half a dozen Ghost societies. Among the Vedda territorial grouping would figure prominently, and in Polynesia distinctions of caste would come to the foreground. In each and every case, however, diverse coëxisting units would have to be considered.

Multiplicity by itself would not be fatal to a generalized scheme of social evolution, for abstractly it is conceivable that at a certain definite stage in the history of the sib organization status groups would supervene, at another age-classes, and so forth. But empirically it turns out that the several types of social unit are combined in a purely capricious fashion. In one region we find secret societies with sibs; in another, sibs but no secret societies; in a third, a secret society without sibs; a fourth tribe has either or both features in combination with all sorts of associations; a fifth lacks both. Upon what principles can be fixed the chronological order of the observed combinations? Shall we say that Andamanese siblessness plus status grouping is anterior to Maidu siblessness and lack of status grouping plus a secret organization? And is the Melanesian union of mother-sibs, sex dichotomy with graded clubs, and Ghost societies, earlier or later than the Hidatsa complex of mother-sibs, military age organizations and bundle societies? An attempt to embody the exuberant variety of phenomena in a single chronological sequence seems hopeless. Probably even adherents of unilinear evolution would admit that the totality of social manifestations cannot be dealt with in this fashion and would be content with maintaining that only each distinct type of social unit or phenomenon taken by itself tends to develop through a fixed series of stages.

But this contention has been proved erroneous for practically every department of social organization. Its fallacy becomes patent as soon as we place side by side the institutions of tribes in distinct areas but on the same general level of cultural advancement. The aboriginal Australians were economically hunters and seed-gatherers, and that was the condition of the Paviotso of Nevada, both representing technologically the Neolithic stage of European archaeologists. Yet, whatever branch of their social life we compare, there is complete dissimilarity. The Australians have sibs, moieties, totemism, classes; among the Paviotso not even the faintest germ of these institutions is to be detected so that there is no reason to assume that they ever would have risen or fallen to a similar form of organization. Politically, too, there is no suggestion of resemblance: there is no Paviotso body with powers comparable to those of the Australian gerontocracy; on the other hand, there is nothing in Australia comparable to a director of the rabbit-hunt, in whom is vested what meager central authority exists in Nevada. Australians and Plateau Shoshoneans prove not only different but incommensurable; they represent not one line of development but two separate lines. If it be suggested that these are arbitrarily selected cases, let others be substituted. The Andamanese represent the same stage of general advancement and they are sibless like the Paviotso. But to their division into married couples, bachelors and spinsters there is no parallel among the Nevada people; and though the segregation of bachelors occurs in Australia, this partial resemblance was found to be probably the result of historical connection with the same peoples rather than of independent, spontaneous evolution.

There is no loop-hole for the specious plea that general cultural advancement and social advancement may proceed in mutual independence of each other. That argument has already been examined in another context and its worthlessness appears when peoples are grouped precisely according to the complexity of their *social* institutions. From that angle, the Negroes and the Polynesians, who would occupy quite different rungs technologically, may be regarded as roughly equivalent. Yet to compare Uganda and Hawaii is to pass from one cultural universe to another: the Africans are devoid of the Polynesian caste system founded on divine lineage; and throughout Polynesia not a trace appears of that complicated jurisprudence that is so marked a trait of Negro Africa. If the assumed laws of social evolution operate neither among peoples of like general condition nor among peoples of generally like complexity of social organization, where can they possibly be conceived to operate?

But what of the resemblances that undoubtedly do occur in widely separated areas? Is it not an inherent law that produces polyandry in Eskimo and Toda communities or sibs among the Pueblo and the Gros Ventre Indians? At this point it is desirable to discriminate more sharply than has hitherto been done between the theory of independent development, which I have again and again advocated, and a belief in laws regulating the independent reproduction of the same *series* of stages which I now at the close of my investigation formally abjure. Undoubtedly there are certain conditions that may recur in different areas and produce similar results. Scarcity of women and polyandry were seen to be thus causally linked, but as I have already shown in the appropriate place the parallelism is of strictly limited scope. The common cause of polyandry is female infanticide, but the cause of infanticide was seen to vary, while the implications of polyandry again show divergence in the two regions after the brief span of likeness. Gen-

CONCLUSION 433

erally speaking, the duplication of conditions may indeed produce the duplication of one sequence but there the matter ends. For the course of cultural evolution depends not on that single element of similarity but on the whole complex of associated features as well, and since *these* are not alike nor indeed well can be alike in peoples with a distinct body of cultural traditions, the effect is almost inevitably divergence so far as any advancement occurs at all. But it should be noted that often enough such advancement is not observed; development terminates in a blind alley with no possibility of further parallelism. When we have recognized how a like social point of view can produce a similar term of opprobrium among Australian blacks and Crow Indians (p. 11), that is as far as we can go. There is no further social result flowing from the use of similar vituperative epithets, nor can any further consequence therefrom be readily imagined. At this juncture it is well to revert to the linguistic analogy of the introductory chapter. When the Shoshoni and the Greeks independently evolve a dual number, this is the result of similar classificatory processes, but what is the general import of the isolated resemblance? Precisely nil. It has not inaugurated a series of morphological changes making both languages conform to a common linguistic pattern. To be sure, it is conceivable that a classification of the type mentioned might be correlated with certain other features that are descriptively distinct though psychologically linked. The total resemblance in structure would nevertheless remain remarkably slight. Now this example illustrates my conception of the independent development of sociological or cultural traits. Independent development occurs; but its products have a negligible influence on the total course of events in their respective series, which remain essentially distinct.

The occurrence of convergent evolution—of like results achieved through different channels—might be cited as evidence of laws consummating predestined ends. But in by far the greater number of instances the likeness dissolves on closer scrutiny into a superficial or only partial resemblance. Thus teknonymy appeared as a possible result of a system of status designations, of feminine inferiority, or of a paucity of kinship terms. Evidently the import of the custom is quite different in these cases; or rather there are three customs which it is sometimes convenient to call by a common name. In the same way we find it convenient to group together as democracies the polities of ancient Athens and of the United States. This sets them apart for certain purposes from certain other constitutions but implies no recognition of either genetic or psychological affinity. But even where genuine likeness has been achieved we find divergence setting in after convergence, as in the case of polyandry.

Thus neither the examples of independent evolution from like causes nor those of convergent evolution from unlike causes establish an innate law of social progress. One fact, however, encountered at every stage and in every phase of society, by itself lays the axe to the root of any theory of historical laws—the extensive occurrence of diffusion. Creating nothing, this factor nevertheless makes all other agencies taper almost into nothingness beside it in its effect on the total growth of human civilization. An explanation of the ultimate origin of the Omaha sib would account for *one* sib organization; transmission accounts for that organization among a dozen tribes or more. Diffusion not merely extends the range of a feature, but in so doing it is able to level the differences of race, geographical environment, and economic status that are popularly assumed as potent instrumentalities in cultural evolution. Through diffusion the Chinese come to share Western notions of government; through diffusion the Southern Plains Indians come to share with the Iroquois of the Woodlands a type of sib that distinguishes them from their fellow-Siouans living under the same geographical conditions; through diffusion fishermen, reindeer nomads, and tillers of the soil come to entertain the identical conception of feminine disabilities. Any conceivable tendency of human society to pursue a fixed sequence of stages must be completely veiled by the incessant tendency to borrowing and thus becomes an unknowable noumenon that is scientifically worthless. Strangely enough, it was a jurist who clearly recognized this fact at a time when anthropologists were still chasing the will-o'-the-wisp of historical laws; and Maitland's memorable words in *Domesday Book and Beyond* may well be quoted in full: "Even had our anthropologists at their command material that would justify them in prescribing that every independent portion of mankind must, if it is to move at all, move through one fated series of stages which may be designated as Stage A, Stage B, Stage C, and so forth, we still should have to face the fact that the rapidly progressive groups have been just those which have not been independent, which have not worked out their own salvation, but have appropriated alien ideas and have thus been enabled, for anything that we can tell, to leap from Stage A to Stage X without passing through any intermediate stages. Our Anglo-Saxon ancestors did not arrive at the alphabet or at the Nicene Creed, by traversing a long series of 'stages'; they leapt to the one and to the other." Present ethnographical knowledge warrants us in extending Maitland's argument; we know that the relatively stationary no less than the relatively progressive peoples have evolved their culture through contact with alien ideas, and that accordingly the conditions for the operation of social laws among independent peoples nowhere exist. By all means let us register such sequences as may be found to recur in separated regions, but let us not dignify these strictly limited and sometimes trivial relations, such as that between polyandry and a paucity of women, by the pretentious title of historical laws.

To recognize the complexity and singularity of cultural

phenomena, mainly as a consequence of diffusion, is then to abandon that quest of short-hand formulas prescribed by Professor Pearson, and it will be abandoned not from any foolish disdain for a simplification of facts but because we prefer to have the facts unsimplified than a simple statement that fails to correspond with them. The evolutionary views until recently current among anthropologists are of the category of those 'laws' denounced by Sir Henry Maine when in 1861 he wrote as follows: "Theories, plausible and comprehensive, but absolutely unverified, . . . enjoy a universal preference over sober research into the primitive history of society and law." The period has come for eschewing the all-embracing and baseless theories of yore and to settle down to that sober historical research involved in the intensive study of specific regions.

Must we, then, resign all hope of rising from a contemplation of unique series of events to an interpretation? By no means. First of all the renunciation of historical laws does not imply the renunciation of uniformities *independent of the time factor* and veritably inherent in the essence of social existence. The universality of borrowing is itself a generalization of this type, as is the implied aversion from or inability for creative effort, which in turn is correlated with the persistence of cultural features once established. Secondly, it is precisely the singular combination of traits forming the context or past history of a given feature that, in conjunction with such general sociological principles as these, furnishes an interpretation of its meaning, *as nothing else whatsoever can*. An example from Maine, that champion of sane historical methods, will elucidate the point. Maine was confronted with the fact that the later Roman republic dispensed with the death penalty, a fact which had led to explanations based on the supposed psychology of the Romans. But Maine discovered that at the time in question permanent judicial bodies were commissions holding a delegated authority from the legislative assembly, which itself lacked power of inflicting capital punishment, hence could not delegate such authority to one of its creatures. The interpretation completely clarifies the problem, carries immediate conviction, and at once exposes the speciousness of any type of explanation not founded on similar principles. When we desire to understand Masai age-classes or Hidatsa age-societies, we shall do well to follow not Morgan or Schurtz, but Maine; to saturate ourselves with the spirit and history of Masai and Hidatsa culture, respectively, and with that of their neighbors, rather than to fly for aid to a chimerical law of social evolution.

The principles that underlie the growth of social organization do not differ from the principles operative in culture generally. It was once believed that the stages which archaeological research reveals in western Europe must be stages mankind have everywhere been obliged to traverse. But the case of African technology suffices to disprove the assumption: the Africans did not pass from a Stone Age to an Age of Copper and Bronze and then to an Iron Age; whether through autochthonous advancement or through borrowing from Asiatic sources, they passed directly from the manufacture of stone tools to the manufacture of iron tools. In another phase of material civilization the American natives, except in Peru, completely failed to domesticate animals for economic use, clearly proving that, as in Yucatan and Mexico, a fairly complex cultural structure can be reared without resting on domestication as one of its supports. In the absence of an inherent law of evolution, then, social history merely conforms to the facts of culture history generally.

There is nevertheless an important difference not so much objectively as from the point of view of the appraising observer between the history of material culture and that of social organization. In the former there are periods of retrogression or stagnation alternating with eras of advancement, and the very use of these words implies criteria for judging progress. Nor is it difficult to fathom their foundation. Tools are contrivances for definite practical purposes; if these are accomplished more expeditiously and efficiently by one set of tools, then that set is better. Hence it is a purely objective judgment that metal axes are superior to those of stone. So economic activity has for its object the sustenance of human existence, and when the possibilities for supporting life are enlarged, as by the domestication of an eatable and milkable species, we are justified in speaking of a *progressive* change. But in the sphere of social life there is no objective criterion for grading cultural phenomena. The foremost philosophers are not agreed as to the ultimate ideals to be sought through social existence. Within a century Western thought and action have swung from one pole to the other, from the extremes of Manchesterian individualism to the extremes of state socialism; and the student's evaluation of, say, the communistic bias of Eskimo society will not be the same if he is a disciple of Herbert Spencer as it would be if he were a disciple of Prince Kropotkin. Democracy has become a slogan of modern times, but it has also roused the impassioned protests of men of genius and of reactionary biologists, some of whom doubtless cast wistful glances in the direction of Micronesia, lamenting the decay of that spirit of loyalty to superior rank so nobly preserved in the Marshall Islands. Again, the unqualified emancipation of woman may be the only goal consistent with strict individualism, but what if individualistic aspirations are subordinated to others, say, to the perpetuation of traditional family ideals or to eugenic aims? Here, too, judgment of primitive conceptions must depend on one's subjective reaction to moot-problems of modern speculation. Even where the verdict of modern society tends to unanimity, the critical investigator cannot accept it as absolutely valid. It is not obvious that obligatory monogamy is in an absolute sense the most preferable form of marriage, least of all when it is tempered with a system of libertinage producing something not wholly different from the system of the Masai.

In short, the appraisal of sociological features is wholly different from that of technological features of culture. The latter may be rated according to the closeness with which they accomplish known ends; the former have unknown ends or ends whose value is a matter of philosophic doubt, hence they can be graded only on subjective grounds and must scientifically be treated as incommensurable.

Of course it is true that social organizations differ in complexity, but that difference fails to provide a criterion of progress. When the Andamanese evolved or borrowed the notion of segregating bachelors from spinsters, and both from married couples, their social culture gained in complexity, but it is not easy to prove that it experienced either improvement or deterioration. If our enlightened communities coped as successfully with, say, the problem of maintaining order as ruder peoples in a simpler environment, then it might be conceded that our complex administrative machinery represents an intellectual advance. But the condition is contrary to fact, and our cumbersome method of preserving the peace and the more elegant solution of the same problem in simpler circumstances remain incommensurable.

When from definite customs and institutions we turn to the dynamics of social history, the result is again the impossibility of grading cultures, but for a different reason. Institutions are generally different and not comparable; processes are not only comparable but identical in the simpler and the higher civilizations. Thus we find the co-operative motive and the need for congenial companionship incarnated in a variety of forms among primitive peoples and at times even simulating the semblance of quite modern institutions, as in the case of the Samoan trade unions. As an invariable component of primitive life we further encounter the eternal striving for prestige, which is thus clearly a characteristic of all social aggregates. The peacock theory of primitive man does away with that shopworn commonplace that primitive society wholly merges the individual in his group. It is true that at bottom it despises individuality, for it prizes variation only in a direction it has predetermined and conformity to its standards is the price exacted for recognition. But in this respect primitive and civilized society coincide in principle, however they may differ in detail. History records a transfer of power from one mystically sanctified source of authority to another, from a church to a book, from a book to a state, or to an intangible public opinion. But with unfailing tenacity every society from the simplest to the most complex has adhered to the principle that the one unpardonable sin consists in setting up one's private judgment against the recognized social authority, in perpetrating an infraction of tribal taboos. When, therefore, Sir Henry Maine points out the growing importance of contractual instead of status relations in modern society, his argument is of formal rather than of substantial significance for the history of individual freedom. In the disposal of his property an Ewe is not so free as an American, in other regards he is freer; and both are hedged about by a set of conventions whose breach may subject them to indignity, ostracism, and death. Neither morphologically nor dynamically can social life be said to have progressed from a stage of savagery to a stage of enlightenment.

The belief in social progress was a natural accompaniment of the belief in historical laws, especially when tinged with the evolutionary optimism of the 'seventies of the nineteenth century. If inherent necessity urges all societies along a fixed path, metaphysicians may still dispute whether the underlying force be divine or diabolic, but there can at least be no doubt as to which community is retarded and which accelerated in its movement toward the appointed goal. But no such necessity or design appears from the

CONCLUSION

study of culture history. Cultures develop mainly through the borrowings due to chance contact. Our own civilization is even more largely than the rest a complex of borrowed traits. The singular order of events by which it has come into being provides no schedule for the itinerary of alien cultures. Hence the specious plea that a given people must pass through such or such a stage in *our* history before attaining this or that destination can no longer be sustained. The student who has mastered Maitland's argument will recognize the historical and ethnologic absurdity of this solemn nonsense. In prescribing for other peoples a social programme we must always act on subjective grounds; but at least we can act unfettered by the pusillanimous fear of transgressing a mock-law of social evolution.

Nor are the facts of culture history without bearing on the adjustment of our own future. To that planless hodgepodge, that thing of shreds and patches called civilization, its historian can no longer yield superstitious reverence. He will realize better than others the obstacles to infusing design into the amorphous product; but in thought at least he will not grovel before it in fatalistic acquiescence but dream of a rational scheme to supplant the chaotic jumble.

END

CORRECTIONS AND ADDENDA

P. 4 f. It is worth noting the skepticism of a great historian like Eduard Meyer (*Kleine Schriften,* 1:29, 32, *1910*) on the subject of historic laws.

P. 15. The view that incest is instinctive must be rejected as without solid foundation.

P. 26. It is worth noting that the Arabs apparently everywhere favor parallel cousin marriage, i.e. with father's brother's daughter. See e.g. Brenda Z. Seligman, Studies in Semitic Kinship, *Bulletin, School of Oriental Studies, London Institution,* III, pt. I, 51-68, 263-279, *1923.*

P. 27. Radcliffe-Brown has introduced the convenient adjectives "matrilateral" and "patrilateral" for the marriage, respectively, with a mother's brother's and a father's sister's daughter. Where both occur jointly, Wm. Lloyd Warner speaks of "symmetrical" cross-cousin marriage; where only one occurs, he designates it as "asymmetrical."

P. 36. Although the simultaneous marriage with a woman and her sister and the marriage with a deceased wife's sister are related phenomena, only the latter should be called "sororate," the former being "sororal polygyny," as suggested by Marcel Granet, *La polygynie sororale et le sororat dans la Chine féodale* (Paris, 1920).

P. 45. John M. Cooper, Temporal Sequence and the Marginal Cultures, *The Catholic University of America, Anthrop. Series,* No. 10:52-57, forcibly argues that *sporadically* polyandry probably occurred in far distant times, "but that it was then, as it is now, exceptional rather than normal."

P. 74 ff. Hahn's generalization goes beyond the facts. Many Oceanian, African, American tribes that farm without ploughs have men do the work of cultivation, wholly or in part. Hahn is almost one hundred per cent right, however, in describing ploughing as a masculine labor. To Laufer's generalization there are a few, but only a very few, exceptions, as among the Batwa of Ruanda. Of course, a shift in the division of labor sometimes occurs. Thus, the Shilluk women on the upper Nile are said to have been formerly the only cultivators.

P. 90, line 3. Read "daughter's husband," not "daughter's *son.*"

P. 110. After some sporadic use of "sib," most anthropologists have reverted to "clan," which has the advantage of being more or less international.

P. 115. Besides the Hopi, some Shoshoneans in California also have a Dakota terminology.

P. 122. Rivers, in the review cited in the Preface to this book, was not satisfied with the argument for diversity of clan origins, which was also rejected by Ronald L. Olson, Clan and Moiety in Native America, *U. C.,* 33:351-422, 1933. Cf. R. H. Lowie, Some Moot Prob-

CORRECTIONS AND ADDENDA 442a

lems in Social Organization, *American Anthropologist,* 36:321-330, 1934.

P. 127. Kroeber's scheme concerning major groupings of Pueblo clans was not accepted by Elsie Clews Parsons, who also felt that he had underestimated the part played by Zuñi clans (*American Anthropologist,* 20:98-104, 1918).

P. 151. Mrs. A. W. Hoernlé, The Social Organization of the Nama Hottentots of Southwest Africa (*American Anthropologist,* 27:1-24, 1925), proves that the Hottentots have patrilineal clans.

P. 158. In the article quoted in the Preface, Kirchhoff (on K. Th. Preuss's findings) shows that the Witoto of the Northwest Amazons have a full-fledged patrilineal clan organization (p. 175 f.).

P. 161. The Australians seem to be almost always, not merely "at least often," permanently patrilocal.

P. 217. Present evidence indicates that among the Pueblos land did belong to the clan (sib).

P. 219. The question of clans in Mexico remains vexed. Some tribes probably had them.

P. 235. Cf. R. H. Lowie, "Incorporeal Property in Primitive Society," Yale Law Journal, 37:551-563, *1928.*

P. 251. As a synonym of junior-right, "ultimogeniture" is sometimes used.

P. 309. Facts on the Poro are conveniently summarized in George W. Harley, Notes on the Poro in Liberia, Papers of the Peabody Museum of American Archaeology and Ethnology, Harvard University, 19:1-36, *1941*

P. 351. For the Natchez and other Southeastern Indians, see John R. Swanton, The Indians of the Southeastern United States, Bureau of American Ethnology, Bulletin 137, *1946.*

P. 361. On Polynesian government, the numerous Bulletins of the Bernice P. Bishop Museum, published during the last twenty years, provide valuable data.

P. 369. The symposium edited by Fortes and Evans-Pritchard (see Preface) is most valuable on African forms of government.

P. 436, line 5. Read "we prefer the facts unsimplified to a simple statement."

P. 444. Insert: Bogoras, W., The Chukchee. Leiden and New York, *1910.*

BIBLIOGRAPHY

Note.—This Bibliography includes all the literature cited in this work. The following abbreviations are used to designate serial publications:

Amer. Anth.	American Anthropologist
Amer. Anth., Mem.	Memoirs of the American Anthropological Association
A. M. N. H.	Anthropological Papers of the American Museum of Natural History
A.M.N.H., Bull.	Bulletin of the American Museum of Natural History
A.M.N.H., Hd.	Handbook Series of the American Museum of Natural History
A.M.N.H., Mem.	Memoirs of the American Museum of Natural History
B.A.E.	Annual Report of the Bureau of (American) Ethnology
B.A.E., Bull.	Bulletin, Bureau of American Ethnology
Can. Geol. Sur., Mem.	Memoir, Canada Department of Mines, Geological Survey
Can. Geol. Sur., Mus.	Museum Bulletin, Canada Department of Mines, Geological Survey
Can. Sum. Rept.	Summary Report of the Geological Survey, Canada
Field Mus.	Anthropological Series, Field Museum of Natural History
J.A.F.L.	Journal of American Folk-Lore
J.A.I.	Journal of the (Royal) Anthropological Institute of Great Britain and Ireland
Reports	Reports of the Cambridge Anthropological Expedition
U. Cal.	University of California Publications in American Archaeology and Ethnology
Z. vgl. R.	Zeitschrift für vergleichende Rechtswissenschaft

Adair, J.
 1775. The History of the American Indians. London.
Alldridge, T. J.
 1910. A Transformed Colony: Sierra Leone. London.
Annual Archaeological Report. Toronto, 1906.
Baden-Powell, B. H.
 1896. The Indian Village Community. London.

443

Bandelier, A.
　　1878. On the Distribution and Tenure of Lands and the Customs with respect to Inheritance, among the Ancient Mexicans. Reports of the Peabody Museum, II, No. 2, 385-448.
Barrett, S. A.
　　1917. Ceremonies of the Pomo Indians. U. Cal., XII, 397-441.
Barton, R. F.
　　1919. Ifugao Law. U. Cal., XV, 1-127.
Bleek, W. I., and Lloyd, L. C.
　　1911. Specimens of Bushman Folklore. London.
Boas, F.
　　1888. The Central Eskimo. 6 B.A.E., 409-669.
　　1897. The Social Organization and Secret Societies of the Kwakiutl Indians. Report of the U. S. National Museum for 1895. 315-733.
　　1907. The Eskimo of Baffin Land and Hudson Bay. A.M.N.H., Bull., xv.
　　1911. The Mind of Primitive Man. New York.
　　1916 (a). Tsimshian Mythology. 31 B.A.E.
　　1916 (b). The Origin of Totemism. Amer. Anth. XVIII, 319-326.
Brown, A. R.
　　1913. Three Tribes of Western Australia. J.A.I., XLIII, 143-194.
Castren, M. A.
　　1853. Reiseerinnerungen aus den Jahren 1838-1844. St. Petersburg.
Codrington, R. H.
　　1891. The Melanesians: Studies in their Anthropology and Folk-Lore. Oxford.
Cole, F. C.
　　1913. The Wild Tribes of Davao District. Field Mus. XII. 49-203.
Cunow, H.
　　1894. Die Verwandtschafts-Organisationen der Australneger. Stuttgart.
　　1912. Zur Urgeschichte der Ehe und Familie. Stuttgart.
Cranz, D.
　　1765. Historie von Grönland. Barby.
Czaplicka, M.A.
　　1914. Aboriginal Siberia. Oxford.
Dixon, R. B.
　　1905. The Northern Maidu. A.M.N.H., Bull. XVII, 119-346.
　　1907. The Shasta. Ibid., 381-498.
Dorsey, J. O.
　　1884. Omaha Sociology. 3 B.A.E., 211-370.
Ellis, A. B.
　　1890. The Ewe-speaking Tribes of the Slave Coast of West Africa. London.
Ellis, Wm.
　　1831. Polynesian Researches. London.
Erdland, P. A.
　　1914. Die Marshall-Insulaner. Anthropos-Bibliothek. Münster i. W.
Ferguson, W. S.
　　1918. The Zulus and the Spartans. Harvard African Studies, II, 197-234.

Fletcher, A. and La Flesche, F.
  1911. The Omaha Tribe. 27 B.A.E.
Frazer, J.
  1892. The Aborigines of New South Wales. Sydney.
Frazer, J. G.
  1910. Totemism and Exogamy. 4 vols. London.
  1911. The Golden Bough. 3d. ed., pt. II. London.
  1912. Psyche's Task. London.
Franciscan Fathers, The.
  1910. An Ethnologic Dictionary of the Navaho Language. St. Michaels.
Freire-Marreco, B.
  1914. Tewa Kinship Terms from the Pueblo of Hano. Amer. Anth., XVI, 269-287.
Freud, S.
  1912, 1913. Ueber einige Uebereinstimmungen im Seelenleben der Wilden und der Neurotiker. *Imago*, 17-33; 213-227; 1913, 1-21, 357-408.
Frobenius, L.
  1913. Und Afrika Sprach. 1. Berlin-Charlottenburg.
Gifford, E. W.
  1916. Miwok Moieties. U. Cal., XII, 139-194.
  1918. Clans and Moieties in Southern California. U. Cal., XIV, 155-219.
Goddard, P. E.
  1903. Life and Culture of the Hupa, U. Cal., I, 1-88.
  1913. Indians of the Southwest. A.M.N.H., Hd.
Goldenweiser, A. A.
  1910. Totemism; an Analytical Study. J.A.F.L., XXIII, 179-293.
  1912. On Iroquois Work. Can. Sum. Rept., 464-475.
  1913. On Iroquois Work. Can. Sum. Rept., 365-373.
  1918. Form and Content in Totemism. Amer. Anth. XX, 280-295.
Gurdon, P. R. T.
  1907. The Khasis. London.
Hahn, Ed.
  1905. Das Alter der wirtschaftlichen Kultur der Menschheit. Heidelberg.
Hartland, E. S.
  1917. Matrilineal Kinship and the Question of its Priority. Amer. Anth. Mem., IV, 1-90.
Hawkes, E. W.
  1913. The "Inviting-in" Feast of the Alaskan Eskimo. Can. Geol. Sur., Mem. 45.
  1916. The Labrador Eskimo. Can. Geol. Sur., Mem. 91.
Hearne, S.
  1795. Journey from Prince of Wales Fort in Hudson's Bay to the Northern Ocean. London.
Hobhouse, L. T.
  1915. Morals in Evolution. London.
Hocart, A. M.
  1913. The Fijian Custom of Tauvu. J.A.I., XLIII, 101-108.
  1915. Chieftainship and the Sister's Son in the Pacific. Amer. Anth., 631-646.

Hodson, T. C.
    1911. The Naga Tribes of Manipur. London.
Hollis, A. C.
    1905. The Masai. Oxford.
    1909. The Nandi. Oxford.
Howitt, A. W.
    1904. The Native Tribes of South-east Australia. London.
Jesuit Relations and Allied Documents. 1896-1901. Edited by Reuben Gold Thwaites. 71 volumes.
Jochelson, W.
    1908. Material Culture and Social Organization of the Koryak. A.M.N.H., Mem. x.
    1910. The Yukaghir and the Yukaghirized Tungus. A.M.N.H., Mem., xiii.
Junod, H. A.
    1912. The Life of a South African Tribe. 2 vols. Neuchatel.
Keysser, Ch.
    1911. Aus dem Leben der Kaileute, *in* Neuhauss, R., Deutsch Neu-Guinea, iii. Berlin. 1-242.
Kingsley, M. H.
    1904. Travels in West Africa. London.
Kohler, J. 1897.
    Urgeschichte der Ehe. Z. vgl. R. xii.
Krämer, A.
    1902. Die Samoa-Inseln. Stuttgart.
Krause, A.
    1885. Die Tlinkit-Indianer. Jena.
Kroeber, A. L.
    1904. The Arapaho. A.M.N.H., Bull., xviii, 1-229, 279-454.
    1908. Ethnology of the Gros Ventre, A.M.N.H., i, 145-281.
    1917 (a). Zuñi Kin and Clan. A.M.N.H., xviii, 39-205.
    1917 (b). The Tribes of the Pacific Coast of North America. XIX International Congress of Americanists. 385-401.
Lang, Andrew.
    1885. Custom and Myth. London.
Laufer, B.
    1900. Preliminary Notes on Explorations among the Amoor Tribes. Amer. Anth., 297-338.
    1917. The Beginnings of Porcelain in China. Field Mus., xv, 79-177.
Lehner, St.
    1911. Bukaua, *in* Neuhauss, Deutsch Neu-Guinea, iii, 397-485. Berlin.
Lowie, R. H.
    1912. Social Life of the Crow Indians. A.M.N.H., ix, 179-248.
    1913. Societies of the Crow, Hidatsa and Mandan Indians. A.M.N.H., xi, 145-358.
    1915. Exogamy and the Classificatory System of Relationship. Amer. Anth., 223-239.
    1916. Plains Indian Age-Societies: Historical and Comparative Summary. A.M.N.H., xi, 877-984.
    1917 (a). Notes on the Social Organizations and Customs of the Mandan, Hidatsa and Crow Indians. A.M.N.H., xxi, 1-99.

BIBLIOGRAPHY

    1917 (b). Culture and Ethnology. New York.
    1919 (a). The Matrilineal Complex. U. Cal., XVI, 29-45.
    1919 (b). Family and Sib. Amer. Anth., 28-40.
Maclean, Colonel.
    1858. A Compendium of Kafir Laws and Customs. Printed for the Government of British Kafraria. Mount Coke.
Maine, H.
    1861. Ancient Law. London.
Malinowski, B.
    1913. The Family among the Australian Aborigines. London.
Man, E. H.
    1883. On the Aboriginal Inhabitants of the Andaman Islands. London.
Marett, R. R.
    1912. Anthropology. Home University Library.
Markham, Clements.
    1892. A History of Peru. Chicago.
Martin, R.
    1905. Die Inlandstämme der Malayischen Halbinsel. Jena.
Merker, M.
    1910. Die Masai. Berlin.
Mooney, J.
    1907. The Cheyenne Indians. Amer. Anth., Mem., I, 361-442.
Morgan, L. H.
    1871. Systems of Consanguinity and Affinity of the Human Family. Smithsonian Contributions to Knowledge, XVII.
    1877. Ancient Society. New York.
Murdoch, J.
    1892. Ethnological Results of the Point Barrow Expedition. 9 B.A.E., 19-441.
Nelson, E. W.
    1899. The Eskimo about Bering Strait. 18 B.A.E., 19-518.
Parkinson, R.
    1907. Dreissig Jahre in der Südsee. Stuttgart.
Parsons, E. C.
    1916. Avoidance in Melanesia. J.A.F.L., XXIX, 282-292.
Philbrick, F. S.
    1918. (Translator) Huebner, R. A History of Germanic Private Law. Boston.
Powers, S.
    1877. Tribes of California. Contributions to North American Ethnology, III.
Radloff, W.
    1893. Aus Sibirien. I. Leipzig.
Restrepo, Vicente.
    1895. Los Chibchas antes de la conquista española. Bogota.
Radin, P.
    1911. The Ritual and Significance of the Winnebago Medicine Dance. J.A.F.L., XXIV, 149-208.
    1915. The Social Organization of the Winnebago Indians, an Interpretation. Can. Geol. Sur., Mus., No. 10.
Reports of the Cambridge Anthropological Expedition to Torres Straits, Vols. v and VI. Cambridge, 1904, 1908.

Rivers, W. H. R.
    1906. The Todas. London.
    1914 (a). Kinship and Social Organization. London.
    1914 (b). The History of Melanesian Society. 2 vols. Cambridge.
    1915. "Marriage"; in Hastings' Encyclopaedia of Religion and Ethics. VIII.

Rockhill, W. W.
    1891. The Land of the Lamas. New York.

Roscoe, J.
    1907. The Bahima: a Cow Tribe of Enkole in the Uganda Protectorate, J.A.I., 93-118.
    1911. The Baganda. London.

Roth, W. E.
    1903. North Queensland Ethnography. Bulletin 5. Brisbane.
    1906. North Queensland Ethnography. Bulletin 8. Brisbane.
    1915. An Inquiry into the Animism and Folk-Lore of the Guiana Indians. 30 B.A.E., 117-384.

Routledge, W. S. and K.
    1910. With a Prehistoric People. London.

Russell, F.
    1908. The Pima Indians. 26 B.A.E., 17-389.

Sapir, E.
    1911. Some Aspects of Nootka Language and Culture. Amer. Anth., 15-28.
    1913. A Girl's Puberty Ceremonial among the Nootka Indians. Transactions, Royal Society of Canada, 3d series, 67-80.
    1915. The Social Organization of the West Coast Tribes. *Ibid.*, 355-374.

Schinz, W.
    1891. Deutsch-Südwest-Afrika. Oldenburg.

Schmidt, M.
    1905. Indianerstudien in Zentralbrasilien. Berlin.

Schultze, L.
    1907. Aus Namaland und Kalahari. Jena.

Schurtz, H.
    1902. Altersklassen und Männerbünde. Berlin.

Seligmann, C. G. and B. Z.
    1911. The Veddas. Cambridge.

Skeat, W. W., and Blagden, C. O.
    1906. Pagan Races of the Malay Peninsula. 2 vols. London.

Skinner, A.
    1913. Social Life and Ceremonial Bundles of the Menomini Indians. A.M.N.H., XIII, 1-165.

Speck, F. G.
    1909. Ethnology of the Yuchi. University of Pennsylvania, Anthropological Publications of the University Museum, I, 1-154.
    1915 (a). Family Hunting Territories. Can. Geol. Sur. Mem., 70.
    1915 (b). The Family Hunting Band as the Basis of Algonkian Social Organization. Amer. Anth., 289-305.
    1918. Kinship Terms and the Family Band among the Northeastern Algonkians, Amer. Anth., 143 *seq.*

BIBLIOGRAPHY

Spencer, B., and Gillen, F. J.
    1899. The Native Tribes of Central Australia. London.
    1904. The Northern Tribes of Central Australia. London.
Spieth, J.
    1906. Die Ewe-Stämme. Berlin.
Spinden, H. J.
    1908. The Nez Percé Indians. Amer. Anth., Mem., II, 165-274.
    1917. Ancient Civilizations of Mexico and Central America. A.M.N.H., Hd.
Stack, E., and Lyall, C.
    1908. The Mikirs. London.
Stair, J. B.
    1897. Old Samoa. Oxford.
Stevenson, M. C.
    1909. The Zuñi Indians. 23 B.A.E.
Swanton, J. R.
    1905 (a). Contributions to the Ethnology of the Haida, A.M.N.H,. Mem., VIII.
    1905 (b). The Social Organization of American Tribes. Amer. Anth., 663-673.
    1906. A Reconstruction of the Theory of Social Organization. Boas Anniversary Volume. 166-178. New York.
    1908. Social Condition, Beliefs, and Linguistic Relationship of the Tlingit Indians. 26 B.A.E., 391-485.
    1911. Indian Tribes of the Lower Mississippi Valley. B.A.E., Bull. 43.
    1912. A Foreword on the Social Organization of the Creek Indians. Amer. Anth., 593-599.
Tafel, A.
    1914. Meine Tibetreise. Stuttgart.
Talbot, P. A.
    1912. In the Shadow of the Bush. London.
Teggart, F. J.
    1918. The Processes of History. New Haven.
Teit, J.
    1900. The Thompson Indians of British Columbia. A.M.N.H., Mem., II.
    1909. The Shuswap. *Ibid.*, IV.
Thalbitzer, W.
    1914. The Ammassalik Eskimo. Copenhagen.
Theal, G. Mc.
    1907. History and Ethnography of Africa South of the Zambesi. London.
Thomson, Basil.
    1908. The Fijians. London.
Thurnwald, R.
    1910. Das Rechtsleben der Eingeborenen der deutschen Südseeinseln. Berlin.
    1912. Ermittlungen über Eingeborenenrechte der Südsee. Z. Vgl. R. XXIII, 309-364.
Torday, E., and Joyce, T. A.
    1910. Les Bushongo. Brussels.

Tregear, E.
    1904. The Maori Race. Wangani.
Turner, B.
    1884. Samoa. London.
Tylor, E. B.
    1889. On a Method of Investigating the Development of Institutions; applied to Laws of Marriage and Descent. J.A.I., XVIII, 245-272.
    1896. The Matriarchal Family System. Nineteenth Century, XL, 81-96.
Von den Steinen, K.
    1897. Unter den Naturvölkern Zentral-Brasiliens. Berlin.
Waitz, Th., and Gerland, G.
    1872. Anthropologie der Naturvölker. VI. Leipzig.
Webster, H.
    1908. Primitive Secret Societies. New York.
Weule, K.
    1908. Wissenschaftliche Ergebnisse meiner ethnographischen Forschungsreise in den Südosten Deutsch-Ostafrikas. Berlin.
Whiffen, T.
    1915. The Northwest Amazons. New York.
Wilson, G. L.
    1917. Agriculture of the Hidatsa Indians. University of Minnesota. Studies in the Social Sciences, No. 9. Minneapolis.
Wissler, C.
    1911. The Social Life of the Blackfoot Indians. AM.N.H., VII, 1-64.
Zahn, H.
    Die Jabim, *in* Neuhauss, Deutsch Neu-Guinea, III, 289-394.

INDEX

ADOLESCENT ceremonies, for girls, 319.
Adoption, Andaman Islands and Torres Straits, 167; of children, 77; part played in sib membership, 115-116.
Adultery, punishment for, 415, 424.
Age-classes, 313-319; and four class system, 269; Cunow on, 257; Hidatsa, 293, 295; Masai, 271, 273, 274-275, 293-294; Omaha, 321-322; Plains Indian, 334-335; in Schurtz's scheme, 298-299, 302, 314-319; secondary, 322, 329, 332.
Age, factor, in African and American tribes, 315; factor, in Australian organization, 264, 315; factor, Dakota comrades, 320; factor, within the family, 314; factor, Plains military societies, 322; grading by, Andaman Islands, 259; purchase and rank, in Plains Indian societies, 325-329.
Age-grades, Australian class system, 269-270; Hidatsa, 292.
Age-groupings, Plains societies, 324-325.
Age-societies, Plains Indian, 324-335; interpreted, 334f. See also Age-classes.
Agriculture, and horticulture, 193, 194, 197; division of labor in, 75; woman's share in, 160, 179, 183-184, 218.
Alliances, between North American tribes, 388.
Animal names, for sibs, Admiralty Islands, 120; Buin, 120, 137-138; Iroquois, 143-144; Winnebago, 118; Northwest Coast moieties, 128.

Aristocracy, basis among Plains Indians, 340-341; basis, New Zealand, 341; in primitive society, 355. See Caste.
Associations, 257-337, 394-396; in Andamans, 258 seq.; coexisting with sibs among Crow, 427 seq.; defined, 257; historical survey of, 257-258; rarity in Asia, 310; relation to political organization, 395f.; relation to sibs, 257, 262; theory of, 297-337; varieties of, 319-323; women's, Hidatsa, 294-295; women's, in North America, 305.
Autocracy, African rulers, 375, 376; Natchez, 383.
Avoidance, Frazer's interpretation of rules of, 91, 93, 97; parent-in-law, Tylor's interpretation of, 94-97; psychoanalytic motivation in parent-in-law taboo, 91-94.
Avunculate, 248; defined, 81-84; and cross-cousin marriage, 172; examples of usages connected with, 82-83; and matrilineal and patrilineal descent, 171-173; in Oceania, 179; and privileged familiarity, 100.

BACHELORS' kraals, Masai, 273-274.
Bachelors segregated, Andamans, 259, 316f.; Australia, 264; Bororo, 50; Masai, 50, 271; North America, 317; Zulu, 316, 374.
Baden-Powell, on joint ownership of land in India, 232f.
Bandelier, on Mexican land tenure, 218f.
Betrothals, infant, 18, 52.

452 PRIMITIVE SOCIETY

Bilateral family, universality of, 78.
Bilateral kin group, 64-68.
Blood feuds, 368, 400, 404, 414.
Blood-kin, prohibition against marriage of, 15-16.
Blood-money, 404.
Boas, on totemism, 139, 145; on Tripartite organization of Northwest Coast tribes, 136-137.
Borough-English. See Junior-right.
Bravery, influence on prestige, Bagobo, 342; Masai, 341-342; New Zealand, 341; Plains Indian, 339-342.
Bride-price, and dowry, in North America, 21-22; Kai, 20; influence of patrilocal and matrilocal residence, 72-73; influence of practice of polygamy, 42; Thonga, 20-21.
Bride-purchase, in Siberia, 178.
Brother-in-law and sister-in-law, privileged familiarity between, 100, 101.
Brother-sister marriage, 15.
Brown, on Australian family, 66-67; on Australian kinship usages, 80-81; on Australian four-class system, 268.
Bull-roarer, 265-266, 311-313; its equivalent, 280.
Bundles, ceremonial, Hidatsa, 295, 305.
Burial customs, influence on rules of inheritance, 244.

CASTE, 345-355; affects prestige, 341, 345 seq., 353 seq., 362-367; affects property rights, 234; system, Marshall Islands, 227, 365-366.
Caste, system, 345-355; affects prestige, 341, 345 seq., 353 seq., 362-367; affects property rights, 234; Africa, 349-351; Maori, 345-347; Marshall Islands, 227, 365-366; Natchez, 351-353; New Zealand, 341; Northwest Coast, 353-355; Polynesia, 345; Samoa, 347-349.

Ceremonial, chambers, Pueblo, 308; functions of sibs, 119-121, 127; life, Hidatsa, paternal kin in, 65; objects, ownership and transfer of, 239; organizations, Zuñi, 281-282; paraphernalia, 272, 279, 290; privileges, individual ownership of, 237; privileges, transfer and ownership of, 239-243.
Ceremonies, for absolution from taboos, Andamans, 260-261; women's position in, 197.
Chattels, laws relating to, 233-235.
Chiefs, Africa, 221, 350, 370 seq., 423, 424; Algonkian, 384; Australia, 360; California, 342-343; 404; Crow, 384-385; Dieri, 260; Marshall Islands, 365-366; Melanesia, 367; Natchez, 351-353, 383; New Guinea, 369; New Zealand, 228, 362-363, 345-346; North America, 384-387; northwest coast of N. America, 353, 383-384; Oceania, 225-229, 345 seq., 362 seq.; Plains Indian, 339; Polynesia, 225, 345; Samoa, 347, 363-365; Solomon Islands, 367-369.
Chieftaincy, succession of, Buin, 121.
Children, adoption of, 78; individual ownership of property, 233-234; relations with maternal uncle, 82-83; relations with paternal kin, 83-84; status, in matrilocal household, 71, 72; status, in matrilocal and patrilocal residence, 159; status, in patrilocal household, 70, 71; tendency to stabilize marriage, 69.
Chronology, family and sib, 147-150, 165; levirate, sororate and sib, 163-164; matrilineal and patrilineal stages of culture, 169-183.
Civil law, Kafir, 422-424; paucity of, 397.
Circumcision, Masai initiation, 271-273.
Clans, defined, 111. See mother-sibs.

Classes, distinction of, by primitive man, 338; social, Africa, 349-351; New Zealand, 346-347; Northwest Coast, 353-354; Samoa, 347-349.
Class system, Australia, 267-270.
Clubs, graded, Banks Islands, 276-277; graded, Oceania, 316; military, Crow, 288-291; in Schurtz's scheme, 300; secular, Crow, 287-288. See also Men's Clubs, Secret Societies, Men's Tribal Society.
Collateral inheritance, 249f., 371.
Collective ownership, of property, Hidatsa, 218.
Collective responsibility, for crime, 399-400; Africa, 418, 422; in Australia, 407; Ifugao, 411-412.
Communal hunting, Plains Indians, 385.
Communism, primitive, 205-210; based on communal solidarity, 208; coexistent with individualism, 209f., 216, 233; connected with food, 210; distinguished from joint ownership, 206; distinguished from hospitality and moral obligations, 207; as to land, 229-233.
Compensation, for crimes, 403-404, 423.
Composition. See weregild.
Comrades, Dakota, a form of association, 320.
Consanguine family, 56-58.
Convergence, 433f.; junior right a case of, 254.
Convergent evolution, 254; Siberian parent-in-law taboo, 103-104; in teknonymy, 109; in totemism, 140-141.
Council, governing, Africa, 372, 376f.; America, 386f.; Australia, 358, 359f.; Central Australia, 360-361; as court, 421; Dieri, 359-360; Ewe, 377; Iroquois, 388; Natchez, 383; Northwest Coast, 384; Omaha, 416; Samoa, 363; Thonga, 372-373.
Court etiquette, Ewe, 377; procedure, 420 seq.; Thonga, 373.
Courts, Uganda, 424-425.
Cousins, classification into parallel and cross, 134.
Cousin-marriage, 15-18.
Couvade, 174-175.
Crests, Northwest Coast tribes, 128-129.
Crimes, Australian methods of dealing with, 406-409; collective responsibility for, 399-400; expiation for, 407-408; recognized, in Australia, 408-409; recognized by Omaha, 416; and torts, 398, 401 seq., 422; voluntary and involuntary, 401-402.
Criminal law, Kafir, 422-424; motive, 400-402.
Cross-cousin, defined, 26; marriage, distribution, 26-29; marriage, discussion of origin of, 28-31; marriage, and the avunculate, 172; marriage, influence on classification of kinship, 31-32; marriage, and sib exogamy, 148; privileged familiarity between, 101.
Cunow, on age-classes, 257, 266; on Australian class system, 268-270; on Hawaiian kinship systems, 58-59.

Dance organizations, Omaha, 321-322.
Democracy, East African, 278; Masai, 351; in North America, 219-220, 338-339, 351, 383, 384; and primitive society, 389-390.
Descent, Khasi, 190; Maori, 345-346; matrilineal, influence on position of women, 189; matrilineal and patrilineal, 166-185; Melanesian, 393-394; Plains Indians, 124-125; rules of, 177; rules of, influence on inheritance, 173, 247; rules of, sib systems east of the Mississippi, 123-124; rules of, and transmission of property, 167-169.
Despotism, Africa, 224, 370, 373, 377 seq.; Hawaii and Marshall Islands, 227, 365f.

Diffusion, 434f.; age-societies, 329; and the avunculate, 171-172; of culture, explanation of theory of, 8-13; of resemblances in sib systems east of Mississippi, 123-124; importance in all problems, 302; influence on cultural traits, 176; influence on elaboration of graded series of societies, 329-333; junior-right usage, 254; levirate, sororate, and sib, 163-164; parent-in-law taboos, 85-86, 88-91, 93-94; and Schurtz's scheme, 302; of teknonymy, 108.

Divination, 406, 422.

Divorce, 19, 68, 69, 71.

Domestication, of animals, a masculine achievement, 75, 183-184, 194.

Dual organization, and Dakota kinship terminology, 134, 135; defined, 118; simplest conceivable, 135; Southwestern sib system, 127.

ECONOMIC, basis of marriage, 64-66; conditions, influence on matrilocal or patrilocal residence, 72, 73; interpretation, of woman's position, 193-201; interpretation, criticised, 356.

Elders' class, Australia, rule of, 359.

Endogamy, defined; tribes having, 16-17, 160.

Endogamous, groups, 30; moieties, 132-133, 136.

Environment, examples of adaptation to, 8.

Ethics, and law, differences between, Plains Indians, 207-208.

Evidence, 402, 404-406.

Evolutionary doctrine, influence on theories of social phenomena, 55-56.

Exogamy, effect on marriage customs 148; Blackfoot, 124; Crow, 113; defined, 16; and endogamy, not mutually exclusive, examples, 17; Gros Ventre, 125; Hupa, 112; Iroquois, 113; law of, 113-114; and lesser and greater sibs, 132; Melanesia, 105; Miwok, 113; and the sib system, 114; in sibs east of Mississippi, 123; and totemism, 141; Zuñi sibs, 127.

Exogamous groups, Northwest Coast tribes, 130; quarters, Northwest Coast tribes, 129.

Expiatory combat, 407f.

FAMILIARITY, privileged, 98-101.

Family, the, 63-77; bilateral character of, 63-64, 111, 147; individual, a social unit, 66; influence of avunculate on, 82-83; life, influence of kinship usages on, 81; polygynous, 44-45; priority of the, 147-156; and sib, distinction between, 112-113; unit, looseness of, 68.

Fatherhood, determination of, in fraternal polyandry, 47-48.

Father-sibs, defined, 112; development of, in Siberia, 178; exogamous, 118, 120, 136, 176.

Father's sister, social relations with nephew, 83.

Feasting societies, Omaha, 321.

Feuds, Eskimo, 414; Ifugao, 411.

Fines, 409 seq., 423, 402-403, 424.

Four-class system, Australia, 267.

Fraternities, Zuñi and Hopi, 283-286, 336.

Frazer, on the levirate, 62; on rules of avoidance, 91, 93, 97; on social behavior of relatives by blood and marriage, 101; on teknonymy, 108; on totemism, 141-142.

Freire-Marreco, on Pueblo family life, 71.

Freud, on psycho-analytic motivation of parent-in-law taboos, 91-94.

Fruit trees, special ownership law in Africa, 223; in Oceania, 226.

GENEALOGIES, Polynesian, 346.

Gentes, defined, 111. See father-sibs.

Gerontocracy, Australia, 359-360.

Ghost organizations, Banks Islands, 278, 307-308, 363.
Gifford, on Miwok cross-cousin marriage, 28, 30-31; Miwok kinship terms, 38; on sib systems of California, 128.
Goldenweiser, on totemism, 139-141, 143.
Government, Africa, 369-382; Australia, 359-361; democracy and primitive organizations, 389 seq.; Melanesia and New Guinea, 367-369; North America, 383-389; Polynesia and Micronesia, 361-367.
Grades, of age-series explained, 329 seq.; of Masai men, 271; of Melanesian club, 276 seq.; Melanesian and Hidatsa compared, 292f. See also age-classes.
Group, marriage, 40, 49, 54, 61-62; ownership of property, 206.
Guilds, Cheyenne women's, 305.

HARTLAND, on priority of matronymic system, 171.
Headman, California tribes, 342, 343.
Historical method, in ethnology, 4-7.
Hobhouse, on bride-buying peoples, 26; on maternal-paternal descent, 180-182; on pastoral life and woman's status, 193.
Hollis, on East African sibs, 137.
House ownership, Hopi women. 216-217.
Hunting territories, joint and individual ownership of, 211-215; owned by Hopi sibs, 117.

IN-BREEDING, primitive repugnance for, 15-16.
Incest, crime in Australia, 408; fundamental social law precluding, 105; result of sophisticated civilization, 58; universal taboo against, 15-16.
Incorporeal property, 235-243; Andamans, 235; hereditary and non-hereditary, 237, 239f.; and individual ownership, 242; Koryak. 236; Nootka, 237; Plains Indians, 238 seq.; Torres Straits, 236.
Independent development, 355, 432; Blackfoot-Gros Ventre sib scheme, 126; castes in Polynesia and the Northwest Coast, 355; cross-cousin marriage, 31; examples of, in various phases of culture, 10-13; name taboo, 89; theory explained, 8-13.
Individual ownership, of chattels, 233-234; in general, 205-210, 233, 235, 243; Hottentot, 215; incorporeal property, 235 seq.; in India, 232f.; Kirgiz, 216; of land, Africa, 221-222; Australia, 214; Fiji, 226; Northeast Algonkians, 211f.; Torres Straits, 227; Vedda, 214; Zuñi, 217.
Industrial occupation, sexual division of labor in, 75.
Infanticide, female, 46, 47-48; influence on polyandry, 46, 48.
Inheritance, 243-255; ceremonial privileges, 117; chieftaincy, Solomon Islands, 368; collateral, 249-250; conjugal, 245; and descent, 167-169, 250; fraternal, Arapaho, 250; fraternal, Thonga, 371-372; hereditary and acquired property. 243; Hidatsa, 243-244; Hopi, 217; hunting grounds, Algonkians, 213; incorporeal property, 237-238, 242; influence on marriage customs, 245; influence of sib on rules of, 245-247; land, in Melanesia, 225-226; Kai, 243, 244; multiple, 246f., 251; Northwest Coast, 354; in Oceania, 180; Ostyak, 200, 245; primogeniture, 248f.; property, Ewe women, 26, reindeer herds, 245; rules Chukchi and Koryak, 177 rules, cross-cousin marriage a result of, 30-31; rules, Eskimo, 253; sib, 245f.; Torres Straits Islands, 227, 243; by women, 244f.

Initiation rites, Andamans, 259-261; Arunta, 318; Australia, 264-266; Banks Islands, 276, 279-281; boys, Solomon Islands, 368; and bull-roarer, 311-313; Crow Tobacco societies, 286-288; diffusion of, 313; Masai, 271-275, 318; Melanesia, 276, 368; not tribal in North America, 318; Zuñi, 282.

Instability of family unit, 68-70.

JOINT-OWNERSHIP, of property, 206.
Joking-relatives, 385.
Joking-relationship, Crow and Hidatsa, 100, 101.
Junior levirate, distribution, 32-33; parallel to, in the sororate, 36-37; taboos connected with, 102, 103, 104; theory of origin, 35.
Junior-right, 251-254; and convergence, 254; with primogeniture, 251f.
Justice, Africa, 318-425; Australia, 406-409; Eskimo, 412-415; Ifugao, 409-412; Plains Indians, 415-416; Polynesia, 416.

KIN, alignment, in matrilocal residence, 71-72, 191-192; in patrilocal residence, 70-71; mother's and father's, 81-84.
Kings, 349, 365, 370 seq.; Africa, 350; Dahomi, 380-381; Ewe, 376-377, 378; Hawaiian, 417; powers of, 359; supreme judge, 417, 424; Thonga, 371-372; Yorubaland, 381; Zulu, 373-375.
Kinship, avunculate a definite type of, 172-173; basis of the sib, 111; classification, influence on cross-cousin marriage, 32; group, as judicial body, 397; Hidatsa, 65, 84; and law, Ifugao, 391-392, 409-412; organization, see sib; and political organization, 395-396; among siblings, 114; systems, distinguishing lineal and collateral kin, 155; Hawaiian, 58-59; influence of sib organization upon, 162; terminology, Australian, 270; Dakota, 60, 61, 114-115; Dakota and the sib, 134, 162-166; Crow, 60; Crow sib-mates, 117; as evidence of universality of the family unit, 64; factor in marriage prohibitions, 16; Hawaiian, 57, 154; Hidatsa, 60; influenced by levirate and sororate, 37-38; influence of sib, 113; Miwok Paviotso, 16; Siberian, 103; Yahi, 37-38; Wishram, 37; reciprocal, 270; Thonga, 64; Torres Straits Islanders, 65; usages, 80-109.
Kohler, on group marriage, 61.
Kroeber, analysis of Southwestern sib system, 127; on Pacific Coast separations, 387; on Pueblo ceremonial organization, 282-286; on Pueblo matrilocal units, 73; on sibs and societies, 283 seq.

LABOR, sexual division of, 66, 74-75, 160-161, 187, 198, 202; Andamans, 262; importance in social history of mankind, 183; Kirgiz, 76; Thonga, 76; Toda, 76.
Land, African tribes, ownership of, 221-225; Australian attitude toward ownership, 213-214; communal ownership of, 206, 231; division of conquered, New Zealand, 228; hereditary, 225; joint ownership of, 229, 231, 232; joint ownership, Ifugao, 229; ownership, in ancient Mexico, 218-219; ownership by sib denied, 216-217; ownership, in South America, 219-220; tenure, 210-233; tenure, Africa, 221-225; tenure, in America, 216-220; tenure, feudal, 224, 227; tenure, among hunting tribes, 211-215; tenure, Ifugao, 229-231; tenure, India, 231-233; tenure, individual or communal, 211 seq., 229-233; tenure, among pastoral peoples,

INDEX

215f.; tenure, in Oceania, 225-229; tenure, among tillers, 216-233; transfer, in Africa generally, 221; transfer, among Ewe, 223; transfer, Fiji, 226; transfer, Ifugao, 230-231; transfer, impossible in Mexico, 219.
Laufer, on primitive ceramics, 75; on Chinese family life, 76.
Laws, civil, 397; criminal, 397-399; Ewe, 377; fundamental, precluding incest, 105; sociological and historical, see unilinear evolution; underlying civilization, 5-6.
League of the Iroquois, 388-389.
Legends, local, proprietorship of, 236.
Legislative functions, primitive communities, 358.
Levirate, 156, 174; Crow, 102; defined, 19; distribution of, 32-36; Frazer interprets as a relic of group marriage, 62; Hidatsa, 21; influence on Dakota terminology, 114; influence on kinship classifications, 61, 163-165; influence of marriage by purchase, 34; influence on social relations, 81.
Lineage, importance in the Northwest Coast, 354-355.
Licensed wife stealing, 68.
Live stock, property rights in connection with, 234-235.

Magic formulas, individual ownership of, 236.
Majority vote, absence of, 369, 387.
Maine, comparison of rude and mature jurisprudence: crimes and torts, 397 seq.; on collective ownership, 206; his historical method, 436; on inheritance of land, 243; on joint ownership, especially of land, 206, 231; on political organization of society, 391.
Maitland, on diffusion and sociological laws, 435.
Marriage, 14-38; on the Amazon, 165; Australian, 266-268; by capture, 23-24; economic basis of, 64-66; by exchange, 17; form of, Dieri, 52-54; Hupa, 70-71; individual, not influenced by sexual communism, 50, 51, 52; Kai, 82; Kariera, 172; Koryak, 22; Makonde, 82; by mutual consent, 24; Natchez, 352; prohibitions, 15-17; by purchase, 17, 19-21, 24-25; Ostyak, 200; Reindeer Chukchi, 200; regulations, Australian, 105; regulations, Melanesia, 105; regulations, for relatives by, 84-97; Thonga, 82; Tibetan, 46; transfer of property in, 205; Zulu, 374.
Masked Dancer society, Zuñi, 281-283.
Mate, means of acquiring, 17-26.
Maternal uncle, relations with nephew, 82-83.
Mating, preferential, 26-38.
Matriarchate, the, 189-191; Iroquois, 190; among Khasi, 189, 190; not consequence of mother-sibs, 189f.; Pueblo, 190.
Matrilineal descent, influence of property rights upon, 160; Hopi, 176; Northwest Coast tribes, 128; Zuñi, 127.
Matrilineal groups, 168.
Matrilineal kinship group, influence of matrilocal residence on, 159.
Matrilocal marriage, influence on parent-in-law taboos, 94, 96.
Matrilocal residence, 159; causal connection with teknonymy, 107, 108; Eskimo, 73; Hidatsa, 72; Hopi, 42, 164; influence on kinship system, 164; influence on practice of polygyny, 42; Kai, 102; Khasi, 72; Ovambo, 72; Pueblo, 192; and woman's position, 191-192; Yukaghir, 72-73, 178, 192.
Matrilocal tribes, 70-72.
Matronymic groups, 64-65.
McLennan, on Hawaiian kinship system, 59.
Men's clubs, Crow, 287; Melanesia, 276; see also Military

societies, Associations, Secret Societies.
Men's clubhouse, Banks Islands, 276; genetic connection with bachelor's dormitory, 257.
Men's house, 197, 299, 306, 307, 308, 315-316, 317, 368; in Schurtz's scheme, 299.
Men's tribal society, in Australia, 263; Melanesia, 275; Pueblo Indians, 282.
Menstruation, primitive horror of, 203.
Merker, on African sibs, 137.
Military, associations, Crow, 288-291; Hidatsa, 292-296; clubs, Hidatsa, 241; organizations, Hidatsa, 292-293; renown, quest for; Bagobo, 341; Masai, 342; New Zealand, 341; Plains Indians, 339-341; societies, Crow, 288-291; societies, Hidatsa, 292 seq., 342, seq.
Moieties, Australian, 266-267; and Dakota type of kinship nomenclature, 134; defined, 118; Eastern North America and Plains sibs, 125; exogamous patrilineal, Miwok, 119; exogamous and non-exogamous, 132-133; group, sibs east of the Mississippi, 123; Iroquois, 132; Northwest Coast tribes, 136-137; theory of origin of, 135-137; Winnebago, 118.
Monarchical government, Africa, 369-370; Congo, Ewe, 376-380; Thonga, 370-373; Yorubaland, 381-382; Zulu, 373-375.
Monarchy, and land law, 221, 224. See Kings, Despotism, Chiefs.
Monogamy, Andamans, 167; Eskimo, 41; Hopi, 42; Kai, 42; Kikuyu, 41; Kirgiz, 42; Yukaghir, 42; Zuñi, 42.
Morgan, atomistic theory of society, 257, 338, 390, 427; cf. with Schurtz, 301 seq.; criticism of his theories on the family and the sib, 147-151; on democracy, 356, 389; on descent and transmission of property, 169; on development of human marriage, 55-62; on development of lesser and greater sibs, 130-131; on the exogamic sib, 147-148; on group marriage, 61-62; inadequacy of his scheme of organization of primitive society, 257; on the levirate, 62; on marriage, 55-62; on origin of sib organization, 122; on primitive democracy, 338, 351, 389; on primitive political organization, 390, 391; on priority of matrilineal descent, 166; on stability of kinship terms, 155.
Mother-sibs, defined, 111, 112; development of, Hidatsa, 160; exogamous, Crow, 116; and father-sibs, 166-185; Hopi, 116, 117; relative priority of, in Oceania, 179.
Motive, criminal, 400f.
Murder, not always a crime, 407; in the Plains, 415; punishment for, 404, 414, 416, 417.

NAMES, animals, for sibs, 137-138; avoidance of use of, of those under taboo, 86-88; Eastern North American sibs, 125; individual ownership of, 236, 237; individual and personal, Iroquois sibs, 143; Miwok moieties, 119; Mohegan sibs, 131; personal, Miwok, 119; sibs, Crow; sibs, Hopi, 117; sibs, east of the Mississippi, 123, 124; taboos, 89-90, 106; Winnebago father-sibs, 118-119.
Naming customs, 83, 84, 119.
Nicknames for social units, 116, 126.

OATHS, 405; Ewe, 421-422.
Ordeals, 405, 406, 412, 418, 419, 422; Australian initiation, 265; Banks Islands, 280-281; Ewe, 419-420; Hawaii, 418; Masai, 271; Thonga, 422.
Orphans, status among primitive peoples, 11-12.

INDEX

Parallel cousins, 29; defined, 26; marriage tabooed between, 165.
Parallelism. See Independent Development.
Parent-in-law taboos, occurrence in different regions, 85-86, 87, 88, 93-94, 103-104, 105-106.
Parsons, rejects Frazer's theory of social taboos, 104; on teknonymy, 262.
Pastoral life, woman's status in, 193, 195, 198.
Paternal kin, usages connected with, 81, 83-84.
Paternal sibs, Siberia, 177-178.
Patrilineal, groups, 168, 172; segregation of kin, Algonkian tribes, 160; tribes, 171.
Patrilocal, groups, of women, 160-161; residence, 70-74; residence, on the Amazon, 165; residence, among the Australians, 161; residence, Eskimo, 73; residence, Hupa, 112, 157-158; residence, Koryak, 72-73; residence, influence on parent-in-law taboo, 95-96; residence, among matrilineal people, 159; residence, in Oceania, 180; residence, Siberia, 178; tribes, 70-71.
Patronymic groups, 63-64, 65.
Pawning, of land, 230; of person, 234.
Pearson, on sociological laws, 4, 436.
Penalties, exacted for crimes, 399-400, 417.
Philbrick, on the sib, 111.
Plundering expeditions, against criminal, 417-418.
Police organization, Plains Indians, 385-386, 415f.
Political functions, Ostyak sibs 120; Winnebago sibs, 119, 121.
Political organization, 358; Africa, 221-225, 369-383; America, 220; and associations, 395f.; Australia, 359-361; Bakuba, 380-381; coexistence with sibs, 392 seq.; Dahomi, 379-380; defined, 358-359; Ewe, 376-378; lack of among Ifugao, 391f.; Maine's and Morgan's theory of, 390, 391; Melanesia and New Guinea, 367-369; Natchez, 383; New Zealand, 362-363, 365; Northwest Coast, 383-384; in Oceania, 22; Samoa, 229, 363-367; Thonga, 370-373; Yorubaland, 381; Zulu, 373-377.
Political society, Schurtz on origin of, 394-396.
Polyandry, 45-49, 205; Chukchi, 52; distribution of, 45; economic influence on, 45-46; fraternal variety, 46-48; Toda, 49, 167.
Polygamy, 40-62, 205; defined, 40; influenced by biological and economic conditions, 40, 42, 45.
Polygyny, 205; analysis among Reindeer Koryak, 43-44; defined, 40; distribution, 40-41, 43, 44, 48; economic conditions influence, 43-44; limitation by matrilocal residence, 72; motives for, 42-44.
Population, proportion of male and female, Eskimo, 40-41; Toda, 46-47.
Potential mates, licensed familiarity between, 102.
Preferential mating, distribution, 17-18.
Primogeniture, 248-255; Maori, 346; New Zealand, 345, 362; Nootka, 354, 355; Samoa, 349; Thonga, 371-372.
Privileged familiarity, 99-101, 103.
Progress, 437 seq.
Prohibitions, marriage, 15-17.
Property, 205-255; collective ownership of, 206; concepts, basis of levirate, 34-35; conveyance, by Ewe, 223; and cross cousin marriage, 31; Crow, 168; Hidatsa, 168; and the Hopi sib, 117; individual ownership of, 208; inheritance of, 189, 190; influence on rank on the Northwest Coast, 354; Navaho, 168; ownership, by woman, 160, 161; ownership, Yuchi, 217; ownership, Zuñi, 217; rights, Banks Island

club, 277; rights, influence on establishment of unilateral lines of kin, 165; rights, influence of sib organization, 245-248; rights, New Zealand, 228-229; rights, of women, 202; sale of, Ewe, 223; transmission of, means of establishing unilateral descent, 157, 158-159, 167; transmission of, Morgan's theories on, 166; transmission, among patrilineal and matrilineal tribes, 167-168.
Psychological interpretation for cultural data, 93-94.
Puberty, in North America, 318-319; coincident with Initiation, 261, 310. See Initiation.
Public opinion, in primitive society, force of, 385, 398, 407, 409 seq.
Punishment for crimes, Ifugao, 412; Uganda, 425.
Purchase, ceremonial privileges, Plains age-societies, 328; concept, in marriage, 22, 23; of foreign societies, influence on graded systems in the Plains, 329-331; importance in entrance to Hidatsa military organizations, 292-293; membership in club, 242, 276, 286, 292, 300, 324.

RANK, 338-357.
Reciprocal services, between moieties, 133-134.
Relations, social, relatives by blood and marriage, 80-81.
Religious functions, Ostyak sibs, 120.
Ritualism, Hopi, influence on sib system, 117; importance of Iroquois woman in, 197; Toda women excluded from, 187.
Rituals, individual ownership of, 237.
Rivalry, Crow military associations, 290-292.
Rivers, on Dakota type of kinship terminology and the sib system, 114; on kinship usages, 81, 83; on Polynesian and Melanesian sib systems, 154; theory of origin of cross-cousin marriage, 30; on Toda exogamous marriages, 136.
Royalty, Africa, 349f., in North America, 351f., and ownership of lands, 221, 224; Polynesia, 346.

SAPIR, on influence of sororate and levirate on kinship, 37.
Schurtz, on associations, 257; compared with Morgan as to method, 301 seq.; criticised, 304 seq.; his scheme expounded, 297 seq.; on political organization, 395-396.
Segregation of unmarried, 76-77.
Sex dichotomy, 196, 197, 263, 275, 303-313, 316; in Australia, 258; Banks Islands, 275.
Sexes, segregation of, 306-307; Africa, 310; Andaman Islands, 259, 317; Australia, 263, 310; California, 307; Chipewyan, 309; Masai, 271; Melanesia, 310.
Sexual communism, 49-55; Australia, 52, 55; Bororo, 50, 51; Chukchi, 51-52, 55; hypothetical, 55-62; Masai, 50-51; Toda, 54.
Shamanism, 342-345; in Australia, 308; in North America, 307-308.
Sibs, 111-146; Australia, 156, 393; Crow, 130; and Dakota terminology, 162-166; defined, 111-112, 157; and democracy in primitive organizations, 389-390; diffusion in Australia, 152; diffusion in North America, 122-130, 150, 152, 176; distribution of, 148; distribution in Asia, 151; diversity of functions of, 122; exogamous matrilineal, Buin, 120; exogamous, Morgan's theories concerning, 147-148; exogamous patrilineal, 121; fundamental units of Crow social organization, 131; of higher order, 130-137; history of the, 147-185; inferior, 351, 390;

INDEX

Iroquois, 143, 388; Kariera, association with plants and animals, 138; linked, 127, 130, 131; Masai, 271; membership in, influence of marriage on, 115; organization, Blackfoot, 124; organization, California, 128; organization, Gros Ventre, 124; organization, influence on transmission of property, 205; organization, lacking among Fuegians, 151; organization, Masai, 270-271, 275; organization, in North America, 122-123; organization, and kinship systems, 162; origin of lesser organization, tripartite, Mohegan, 131; organization, relation to Pueblo fraternities, 283-285; organization, Siberia, 177-179; organization, types of, 116-122; organization, unity or diversity of origin, 122-130; patrilineal, California, 128; and greater units, 130-131, 157-162; as proprietary unit, 216 seq., 224, 245; restricted distribution of unilateral, 147; and secret societies, 283; survival after contact with Caucasians, 153.

Sib system, Admiralty Islands, 121; alleged effects on marriage system, 148; Blackfoot, 126; Buin, 120-121; California, 153-154; correlation with Dakota type of kinship terminology, 150; Crow, 116-117; distribution in Africa, 151-152; diversity in North America, 126; east of the Mississippi, 123-124; Gros Ventre, history of, 125-126; Hopi, 117; independent development throughout the world, 129; Kariera, 121; lacking in the Andaman Islands, 151; Melanesia, 120; northwestern plains of North America, 124-125; northwest coast of North America, 128-129; in the Southwest, 127; Winnebago, 118; Zuñi, 127.

Siblings, defined, 26; restriction of intimacy between, 102; usages connected with father's, 84.

Singing contests, Eskimo, 413.

Sins, and crimes, 398, 414.

Sisters, exchange of, in mating, 18.

Slavery, 346f., 350, 353, 356; Africa, 234, 350; Maori, 346-347; Northwest Coast, 353.

Smith, G. Elliót, theory of origin of totemism, 138.

Social, grouping, Banks Islands, 276-277; Masai, 271-275.

Social intercourse, restrictions in, 97-99.

Social organization, Andaman Islands, 258-262; Australia, 262-270; Banks Islands, 275-281; Crow, 286-292; evolution compared with that of material culture, 437 seq.; Hidatsa, 292-296; interrelations of various aspects of, 14; intricate, found with rude cultures, 149; Masai, 270-275; Pueblo Indians. 281-286.

Social progress, distinguishing stages of, in Australia, 264.

Social relations, influence of kinship usages on, 80-81.

Social restrictions, connection with sexual restrictions, 102.

Social status, stages of, Masai, definite usages linked with, 271-272.

Social stratification, Marshall Islands, 365-366.

Social usages, importance of maternal and paternal kin in, 65.

Social and sexual taboos, psychological interpretation of, 104, 105.

Societies, graded, Plains, 326-332; women's, Africa, 309-310.

Societies, secret, Africa, 309, 381, 419; Banks Islands, 278-281; California, 307, 308; Central Algonkian, 305; Hidatsa, 295; Melanesia, 278 seq., 336; Omaha, 320; Pueblo, 282; in Schurtz's scheme, 300.

Society membership, form of property, 240, 241f.

Songs, individual ownership of, 235-236.
Sorcery, Ewe, 419-420; Thonga, 422.
Sororate, Crow, 102; defined, 18; distribution of, 32-37; Hidatsa, 44; influence on Dakota type of terminology, 114; influence on kinship terminology and classification, 61, 163; influence on social relations, 81; Kariera, 18; Morgan interprets as a relic of group marriage, 62.
Speck on individually owned hunting grounds, 158, 160, 211f.
Spinsters segregated, Andamans, 259.
Spouses, status of, in matrilocal and patrilocal residence, 70-71, 72.
Status terms, in Andamans, 259, 262; in Australia, 264; Masai, 271.
Suitor's test, Arawak, 22-23; Koryak, 23-24.
Supernatural experiences, common, associations based on, Plains Indians, 320-321.
Swanton, on cross-cousin marriage, 31; on the sib, in North America, 150.

Taboos, barring social intercourse, 97-99; food, Australian, 264-265; food, Toda, 75; against incest, universal, 15; connected with initiation in the Andamans, 260, 261; against killing or eating totem animals, 139; kinship, 97-98; and license, 101-107; New Zealand, 362-363; Oceania generally, 363; parent-in-law, 84-97, 107; Polynesian chief's prerogative, 362f.; protection of property, 279, 363; social and sexual, correlation between, 104; transgression of, punishment for, 414.
Teggart, on political organization, 395.

Teknonymy, defined, 107; examples of practice, 107-109; explanation of, 262; and status terms, 262.
Territorial organization, Australia, 393; Melanesia, 393-394. See Political Organization.
Territorial rights, jealousy regarding, 394.
Theft, punishment for, 424.
Three-class division of society, Ifugao, 402.
Thurnwald, on Buin sib system, 120.
Tobacco, planting, Crow, ownership and transfer of privilege, 240-241; society, 286; society, women's place in, 305.
Torts, 398 seq.
Totemism, 137-145, 264; Arunta, 138; British Columbia, 140; Central Australian type of, 140; diffusion of, 138; Goldenweiser on, 140; Iroquois, 143; theories of origin of, 138-139; and the sib, 142.
Trade unions, Cheyenne, 305; Samoan, 348.
Tribal organization. See Political Organization, Sib, 390-396; Ifugao. 391-392.
Tripartite division of society. 258, 259, 261-262, 298.
Tylor, on cross-cousin marriage, 29-30; on Dakota type of kinship terminology and sib system, 114; interpretation of parent-in-law avoidance, 94-97; on the levirate, 32, 33-34, 36; matrilineal and patrilineal stages of culture, 169-183; on matrilocal residence, 159; on primitive marriage, 35; on teknonymy, 107-108.

Unilateral, descent, most effective means of establishing, 157; reckoning of kinship, 161-162.
Unilinear evolution, 301 seq., 334, 336f., 430f.

Vision, importance of influence on

Plains societies, 332; ownership of privileges secured through, 238; quest of, an individual affair in the Plains, 318-319.
Visionary experiences, individual character of proprietary rights, 242.

WEALTH, 342-345; conception of, among various peoples, 343-344; determines penalties, 402; influence on prestige, 277, 343f., 368.
Webster, on associations, 257.
Weregild, 402-404.
Witchcraft and justice, 414, 419f.
Wives, abduction of, Crow, 290-292; exchange of, 51-52; surrender of, 49.
Wife-stealing, licensed, Crow, 68.
Woman, excluded from activities of men, 74, 75, 77; excluded from mysteries, 263, 279; Von den Steinen's and Radin's explanation, 304; as herd owner, 200-201; as house owner, 190, 216, 246; individual ownership of property by, 233-234; inferiority of, differences in character among Chukchi, Ostyak, and Oceanians, 196; as inheritor, 200, 245; isolation of, Banks Islands, 77; as land owner, 214, 218, 224; as owner of chattels, 233, 245; and property rights, in Africa, 224-225; segregation of, 197; segregation during menstruation, 203.
Woman, position of, 74-76, 183-203; Andamans, 187, 193, 201; Australia, 202, 263, 189; Africa, 189; Bantu, 201; Central Asia, 187, 201; Chinese, 188, 201; Ewe, 20; influence of economic conditions, 193 seq.; influence of maternal sibs, 189 seq.; influence of matrilocal residence, 191; influence of pastoral life, 193-195; influence of stage of civilization, 201-203; influence on teknonymy, 109; Iroquois, 201; Kai, 20; Kirgiz, 19; legal and real status of, 186, 188; Maritime and Reindeer Chukchi, 199-200; Ostyak, 200; and property rights, 202; in social organization, 303-313; Siberia, 187-188; Thonga, 20; Toda, 187; Vedda, 193, 201.
Women's societies, African, 309; Cheyenne, 305; Hidatsa, 294; Pueblo, 305.